THE TEPEHUAN
OF CHIHUAHUA
Their Material Culture

Campbell W. Pennington

THE TEPEHUAN
OF CHIHUAHUA
Their Material Culture

University of Utah Press
Salt Lake City

FOR
THOSE STUDENTS
CONCERNED WITH
HOW SURVIVING
ABORIGINAL PEOPLES
UTILIZE THEIR
ENVIRONMENTS

CONTENTS

PREFACE

The Tepehuan Indians of Mexico can be divided geographically into two groups: the southern Tepehuan who inhabit portions of the states of Nayarit and Jalisco, and the northern Tepehuan who live in scattered settlements south of the Río Verde in the state of Chihuahua. Probably in prehistoric times, they were not geographically divided; their lands must have included that stretch of territory between the now-separated groups.

Although there are several publications available on the historic Tepehuan, only a few of these are of recent date, and most of them concentrate on the southern group. The northern Tepehuan have been studied, but for the most part, attention has been given only to those Indians living in and around mestizo settlements. Clearly, these Indians reflect more than a little integration with the mestizos and are not an adequate representation of the way of life followed by most northern Tepehuan.

In this monograph, based upon two summers of field work among the Chihuahua Tepehuan (in 1960 and 1965), I have attempted to present a detailed account of northern Tepehuan material culture as it existed in the 1960's. I have also attempted to indicate the approximate age of certain elements of that culture by using data available in archival materials and in reports of archeological investigations in what once was the Tepehuan northern habitat. Unfortunately, archival material is scanty—no doubt because the Tepehuan of central and southern Durango were rapidly absorbed into the mestizo complex after large-scale penetration of the area by Spaniards both before and after 1600. Jesuit records for the period prior to that order's expulsion from Mexico in the 1760's indicate that northern Durango was, in part, Tepehuan country, but there is little in the ecclesiastical record to indicate how the aboriginal Tepehuan lived. Also, the exceedingly rough portion of Chihuahua south of the Río Verde inhibited significant penetration of that isolated Tepehuan area by Jesuit missionaries until after 1700. Hence, the Jesuit materials—important as a primary source for Tarahumar customs in the early historical period—are not particularly useful for the Tepehuan. Franciscans labored among certain of the southern Tepehuan during the colonial period, but the available record includes almost nothing relative to the material culture of these people.

Data presented herein are incomplete in that they are essentially concerned with the material culture of the northern Tepehuan; I do not feel competent to report on matters other than those pertaining to how they utilize the resources of their rather bleak and inhospitable environment. However, social customs are frequently referred to, particularly when utilization of the material environment is involved. Urgently needed is a comprehensive sociological study of the Chihuahua Tepehuan to be completed before they are integrated further with Mexican cultural life. The integrating forces are both social and economic: the federal government continues to be active among surviving aboriginal peoples, and lumber interests have begun to encroach upon Tepehuan territory. There is no doubt that the government station at Guachochic, located immediately north of the Río Verde, has had and will continue to have influence upon the Indian way of life. Within the past five years a lumber road has been constructed between Hidalgo del Parral and Guadalupe y Calvo, and undoubtedly within the next few years, an extension of this road will bring lumber interests into the Tepehuan heartland, the northern portion of the great Mesa de Milpillas.

Whatever has been accomplished in this study could not have been done without the generous assistance of many people within the United States and Mexico. The late J. Alden Mason was most helpful with suggestions relative to linguistic matters; and the most competent of contemporary students of the Tepehuan language, Burton William Bascom of Baborigame, Chihuahua, and Santa Ana, California, not only checked the Indian terms used herein, but also permitted me to make a photocopy of his copy of that rare, eighteenth-century Tepehuan dictionary, the *Arte de la Lengua Tepehuana*, written by Padre Benito Rinaldini and published in 1743. The Indian terms, as I have presented them, are phonetic transcriptions and are by no means as accurately transcribed as those terms presented by Bascom in his 1965 study of the Piman languages. Bascom is a trained linguist—I am not—and, moreover, there are dialectical differences among the northern Tepehuan which are readily apparent when one travels through southern Chihuahua. The phonetic transcriptions made in 1960 were rechecked during the field season of 1965 and are believed to be essentially correct. The reader is cautioned, however, about one point: I have attempted, insofar as possible, to determine the Indian terms for all elements of Tepehuan material culture discussed within this monograph. In many instances, it is obvious I obtained only literal translations of the Spanish terms for these elements. For example, *Zornia diphylla* is known among the mestizos as *yerba de la víbora*. The plant is known among the Tepehuan as *kói* (*víbora*) *vasógadï* (*yerba*), a literal translation of the mestizo term. Since there is value in recording these literal translations, I have done so. In other cases, the Indian term, as presented, is not to my knowledge related to the mestizo term.

A vast debt is owed to botanists who kindly identified plants collected in 1960 and 1965: Edgar Anderson, Lyman Benson, Annetta Carter, D. S. Correll, Hugh Cutler, Hazim Daoud, Charles B. Heiser, Marshal Johnston, Lawrence Kaplan, Charles T. Mason, N. T. Mirov, Harold Moldenke, C. H. Muller, Gene Newcomb, Gerald B. Ownbey, Marion Ownbey, J. Roy Quinby, Jonathan Sauer, J. C. Stephens, Jason R. Swallen, John M. Tucker, William Turner, M. A. Wahl, W. A. Webber, Thomas Whitaker, and Carroll E. Wood. Most of the specimens are vouchered in the University of Texas Herbarium, Austin, Texas.

I gratefully acknowledge the hospitality and advice extended by Padre Mauricio Rivera Romera at the Chinatú Mission while I was en route to the Tepehuan country in 1960. The field work could not have been accomplished without the generous assistance and cooperation of the schoolmaster at Llano Grande in 1960, Señor Ignacio Gonzáles, or without the assistance freely given by Martín Barro Julian (Tepehuan), Jesús Chaparro Holquín (three-quarters Tepehuan), José Benito Gonzáles Montijo (of Tepehuan extraction), Manuel Acosta Naverette (three-quarters Tepehuan), and Don Sotero Montijo who was born about ninety years ago at Nabogame and who married a Tepehuan. Difficulties encountered during the field season of 1965 were mitigated by the assistance of Don Gilberto Gonzáles Músquiz and Señor Jesse Aguayo of Chihuahua City and by the kindness of Rosario Díaz who provided shelter during the rainy season at Baborigame. Ignacio Gonzáles Montijo provided a base of operations at La Ciénega on the Mesa de Milpillas. Apolonio Loera was a particularly valuable informant during the field season of 1965.

Professor Lorrin Kennemar of the University of Texas Department of Geography kindly made working space available while I was utilizing materials in the Latin American Collection at the University during the spring of 1963 and the summer of 1967. I acknowledge the courtesies shown me by Dr. Nettie Lee Benson, Librarian of the Latin American Collection at the University of Texas. Editors of *América Indígena* have graciously permitted me to use certain of my materials published in January 1963. The field season of 1960 was supported by the American Philosophical Society and the University of Utah; field work in 1965 was, in part, supported by the Research and Projects Office of Southern Illinois University. I gratefully acknowledge the cartographic work executed by Daniel R. Irwin, Tso-Hwa Lee, John McHale, and George Burson of the Southern Illinois University Department of Geography.

Campbell W. Pennington

Department of Geography
Southern Illinois University
Carbondale, Illinois 62901
1969

CHIHUAHUA TEPEHUAN COUNTRY—1960's

1
THE TEPEHUAN

Tucked away in the rugged and inhospitable terrain of southern Chihuahua, Mexico, between the Río Verde and the settlement of Redondeados are about 8,000 Tepehuan, the most northerly remnant of an aboriginal people who once occupied a vast stretch of territory that extended eastward from the Sierra Madre Occidental and from what is now Chihuahua southward into Nayarit and Jalisco. The Chihuahua Tepehuan and their immediate neighbors to the north, the Tarahumar, constitute the most numerous of the surviving Indian groups within the northern portion of the Sierra Madre Occidental. Elsewhere in the area, there are only a few Pima Bajo and Varohío.

INTRODUCTION

In the past sixty-seven years, three major publications concerning the Tarahumar have been published: those of Lumholtz,[1] Bennett and Zingg,[2] and Pennington.[3] In addition, there are a number of shorter publications, such as the brief monographs of Basauri[4] and Plancarte.[5] The scholarly Tarahumar grammar written by Brambila[6] and the Tarahumar dictionary compiled by Thord-Gray[7] have supplied a great amount of information concerning the Tarahumar language. Gentry has contributed an ethnographic survey of the Varohío,[8] and Mason and Brugge made brief comments on the Pima Bajo.[9]

The Chihuahua Tepehuan are little known apparently because it was believed that they had become completely integrated with the mainstream of mestizo cultural life and because most writers, except Lumholtz[10] and Mason,[11, 12] have concerned themselves with the remnants of aboriginal Tepehuan located far to the south in the states of Durango, Nayarit, and Jalisco. Cerda Silva,[13] Gámiz,[14] and Basauri[15] hardly acknowledged the existence of several thousands of Tepehuan in southern Chihuahua. Even the location of these northern Tepehuan is not shown correctly on the most recent map of their aboriginal and contemporary distributions.[16]

In spite of having received slightly more attention, the southern Tepehuan are as little known as their northern relatives. It is true that the above-mentioned publications of Basauri, Cerda Silva, and Gámiz make brief mention of the material culture of the Tepehuan far to the south, but as Mason has already noted,[17] most of the data seem to have been taken from Lumholtz' *Unknown Mexico* published in 1902. Furthermore, the material as presented by Gámiz in 1948 is exceedingly suspect in view of archeological evidence and traditional history. Mason's study of the Tepecano language,[18] published in 1917, contains little ethnographic material. The rather complete data offered by Lumholtz in 1902 and the brief summaries of southern Tepehuan material culture presented in 1948 and 1952 by Mason and in 1963 by Riley and Winters constitute the only reliable information on the southern Tepehuan.

The important contributions to the study of Chihuahua Tepehuan in recent years have been those of Bascom and Mason: Bascom has written a scholarly study of the linguistic relationship between idioms in the speech of contemporary northern and southern Tepehuan,[19] and Mason's publications are the only contributions of data concerning material culture of the Chihuahua Tepehuan since the time of Lumholtz. His brief but important papers suggest that the Indians have become integrated with mestizo life. However, my two summers of field study, undertaken in 1960 and 1965, yielded evidence that the Tepehuan of Chihuahua have by no means been entirely integrated and that they still follow many ancient customs. Within this monograph, I have disagreed with certain statements made by Mason; however, it must be remembered that he visited only Baborigame which is essentially mestizo in population. Indicating just how much the Indians living near Baborigame had been absorbed into the mestizo complex, he wrote that "doubtless extensive research among them [the outlying Tepehuan] would provide a considerable body of ethnographic material, customs, practices and beliefs passed down from former years. . . ."[20]

Although no important archeological investigations have been conducted in the Tepehuan habitat area of Chihuahua, significant findings have been made in the old Tepehuan country of Durango on the Río Zape. Cultural material from a cave site, the oldest of which has been radiocarbon dated at about 600 A.D., has been reported by Brooks and his associates. It is true that they did not identify cultural material from the Río Zape site as being Tepehuan in origin. In their summary, they simply noted that "the vegetable material [associated with the artifacts] collected from excavations in the cave . . . indicates that the inhabitants were dependent upon the bean-corn-cucurbit complex as their main source of food supplies. . . ."[21] Thirty years ago, Brand raised the question of whether or not "archeologic vestiges" at Zape should be linked "with any historic people of the area."[22] Perhaps this thought should now be applied to materials recovered from the Zape site by Brooks and his associates. However, it is assumed herein that the materials excavated by Brooks and his colleagues are Tepehuan in origin; the assumption is based upon the lack of available evidence that people other than the Tepehuan inhabited what is today northwestern Durango in the period around 600 A.D. Some of the materials recovered from the Zape site are clearly related to the present-day culture of the Chihuahua Tepehuan, and furthermore, we know that at the time of White-Indian contact there were many Tepehuan in what is now northern Durango.

Today, the Tepehuan of Chihuahua refer to themselves as *ódami* (Indian people), a term that apparently was in common use during the eighteenth century when Padre Benito Rinaldini recorded the word as *odame* (*gente* or *nación*).[23] Tepehuan of southern Durango also refer to themselves as *ódami*.[24]

Little is known of the exact origin of the name *Tepehuan*. Pérez de Ribas wrote in the seventeenth century that the name was derived from the Mexican (Náhuatl) word *tepetl* that meant mountain or from *tetl* that meant rock or boulder.[25] In either case, he thought the name suitable since the Indians were by nature hardy and rough like the area they inhabited. An eighteenth-century account of Indé states that the word stems from *tepetl* or *tetl*.[26] In the nineteenth century, Pimentel wrote that some authorities believed *Tepehuan* to be derived from a Mexican word *tepehuani* that meant *conquistador*.[27] Other students of Mexican aboriginal languages believed that the word was a combination of *tepetl* (mountain) and the suffix *-hua*, which in the Mexican tongue indicated possession; *Tepehuan* meant "people of the mountains." Yet other students believed that it was a Tarahumar word, being derived from *pehua* or *pegua* which meant hard (*duro*).[28]

Today, the Chihuahua Tepehuan are clustered in the extreme south of the state, but how long this group has occupied the area between Guadalupe y Calvo on the south and the great canyon of the Río Verde on the north cannot be determined. The Indians state that they do not know when their ancestors arrived in Chihuahua and that they know nothing of their ancestors' origins. Presumably, ancestors of at least some of the Chihuahua Tepehuan entered the area immediately south of the Río Verde in the early seventeenth century either from what is now northwestern Durango or from the northeast. There is evidence in an eighteenth-century report written by Rinaldini that the uplands near Baborigame and Nabogame were settled by Tepehuan who retreated into that relatively inaccessible region during the great rebellion that began near Guadiana (now, Durango City) and ultimately spread for hundreds of miles north and south in the period between 1616 and 1618.[29] Tepehuan once lived in the upper San Pablo Valley and at San Gerónimo de Huejotitlán, both of

which are located somewhat to the north and northeast of the present Tepehuan habitat. Some of these people might have retreated to southern Chihuahua after the rebellion spread from Guadiana northward into the main gateway
between the Tepehuan and Tarahumar country.[30] The Indians referred to by
Rinaldini could hardly have come from the vicinity of what is today Hidalgo
del Parral or the land immediately south of that city since there is nothing in
the historical record to indicate that this area was actually occupied by aboriginal Tepehuan. Indeed, there is some evidence that the country south of Parral
was not occupied at all in immediate pre-Conquest times. The famous Misión
San Miguel de Las Bocas (located near present-day Villa Ocampo, Durango)
was founded in 1630[31, 32] for a specific purpose: to care for the Tarahumar and
the Tepehuan who were brought into the region for work on the Spanish farms
that were producing food for the mining community located at Parral about
fifteen leagues north of Las Bocas. However, it should be noted that there are
undated occupation sites along the Río Florido a few miles from Villa
Ocampo.[33] The Tepehuan mentioned by Rinaldini undoubtedly did not come
from the west since the western lands were held by the Tubar and the Zoe in the
early seventeenth century.[34]

Chihuahua Tepehuan state that when their ancestors arrived in Chihuahua
the country was occupied by the Cocoyome, a tribe that planted blue maize; it
was from the Cocoyome that they obtained their *maíz azul*, so prized today.
The Cocoyome traded this maize for Tepehuan children who were esteemed as
food. If maize was lacking, the Cocoyome stole a Tepehuan child or pregnant
woman, who was then killed and roasted before being eaten at festivals. According to legend, the Cocoyome did not eat each other as did their neighbors
on the north, the Tarahumar. The Cocoyome had no arms except the bow and
arrow. It was from the Cocoyome that the Tepehuan learned of certain games:
palillo, *quince*, and *cuatro*. The Cocoyome lived in small multiroomed dwellings located in caves.[35] According to present-day Tepehuan, the Cocoyome
were excellent farmers, planting corn, calabazas, *guajes*, and beans, especially
the *frijol yurimun*.[36] When asked what became of the Cocoyome, the Tepehuan
state that all of the Cocoyome died when, one day, the skies rained blood.[37]

The absence of origin and migration tales in their oral tradition and a lack
of archeological evidence make impossible a precise statement about how long
the Tepehuan have occupied the extreme-southern portion of Chihuahua.
However, on the basis of data available in historical documents, we may state
that there must have been considerable numbers of them living south of the
Río Verde during the seventeenth century. Ancestors of some of these
seventeenth-century Indians were undoubtedly living south of the Río Verde
long before the arrival of Spaniards in northwestern Mexico.

Most of the Chihuahua Tepehuan are at present located in the *municipio* of Guadalupe y Calvo, with a few of them in the *municipio* of Morelos (see Map I for locales that are known to include Tepehuan).[38] Very few Tepehuan live north of the Río Verde. Except for the presence of colonial Tepehuan in the San Pablo Valley and in the valley of the Río Valle de Allende, the Río Verde seems to have long been an important dividing line between the Tepehuan and the Tarahumar.

The Tepehuan are scattered throughout an area that includes about 10,500 square kilometers (the *municipios* of Morelos and Guadalupe y Calvo), but their greatest concentration is in the northern portion of the great Mesa de Milpillas, which actually includes three mesas: Llano Grande, La Reforma, and Orilla de La Mesa. An important secondary cluster is located along a northwest-southeast line in the drainage basin of the Río Basonopa, bounded by Dolores on the south and Basonopa on the north. Four additional clusters are located on the northern and western margins of the major Tepehuan country: in and about Gueráchic on the Río Verde; in the country between Real La Dura and Real Morelos on the northwest; in and about Santa Rosa, which is about thirty-eight kilometers west of Baborigame, almost on the border between Chihuahua and Sinaloa; and in the vicinity of Tohayana located about fifty-five kilometers west of Guadalupe y Calvo. There are almost no Tepehuan living in the immediate vicinity of Guadalupe y Calvo, but there are scattered settlements to the southeast of that city at Redondeados. According to Indian officials at La Ciénega (on the Mesa de Milpillas), there are Tepehuan living just south of the border between Chihuahua and Durango and west of the southwestern Chihuahua-Sinaloa border. On the east, Chinatú is essentially Tarahumar, but there are numerous Tepehuan living between the Tarahumar mission at Chinatú and Santa Rosalia located on the edge of the Mesa de Milpillas to the west.

The Chihuahua Tepehuan do not live in villages; rather, their habitations are scattered here and there on ejido lands in the uplands and along canyon streamways. As Mason has pointed out, the only grouping occurs when close relatives construct houses fairly close to one another.[39] Baborigame and Nabogame are rather old settlements that date back at least to the early eighteenth century, but these "villages" were established among the Tepehuan when Jesuit missionaries gathered the Indians together at places where they might better be brought under control.[40] The mestizo (*óbbi* or *óbai*, foreign people) element is dominant at Baborigame today. Nabogame is essentially Tepehuan, but the site cannot be considered a true village since the Indian habitations are scattered along the Río Nabogame that runs through the valley where the old mission is located. It appears that most of the Tepehuan adhere to the custom of their ancient relatives in northern Durango with respect to location of habita-

tions. Pérez de Ribas repeatedly refers to the scattered nature of Tepehuan settlements north of Durango City in the early seventeenth century, noting that
the Indians were strung out along the arroyos and rivers or were located near
springs which were present in this area.[41]

Generally, the unmixed Tepehuan are found along canyon streams everywhere in Chihuahua south of the Río Verde except in the rough country south
of that river. They are also found along fringes of the northern portion of the
Mesa de Milpillas, particularly where the Arroyo de Milpillas trenches the mesa
and upon the high and flattish summits of the broken country just south of the
Río Verde. It appears that unmixed Tepehuan dominated the Mesa de Milpillas
about sixty-eight years ago; but, today, the flatter and better lands of the mesa
have been alienated by mestizo families who have pushed the Indians toward
the margins of the mesa except in the Arroyo de Milpillas where the Indians
were so numerous that alienation of their lands was impossible.

For the most part, the Tepehuan tend to be sedentary folk whether they
live in the uplands or in the canyons. There are certain exceptions as when a
man has two wives, a common occurrence. In this case, he may maintain two
homes, one in the upland and another in the canyon country. Usually it is the
husband and perhaps several of the older children who move back and forth
from upland to canyon or from canyon to upland; sometimes it is entire families, those more interested in herding than in tillage, who may move from one
portion of the upland to another or from the upland to the canyon country in
search of better pasture. Such moves are rarely permanent, and most families
tend to return to a home base.

Present-day southern Tepehuan are located, for the most part, in the municipalities of Mezquital and Pueblo Nuevo in Durango and in the municipality
of Huajicori in Nayarit.[42, 43, 44] Remnants of the Tepecano who are, without
doubt, linguistically related to the southern (Durango and Nayarit) and northern (Chihuahua) Tepehuan are found in the vicinity of Azqueltán in northern
Jalisco.[45]

THE SIXTEENTH-CENTURY TEPEHUAN AND THEIR NEIGHBORS

The exact distribution of the sixteenth-century Tepehuan cannot be determined from a study of twentieth-century place-names in Mexico since Tepehuan names for locations have not survived as have the Indian names in the old
Tarahumar country. A few place-names of obvious Tepehuan origin are certain;
most of these are found in the Tepehuan country of southern Chihuahua,
where three Tepehuan language suffixes (-kïrï, -kamo, and -karu) mean "place
of" (*lugar de*) when combined with terms for natural phenomena. Nabogame is

derived from *navokamo*, which is clearly a combination of *návoi* (*nopal*) and *-kamo* (*lugar de*). Baborigame is derived from *vavúlikamo*, a combination of *vavúli* (*chalote*) and *-kamo*.[46] Basonopa is a corruption of *vasoákamo*, a combination of *vásoi* (*zacate*) and *-kamo*. It is certain that the northern Tepehuan have, for a long time, named sites according to natural phenomena. Padre Rinaldini noted in the eighteenth century that *upivagaquer* meant *lugar de nogales*;[47] the term is clearly related to the current place-name *ipïvïkïrï*, which is derived from *ipïvï* or *ipiokai* (*nogal*) and *-kïrï*. Present-day Tepehuan state that *-kïrï* is the preferred designation for "place of," and it is undoubtedly related to Rinaldini's *gáre* (*á aquel lugar*) or *igure* (*aqui, á este lugar*).[48]

The Chihuahua Tepehuan commonly refer among themselves to specific locales according to natural phenomena. *Bokuripikïrï*, or *lugar de tescalama*, stems from *bokuripi* (*tescalama*) and *-kïrï*. *Čikulikïrï* is derived from *čikuli* (*chicura*, an upland *cebollín silvestre*), and *-kïrï*. *Dïvïraikïrï*, or *lugar de tierra ceniza*, is derived from *dïvïrai* (*tierra ceniza*) and *-kïrï*. *Ivakïrï* is literally *lugar de quelite*, being derived from *ívagi* (*quelite*) and *-kïrï*. *Upáraikïrï*, or *lugar de algarroba*, is derived from *upárai* (*algarroba*) and *-kïrï*.

No data are available concerning place-names among the southern Tepehuan, but the Tepecano of Azqueltán, Jalisco, also designate localities according to local phenomena; the suffix *-tám* is used to indicate "place of" or "place where."[49]

Not much archeological evidence for an accurate determination of the limits of the immediate pre-Conquest Tepehuan is available at the present time. There are no archeological data to indicate the antiquity of the Tepehuan in southern Chihuahua. Kelley has reviewed, in broad outline, the important archeological sites within or peripheral to what is known to have been northern Tepehuan country during colonial times.[50] Among the sites mentioned are those along the upper Río Florido and at Zape; however, only the Zape site has yielded evidence that may provide a link with the culture of the northern Tepehuan.[51] In the south, Riley and Winters have found in central and southern Durango similarities between finds in certain Chalchihuites sites and some aspects of the present-day southern Tepehuan culture, particularly with respect to pottery, pipes, and incense burners.[52] This evidence, although slight, does constitute justification for the inclusion of at least portions of central and southern Durango as prehistoric Tepehuan country. However, judging from data available in historical documents, it would seem that the immediate pre-Conquest Tepehuan did not occupy that country where the southeastern border of Durango abuts upon Zacatecas as indicated upon Riley and Winters' map showing distribution of the Tepehuan and the Tepecano at the time of conquest.[53]

Existing differences between northern (Chihuahua) and southern (Durango and Nayarit) Tepehuan with respect to culture and language prompted Mason[54] to pose the question of whether linguistic maps[55] showing aboriginal Tepehuan as continuous and undivided (southern Chihuahua to Nayarit and Jalisco) are, in fact, correct. Mason wrote that the "languages of the two [groups, the northern and southern Tepehuan,] are quite different and almost certainly not mutually intelligible." However, he noted that the "languages of the Southern Tepehuan and the Tepecano are very close, apparently only dialectically different."[56] This statement was based on the fact that in 1911 Mason found languages of the southern Tepehuan and the Tepecano mutually intelligible.

It is quite true that, at present, there are differences between languages spoken by the Tepecano, the southern Tepehuan, and the northern Tepehuan. Mason quickly recognized this when he compared his Tepecano and southern Tepehuan data with linguistic data pertaining to the northern Tepehuan that he found in Rinaldini's dictionary.[57] Mason's assumption that northern and southern Tepehuan languages are not mutually intelligible seems to be correct since Bascom noted that at a linguistic workshop held in 1959, a northern Tepehuan and a southern Tepehuan could not communicate extensively with each other except in Spanish.[58] However, isolated Indian words were readily understood. Bascom concurs with Mason's assumption that the Tepecano language is no more than a dialect of southern Tepehuan,[59] and in a scholarly analysis of the Tepehuan and Piman languages, he makes clear that the modern northern Tepehuan and southern Tepehuan (including Tepecano) are daughter languages of an ancient language that must have been widely diffused in northwestern Mexico.[60]

These linguistic data constitute but slight evidence for the exact determination of boundaries for the sixteenth-century Tepehuan. However, herein it is assumed that, in pre-Conquest times, there was probably a close linguistic and perhaps even a close cultural relationship between aboriginal peoples who survive today as the northern Tepehuan, the southern Tepehuan, and the Tepecano. Therefore, early references in the civil, military, and ecclesiastical records to the Tepehuan and the Tepecano may be used to map aboriginal distribution of the Tepehuan in the sixteenth century, particularly in view of a comment in a seventeenth-century document concerning the Tepehuan of northern Nayarit and southern Durango. This document makes clear that the term *Tepecano* referred to the Tepehuan who lived in the mountains. In referring to those Tepehuan who lived "cercada la Nassión Chora Nayalyta [the Cora of the Sierra Nayarit] ... ," Antonio Arias y Saavedra commented that the Indians "salen al Valle del Súchil á la Poana i á otras labores de aquel Reino á sacatecas, xombrerete, y otros que por allá les llaman tepecanos que quiere desir Serranos."[61]

General comments found in accounts of the great religious chroniclers (Pérez de Ribas, Alegre, and Arlegui) concerning distribution of Indian groups are of dubious value in mapping aboriginal habitats in northwestern Mexico. This is so because each chronicler tended to outline only the area in which his particular order was operating and, moreover, Jesuit and Franciscan missions overlapped in the Tepehuan country. The Jesuit Pérez de Ribas noted in the middle of the seventeenth century that the Tepehuan lands were among the most extensive of Indian lands in New Spain, reaching as far as New Mexico and falling within the jurisdiction of Nueva Vizcaya and the episcopate of Guadiana (Durango City). He stated that settlements of the Tepehuan began about thirty leagues north of Guadiana, with the first important pueblo being Santiago Papasquiaro. However, the Tepehuan frontier was only about fifteen or sixteen leagues north of Guadiana.[62] Another Jesuit chronicler, Alegre, wrote in the eighteenth century that the Tepehuan lands extended from about twenty-five degrees to twenty-seven degrees of latitude; the Indian pueblos began about twenty-five leagues north of the capital (Guadiana) of Nueva Vizcaya.[63] Both Pérez de Ribas and Alegre ignored the Tepehuan who lived south and west of Guadiana. The Franciscan Arlegui was more correct in his comment on distribution of the Tepehuan than Pérez de Ribas or Alegre. He wrote in the eighteenth century that the lands of the Tepehuan extended from the vicinity of Acaponeta (Nayarit) to the Sierra del Mezquital and thence almost to Parral.[64] Chronicles of Jesuit and Franciscan missionary activity in Mexico can be very valuable as source materials for specific locations of Indians: where early letters, now missing from archives, are quoted in full, they give information as to the precise location of certain of the Tepehuan during the early colonial period.

Boundaries of the lands occupied by the sixteenth-century Tepehuan and their neighbors are shown on Map II. With few exceptions, all of the locations mentioned in the following sections may be found on this map.

THE EASTERN BORDER

Portions of the eastern border and the heartland of aboriginal Tepehuan country were penetrated by Spaniards in 1552 and 1554, but there are apparently no specific references to the Tepehuan in the record of these *entradas*. Giñéz Vazquez de Mercado reached the vicinity of the modern city of Durango in 1552 by way of San Martín de Cayn, Sombrerete, and Chalchihuites.[65] In 1554, Francisco de Ibarra traversed the country between Zacatecas and the Río Nazas and discovered mines at Fresnillo, Chalchihuites, Sombrerete, San Martín de Cayn, Nieves, Aviño, San Lucas, and Ranchos. Ibarra's party also explored the country in the vicinity of Guatimapé (west of Laguna de Santiaguillo) and the Valle de Guadiana.[66] An account of Ibarra's discoveries in 1554 contains repeated references to *naturales* within the territory explored, but no specific people are mentioned for eastern Durango.[67]

It is in Pedro de Ahumada's *Relación* of 1562 that the earliest specific information concerning people along the eastern Tepehuan border from Nochistlán to Sombrerete is found.[68] Semisedentary Cazcan were reported at Nochistlán and Teocaltiche. Zacateco were reported at Chalchihuites, Sombrerete, San Martín de Cayn, Aviño, Peñón Blanco, Mezquital, and Poanas. The Huachichile were divided by Ahumada into three groups: Primeros, Segundos, and Terceros; these nomadic people were accustomed to making sporadic forays into the country of the semisedentary Cazcan and Zacateco. Huachichile were specifically reported in the vicinity of Mazapil and Salinas (in northeastern Zacatecas). Ahumada was very explicit in noting that the lands of the Zacateco extended almost to Guadiana (the valley in which Durango City is now located) "que confina con los Tepeguanes."[69] Another account of Ahumada's exploits refers to Cazcan at Tlaltenango and states that the Huachichile and the Zacateco were "indios que confinan con las minas de los Zacatecos y san martín y aviño."[70] These specific references corroborate statements made by Tello[71] concerning Cazcan at Teocaltiche, Tlaltenango, and Nochistlán in 1541 and 1542. In addition, Tello recorded Cazcan at Noxtlán, Juchipila, Teul (in the Mixton Sierra), Cuixpalan, Epatlán, Tepeaca, and Tzotzocola; none of these sites, except Juchipila and Teul, can be found on modern maps. He placed Zacateco near Teocaltiche and Nochistlán in 1541 and 1542. Additional evidence concerning distribution of the little-known Cazcan is found in a list of Cazcan pueblos held *encomiendo* in 1550;[72] these pueblos included Yahualica, Apozol, Mexticacán, Juchitlán, Mezquituta, Tracache, Moyahua, Nochistlán, Juchipila, Tequicistlán, Teul, Mezicicate, Tlaltenango, and Xalpa, most of which may be readily located on modern maps. Ponce placed Cazcan at Juchipila and Teul in 1587, noting that at Teul "todos hablan la lengua cazcana."[73]

A letter of Jerónimo de Ramírez written in 1594[74] refers to Jesuit activity among Indians at Cuencamé (located south of the Río Nazas), which Decorme places within Zacateco country.[75] That the lands of the Zacateco extended northward to the Río Nazas seems certain since the Jesuit *anua* of 1596 refers to the Zacateco as being along that river.[76] Moreover, Martín Peláez recorded Zacateco along the Nazas in 1605.[77]

According to Juan Miranda, there were Tepehuan living near the San Buenaventura mines located in Zacateco country about ten leagues south of Nombre de Dios in 1572.[78] However, these Indians had undoubtedly been brought from the west into the area to work in the Spanish mines. The *Memorial* of 1563 repeatedly refers to Chichimec being in the vicinity of Nombre de Dios,[79] which was founded in 1562 for the purpose of protecting Spanish miners near Aviño, Peñón Blanco, and San Martín de Cayn.[80] Mexican, Tarascan, and Zacateco Indians were settled at Nombre de Dios in order to entice the marauding Chichimec into a more settled way of life. There is no mention of the Tepehuan. In the sixteenth century, the term *Chichimec* was commonly applied to Indians who had no permanent settlements, and there is no evidence that the essentially sedentary Tepehuan were ever referred to as "Chichimec." Those Chichimec mentioned in the *Memorial* of 1563 were, undoubtedly, wandering bands of semisedentary Zacateco, Cazcan, and Huachichile who had not been pacified. The rapid assimilation of the Chichimec into the neighborhood of Nombre de Dios is revealed in an account of the villa some fifty years after its founding, by which time four languages were spoken: Tonalteco, Tarascan, Náhuatl, and Spanish;[81] the Tepehuan language is not mentioned.

The Jesuit *anua* of 1596 refers to lands occupied by the Lagunero in the vicinity of the great lagoon that characterized the mouth of the Río Nazas at the time of the Conquest; these people were said to live to the northeast of Cuencamé beyond the Río Aguanaval and to be a folk who had no houses and who did not till the soil but existed on products of the hunt instead.[82] The most westerly extension of these Indians was apparently in the vicinity of Nazas (on the Río Nazas). Martín Peláez refers to Lagunero who lived on the margin or limit (*orilla*) of the Río Nazas in 1605.[83] The term *Lagunero* was used by early missionaries to include all of the numerous groups that lived in the vicinity of the now-desiccated Laguna de Mayran, known as the Laguna Grande de San Pedro in the late sixteenth century,[84] and was probably used as well to include those people who lived in the vicinity of the former Laguna de Viezca.

The *anua* of 1598 refers to Iritila, Miopacoas, Meviras, Hoeras, and Maiconeras as living in the vicinity of the Valle de Parras (now, Parras de La Fuente); the Paogas, Caivseras, Vasapalles, Ahomamas, Yanobopas, and Daparabops were living in the lagoon country, that is, near the Laguna Grande de San Pedro. A *nación* called Pachos is also mentioned. This *anua* also states that the fathers at the Misión de Las Parras administered to these Indians in two languages, ". . . á la iritila que es propia de este valle [Valle de Parras] y mexicana, que es general . . ."[85] Mota y Escobar's account of 1602 refers to Mexues, Iritales, Zacatecos, Pachos, Guazahayos, and Ocals as being administered to by fathers of the Misión de Parras. Mota commented that all of these *naciones* spoke the Mexican language as well as *la lengua iritila*.[86] These statements suggest a linguistic relationship among the Indians of the lagoon country and those of the Valle de Parras, and additionally, they suggest a relationship between the Zacateco and the Indians of the lagoon country and the Valle de Parras. However, the question of whether Zacateco country extended as far north as Parras de La Fuente and whether there was a definite linguistic affiliation between the Iritila and the Zacateco cannot be answered with certainty. That there was some linguistic relationship between these two groups seems certain since Father Juan Agustín, who first administered to Indians of the Valle de Parras, was proficient in the Zacateco language and was able to make himself understood when he first reached the Valle de Parras.[87] Because there is a lack of more complete data concerning languages spoken by Indians of the lagoon country and the Valle de Parras, the term *Lagunero* is used herein to designate those Indians who lived on the northeastern border of the Tepehuan country, beyond the Toboso, in the sixteenth century.

The record regarding aboriginal inhabitants in the arid country around Mapimí is unclear. Mota y Escobar recorded Tepehuan at Mapimí shortly before 1602;[88] later, they were referred to as Tepehuan *negritos* by Mateo de Vesga in 1620-1622.[89] To be at Mapimí, these Tepehuan must have been brought from far to the west or southwest, across a great north-south stretch of land dominated by eleven tribes of hostile Indians referred to in seventeenth-century documents as the Toboso. These people inhabited the ranges and mountains east of the camino real that extended from Cuencamé in Durango to Hidalgo del Parral in Chihuahua. Reports by Lope de Sierra Ossorio in 1678 and 1683 indicate that of these eleven hostile tribes, the Toboso were the most brave; hence, all of the Indians in the Toboso area were known by that name.[90,91] The Toboso sallied forth from their accustomed haunts near Cuencamé, El Pasaje, El Gallo, and Cerro Gordo (the present-day Hidalgo, Durango)[92] to raid parties of travelers going to and from Guadiana, Zacatecas, and Hidalgo del Parral by way of the most easterly route. There seems to be little evidence that the Tepehuan ever penetrated into what is herein designated as Toboso country in spite of the fact that the Tepehuan and the Lagunero raided Spanish mining camps at Mapimí during the great rebellion that began in 1616.[93] The available evidence suggests that the Indians known in the seventeenth century as the Toboso dominated a great triangle of land marked by Cerro Gordo, El Gallo, and Mapimí and that they lived north of the Río Nazas, roaming at times, however, into Zacateco country as far south as El Pasaje and Cuencamé.

According to Juan de Miranda, the Concho Indians lived about ten or twelve leagues north of Santa Bárbara, and the Salinas were located about five or six leagues *abajo* (to the south or southeast?) of the river that headed in the mountains west of Santa Bárbara.[94] Mota y Escobar described the Concho as a large group living near the Valle de San Bartolomé in 1602.[95]

THE NORTHERN BORDER

The area between the Río de Balleza and the Río Valle de Allende can be considered a gateway between Tepehuan lands to the south and the Tarahumar lands to the north. There was mingling between the two groups not only in this transitional area, but also in the area south of the Río Verde. There are records of both the Tepehuan and the Tarahumar living at San Gerónimo de Huejotitlán in 1669[96] and 1690.[97] Both were also reported at Cinco Llagas,[98] Nabogame, Chismal (a *visita* of Nabogame), Chinatú, and Santa Ana[99] (located near the Real de San Nepomuceno). The Tarahumar held Satevó north of the Río Verde. Except for the above-named locales where both groups were to be found, the lands south of the Río Verde were essentially Tepehuan dominated by the eighteenth century and, in all probability, had been for some time.

In order to avoid repetition and to present a unified body of data on the Tepehuan in the northern borderland, a more complete record for these Indians is given in the section on the Tepehuan heartland.

THE WESTERN BORDER

The high country near the juncture of the Río Verde and the Río Urique was held in the sixteenth century by the Tubar and the Zoe, who may have first been mentioned in a letter written by Padre Juan Calvo and quoted by Pérez de Ribas.[100] Calvo was living at Tecorato (near present-day Yecorato, Sinaloa) in the second decade of the seventeenth century and wrote of the Tubaris who lived in the highlands of the Río Cinaloa country.[101] To the south and southwest of the Tubar were the Zoe. Calvo commented that both groups were termed *indios serranos* and that each group spoke a distinct language. A report made by Ignacio Lizasoain in 1763 records the Tubar at Tubares and San Andrés de Tubares.[102] Tamarón y Romeral's survey of 1765 places Tavares (Tubar) at Cinco Llagas, Tovares (undoubtedly present-day Tubares, Chihuahua), and San Miguel de Tubares.[103] The Franciscan Fathers' report of 1778 records Tubar at Concepción (south of Cerocahui, Chihuahua), San Ignacio (near the Río Batopilas), San Miguel de Tubares, and San Andrés.[104] Alcocer located the Tubar at Concepción de Tubares, San Miguel de Tubares, and San Andrés in 1788.[105] In the nineteenth century, Lumholtz found remnants of the Tubar at Morelos (present-day Real Morelos, Chihuahua), San Andrés, Tubares, and San Miguel.[106] The Zoe must have been absorbed into the mestizo complex long ago as no reference to them has been found in documents of the eighteenth century.

Both Sauer[107] and Decorme[108] have summarized the considerable evidence in civil and ecclesiastical records of the late sixteenth and early seventeenth centuries concerning the multiplicity of tribal units in Sinaloa located south of the Tubar and the Zoe, west of the Tepehuan, and northwest of the Acaxee. These people included the following: the Chicorato in the northeast (in the vicinity of present-day Chicorato); the Yecorato in the northwest at Sumupa, Comanito (the modern Cacalotlán), and San José Gracia; the Bacoburito at Bacoburito; the Teuchiapa in the east at Tecuciapa; and the Bacapa in the south at Huacapa. All of these people reportedly spoke rather distinct languages (dialects?), but since the languages were clearly affiliated with the Cáhitan language, Sauer has included all of these people among the Comanito, a sub-group of the Cáhita Indians who dominated the coastal lands far to the west. Sauer quotes Hurdaide material which indicates that the Teuchiapa and Chicorato lived in the headwater country of the Río Sinaloa, adjoining the Tepehuan.[109]

The Tepehuan referred to in the Hurdaide documents were undoubtedly the Oclotani who were identified as Tepehuan in Jesuit letters (*Drey Neue Relationes*) published in 1611.[110] The Oclotani lived east of the Baimoni (the most northerly Acaxee) in settlements which were known to the Jesuits as Santa Cruz, San Lorenzo, San Juan, and San Pedro. None of these settlements can be identified with certainty, but present-day Santa Cruz, Durango, is probably located within what was Oclotani country in the early seventeenth century and was undoubtedly the same place referred to as Ocotlán in numerous early documents. According to the *Drey Neue Relationes*, the Indian name for Santa Cruz was *vuamariana*, derived from the name of a stone idol called *vuamari*; both of these terms are related to the present northern Tepehuan term for yellow (*vúáma*). The letter concerning the Oclotani also mentioned that the Tepehuan of the Valle de Aguila (the upper San Juan Valley of Chihuahua) were at war with the Tarahumar; the Valle de Aguila is almost due north of the city of Santa Cruz, Durango. Furthermore, Padre Juan del Valle recorded the *reducción* of four pueblos in Ocotlán in 1607,[111] one of which was called Santa Cruz. The description of a stone idol, known as *ubamari*, found at this pueblo is remarkably similar to the one given of the idol in the *Drey Neue Relationes*.[112] Padre Juan Fonte, in referring to the *reducción* of the *partido de Ocotlán* in 1607, also mentions an idol called *ubamari* and notes that Ocotlán was renamed Santa Cruz.[113] This Santa Cruz is undoubtedly the same Santa Cruz at which a Jesuit missionary was on permanent assignment in 1748 and 1751;[114] the site was listed as a mission within the *Provincia de Tepehuanes*.

Southeast of the Comanito Cáhita were the lands of the Acaxee, lands which were entered from the west by some of Nuño de Guzman's men in the 1530's and from the east by Francisco de Ibarra in 1564.[115, 116] However, records of these expeditions are not of particular value in defining either the Acaxee country or the border between Acaxee and Tepehuan lands; it is in civil and ecclesiastical records that the aboriginal location of the Acaxee can best be determined.

A report made by Diego de Avila in 1600 indentifies Acaxee at the follow-

ing pueblos: Coscatitlán, Colutla, Estancia Cobos, Birimoa, Tasio, San Gerónimo y Frijolar, Las Vegas, Otatitlán, and Remedios.[117] Of these sites, only Birimoa, Otatitlán, and Remedios can be found on modern maps. The Jesuit *anua*
of 1602 indicates that the Acaxee were living in the vicinity of Las Vírgenes,
Papudos, San Hipólito, Topia, and San Andrés;[118] only Topia and San Andrés
may be found on modern maps of Durango. This document also refers to a
people called the Sabaibo who lived south of the Acaxee; however, these people were Acaxee as will be shown below. Urdiñola's *Memorial* of 1604 records
Acaxee at San Andrés and San Hipólito.[119] In the following year, Martín Peláez
reported Acaxee at Sabaibo (on the Río San Andrés), San Hipólito, Topia, San
Gerónimo, and along the Río Humay.[120] Jesuit letters of 1607 refer to distinct
areas and peoples within the lands of the Acagrenses, the name by which the
Acaxee were called by writers of the letters:[121] the heartland of the Acaxee
country included Topia, San Andrés, Gregorio, San Hipólito, and Tamazula;
towns of the Sabaibo were located to the south and included the pueblos of
Otatitlán and nearby Huejupa; the western Acaxee country was peopled by
Camarones who lived at Chacala and nearby Oso; the Caratapanis lived to the
northwest at Atotonilco, Chanmango, Batoromito, San José, and Humaya; and
the Baimoni lived in the extreme northwest of Acaxee country. The Baimoni
were forced to pay tribute to the Tepehuan who were then known as the Oclotani. Zapata's report of 1678 makes no distinction between the Acaxee and the
Xixime in referring to the Misión de Xixime, but he refers to mission settlements that were clearly Acaxee in the early seventeenth century: Otatitlán, Los
Remedios, San Gregorio, San Andrés, Otaes, El Palamar (on the Río San Lorenzo), Las Vegas, Huejupa, and San Hipólito.[122]

South of the Acaxee country was the land of the Xixime about whom
very little is known. Central and northern portions of the Xixime country may
be determined from civil and ecclesiastical records of the early seventeenth century, but the southern margin of the Xixime lands cannot be defined. The most
northwesterly locale of these Indians appears to have been at Cosalá in Sinaloa;
Xixime were recorded there in 1613.[123] The Jesuit Santarén was administering
to northeastern Xixime at Otaes in 1613, and the Indians were reported there
as late as 1737.[124] Alonso del Valle, in writing of the Tepehuan rebellion in
1618, specifically refers to Xixime at Basis, Zapiuris (present-day Sapioris,
Durango), Guarizame (near what is now Guarisamey, Durango), Yamoriba,
Guapijue, Huahuapa, and Tenchius.[125] The heartland of the Xixime seems to
have been centered around the Río Piaxtla. Living in this same region were the
Hume, an Indian group considered by the missionaries as being distinct from
the Xixime but a group that spoke the same language. The Hume appear to have
dominated the great gorge of the Piaxtla, the Rincón de Zamora, known to
them as the Lengate Nabuco. Alonso del Valle recorded Hume in the following

pueblos in the vicinity of the Rincón de Zamora: Guarisame, Tominstame, Queibos, Yazaboytia, Acuz, Yomocoa, Tomisitua, Zipamoytia, and Mosas,[126] none of which may be found on modern maps. The Jesuits Juan del Valle, Bernardo de Cisneros, and Santarén visited Xixime at Humase (near Guarisamey) in 1611 and 1612.[127]

Almost nothing is known of the Indians who inhabited the mountain country east of what is today Rosario, Sinaloa. Sauer assumes that they were not Tepehuan but were Xixime since they are referred to in early Franciscan documents in connection with the more northerly Xixime.[128]

THE SOUTHERN BORDER

The lands to the north and northeast of what is today Acaponeta, Nayarit, appear to have been Tepehuan by 1600. Tello recorded Tepehuan at Quibinquinta[129] (now, Quiviquinta in Nayarit) in 1596 as did Mota y Escobar in 1602.[130] Francisco del Barrio, in writing of Indian disturbances in 1604, specifically reported Tepehuan north of Acaponeta at Milpillas (Milpillas or Milpillas Grande, Nayarit), Quiviquinta, Tlachichilpan (Tachichilpa), Teititlán, San Sebastian, and Los Caimanes (modern San Francisco Caiman, or Caiman, Nayarit).[131] Tepehuan were reported at Acaponeta in an account of the Tepehuan rebellion in 1617,[132] and they were reported in the vicinity of Acaponeta in 1621 by the Franciscan Tello.[133]

Antonio Arias de Saavedra wrote in the middle of the seventeenth century that the Tepehuan were located "cercada la Nassión Chora Nayalyta [that is, west, north, and east of the Cora who lived in the Sierra de Nayarit]...."[134] They were living at the following pueblos: Acaponeta, Quiviquinta, Milpillas Grande, and San Juan Peyotán (Nayarit); Colotlán, Azqueltán, Mezquitic, and Huejuquilla (Jalisco); in the vicinity of Monte Escobedo (Zacatecas); and at Lajas, Milpillas Chico, Santa María Ocotán, San Francisco Ocotán, and Huazamota (Durango). There were also Tepehuan at locales which are not on modern maps, such as Thenara, Voynara, Moroata, Nyara, Tzenzompia, N[o]xta, Camotán, Quempontyta, Quenta, Sapotlán, San Juan Tuametla, and Nextalpa. This report is of interest because it suggests that the Mezquitic and Colotlán country was transitional between Zacateco and Tepehuan lands; both Mezquitic and Colotlán were recorded as being loci of Zacateco in 1591.[135]

The most southerly extension of the Tepehuan, at least in terms of their distribution on the basis of language, appears to have been at Amatlán (undoubtedly in the vicinity of present-day Amatlán de Jora, Nayarit). The data for Amatlán are rather specific. In 1580, two Franciscans, Andrés de Medina and Pedro de Almonte, began to administer to the Indians in the *serranía de*

Amatlán (*de Jora*), which is the country between the juncture of the Río Grande de Santiago and the Río Guadalupe in the state of Jalisco; Medina was sent to the site because he understood the *lengua Tepehuana*.[136] There were Tepehuan still living at Amatlán in 1620.[137] It is doubtful that they ever lived as far south as San Pedro Analco, which is located southeast of Amatlán de Jora, Nayarit; documents of 1605 and 1606[138, 139] refer to *naturales* Guainamotas and Coras in connection with San Pedro Analco.

Southwestern Tepehuan lands of the sixteenth century adjoined those held by the Cora, Huichol, and related groups, most of whom were known to sixteenth-century Franciscans. These groups are referred to on Map II as the Nayari, a term that was much used, albeit in a somewhat different form, by authors of ecclesiastical and military reports referring to the peoples of Nayarit during the early and late colonial period.[140]

Ponce records a *provincia* called Vaynamota located about twenty-three leagues from Xala[141] (now, Jala in Nayarit); this province extended in a north-south direction and was apparently centered upon the Río Huaynamota, since Ponce noted that the principal pueblo within the province was called Vayna-mota (probably located near the present-day Huaynamota, Nayarit). North of Vaynamota was another province called Vazamota that was peopled in 1587 by many converts. It was probably located in the vicinity of what is now Huaza-mota in Durango and was, without doubt, the same Huazamota recorded as Tepehuan territory by Antonio Arias de Saavedra in the middle of the seventeenth century. South of Vaynamota was another province called Zayabecos that was inhabited by "cannibals." South and west of Vaynamota was a "provincia de indios Chichemecas por baptizar, llamadas Coras."[142] East of Vayna-mota was a province known as Uzares and to the west of Vaynamota lay the province of Tepeque (Tepic).

In regard to languages, Ponce commented that people living in the pueblos of Xalixco (Jalisco City) and Tepequechpán (Tequespespán) spoke Tecual. Those of Vitzuintlán (Ixcuintla) spoke Pinutl, and people who lived north of Centipac (Sentispac) spoke Pinutl or Pinonuquia, which was the same language spoken by the Coras, Canoas, and the Vaynamotecas (the Vaynamota); however, the Indians on the coast spoke a language called Naarinuquia. Within the *guardianía* of Acaponeta (that is, to the west, south, and southeast), the following languages were spoken: Pinutl or Pinome, Guachicanuquia, Guacnuquia, Garinuquia, Iruzanuquia, Naarinuquia, and Neuxinuquia.[143]

These data suggest Naarinuquia as the dominant language along the coast; Tecual in the vicinity of Jalisco City and Tequespespán; and Pinutl, Pinome, or Pinonuquia along the Río Santiago and the Río Huaynamota in Nayarit. A comment made by Antonio Arias de Saavedra in the middle of the seventeenth century indicates that Usare was the language of the province called Uzares, located east of the province of Vaynamota.[144] These data establish a linguistic relationship between peoples who lived south and southeast of Acaponeta, north of Sentispac, and immediately east of the Tepic Plateau. However, this linguistic relationship did not prevent disputes from occurring among the various groups. Francisco del Barrio wrote at length of warfare between the Chora (Cora) and the Guaynamota (Vaynamota), both of whom spoke the same language. The Alicia are also mentioned as a *nación* at war with the Cora. Barrio refers to Guaynamota pueblos along the Río Huaynamota at Sauchiche, Acaritz, Aumata, Vyuisita, Tlaxomulco, and Taullita. None of these places are on modern maps. He reports Cora at Acatlán, which was undoubtedly located near the site of the present-day Acatán de Cañas or within the Sierra de Acatán. There are repeated references to an important Cora center called Anyari or Yanari west of the Río Huaynamota. The Coano lived near Guajacatlán (now, Ahuacatlán in Nayarit).[145]

Tello records the establishment of a settlement of Guisares at Huaximic (now, Huajimic in Nayarit) in 1602;[146] these people had once lived along the eastern border of the Vaynamota country. Santoscoy refers to the Usiliques who took part in an uprising near San Andrés Teul (Zacatecas) in 1591.[147]

In the middle of the seventeenth century, Arias de Saavedra referred to Totorame who lived along the coast west of Xalixco (Jalisco City) and the Huitzole who lived southeast of Acaponeta in the vicinity of San Pedro Ixcatán.[148] These Huitzole were also called Ixchatecos. The relationship between the people of San Pedro Ixcatán and the Tecual-speaking people of Jalisco City is made clear: both groups spoke the same language, *la lengua tequalme* (Tecual). San Pedro Ixcatán was recorded as being peopled by folk who spoke Tequalme as late as 1769.[149]

The sixteenth- and seventeenth-century references cited above establish the relative position of the Cora (Guaynamota or Vaynamota), the Huichol (cited in the literature as Uzares, Alicia, Guisares, Huitzole, Hueitxolme, Usilique, and Ixchatecos), and the Totorame on the southern and southwestern borders of the sixteenth-century Tepehuan.

THE TEPEHUAN HEARTLAND

Distribution of the Tepehuan north of Durango City in the late sixteenth and early seventeenth centuries can be documented by references found in civil and ecclesiastical records. However, the repeated references in these records to pueblos of the Tepehuan should not be taken to mean that the Indians lived in villages. Pueblos referred to by the early missionaries were founded by the fathers at sites where there were Indian milpas or where Indians were working in mines.

It was the Franciscan order that first administered to the northern Tepehuan. A convent was founded in the Valle de San Bartolomé (now, Valle de Allende in Chihuahua) downstream from Santa Bárbara about 1560,[150] and shortly thereafter there were more than three hundred Indian families living near the mission;[151] these people were undoubtedly the Indians referred to as "algunos indios Lepeguanes [Tepehuan] " by Miranda in 1575.[152]

Jesuits first appeared in Durango shortly after 1590 and established their first important mission north of that city at Misión La Sauceda (near present-day Canatlán, Durango) in 1596;[153] and in the following year, missions were established at Santiago Papasquiaro, Atotonilco (where there were five settlements of Tepehuan near the juncture of the Río Tepehuanes and the Río de Santiago), and Santa Catalina (now, Tepehuanes in Durango). In addition, many Tepehuan living near Guanaceví were baptized.[154] The *anua* of 1597 makes clear that the Santiago Papasquiaro site was selected because the Indians came in from the surrounding country to work in mines at Santiago. The Atotonilco Valley was chosen as a mission site because the Indians came from their accustomed retreats in the nearby highlands to work milpas along the river. Jesuits established a center at Guanaceví because the Tepehuan were at work in the mines there. The Jesuit report for 1602 contains references to numerous Tepehuan at Santiago Papasquiaro, Atotonilco, Indé, Zape, Santa Catalina, and Ocotlán[155] (located about forty leagues from Santiago Papasquiaro). Mota y Escobar recorded Tepehuan at Indé, Santa Catalina, and the Valle de San Bartolomé in 1602, noting that those in the Valle de San Bartolomé came from Indé.[156] Several Tepehuan pueblos were administered to by Jesuits in the vicinity of the *partido de Ocotlán* (what may be Santa Cruz, Durango) northwest of Santiago Papasquiaro in 1607.[157]

Important clusters of Tepehuan north of Durango City are indicated by comments in an unsigned account of the great Tepehuan rebellion of 1616-1618;[158] there are specific references to Tepehuan near Guadiana (in villages around the city), La Sauceda (near Canatlán), El Jaral (about two leagues from Guadiana), Guanaceví (in the very center of the northern Tepehuan lands), Indé, San Ignacio (about five leagues from Guanaceví), Santa Catalina (Tepehuanes), Santiago Papasquiaro, Tenerapa (near Santa Catalina), El Tunal (near Guadiana), Guatimapé (near Atotonilco), and Terame (west of Guadiana, toward the Xixime country).

The Tepehuan lands extended west through the mountains in places so much so that the Indian lands overlooked Sinaloa. The ranges that overlooked Sinaloa were portions of the northwest-southeast ranges of the Sierra Madre

Occidental west of the Tepehuan country of northern Durango; these ranges include such peaks as Cerro Canoas, Cerro Huagal, Cerro Tule, Cerro Cebollas, Cerro Blanco, and Cerro Asientos. Lands west of this portion of the Sierra Madre Occidental are adjacent to lands held in the sixteenth century by the Acaxee and the Xixime that were considered within the jurisdiction of Sinaloa in the early historical period.

Juan Fonte recorded Tepehuan in the vicinity of San Juan in the Valle de Aguila,[159] by which name the upper portion of the Río Balleza Valley (now, Valle de San Juan) was known in the first decade of the seventeenth century. Mateo de Vesga reported raids on Spanish farms in the Santa Bárbara Valley by Tepehuan from the Valle de San Pablo (the lower portion of the Río Balleza Valley) in the early 1600's.[160]

Additional information concerning distribution of the Tepehuan in northern Durango during the early seventeenth century is found in the monumental work of Andrés Pérez de Ribas (1576-1655) published in Madrid in 1645 and entitled *Los Triunfos de Nuestra Santa Fe*. Pérez de Ribas knew the west coast missions best from personal experience; he did not reside in Durango except when he passed through the area while en route to and from Mexico City or Sinaloa. However, he became *Provincial* of New Spain in 1638 and in writing his history had access to original sources,[161, 162] much of which he incorporated within his account of Jesuit activity among the Tepehuan. Pérez de Ribas places the Tepehuan in the rough country east of Topia and San Andrés, in Santiago Papasquiaro, Guanacoví, Indé, La Sauceda (Canatlán), Santa Catalina (Tepehuanes), Zape, San Ignacio (near Zape), Atotonilco, Guatimapé, Boyagame (near Santa Catalina), along the Río de Los Ahorcados (the modern Río Tepehuanes), Las Salinas ("distant from Guadiana"), El Tizonazo (San José), Otinapa (west of Durango City), San Pablo (Balleza), Tenerapa (near Tepehuanes), and at El Tunal (near Santiago Papasquiaro).[163]

Zapata's account of 1678 mentions Tepehuan north of Durango at Santiago Papasquiaro, Atotonilco, Santa Catalina (Tepehuanes), Zape, San José Tizonazo, Indé, and Santa Cruz de Nazas (on the Río Oro not far from Indé) in the state of Durango; and at San Pablo (Balleza) and San Gerónimo de Huejotitlán in the state of Chihuahua.[164]

A civil report made in 1715 records Tepehuan at the following sites: San Diego de Canatlán, San Nicolás, Santiago Papasquiaro, San Andrés Atotonilco, Santa Catalina de Tepehuanes, and Zape.[165]

Ignacio Lizasoain's report of 1763 does not refer to Tepehuan being in what is now Durango, but it does indicate that there were many Tepehuan inhabiting the ravines near Nabogame and Baborigame.[166]

Tamarón y Romeral's survey of 1765 specifically refers to *indios* at the following locales north of Durango City: Zape, Santa Catalina (Tepehuanes), Santiago Papasquiaro, Atotonilco, San Nicolás, and Canatlán in Durango; and at Baborigame, Nabogame, Santa Rosalia, and Cinco Llagas in Chihuahua.[167]

The Fransciscan Fathers' report of 1778 mentions Tepehuan at Nabogame, Chismal, Dolores, Santa Ana [near the Real de San (Juan) Nepomuceno], Chinatú, Baborigame, Basonopa, Tohayana, Cinco Llagas, Santa Rosa, and Gueráchic on the Río Verde.[168] It should be recalled that the Tarahumar were also reported at Cinco Llagas, Chinatú, Nabogame, Chismal, and Santa Ana. In 1788, Alcocer recorded Tepehuan at Baborigame, Cinco Llagas, Basonopa, Santa Rosa, Nabogame, and Dolores.[169] Bernardo Tarandoy Cobarruvias referred to Indian families at Zape, Santa Catalina, Santiago Papasquiaro, San Nicolás, Las Bocas, San Gabriel, and San José Tizonazo in Durango; and at Baborigame, Nabogame, Basonopa, Santa Rosalia, San Juan, and Huejotitlán in Chihuahua in 1784.[170] Archival material for the period 1777-1825 in the Franciscan Convento de Guadalupe (located near Zacatecas) includes repeated references to missionary activity among the Tepehuan at Nabogame, Baborigame, Basonopa, and Dolores.[171]

It is clear that most of the country south of the upper reaches of the Río Verde in the state of Chihuahua was dominated by the Tepehuan by the middle of the eighteenth century, but how long these Indians had been there cannot be determined. The previously cited Jesuit document written by Benito Rinaldini in the eighteenth century describes Tepehuan moving into the Baborigame and Nabogame country in flight from the wrath of the Spaniards during the great rebellion which began near Durango City in 1616.[172] Although Zapata's report of 1678[173] mentions only those Tepehuan at San Pablo Balleza and Huejotitlán, there must have been many Tepehuan south of the Río Verde at that date. It is true that a permanent mission was not established at Nabogame until after 1700,[174] but the Nabogame site was known to the Jesuits as early as 1678. In that year it was listed as a *visita* of San Martín Atotonilco.[175] That there were significant numbers of Tepehuan immediately to the south and the northeast of the Río Verde during the first half of the eighteenth century may be evidenced by the fact that Jesuit missionaries were on permanent assignment at Baborigame, Nabogame, San Pablo Balleza, Huejotitlán, and Las Cuevas during the 1740's and 1750's.[176]

Sixteenth-century references document the presence of Tepehuan in the vicinity of what is now Durango City. The account of Ahumada's expedition against the Chichimec in 1562 refers to the Valle de Guadiana as being in Tepehuan territory,[177] and the Franciscans Pedro Espinareda and Juan de Tápia worked there among the Tepehuan in the 1550's.[178, 179] Shortly after the founding of Durango City in 1563 or 1564,[180] these Indians apparently retreated from the Valle de Guadiana or were absorbed as mestizos into the Spanish complex, since the next references to Tepehuan in that immediate area are those found in early seventeenth-century documents that record the great Tepehuan rebellion which began near Durango City in 1616.[181]

The country west of Durango City, between the city and the Xixime pueblos of Humase, Yamoriba, and Zapiuris, was certainly Tepehuan in the late sixteenth century; Alonso del Valle, writing from Guatimapé in 1618, refers to a Tepehuan pueblo called Cocoratame located near the Xixime pueblos.[182] Mateo de Vesga, who wrote of the Tepehuan rebellion between 1616 and 1618, also mentions Cocoratame as a Tepehuan site.[183] Pérez de Ribas places Tepehuan at Otinapa somewhat to the west of Durango at the time of the rebellion.[184]

The general distribution of the Tepehuan living south of Durango City in the very early colonial period was given in the section describing the southern border of the Tepehuan. As cited previously, the civil and ecclesiastical records make clear that the Tepehuan were living at or near Quiviquinta, Tachichilpa, Milpillas, Los Caimanes, Acaponeta, San Juan Peyotán, and Amatlán de Jora in Nayarit; at or near Colotlán, Azqueltán, Mezquitic, and Huejuquilla in Jalisco; at or near Monte Escobedo and San Andrés Teul in Zacatecas; and at or near Lajas, Milpillas Chico, Huazamota, Santa María Ocotán, and San Francisco Ocotán in Durango. In addition, there were Tepehuan living at or near numerous locales which cannot be found on modern maps: Teititlán, San Sebastian, Thenara, Voynara, Moroata, Nyara, Tzenzompia, Noxta, Camotán, Quepontyta, Quenta, Sapotlán, San Juan Tuametla, and Nextalpa. These records further suggest that some early sites, which were apparently not Tepehuan in immediate pre-Conquest times, became Tepehuan in the early seventeenth century. Mezquital, recorded as Zacateco country in 1562,[185] was peopled by Tepehuan in 1617 as was Tajicaringa.[186]

References to the Tepehuan at Santiago Bayacora, El Tunal (near the city of Durango), Mezquital, Yonora, Xoconoxtle, Santa María Ocotán, Teneraca, San Francisco Ocotán, San Pedro Jícara, Huazamota, San Bernabé, San Antonio, San Lucas de Galpa, Lajas, Milpillas Chico, Tajicaringa, Ylamatech, and Pueblo Nuevo by Tamarón y Romeral in 1765[187] constitute additional evidence of important clusters of Tepehuan south of Durango City in pre-Conquest times.

POPULATION

There are insufficient data for estimating accurately the number of Tepehuan who lived during the sixteenth century in the area extending from what are today northern portions of Jalisco and Nayarit in the south to southern Chihuahua in the north, and furthermore, some of the population data for the early seventeenth century are questionable.

Without doubt there were many Tepehuan living in what is now the state of Durango in the early part of the seventeenth century, but there were probably not as many Indians as is suggested in at least one account of the Tepehuan rebellion of 1616-1618. Arlegui is apparently responsible for the oft-repeated statement that Governor Gaspar de Alvear y Salazar went out to battle 25,000 Tepehuan warriors on the plains of Cacaria just north of Guadiana in November of 1616.[188] The Zapata report of 1678 makes clear that the average size of the Tepehuan family was 3.4 persons in the seventeenth century.[189] Therefore, if it is assumed that at least 20,000 of the alleged 25,000 warriors were heads of families, then there would have been about 68,000 Indians within central Durango during the early seventeenth century. This figure seems extremely high when civil and ecclesiastical records are examined. A civil report of 1625 indicates that Jesuit and Franciscan missionaries administered to 2,732 baptized Indians at Indé, Santa Catalina, Guanacevi, Valle de San Bartolomé, and La Sauceda; there were more than 1,000 Indians in the Valle de San Bartolomé alone.[190] The total figure does not suggest the presence of a great number of Tepehuan north of Durango City in the early seventeenth century. However, the figure is obviously inaccurate with respect to the total number of Tepehuan living north of Durango City since only baptized Indians are referred to.

The Zapata report of 1678 lists a total of 1,820 Indians at the following missions: Santiago Papasquiaro, Atotonilco, San Nicolás, Santa Catalina, Tepehuanes, Zape, and San José Tizonazo (Durango) and at San Pablo Balleza and San Gerónimo de Huejotitlán (Chihuahua).[191] This figure represented a total of 526 families under mission control.

An eighteenth-century report made by Padre José Echeverría in 1731 gives a total of 418 Indian families under mission control at Las Bocas (near present-day Villa Ocampo, Durango), San José Tizonazo, Santa Cruz (de Nazas), Zape, Santiago Papasquiaro, San Nicolás, and Atotonilco.[192] This report seems to be reasonably accurate with respect to the actual number of Indian families at the missions since Echeverría made a distinction between *españoles* and *indios ladinos ó mestizos*.

The first report that gives rather precise data concerning numbers of Tepehuan families at or near the old Jesuit missions north of Durango City after the missions were secularized in 1753[193] is that of Tamarón y Romeral, whose survey of 1765 recorded a total of 346 Indian families at Zape, Santa Catalina (Tepehuanes), Santiago Papasquiaro, Atotonilco, San Nicolás, and Canatlán (Durango) and at Baborigame, Nabogame, Santa Rosalia, and Cinco Llagas (Chihuahua).[194] The Chihuahua centers of Baborigame and Santa Rosalia contained about one-half of the Tepehuan referred to, a total of 168 families and 590 people.

Apparently, the sole late eighteenth-century report of Tepehuan population near or at the former Jesuit missions of northern Durango and southern Chihuahua is that made by Bernardo Tarandoy Cobarruvias, who recorded in 1784 a total of 226 families at Zape, Santa Catalina, Santiago Papasquiaro, San Nicolás, Las Bocas, San Gabriel, and San José Tizonazo in Durango.[195] In comparison, there were 391 families listed for the Chihuahua missions of Baborigame, Nabogame, Basonopa, Santa Rosalia, San Juan (Balleza), and San Gerónimo de Huejotitlán.

These data suggest that by 1800 the Tepehuan, as such, had virtually disappeared from the scene in northern Durango[196] and that they were more numerous in the southernmost part of Chihuahua, where they persist today.

There are no adequate data from which we may determine exactly how many Tepehuan there are in southern Chihuahua at the present time. According to the census of 1960, there were 33,050 inhabitants in the *municipios* of Guadalupe y Calvo and Morelos,[197] where most of the northern Tepehuan live. Of these people, approximately 3,718 out of a total of 26,751 people in the *municipio* of Guadalupe y Calvo were reported to speak a *lengua indígena*; some 970 people out of a total of 6,299 inhabitants in Morelos were said to speak an Indian dialect. The total number of assumed aborigines (4,688) is a more realistic estimate of the number of Tepehuan than that found in the census data of 1940, 1945, and 1950. The 1940 census lists a total of 2,491 Tepehuan in Chihuahua.[198] A special census, apparently conducted by the *Instituto Nacional Indigenista* in 1945, recorded a total of 3,379 Tepehuan.[199] According to the census of 1950, the *municipio* of Guadalupe y Calvo had a total of 1,746 people who spoke both Spanish and a *lengua indígena*; a total of 420 people spoke only an Indian dialect.[200]

Lack of agreement as to exactly what constitutes an *indígena* and a mestizo, not only among the Indians and mestizos of western Chihuahua but also among the census takers as well, precludes an accurate determination of the number of Tepehuan in southern Chihuahua. Even if there were agreement among census takers as to what is an *indígena* and what is a mestizo, the census records for much of western Chihuahua would most likely be incorrect: census takers are loath to enter the area occupied by the Tepehuan even when the recorders are native Chihuahuans.[201]

Evidence for the belief that there are more Tepehuan than official records indicate is found in data concerning Indian and mestizo families at Llano Grande in 1960. At that time, forty-seven families were said to be Tepehuan, where-

as thirty-four were said to be mestizo. The average size of the present-day Tepehuan family is six, which means that there were about 282 Indians at Llano
Grande in 1960. That there were more is highly probable since many of the
important mestizo families have one parent who is Tepehuan or of Tepehuan
extraction but who is counted as a mestizo. Wealthy families are considered to
be mestizo, and members of such families rarely consider the parent of Tepehuan extraction or origin as being Indian. At least, such is not referred to in
conversation. Since Llano Grande is but one of the thirty-odd "communities"
of Tepehuan, and since some of these "communities," such as Santa Rosa, are
certainly more Indian than mestizo in population, it is quite likely that there
are more than 8,000 Tepehuan living in southern Chihuahua today.[202]

There is little in the early record concerning the number of Tepehuan living south of Durango City. Tamarón y Romeral's report of 1765 is apparently
the first report that gives somewhat exact data concerning the Tepehuan of
southern Durango. This account records a total of 2,174 people and 679 families at or near the following sites: Santiago Bayacora, El Tunal (near the city of
Durango), Mezquital, Yonora, Xoconoxtle, Santa María Ocotán, Teneraca, San
Francisco Ocotán, San Lucas de Galpa, Milpillas Chico, Tajicaringa, Ylamatech, and Pueblo Nuevo.[203] The Cobarruvias account of 1784 lists 105 families
at Huazamota.[204] For the nineteenth century, there is the statement of Lumholtz that there were about 3,000 Tepehuan in southern Durango; these Indians were living at San Francisco de Lajas, Tajicaringa, Santiago Teneraca, Milpillas Chico, Pueblo Viejo, Santa María Ocotán, and San Francisco Ocotán in
the 1890's.[205]

Pastor Rouaix stated that Tepehuan were living at Santa María Ocotán in
1910 but gave no data with respect to numbers. He noted, however, that *indígenas primitivos* had entirely abandoned San Francisco Ocotán, San Pedro
Jícaro, Tajicaringa, Yonora, Milpillas (Chico), and (San Francisco de) Lajas.[206]
Mason interviewed Tepehuan at Santa María Ocotán and nearby Xoconoxtle in
1948 but made no statement concerning population.[207] Riley and Hobgood
found Tepehuan in the vicinity of Santa María Ocotán, Candelaria, Aquitazar-
ca, Xoconoxtle, and Teneraca in 1958.[208]

A partial clue to approximately how many Tepehuan there are in the
southernmost part of Durango is found in the census data of 1960.[209] Within
the *municipios* of Mezquital and Pueblo Nuevo, a total of 1,511 persons were
reported to speak only a *lengua indígena*; a total of 1,298 persons were reported to speak both Spanish and a *lengua indígena*. These data suggest the presence of at least 2,809 Tepehuan in these southern Durango *municipios* that
historically have been essentially Tepehuan.

In the state of Jalisco, at least two of the Tepehuan centers identified by

Arias de Saavedra in the middle of the seventeenth century (Huejuquilla, Azqueltán, Mezquitic, Monte Escobedo, and Colotlán)[210] persisted as Indian sites until recent times. Lumholtz visited the Tepecano (Tepehuan) in the vicinity of Azqueltán, Mezquitic, and Nostic in the late nineteenth century,[211] and Mason interviewed the Tepecano at Azqueltán in the early part of the twentieth century.[212]

In the state of Nayarit, San Juan Peyotán, which was recorded as a Tepehuan site by de Saavedra in the middle of the seventeenth century,[213] retained its identity as an Indian center until late in the eighteenth century; the Cobarruvias document of 1784 records thirty-nine Indian families at the site.[214]

Most of the Tepehuan who, according to late sixteenth- and early seventeenth-century documents, were found in the northwestern portion of Nayarit at Acaponeta, Teititlán, Milpillas (Chico or Grande), San Sebastian, Los Caimanes, Tachichilpa, and Quiviquinta must have been absorbed early into the mestizo complex; however, there were some Indians identified by Lumholtz as Tepehuan at Milpillas Grande and Quiviquinta in the late nineteenth century.[215]

According to the census of 1960, there were 6,715 inhabitants within the *municipio* of Huajicori located in the northernmost part of Nayarit;[216] this *municipio* includes the colonial Tepehuan centers of Caimán, San Francisco de Caimán, Huajicori, Quiviquinta, and Milpillas Grande. Of the total population, 15 persons spoke only a *lengua indígena* and 504 spoke both Spanish and a native language. Since Lumholtz encountered Tepehuan at Quiviquinta and Milpillas Grande in the late nineteenth century,[217] we may assume that these people, who in 1960 spoke a *lengua indígena*, were probably Tepehuan.

The northern prong of Jalisco, which is wedged in between portions of Zacatecas and Nayarit and is adjacent to the old Tepehuan country of southern Durango, includes territory that was certainly Tepehuan during colonial times. The old colonial centers of Mezquitic, Colotlán, Huejuquilla, and Azqueltán are located within this territory which, today, includes the *municipios* of Bolaños, Colotlán, Huejucar, Huejuquilla El Alto, Mezquitic, Santa María de Los Angeles, Totatiche, and Villa Guerrero. According to the census of 1960, these *municipios* contained a total of 69,878 inhabitants.[218] Linguistic data pertaining to idioms suggest that 6,818 spoke a *lengua indígena* in 1960. Presumably, most of these people—if not all—were Tepehuan in origin.

Therefore, within the old Tepehuan country south of Durango City there are some 10,131 Tepehuan: 2,809 in southern Durango, 504 in Nayarit, and 6,818 in Jalisco. This figure is somewhat higher than that suggested in 1965 by Bascom, who accounted for approximately 8,000 Tepehuan and Tepecano in

the municipalities of Mezquital and Pueblo Nuevo in Durango, in the municipality of Huajicori in Nayarit, and near Azqueltán in northern Jalisco.[219]

THE PHYSICAL ENVIRONMENT OF THE CHIHUAHUA TEPEHUAN

The Chihuahua Tepehuan, along with the mestizos, occupy an area that
encompasses about 10,500 square kilometers, most of it within the *municipios*
of Morelos and Guadalupe y Calvo. This area contains rather distinct physiographic divisions and several pronounced types of vegetation zones. No attempt has been made herein to indicate on a map the areal distribution of the
two most important physiographic divisions of southern Chihuahua: the canyon lands and the rolling uplands, each of which consists of somewhat distinct
subdivisions. This is particularly true for the rolling uplands which are comprised of features locally termed *mesas* and *llanos*.[220] Nor has an attempt been
made to map principal vegetation zones found within the Indian habitat in
spite of the fact that the floral complex of southern Chihuahua includes elements that with some justification could be described by Gentry's terms for
upper portions of the Río Mayo country: Pine Forest, Oak Forest, and Short-
tree Forest.[221] Ecological factors have caused such a complicated distribution
of vegetation types in southern Chihuahua that the above terms must be used
with caution. They are, however, useful terms and are applied herein only in a
very general sense.

Southern Chihuahua is part of the Sierra Madre Occidental, that great upland mass stretching from north-northwest to south-southeast and separating
the high interior plateau of northern Mexico from the western coastal plains.
The dominant lithologic element in southern Chihuahua consists of several
thousands of feet of volcanic materials that cover older and folded strata. The
volcanic materials, which have been slightly tilted, are marked here and there
by granitic intrusions, particularly in the west. The lower portions of northern
and western canyons are distinguished by exposures of very ancient granites,
whereas upper portions of the Sierra Madre Occidental are characterized by
frequent exposures of gray volcanic tuff.

When approached from either the west or the east, the Sierra Madre Occidental appears to be exceedingly rough and difficult country. However, not
all of the country occupied by the Chihuahua Tepehuan should be considered
topographically rough and difficult. Admittedly, there is a great amount of
rough terrain, particularly in the broken country immediately south of the Río
Verde Canyon and within the western margins of the Tepehuan country; the
highest peak of northern Mexico (Cerro Mohinora, about 11,500 feet in eleva-

tion) is located just southwest of Guadalupe y Calvo. However, there are significantly extensive portions of southern Chihuahua that are characterized by
rather smooth-topped ridges and wide and flat valley floors, and in some locales, there are mesas and llanos that are areally quite large. One such mesa, the
Mesa de Milpillas, extends in unbroken fashion in a north-south direction for
many miles.

The average elevation of the southern Chihuahua portion of the Sierra
Madre Occidental is about 7,800 feet; however, within the country south of the
Río Verde the deviation from this average may be as much as a thousand feet,
as in one of the very deep canyons immediately west of the Mesa de Milpillas
(east of Cinco Llagas).

LAND FORMS AND VEGETATION

Canyon Country. Before the development of airstrips in the Tepehuan
country (these airstrips are usually nothing more than meadows from which
boulders have been removed) and the completion of a lumber road from Hidalgo del Parral to Guadalupe y Calvo, the canyon country on the west, north, and
east of the southern Chihuahua Tepehuan country inhibited penetration of either of the two extreme-southern *municipios* of Chihuahua. Except for mining
and trade activities, there was little in-and-out traffic. What traffic there was
had to contend with the enormously intricate and sometimes very deep canyon
systems along the Río Chinatú (on the east), the Río Verde (on the north), and
the headwater streams of the Río Sinaloa, such as the Río Basonopa and the
Río Petatlán (on the west);[222] all of these rivers have carved rough terrain into
the tilted lava flows that dominate the lithology of southern Chihuahua. The
Río Verde has developed a canyon system that is almost as deep and certainly
as rugged as the better-known Río Urique Canyon to the north. Also, the Río
Verde Canyon, particularly at middle elevations, has a greater profusion of
volcanic dikes than the Urique Canyon. Again like the Urique, the middle and
upper canyon slopes of the Verde are marked by great benches of very resistant
volcanic materials. These benches usually have steep escarpments (locally
called *bufas*) on their outer margins, and they, as well as the dikes, must be
skirted in descending or ascending the canyon. Talus slopes, devoid of vegetation for the most part, have formed on the lower portions of both dikes and
escarpments. Upper portions of the great sloping benches of the Río Verde
Canyon are mantled with a thin cover of soil, and middle and lower portions of
the benches are covered with rock debris except where the gradient is such that
exposed rock has remained *in situ* and weathered into soil. Except on the
benches, or in the immediate vicinity of canyon tributary streams, or where
these streams have deposited soil in their meandering descent to the Verde,

there is little favorable environment for the development of vegetation other than the most hardy (and xerophytic) types. The canyon bottom of the Río Verde (at least between San Carlos and Gueráchic) lacks a true floodplain with fertile soil. Rather, the stream is bordered by several hundred feet of gravel, sand, and boulders, beyond which the sides of the canyon slope abruptly upward.

Eastern and western canyons that bound the Tepehuan country are more subdued in detail than the canyon of the Verde, but they remain difficult enough with respect to topography to impede access into southern Chihuahua by land routes.

The immediate rim of the canyon country, whether on the east, north, or south, is dominated by species of pines characteristic of the rolling uplands of southern Chihuahua: *Pinus arizonica, P. ayacahuite, P. chihuahuana, P. durangensis, P. Engelmanni, P. leiophylla, P. Lumholtzii, P. reflexa*, and *P. teocote*. None of these appear in pure stands along the rims; they are interspersed with growths of *Cupressus arizonica* and *Pseudotsuga mucronata*. Almost no grasses grow along the canyon rims, but scattered throughout the stands of pine, in favorable ecological situations, there is an understory of vegetation dominated by *Arctostaphylos pungens, Arbutus arizonica, A. xalapensis, Vaccinium confertum, Garrya laurifolia, G. ovata, Salix Gooddingii, Populus tremuloides, Ceanothus depressus, C. coeruleus*, and (in damp areas) ferns. There are a few oaks along the canyon rims—*Quercus omissa, Q. crassifolia, Q. durifolia*, and *Q. coccolobaefolia*—but they are all stunted forms. Unidentified species of the parasitic *Phoradendron* grow upon these oaks.

Almost everywhere along the upper portions of the canyon country that borders the Tepehuan habitat on the east, north, and west, a considerable number of oaks can be seen from the canyon rims. Since they dominate the landscape, these oaks constitute what may loosely be termed an Oak Forest. This Oak Forest is more or less confined to the sloping benches of the canyon country; however, oaks appear downslope in the wetter canyon bottoms. *Quercus chihuahuensis, Q. coccolobaefolia, Q. hypoleucoides, Q. magnoliaefolia*, and *Q. albocincta* are the most common species, with their distribution and number apparently being determined by terrain character and available moisture. At least three types of bunch grasses, *Mühlenbergia dumosa, M. Emersleyi*, and *M. gracilis*, appear here and there among the oaks. *Agave bovicornuta* and at least four other species of agave grow in open, usually rocky, areas in the Oak Forest; also growing here are species of Liliaceae (*Dasylirion simplex, D. Wheeleri, Nolina matapensis, N. durangensis*, and *Yucca decipiens*). *Sabal uresana* appears in better-watered portions of the Oak Forest, chiefly in moist arroyos and along streamways. Lower levels of the Oak Forest slopes are characterized by dense stands of shrubs, among which are conspicuous numbers of *Acacia cymbispina, A. cochliacantha, Mimosa dysocarpa,* and *Hydrangea Oerstedii.* Some of these shrubs grow in colonies of individual species so thick that the movement of pack animals is impeded. At higher levels of the Oak Forest, examples of *Pinus chihuahuana, P. leiophylla,* and *P. Engelmanni* are found.

Below the benches and their predominantly oak environment, the canyon slopes are much steeper, there is less available moisture, and the soil is poor. The landscape is dominated by smaller trees and by shrubs—particularly such trees as *Ceiba acuminata, Bursera grandifolia, Willardia mexicana, Caesalpinia platyloba, Lysiloma Watsoni, Acacia Farnesiana, A. pennatula, A. cymbispina, Haematoxylon brasiletto,* and *Ipomoea arborescens.* Among the species of shrubs that appear in great numbers in this Short-tree Forest are *Mimosa dysocarpa, Acacia cochliacantha, Erythrina flabelliformis, Eysenhardtia amorphoides, Calliandra rupestris,* and *Hydrangea Oerstedii.* More arid portions of the Short-tree Forest are characterized by species of *Dasylirion, Nolina,* and *Yucca;* and it is here that certain cacti—such as *Opuntia* and *Echinocereus* species and *Pachycereus pecten-aboriginum*—begin to appear downslope from the pine-dominated uplands. *Bromus arizonicus* and *B. molliformis* are common grasses growing in this Short-tree Forest complex along with the harsh bunch grasses, *Mühlenbergia gracilis* and *M. Emersleyi.*

What is herein described as the Short-tree Forest is more extensive in canyon country to the north and the west. The eastern Tepehuan canyon country is dominated more by species of oak which are interspersed by stands of shrubs. In the western and northern canyon country, however, the Short-tree Forest reaches down almost to the lowermost elevations occupied by the Tepehuan, and the predominantly deciduous vegetation growing on its slopes contrasts strongly with the evergreen and deciduous vegetation of the streamways and canyon bottoms typical of canyon country at lower elevations. The green strips that mark the streamways and canyon bottoms often extend up into higher elevations of the canyon country, thereby giving variety to the landscape particularly when the deciduous vegetation of the upper slopes has lost its foliage. Trees which are common along main canyon tributary streams at middle and somewhat lower elevations of the canyon lands include the following: *Juglans major, Coutarea pterosperma, Magnolia Schiedeana, Pithecellobium dulce, Randia echinocarpa, R. laevigata, Ficus cotinifolia, F. padifolia, F. Goldmannii, F. radulina, F. petiolaris, Morus microphylla, Haematoxylon brasiletto, Achras zapota, Karwinskia Humboldtiana, Sambucus caerulea, Cupressus arizonica, Tabebuia Palmeri, Hura crepitans, Arbutus arizonica, A. xalapensis, Salix Bonplandiana, Licania retifolia, Quercus chihuahuensis, Q. candicans, Q. coccolobaefolia, Q. hypoleucoides, Q. magnoliaefolia,* and *Q. albocincta.*

Rough margins of these streamways are often characterized by stands of shrubs which include *Caesalpinia pulcherrima*, *Baccharis glutinosa*, *Tithonia fruticosa*, *Solanum madrense*, *Franseria ambrosioides*, *Fouquieria fasciculata*(?), *Buddleia cordata*, *B. tomentella*, and *B. sessiliflora*. *Vitis arizonica* is one of the numerous vines found in the lower portions of canyons. Grasses common to the canyons include *Phragmites communis*, *Arundo donax*, and *Aristida ternipes* var. *minor*.

The great variety of vegetation associated with the canyons proper is indicated by the following list of trees and shrubs that grow in stands or as isolated forms within an area along the Río Verde hardly one mile in length and one-quarter mile in width: the introduced Asiatic mango (*Mangifera indica*), *Sebastiana Pringlei*, *Sapium biloculare*, *Alnus oblongifolia*, *Piscidia mollis*, *Jatropha cordata*, *Fouquieria fasciculata*(?), *Haematoxylon brasiletto*, *Pithecellobium dulce*, *Pachycereus pecten-aboriginum*, *Prosopis chilensis*, *Acacia Farnesiana*, *Randia echinocarpa*, and species of *Ficus*.

Rolling Uplands. The term "rolling uplands" best characterizes the topography of the Chihuahua Tepehuan country, and within these uplands there is a great variety of individual physiographic features and concomitant types of vegetation. The rolling uplands merge almost imperceptibly with the Río Verde canyon country on the north and with the canyon country that is bounded by the Río Chinatú on the east and the headwater streams of the Río Sinaloa on the west. The rolling uplands, broken here and there by such streams as the Río Basonopa and the Río Los Loera, extend south of the Chihuahua Tepehuan habitat to beyond Guadalupe y Calvo.

Within the uplands, streams flowing in a general north-south direction have so dissected the several thousand feet of tuff that large segments of the Indian country are separated from one another by miniature replicas of the deeper and more intricately cut canyons on the north and west. A further distinction is given the rolling uplands by an area that is termed herein "broken country"; it is located on the north side of the Tepehuan lands between the rolling uplands proper and the canyon of the Río Verde. This *quebrado* country extends in finger-like extensions into the rolling uplands for varying distances. Some 50 percent of the ridges in the broken country are exceedingly sharp in detail, and the valley slopes are commonly so steep that occupation by farm folk is impossible. Within the broken country on its northern salient few valley bottoms can be farmed; they are not wide enough for sufficient soil to have been deposited by the streams. Much rock is exposed in the steep and narrow valleys, and the soil is very thin for the most part. However, in the southern extensions of this broken country there are a few wide and flattish valleys, locally termed *llanos*; Baborigame and Nabogame are located in such llanos. Some of the ridges in the upper portions of the broken country have been flattened by erosional activity and, when cleared of timber, support fine stands of grass; these pastures are locally called *savannas*. Vast areas of the rolling uplands literally "stand up" above their canyons and dominate the landscape. This situation probably accounts for the term *mesa* being used for much of the central Tepehuan country—as for example, the Mesa de Milpillas. The tops of these mesas have a gently rolling terrain, broken here and there by wide and shallow arroyos or washes.

Although barely one-third of the rolling uplands south of the Río Verde may be said to be pine-clad, there are at least nine species of pine growing in the uplands of southern Chihuahua. *Pinus chihuahuana* is one of the more widely distributed, being restricted, however, to well-drained slopes. *Pinus Engelmanni* and *P. reflexa* are generally found in areas where the soil is deeper. *Pinus arizonica* is one of the few pines to appear in great stands. *Pinus ayacahuite*, one of the more numerous pines of southern Chihuahua, appears at higher elevations in the rolling uplands. *Pinus durangensis* is apparently more plentiful in the vicinity of Guadalupe y Calvo than toward the Río Verde on the north. The *pino triste* (*Pinus Lumholtzii*) is perhaps the most distinctive pine of southern Chihuahua and appears in areas of exceedingly poor soil, either in the thin soil of the rolling uplands proper or along the edges of arroyos or washes where soil is all but lacking. *Pinus teocote* appears in areas where there are virtually no other pines. It grows at random with one tree rather distant from another. Scattered specimens of *Pinus leiophylla* are found in eastern Tepehuan country. Better-watered margins of the Pine Forest country, particularly where the uplands break away into wide and shallow washes, permit the growth of *Juniperus pachyphloea* and *Pseudotsuga mucronata*. Scattered stands of *Populus tremuloides* are along the western margins of the pine-clad areas, especially where the slopes are shaded.

Where adequate sunshine reaches the forest floor of the pine-clad country and where soil and moisture conditions are suitable, a number of flowering plants lend variety to the landscape. The flowering plants found among the pine stands in the western portion of the Mesa de Milpillas are *Baccharis glutinosa*, *Buddleia sessiliflora*, *Daucus montanus*, *Eryngium Carlinae*, *Ranunculus Forreri*, *R. micranthus*, *Senecio* sp. af. *actinella*, *Verbena carolina*, *Stevia serrata*, *Begonia gracilis*, *Pentstemon barbatus*, *Gaultheria glaucifolia*, and *Chimaphila dasystemma*.

Here and there in the pine country is an understory of vegetation that is characterized by such shrubs as *Holodiscus dumosus*, *Arctostaphylos pungens*, *Arbutus glandulosa*, *A. arizonica*, *A. xalapensis*, *Vaccinium confertum*, *Garrya laurifolia*, *G. ovata*, *Ceanothus depressus*, *C. coeruleus*, *C. azureus*, and *Bouvar-*

dia glaberrima. These shrubs grow in sunny exposures within the pine stands and under trees in the arroyos and washes that have cut the edges of the pine-clad terrain.

There are apparently no areally extensive stands of oak within the rolling uplands. However, clusters of oaks are often found in protected situations among stands of pines. Pines alone occupy the higher and more windy positions. Upland oaks in southern Chihuahua include *Quercus albocincta, Q. arizonica, Q. chihuahuensis, Q. candicans, Q. coccolobaefolia, Q. crassifolia, Q. durifolia, Q. Endlichiana, Q. hypoleucoides, Q. magnoliaefolia, Q. omissa, Q. rugosa, Q. Urbanii,* and *Q. viminea. Struthanthus diversifolius* and *Phoradendron scaberrimum* are two common parasitic plants that grow upon these upland trees.

Washes or arroyos that fringe the edges of the uplands have scattered specimens of pines that are common to the uplands proper, as well as significant numbers of *Alnus oblongifolia, Morus microphylla, Juglans nogal, Fraxinus velutina, Prunus capuli, P. serotina,* and *P. virens.* Water courses that cut through the upland llanos or meadows are often bordered by thickets of *Salix Gooddingii,* and where these streams break away from the uplands, their borders are marked by *Aquilegia Skinneri, Oenothera rosea, Oxalis albicans, Begonia gracilis, Cologania humifusa, Fragaria mexicana, F. vesca, Potentilla Thurberi,* and *Salvia azurea.*

Upland meadows, mesas, and llanos are characterized in some instances by grasses that form a very heavy sod, difficult to prepare for tilling. Grasses that are common to the llanos near Baborigame and Nabogame include *Panicum bulbosum, P. texanum, P. plenum, Mühlenbergia dumosa,* and *M. gracilis.* Usually, a woodland of oak, *madroño,* and pine surrounds the llanos and mesas, which frequently have stands of *Arctostaphylos pungens* and species of *Arbutus* growing in well-drained, shallow depressions in their central portions. In wet areas of the llanos and mesas, there are significant numbers of *Ranunculus micranthus, Potentilla Thurberi, Tauschia nudicaulis,* and *Chromolepis heterophylla* growing.

CLIMATE

Statistical data on the climate in southern Chihuahua are not available; therefore only generalizations based on personal observations and on comments by the local inhabitants may be made concerning the year-round weather conditions.

Rolling Uplands. On a month-to-month basis, the climate in the rolling uplands is only slightly different from what it is in the canyon country, but the total effect of these differences is great enough that the native people refer to the uplands as *tierra templada* and the canyon country as *tierra caliente*. The variations in temperature range and total precipitation between canyon country and uplands are undoubtedly due to the combined influences of altitude and topography. Even the most casual observer in northern and western canyon lands notes that some slopes are clad with vegetation requiring more precipitation than that growing upon other slopes. And to a degree, this is also true for the rolling uplands. Rain storms are apparently generated in the uplands, and as they move toward the west or east, their paths are significantly affected by the great *bufas* in the canyons. Such is the case in the canyon of the Río Verde. Lower portions of the canyon lands experience an occasional drought and, rarely, a frost. By comparison, the uplands experience much more frost, and there are sometimes extended periods of drought that are responsible for successive crop failures.

According to the statements of mestizos and Tepehuan living in or near Baborigame, which is located on one of the upland llanos at an elevation of about 5,900 feet, January is the coldest month of the year. Ice may form in arroyos and remain for several days. Snow may fall several times during the month, and it has been known to pile up as much as one and one-half feet in the higher passes near Llano de Baborigame. There is no evidence that the snow cover ever stays on the ground for more than a few days. Temperature conditions during February are much the same as during January, and a light snowfall that melts upon striking the ground is the usual form of precipitation. March has little change in temperature conditions, but snow is not expected after the middle of the month. However, ice may continue to form on streams in the vicinity of Llano de Baborigame or Llano Grande, which is located south of Baborigame on the Mesa de Milpillas. Commonly, there is rainfall during March, and by the middle of April, rains occur every other day on the average. Rain continues to fall at intervals during May, and frost may occur until late in the month. The frost danger is past by mid-June, and the period of *las aguas* begins toward the last of June. July is quite cool and, for the most part, is a month of downpours that are frequently accompanied by hail.[223] The total amount of precipitation diminishes steadily each month after July—although at Baborigame, August, September, October, and November are apparently never characterized by serious drought. October and November are quite cool, and the first freeze of the winter occurs by mid-November. Freezes continue throughout December.

Statements by mestizos and Indians that the llanos at Baborigame and Nabogame never experience serious drought are echoed by the types and amount of vegetation associated with such upland locales; there seems to be a significant amount of moisture throughout the year. Moreover, the Indians insist that they cannot recall the drying up of springs in the vicinity of Baborigame and Nabogame.

Drought in the uplands seems to be associated mostly with flatter portions of the terrain, as upon the great Mesa de Milpillas and its southern extension toward Guadalupe y Calvo. The Tepehuan who live at Llano Grande and La Ciénega on the Mesa de Milpillas refer to droughts that have persisted for seven years.

Canyon Lands. According to the Tepehuan who live at Santa Rosa—located about two days' travel by mule west of Baborigame in one of those deep and difficult canyons that dissect the rolling uplands in a north-south direction—January is a cold month, and ice occasionally forms in the arroyos. Snow may fall several times during the month, but it rarely remains on the ground for more than a few hours. February is characterized by continued cold, and ice forms in the streams. The cold weather persists until well into March, but less ice forms. April and May may be described as moderate months with regard to temperature, but June is exceedingly hot, and the heat is not alleviated until showers begin to fall toward the end of the month. July is noteworthy as the month of *las aguas*, and there is much flooding of streams. August temperatures vary but little from those of July; however, the precipitation is considerably less than in July. By mid-September, the temperature regimen is quite pleasant; there is little rainfall during the month. October is described as a mild month with respect to temperature, and rainfall is exceedingly rare. November is somewhat cold with little or no precipitation; ice may form in the streams. The same type of weather continues during December but with more ice forming in the streams than in November.

The available evidence suggests that the climate of Chihuahua south of the Río Verde is generally one of moderate temperatures for most of the year with an unequal distribution of rainfall throughout the entire year. Low temperatures in uplands and canyons during some months, freezes that occur in both areas, frosts that occur with regularity in uplands toward the beginning of planting time, hail in the uplands, occasional drought in both uplands and canyons, and the excessive heat of some portions of the northern and western canyons do make life uncomfortable and at times hazardous with respect to crop damage. However, the present-day Tepehuan have demonstrated that they, like their ancestors, can withstand these difficulties.

CHAPTER 1 NOTES

1— Lumholtz (1902). See note at beginning of Bibliography.

2— Bennett and Zingg (1935).

3— Pennington (1963)b.

4— Basauri (1929).

5— Plancarte (1954).

6— Brambila (1953).

7— Thord-Gray (1955).

8— Gentry (1963).

9— Mason and Brugge (1958).

10— Lumholtz (1902).

11— Mason (1948).

12— Mason (1952).

13— Cerda Silva (1943).

14— Gámiz (1948).

15— Basauri (1940).

16— Riley and Winters (1963), 178.

17— Mason (1952), 35-37.

18— Mason (1917).

19— Bascom (1965).

20— Mason (1952), 34.

21— Brooks et al. (1962), 369.

22— Brand (1939), 89-90.

23— 1743: Rinaldini (1743), 65. Lumholtz [(1902), I, 425] wrote that the Tepehuan called themselves *ódami* but was unable to determine the meaning of the word; in Lumholtz' time (the 1890's), they were known by the neighboring Tarahumar as *saeló*, a designation meaning "walking-stick insects." This term is apparently unfamiliar to present-day Tarahumar and Tepehuan.

24— Basauri (1940), I, 356.

25— 1645: Pérez de Ribas (1944), III, 136.

26— 1777: Relación de Indé.

27— Pimentel (1874), I, 221.

28— The Tarahumar word for *duro* is *bewari* or *bewariki*.

29— Circa 1750: Relación de la fundación y aumento y estado presente de estas dos misiones Nabogame y Baborigame. It is certain that this document was written prior to 1755, for Rinaldini died between 1751 and 1755 [1780: Alegre (1958), II, 358, note 40].

30— There can be no doubt about Tepehuan living in the upper San Pablo Valley in the early seventeenth century. Mateo de Vesga refers to raids upon Santa Bárbara farms by Tepehuan and Tarahumar of the San Pablo Valley [1620-1622: "Papeles . . . ," in Hackett (1926), II, 123]. The Jesuit record (1678: Relación de las Misiones . . . ; 1690: Padrón de las personas de confesión . . .) and material in the Parral Archive (1699: Registro de un sitio . . .) refer to Tepehuan at San Gerónimo de Huejotitlán in the seventeenth century.

31— 1662: Carta Anua.

32— 1685: Autos de la fundación de un pueblo. . . .

33— For a discussion of these sites see Kelley [(1956), 132].

34— 1645: Pérez de Ribas (1944), I, 250-52, 352.

35— Tepehuan who live near Nabogame, Baborigame, Santa Rosa, and La Ciénega are familiar with caves containing dwellings with partitioned walls. I saw only one of these cave sites, located about four hours by horse from La Ciénega. The partitioned walls had been pushed over by vandals, and scattered about the cave were human remains which had been dug up. Potsherds and scraps of petates were abundant. The Tepehuan are very reluctant to take visitors to such caves.

36— Insistence by some of the modern Tepehuan that the Cocoyome cultivated the *frijol yurimun* is of interest, for in northwestern Mexico this term invariably refers to the Old World cowpea (*Vigna sinénsis*); hence, some credence may be given to the Rinaldini account of a rather late entry into the Nabogame and Baborigame sites by some Tepehuan. Moreover, if Rinaldini's account be correct then the use of *Vigna sinénsis* by the immediate predecessors of at least some of the Tepehuan south of the Río Verde bespeaks a rapid spread of the plant, probably by Spaniards who reached the west coast, northern Durango, and southern Chihuahua in the late sixteenth century.

37— The Tepehuan account of the Cocoyome differs distinctly from that given to Lumholtz by the Tarahumar. According to Lumholtz, the Cocoyome once lived in the vicinity of Zapuri, Huerachic (Gueráchic), and Tuaripa. The Tarahumar were rather vague as to their relations with the Cocoyome, some stating that the Cocoyome were ancestors of the Tarahumar, others noting that the Cocoyome were ancient enemies of the Tarahumar. The Cocoyome were, however, the "first people in the world, were short of stature and did not eat corn. They subsisted mainly upon herbs, especially a small agave called *tschwai* [properly, *čawé*]. They were also cannibals, devouring each other as well as the Tarahumares. . . . As they had no axes of iron they could not cut any large trees and were unable to clear much land for the planting of corn. They could only burn the grass in the arroyos in order to get the fields ready." The Tarahumar also informed Lumholtz that "long ago, when the Cocoyomes were very bad, the sun came down to the earth and burned nearly all of them; only a few escaped into the big caves" [Lumholtz (1902), I 192-93].

38— These locales were determined by field reconnaissance in 1960 and 1965 and by statements made by responsible mestizo and Tepehuan informants. Census data are of no value in determining exactly where the Indians live.

39— Mason (1952), 41.

40— Circa 1750: Relación de la fundación y aumento y estado presente de estas dos misiones Nabogame y Baborigame. Missions were established at Nabogame and Baborigame by 1707.

41— 1645: Pérez de Ribas (1944), III, 137, 148.

42— Basauri (1940), I, 37.

43— Cerda Silva (1943), 545.

44— Mason (1948), 292.

45— Mason (1917), 311.

46— Lumholtz [(1902), I, 423, 430] states that Nabogame is derived from *Novageri* which means "where nopals [*návo*] grow"; Baborigame is derived from *Vawúlili*, "where there is a large fig-tree."

47— 1743: Rinaldini (1743), 93.

48— Ibid., 1, 11.

49— Mason (1917), 313, 325-26.

50— Kelley (1956), 128-32.

51— The material from the Zape site is discussed in Brooks et al. (1962).

52— Riley and Winters (1963), 177-85.

53— Ibid., 178.

54— Mason (1952), 34, 38-39. Differences in material culture of the northern and southern Tepehuan were clearly recognized by Lumholtz [(1902), I, 422-36, 457-70] in the 1890's.

55— See particularly those maps in Thomas and Swanton (1911) and in Sauer (1934).

56— Mason (1952), 37.

57— 1743: Rinaldini (1743). Mason [(1952), 38] states that Rinaldini composed this dictionary at Zape. This is probably incorrect, for Rinaldini spent most of his years as an active missionary among the Tepehuan of southern Chihuahua at Nabogame. He was assigned to this mission in 1724 and remained there for more than twenty years [Decorme (1941), II, 234, note 19]. Rinaldini's last years were apparently spent at Huejotitlán, located far to the northeast of Nabogame, in Chihuahua. There is a record of his assignment there in 1748 and 1751 [Burrus (1963), 91, 95].

58— Bascom (1965), 160, note 4.

59— Ibid., 162, note 8.

60— Ibid., 1-200. We know almost nothing of the time when the daughter languages diverged from the parent language. Riley and Winters [(1963), 184] suggest that the two groups (northern and southern Tepehuan) may have been linked by intermediate dialects at the time of conquest. This suggestion is apparently based upon the fact that Riley and Winters believed that there was slight evidence for a variation of southern Tepehuan dialects toward those of the northern Tepehuan. This would mean, of course, that divergence from the parent language probably began long before the Conquest.

61— Circa 1650: "Información rendide . . . ," in Santoscoy (1899), 13.

62— 1645: Pérez de Ribas (1944), III, 136-37, 189.

63— 1780: Alegre (1956), I, 467.

64— 1737: Arlegui (1851), 175.

65— Mecham (1927), 56.

66— Ibid., 61, 67-69.

67— 1554: "Relación de los descubrimientos conquistas y poblaciones . . . ," in *Col.* (1870), XIV, 463-70.

68— 1562: "Relación de Pedro de Ahumada," in *Nombre de Dios, Durango* (1943), 53-63.

69— Ibid., 54-56, 59.

70— 1562: "Información acerca de la rebelión de los Indios Zacatecas y Guachichiles . . . ," in *Colección de Documentos Inéditos Para la Historia de Ibero-Americana* (1927), 237, 247.

71— Circa 1650: Tello (1891), 354, 447.

72— See the chart between pages 80-81 in Mendizábel [(1946-1947), V].

73— Circa 1587: "Relación de las cosas que sucedieron al Padre Fray Alonso Ponce . . . ," in *Colección de Documentos Inéditos Para la Historia de España* (1872), LVIII, 35.

74— Quoted in Decorme [(1941), II, 43-45] and in 1780: Alegre [(1956), I, 421-22].

75— Decorme (1941), II, 43.

76— 1596: Carta Anua.

77— 1605: Relación de Martín Peláez.

78— 1572: "Relación hecha por Joan de Miranda . . . ," in *Col.* (1871), XVI, 567.

79— 1563: "Memorial de los Indios de Nombre de Dios, Durango . . . ," in *Nombre de Dios, Durango* (1943), 3, 5, 7, 11.

80— Barlow and Smisor (1943), xvi-xvii.

81— Ibid., xviii-xix.

82— 1596: Carta Anua.

83— 1605: Relación de Martín Peláez.

84— 1596: Carta Anua.

85— 1598: Carta Anua.

86— 1602: Mota y Escobar (1940), 164, 167.

87— 1780: Alegre (1956), I, 579.

88— 1602: Mota y Escobar (1940), 196.

89— 1620-1622: "Papeles . . . ," in Hackett (1926), II, 127. The use of the term *negritos* suggests an intermingling of the Tepehuan and the Negro slaves working in the Mapimí mines.

90— 1678: "El Lizenciado Don Lope de Sierra Ossorio Oidor de la Real Audiencia de Mexico . . . ," in Hackett (1926), II, 213.

91— Circa 1683: "Extracto de papel . . . ," in Hackett (1926), II, 219, 222, 227.

92— Rouaix (1946), 495-96.

93— Dunne (1944), 138.

94— 1575: "Relación hecha por Joan de Miranda . . . ," in *Col.* (1871), XVI, 563-70.

95— 1602: Mota y Escobar (1940), 199.

96— 1669: Registro de un sitio. . . .

97— 1690: Padrón de las personas de confesión. . . .

98— 1765: Tamarón y Romeral (1937), 169-72.

99— 1778: Descripción topográfica. . . . My typescript copy of this document was made from an eighteenth-century copy found in the archives of the Franciscan Convento de Guadalupe near Zacatecas. My copy differs from the version found in *Doc.* [(1857), 4th series, IV, 92-131].

100— 1645: Pérez de Ribas (1944), I, 250-52.

101— Pérez de Ribas referred to the Río Fuerte as the Río Cinaloa, by which name the Fuerte was known in the sixteenth century.

102— 1763: Noticia de la Visita General de P. Ignacio Lizasoain. . . .

103— 1765: Tamarón y Romeral (1937), 170, 172.

104— 1778: Descripción topográfica. . . .

105— 1788: Alcocer (1958), 150-51.

106— Lumholtz (1902), I, 442-43.

107— Sauer (1934), 26-28.

108— Decorme (1941), II, 189-94.

109— Sauer (1934), 27.

110— 1611: Dabertzhofer (1611). I have used the manuscript copy in English translation found in the Bolton Collection, Bancroft Library, University of California, Berkeley.

111— Letter quoted in Decorme [(1941), II, 52-53].

112— 1611: Dabertzhofer (1611).

113— Letter quoted in 1780: Alegre [(1958), II, 153-54]. Additional, albeit uncertain, evidence that Santa Cruz, Durango, was once known as Ocotlán in the early seventeenth century is found in a comment by Pérez de Ribas who stated that the Xixi-me, Acaxee, Ocotlán, and other far-away *naciones* participated in the Tepehuan rebellion of 1616 [1645: Pérez de Ribas (1944), III, 193]. He was clearly referring to people who lived west (the Xixime and the Acaxee) and northwest (Ocotlán) of central Durango, the heartland of the Tepehuan country.

114— Burrus (1963), 90, 95.

115— Mecham (1927), 126-30.

116— 1584: Obregón (1928), 58-66.

117— Decorme (1941), II, 100, note 15.

118— 1602: Carta Anua.

119— 1604: Memorial de Francisco de Hordiñola. . . .

120— 1605: Relación de Martín Peláez.

121— 1611: Dabertzhofer (1611).

122— 1678: Relación de las Misiones. . . .

123— Decorme (1941), II, 120.

124— Ibid., 122, 140.

125— 1618: "Carta del Alonso del Valle, 1618," in *Doc.* (1857), 4th series, II, 92, 95, 119.

126— Ibid., 96, 103.

127— 1780: Alegre (1958), II, 219, 231.

128— Sauer (1934), 19.

129— Circa 1650: Tello (1891), 714.

130— 1602: Mota y Escobar (1940), 85.

131— 1604: Barrio. Relación de las cosas sucedidas. . . .

132— 1617: "Servicios hechos a su Magestad . . . ," in Hackett (1926), II, 95.

133— Circa 1650: Tello (1891), 823.

134— Circa 1650: "Información rendide . . . ," in Santoscoy (1899), 35.

135— Santoscoy (1899), xx.

136— Circa 1650: Tello (1891), 631-32.

137— Ibid., 821-22.

138— 1605: Carta de la Audiencia de Guadalajara. . . .

139— 1606: Real Cedula á la Audiencia de la Nueva Galicia. . . .

140— Sauer [(1934), 5-14] has presented a detailed summary of early references to aboriginal peoples who inhabited what is now the state of Nayarit. Herein, I have utilized only materials that pertain to the border between the Tepehuan and other peoples on the south, and I acknowledge my debt to Sauer for the references.

141— Circa 1587: "Relación de las cosas que sucedieron al Padre Fray Alonso Ponce . . . ," in *Colección de Documentos Inéditos Para la Historia de España* (1872), LVIII, 52-54.

142— Circa 1650: "Información rendide . . . ," in Santoscoy (1899), 35.

143— Circa 1587: "Relación de las cosas que sucedieron al Padre Fray Alonso Ponce . . . ," in *Colección de Documentos Inéditos Para la Historia de España* (1872), LVIII, 57-58, 60, 65, 71. Sauer [(1934), 7] believes that the common ending *-nuquia* may mean "people" or "speech."

144— Circa 1650: "Información rendide . . . ," in Santoscoy (1899), 35.

145— 1604: Barrio. Relación de las cosas sucedidas. . . .

146— Circa 1650: Tello (1891), 733.

147— Santoscoy (1899), xx.

148— Circa 1650: "Información rendide . . . ," in Santoscoy (1899), 9-11, 28.

149— 1769: "Visita de la Misión de San Juan Peyotlán . . . ," in Santoscoy (1899), 49.

150— A land title of 1573 [West (1949), 105, note 14] refers to Tepehuan living in the Valle de San Bartolomé.

151— 1737: Arlegui (1851), 34-35.

152— 1575: "Relación hecha por Joan de Miranda . . . ," in *Col.* (1871), XVI, 566.

153— 1596: Carta Anua.

154— 1597: Carta Anua.

155— 1602: Carta Anua.

156— 1602: Mota y Escobar (1940), 199, 202.

157— 1611: Dabertzhofer (1611). Letter of Juan Fonte is quoted in 1780: Alegre [(1958), II, 153-54]. Letter of Juan del Valle is quoted in Decorme [(1941), II, 52-54].

158— 1616-1618: "Relación breve y succinta de los sucesos . . . ," in Hackett (1926), II, 103, 105, 107, 109, 111, 113. For detailed accounts of this rebellion see Dunne (1944) and Cardoso (1948).

159— Decorme (1941), II, 248-49.

160— 1620-1622: "Papeles . . . ," in Hackett (1926), II, 123.

161— Dunne (1944), 153-54, 190.

162— 1645: Pérez de Ribas (1944), I, 87-90.

163— Ibid., II, 136, 138, 143-44, 147-48, 155, 165, 170, 195, 212, 230, 237-38, 241.

164— 1678: Relación de las Misiones. . . .

165— 1715: Actas de la visita. . . .

166— 1765: Noticia de la Visita General de P. Ignacio Lizasoain. . . .

167— 1765: Tamarón y Romeral (1937), 86, 92-94, 169-71. Santa Rosalia, which is not on modern maps, is probably the Santa Rosalia located on the eastern margin of the Mesa de Milpillas between Nabogame and Llano Grande.

168— 1778: Descripción topográfica. . . .

169— 1788: Alcocer (1958), 151-53.

170— 1784: "Expediente de Real Orden . . . ," in *Crónicas y Relaciones del Occidente de México* (1939), II, 343.

171— 1777-1825: Patentes y comunicaciones. . . .

172— Circa 1750: Relación de la fundación y aumento y estado presente de estas dos misiones Nabogame y Baborigame.

173— 1678: Relación de las Misiones. . . .

174— Circa 1750: Relación de la fundación

y aumento y estado presente de estas dos misiones Nabogame y Baborigame.

175— Decorme (1941), II, 234, note 19.

176— Burrus (1963), 91, 95.

177— 1562: "Relación de Pedro de Ahumada," in *Nombre de Dios, Durango* (1943), 55.

178— Mecham (1927), 83-84.

179— Barlow and Smisor (1943), 54, note 58.

180— The exact date of the founding of Durango is not known. Rouaix [(1946), 137] states that it was founded by Ibarra in 1563. Barlow and Smisor [(1943), 54, note 58] state that the city was founded in 1564. However, there must have been a settlement in the valley in the 1550's, for Pedro de Espinareda began missionary activity at San Juan de Analco in the valley before 1560 [Mecham (1927), 83].

181— See particularly the account in 1616-1618: "Relación breve y succinta de los sucesos . . . ," in Hackett [(1926), II, 101-13] and also in 1645: Pérez de Ribas [(1944), III, 167-206].

182— 1618: "Carta del Alonso del Valle, 1618," in *Doc.*, (1857), 4th series, II, 95, 105.

183— 1620-1622: "Papeles . . . ," in Hackett (1926), II, 121.

184— 1645: Pérez de Ribas (1944), III, 241.

185— 1562: "Relación de Pedro de Ahumada," in *Nombre de Dios, Durango* (1943), 55.

186— 1617: Relación de la guerra de los Tepeguanes. . . .

187— 1765: Tamarón y Romeral (1937), 37, 57-62.

188— 1737: Arlegui (1851), 185-87. The reference to 25,000 Tepehuan appears in Bancroft [(1884), I, 329, note 43], Lumholtz [(1902), I, 450], and Rouaix [(1946), 66].

189— 1678: Relación de las Misiones. . . .

190— 1625: "Razón y minuta de los Yndios . . . ," in Hackett (1926), II, 154.

191— 1678: Relación de las Misiones. . . .

192— Quoted in Decorme [(1941), II, 76-82]. Some of the families enumerated by Echeverría for Las Bocas were undoubtedly Tarahumar. There is ample evidence in seventeenth-century documents that Tepehuan and Tarahumar lived at this site (1662: Carta Anua; 1685: Autos de la fundación de un pueblo . . .).

193— Burrus (1963), 103.

194— 1765: Tamarón y Romeral (1937), 86, 92-94, 169-71.

195— 1784: Expediente de Real Orden . . . ," in *Crónicas y Relaciones del Occidente de México* (1939), II, 343.

196— Evidence for the persistence of some Tepehuan in the state of Durango north of the capital is conflicting, although one might expect to find some of them in the northwest part of the state on the Durango-Chihuahua border. The census data suggest the presence of Indians, but there is no indication as to exactly what Indians are being referred to. According to the census of 1960 [Mexico. . . . *VIII Censo General de Población, 1960. . . . Estado de Durango* (1963), 550-51], the *municipios* of Canatlán, Santiago Papasquiaro, Tepehuanes, Guanaceví, and Indé, all of which were essentially Tepehuan in the late sixteenth century, included a total of 1,582 persons who spoke Spanish and a *lengua indígena*. However, without personal knowledge of these *municipios*, I would hesitate to state that any of these people are even remotely Tepehuan in origin, particularly because there is nothing in the nineteenth-century record (at least not to my knowledge) to suggest their presence in the area immediately north of Durango City. If there were any remnants of the Tepehuan heritage left in the area, they would have been submerged beyond recognition in the long history of cross-blending between the Indian population of certain portions of northern Mexico and peoples brought in from the south and the west. For example, we know that there were more than a thousand Tlaxcaltecan and Tarascan Indians working in the mines at Indé, Topia, and Guanaceví as early as the first decade of the seventeenth century [Dunne (1944), 20] and that some Indian families from Sinaloa and Sonora were settled at Indé during the second half of the seventeenth century according to Zapata (1678: Relación de las Misiones. . . .).

197— Mexico. . . . *VIII Censo General de Población, 1960. . . . Estado de Chihuahua* (1963), 23-24, 614.

198— Plancarte (1954), 101.

199— Ibid., 102.

200— Mexico. . . . *VII Censo General de Población, 1950. . . . Estado de Chihuahua* (1952), 63.

201— I was present when the census was taken at Santa Rosa in 1960 and was permitted to make use of work sheets utilized by the census taker. The recorder, a native of Chihuahua, did not travel up the many arroyos near Santa Rosa in order to determine how many people there were. Instead, a messenger was sent to tell people to come in to a central place for enumeration. In one instance, only ten "heads of families" from one of the arroyos came to be counted. However, a horseback ride several days later disclosed a total of twenty-nine families (all, clearly Tepehuan) living in the arroyo in question. Hence, the recorded figure by no means reflected the true population at Santa Rosa.

202— This figure is much higher than that suggested by Bascom [(1965), 6] who notes that there are approximately 3,500 Tepehuan in southern Chihuahua.

203— 1765: Tamarón y Romeral (1937), 57-62.

204— 1784: "Expediente de Real Or-den . . . ," in *Crónicas y Relaciones del Occidente de México* (1939), II, 341.

205— Lumholtz (1902), I, 469, 473.

206— Rouaix (1946), 261-62.

207— Mason (1948), 292.

208— Riley and Hobgood (1959), 356.

209— Mexico. . . . *VIII Censo General de Población, 1960. . . . Estado de Durango* (1963), 350-51.

210— Circa 1650: "Información rendide . . . ," in Santoscoy (1899), 35.

211— Lumholtz (1902), II, 121-23.

212— Mason (1917), 311.

213— Circa 1650: "Información rendide . . . ," in Santoscoy (1899), 35.

214— 1784: "Expediente de Real Orden . . . ," in *Crónicas y Relaciones del Occidente de México* (1939), II, 341.

215— Lumholtz (1902), I, 469-70. Lumholtz was in error when he recorded Quiviquinta, Santa María Ocotán, and San Francisco Ocotán as being located in Jalisco.

216— Mexico. . . . *VIII Censo General de Población, 1960. . . . Estado de Nayarit* (1963), 185.

217— Lumholtz (1902), I, 469-70.

218— Mexico. . . . *VIII Censo General de Población, 1960. . . . Estado de Jalisco* (1963), 1-2, 996-1000.

219— Bascom (1965), 6.

220— There is virtually nothing in the literature concerning the lithology and structure of Chihuahua south of the Río Verde. A general impression of the complexity of the landscape in Chihuahua may be gained from an examination of comments by Weed (1902) on a portion of the southern Tarahumar country and land near Guadalupe y Calvo, Hovey's comments (1907) on the structure of the Tarahumar country, Brand's rather complete description (1936) of much of central and northern Chihuahua, and

King's résumé (1939) of the lithology of much of western Chihuahua.

221– Gentry (1942), 27-50.

222– The air distance between Guachochic (located north of the Río Verde) and Baborigame (south of the Río Verde) is about thirty miles. However, such is the difficult passage through the canyon of the Verde that three and one-half days of hard mule travel was necessary for the journey from Guachochic to Baborigame in 1965. The return trip was made by air, and the time required was hardly twenty minutes.

223– I was at Baborigame for several weeks during July of 1960 and August of 1965 and can personally attest to exceedingly heavy downpours with hail that did much damage to the corn. Precipitation occurred in the early afternoon and lasted for about an hour. A heavy jacket was required for comfort during the early and late hours of the day all during the summer in the uplands.

2
AGRICULTURE

The Chihuahua Tepehuan depend upon certain basic field crops—corn, beans, and squash—for sustenance; but variety is given to the diet by a minor emphasis on other field and garden products, by utilization of wild plants in season, and to a limited degree by foods obtained from hunting and fishing throughout the year. It is clear that more than 95 percent of the Tepehuan families practice some type of agriculture. However, because the uplands and, occasionally, the canyon lands of southern Chihuahua are characterized by crop failures, the Indians are often forced to work for mestizos by clearing rocks and timber from fields, cutting timber for building or fuel use, building adobe or log habitations, plowing, and herding stock. Occasionally, the Indians seek employment at lumber camps located at or near San Juan or Guachochic. Mestizos commonly pay for Tepehuan labor in "kind," whereas lumber operators pay in cash, which is used for the purchase of clothing and the minimum amounts of corn and beans required to sustain the Indians until the next harvest season.[1] The Indians must seek employment of some sort when the crops fail since there is little food to be garnered even from an intensified use of wild plants as food or in the hunting of game. There are numerous species of wild plants—particularly the *quelites*—eaten by the Indians, but such foods cannot be stored for use at a later time when they are no longer available. Complete crop failures are infrequent in the canyon country to the west, but when partial failures occur, the Indians suffer. They are reluctant to work for mestizos, and they do not ordinarily seek employment in the lumber camps.

THE FIELD CROPS

Gramineae. Maize is beyond doubt the staple foodstuff produced by the Tepehuan and is cultivated by almost all upland and canyon Indians.[2] The origin and history of most types of maize cultivated by the present-day Tepehuan of Chihuahua (see Table I) may conveniently be discussed within the frame of

I— CHIHUAHUA TEPEHUAN MAIZE*

	Locale						
	Cascate	Baborigame	La Reforma	Milpillas	Chinatú	Santa Rosa	Llano Grande
Ancient Indigenous races							
Chapalote (maíz amarillo)	x						
Pre-Columbian Exotic races							
Maíz dulce (maíz viejo, maíz azul)						x	
Prehistoric Mestizo races							
Cónico							
Cónico and other corns (maíz amarillo)					x		
Elote cónico (maíz colorado)							x
Tabloncillo (maíz duro, maíz blanco)						x	
Tabloncillo and other corns							
(maíz pinto)						x	
(maíz amarillo)				x		x	
(maíz fofo)							x
(maíz breve)							x
Tabloncillo perla							x
Tabloncillo perla and other corns (maíz perla)						x	
Vandeño						x	
Modern Incipient races							
Chalqueño (maíz blanco)							x
Chalqueño and other corns							
(maíz canelo, maíz amarillo)			x				x
(maíz viejo)			x		x		
(maíz pepitillo)				x			
(maíz colorado)			x				
(maíz rojo)			x				
Cónico norteño (maíz pinto, maíz de la sierra)					x		x
(cont'd)							

*Common names used by Indians are given in parentheses.

CHIHUAHUA TEPEHUAN MAIZE (cont'd)

	Cascate	Baborigame	La Reforma	Milpillas	Chinatú	Santa Rosa	Llano Grande
				Locale			
Poorly Defined races							
Maíz blando de Sonora (maíz blando)					x	x	x	x
Maíz blando de Sonora and other corns							
(maíz duro)		x					
(maíz chino)		x					
(maíz amarillo)							x
Cristalina de Chihuahua (maíz blando)						x	
Miscellaneous (strains not readily ascribed to the Wellhausen et al. classification of 1952)							
Maíz azul or maíz viejo, an elote corn						x	
Maíz colorado, three mixed varieties						x	
Maíz pepitillo, a mixture of central and western Mexican popcorns					x		
Maíz blando, resembles modern Pima-Papago corns					x		
Maíz chomo, a western Mexican yellow flint mixed with a pointed popcorn						x	
Maíz duro, a western Mexican pointed subdent corn		x					
Maíz azul, similar to American pueblo corns						x	x	
Maíz blando, similar to American pueblo corns						x	x	

reference offered by Wellhausen and his associates, who divide the twenty-five races of maize grown in Mexico into four major groups: the Ancient Indigenous, Pre-Columbian Exotic, Prehistoric Mestizo, and Modern Incipient races.[3] One or more representatives of each of these major groups are cultivated by the Tepehuan of Chihuahua, albeit some are crude forms. Several varieties of maize grown by the Tepehuan are impossible to fit into the Wellhausen et al. classification; in particular are two elote corns, the popcorns, and analogues of corn being cultivated in the American Southwest by the Indians in the upper Río Grande pueblo country and in the old Pima-Papago country.

Among the Tepehuan, maize is known by a general term, *úúnui*, and specific and varietal distinctions are made by color and textural differences. Thus, *maíz amarillo* is *vúáma* (*amarillo*) *úúnui* (*maíz*) or, simply, yellow corn; and *maíz blando* is *abo* (*blando*) *úúnui* (*maíz*) or soft corn. A relative antiquity of *úúnui* as the term for corn is attested to by Rinaldini who referred to *maíz* as *junne* in the eighteenth century.[4]

The Tepehuan at Cascate value a maize that reflects much hereditary influence from one of the most distinctive races of maize in Mexico:[5] the smoky-colored, hard, small-cobbed *chapalote*, a corn that must be at least 2,500 years old in Mexico. Specimens of this race have been found in pre-Christian levels in the Tehuacán Valley.[6] *Chapalote* has thus far been collected as data in the coastal lowlands of northwestern Mexico in the states of Sinaloa and Sonora at elevations from 100 to 600 meters.[7]

Maíz dulce, which the Tepehuan commonly call *maíz viejo* or *maíz azul*, is a blue, sweet corn that traditionally is one of the oldest corns produced at Santa Rosa, where it is grown for the most part as a *temporal* (summer dry-farm) crop in small fields located along streamways. If, however, the summer is exceptionally dry, this essentially lowland corn is irrigated. *Maíz dulce* is said to be used only in the preparation of pinole and *esquite*.

Evidence for the antiquity of *maíz dulce* in Mexico is lacking; but because there is no known corn in Mexico from which it might have been derived through mutation and because of its affinities with South American sweet corns, Wellhausen et al. conclude that the type represents a race introduced into Mexico in prehistoric times and classify it as one of the Pre-Columbian Exotic races.[8] Whatever its precise origin, *maíz dulce* is not widely distributed in Mexico; before the recent record of its presence among the Tepehuan of southern Chihuahua, it was reported only from Jalisco, Nayarit, northern Michoacán, central Guanajuato, and central Durango.[9]

Maíz colorado is an important *temporal* crop produced in the uplands—at Llano Grande for example—where the strain is valued as a roasting-ear corn and for use in preparing *tesgüino*. This corn is *elote cónico*, a subrace of *cónico*, which is the dominant race cultivated on the Mesa Central of Mexico. Wellhausen et al. believe *cónico* to be pre-Columbian in origin[10] and to be one of the Prehistoric Mestizo races that originated through hybridization of an Ancient Indigenous race (*palomero toluqueño*) and a Pre-Columbian Exotic race (*cacahuacintle*) and by further hybridization of both of these races with teosinte (*Euchlaena mexicana*). The relative antiquity of *cónico* is certain since charred remains of this corn found on ancient lava blocks in Mexico have been identified. Like *maíz dulce*, *elote cónico* is not widely distributed in Mexico; except for the isolated occurrence in southern Chihuahua, it seems to be restricted to the southern portion of the Mesa Central.[11] Although no true *cónico* is culti-vated by the Tepehuan, *maíz amarillo*—said to be a very old corn at Chinatú— is identified by Anderson and Cutler as a variety that resulted from the diffusion of *cónico* from central Mexico into the west.[12]

Maíz duro or *maíz blanco*, another very old corn according to the canyon Tepehuan living near Santa Rosa, is cultivated in fields along streamways. This white corn, distinguished by hard-shelled kernels that yield a great amount of soft floury material, is *tabloncillo*, the old, conservative white corn of western Mexico. It is used in the preparation of virtually all corn foods in the Tepehuan diet. Wellhausen et al. classify *tabloncillo* among the Prehistoric Mexico races, but they point out that the corn is not necessarily a primary product of inter-crossing by ancient varieties or of hybridization with teosinte (*Euchlaena mexi-cana*).[13] Rather, they suggest that it is a secondary or perhaps tertiary product of racial hybridization. There is, however, some evidence that it resulted from influences by teosinte on *harinoso de ocho*, a Pre-Columbian Exotic race, and *reventador*, a Prehistoric race. Whatever its origin, *tabloncillo* apparently devel-oped in western Mexico, for it has been reported chiefly in the Jaliscan plains, the coastal plains of Nayarit, coastal Sonora, and southern Baja California at elevations ranging up to 1,600 meters.[14] However, it occurs at a much higher elevation in southern Chihuahua, where it appears with *maíz azul* (*tabloncillo perla*), a distinct subrace of *tabloncillo*. *Tabloncillo perla* is an all-purpose corn that is valued highly by the Tepehuan. Mixtures of *tabloncillo* and other vari-eties are found in profusion in southern Chihuahua: *maíz pinto* (*tabloncillo* plus color from other varieties) at Santa Rosa; *maíz amarillo* (*tabloncillo* and a hard, yellow flint corn) at Santa Rosa and Milpillas; *maíz fofo* (*tabloncillo* and something else that cannot be identified), a soft corn, at Llano Grande; and *maíz breve* (*tabloncillo* plus a small amount of *chalqueño*, a Modern Incipient race) at Llano Grande. All of these varieties serve as multipurpose corns. *Maíz perla* at Llano Grande is a flinty *tabloncillo perla*, another all-purpose corn es-teemed by the Tepehuan.

Maíz blanco, an important all-purpose corn grown at Santa Rosa, is *vande-ño*, a variety reportedly introduced into the Tepehuan country from Sinaloa within the past fifty years. This Prehistoric Mestizo race is a dent corn, presum-ably a derivative or hybridization of two Prehistoric Mestizo races: *olotillo* and *tepecintle*.[15] The center of distribution for *tepecintle* appears to have been Oaxaca, Chiapas, and Guatemala, and that of *olotillo* in Chiapas.[16] *Vandeño* is, today, the common corn on the Pacific Coast from Chiapas to Michoacán, and it has been collected as data along that coast at elevations up to 500 meters as far north as Nayarit and Baja California and as far south as the Gulf Coastal Plain near the Isthmus of Tehuantepec.[17]

The Tepehuan who live near Llano Grande prefer a *maíz blanco* for preparing corn dishes of all sorts; however, it is said not to be suitable for making *tesgüino*. This corn is *chalqueño*, a Modern Incipient race that has developed since the Conquest, apparently as the result of hybridization of two Prehistoric Mestizo races—*cónico* and *tuxpeño*—that grew along the Gulf Coast from Tamaulipas to Yucatán.[18] Today, *chalqueño* is the dominant corn in the southern portion of the Mesa Central at elevations between 1,800 and 2,000 meters.[19]

Within the past twenty years, the Tepehuan living near Llano Grande and La Reforma have widely cultivated *maíz canelo* or *maíz amarillo*, which is a mixture of *chalqueño* and a western yellow flint and is a fast-growing, short-stature corn. According to Indian leaders, this corn was brought to the Tepehuan country from the government station at Guachochic, Chihuahua, located just north of the Río Verde. *Maíz viejo*, which is cultivated near Chinatú and at La Reforma, is *chalqueño* mixed with *tabloncillo*. The Tepehuan at Milpillas favor a *maíz pepitillo*, which Anderson and Cutler identify as *chalqueño* with a large admixture of *tabloncillo*.[20] La Reforma Tepehuan cultivate two varieties of *chalqueño*, one with a strong red flush and another with a pink flush; these corns are known respectively as *maíz colorado* and *maíz rojo*. In addition, the Indians at La Reforma grow a multipurpose corn, a derivation of *chalqueño* and *tuxpeño*, which is another Modern Incipient race (more common to eastern Mexico than elsewhere).[21]

Chalqueño and its derivatives are, for the most part, all-purpose corns among the Tepehuan, but there is a belief that these corns are not particularly suitable for preparing the important corn drink *tesgüino*, so they are not used for this purpose unless preferable types of corn are scarce.

Another Modern Incipient race cultivated by the Tepehuan living near Llano Grande and Milpillas is *maíz pinto* or *maíz de la sierra* that Anderson and Cutler have identified as *cónico norteño*,[22] a race which—until recently collected as data in southern Chihuahua—was reported as being grown only at elevations from 1,600 to 2,100 meters in the northern Baijo (parts of the states of Jalisco, Guanajuato, Aguascalientes, and Queretaro).[23] The Tepehuan consider *maíz de la sierra* to be an old corn, an all-purpose corn, that is highly favored.

Scattered throughout Mexico are races or types of corn that have not been collected in sufficient amounts to provide data warranting a definitive classification and genealogy; they are classified as Poorly Defined races by Wellhausen and his associates.[24] One of these races, *maíz blando de Sonora*, is an exceedingly important all-purpose corn cultivated by the Tepehuan living near Llano Grande, Santa Rosa, Chinatú, and Milpillas, where the corn is known simply as *maíz Blando.* The origin of *maíz blando de Sonora* has not been determined, but Wellhausen and his associates suggest that it may have resulted from introgression of *chapalote* (an Ancient Indigenous race common to the coastal lowlands of Sonora and Sinaloa) and *reventador* (a Prehistoric Mestizo race that is widespread throughout the west coast of Mexico) into *harinoso de ocho* (a Pre-Columbian Exotic race once widely distributed in northwestern and western Mexico).[25]

Within recent years, *maíz blando de Sonora* has been collected at Ures, Sahuaripa, Mazatan, Moctezuma, Suaqui, Santa Ana, Cocospero, Matape, and Bacanora in Sonora at elevations ranging up to 500 meters.[26] Its occurrence in southern Chihuahua offers evidence that it thrives at elevations considerably above 500 meters. *Maíz blando de Sonora* is a flour corn that is relatively ancient in the greater Southwest (southwestern United States and northwestern Mexico); it is quite similar to prehistoric corn from the Cañon del Muerto (Arizona). Corn from this site is presumed to be at least one thousand years old.[27]

Two varieties of *maíz blando de Sonora—maíz duro* and *maíz chino*, both of which are mixed with *cónico norteño* in varying amounts—are cultivated by the Tepehuan at Baborigame in climatic conditions that are perhaps the most harsh of all the Tepehuan country. Llano Grande Tepehuan grow *maíz amarillo*, a flinty form of *maíz blando de Sonora*.

Santa Rosa Tepehuan cultivate yet another Poorly Defined strain, *cristalina de Chihuahua*, which is apparently but one of the many types stemming from a mixture of an old, hard flint or popcorn with teosinte (*Euchlaena mexicana*) and *harinoso de ocho*; this latter corn was probably introduced very early into Mexico from South America.[28, 29]

Maíz azul or *maíz viejo* is an *elote* corn, one of the types cultivated by the Tepehuan that cannot be readily ascribed to the Wellhausen classification and a corn that Santa Rosa Tepehuan claim to be their most ancient corn; the Indians state that it was acquired by their ancestors from the Cocoyome, those legendary folk who are believed to have once lived along the headwaters of the Río Verde. This corn is perhaps the most popular roasting-ear corn grown by the Tepehuan, and according to Anderson and Cutler, it is without doubt a very old corn in western Mexico.[30] It is commonly grown in garden plots located not far from the Tepehuan habitations, but it is also grown in fields.

Three multipurpose varieties of a *maíz colorado* are favored by the Indians who live near Santa Rosa. Anderson and Cutler state that these varieties are very distinctive in color and, to a certain extent, in the shape of the ear but that the varieties are mixed; all three are reminiscent of the old *reventador*, a Prehistoric Mestizo popcorn of western Mexico.[31]

Chinatú Tepehuan cultivate a *maíz pepitillo* that is commonly used as a popcorn and for making pinole. Anderson and Cutler state that this *maíz pepitillo* is definitely not the Prehistoric Mestizo *pepitillo* of Wellhausen and his associates but is a mixture of central and western Mexican popcorns instead.[32] The Chinatú Tepehuan prefer a *maíz blando* for use in preparing certain corn foods (*esquiate, corecos,* and *pozole*) but not for pinole. This *maíz blando* resembles Pima-Papago corns that are mixed with flint corns.

Maíz chomo, which is apparently a western Mexican, yellow flint corn mixed with a pointed popcorn, is cultivated to a considerable extent near Santa Rosa, where the Indians state that the type is one of their oldest corns. *Maíz duro,* an important corn at Baborigame, is claimed to be another old corn and is a western Mexican, pointed subdent corn.

A study by Carter and Anderson suggests that corns grown by prehistoric people in the American Southwest originated in Mexico and reached the Southwest by way of the west coast of Mexico.[33] Subsequently, this stock was modified by introduction of varieties from the Mexican Plateau, and in pre-Columbian times, the Southwestern maize was further altered by varieties from eastern North America. The pueblo corns that eventually developed are represented by analogous types grown by the Tepehuan of southern Chihuahua, particularly *maíz azul* and *maíz blando* which are valued all-purpose corns cultivated near Chinatú and Santa Rosa.

The significance of teosinte (*Euchlaena mexicana*) in the development of maize in Mexico has long been recognized. Familiar to the Tepehuan and the mestizos of southern Chihuahua, teosinte is known among the mestizos as *maíz cocono* or *maíz vihalo* and among the Indians as *kokóñi* (*cuervo*) *úšidï* (*palo* or *árbol*).[34] According to very old Tepehuan, hardly seventy years ago the Indians frequently sought seeds of this plant that commonly grew wild in moist places in arroyos and canyons and planted them in fields along with the corn. The plant had plumes that developed into *espigas*; after three years the *kokóñi úšidï* developed tiny *mazorcas de maíz*, the grains of which were added to corn grains and used in the preparation of tortillas and pinole. *Kokóñi úšidï* is, of course, the *maizillo* or *maizmillo* noted by Lumholtz in the last century. He wrote that the plant grew among the corn at Nabogame and that it had to be weeded out occasionally. He was told that ears developed when the plant was cultivated and that the grain was mixed with ordinary corn (for the preparation of food).[35] Today, *Euchlaena mexicana* is infrequently grown by the Chihuahua Tepehuan and then only in remote locales. However, some of the races of corn being produced by the Tepehuan are clearly contaminated by teosinte (*Euchlaena mexicana*).[36]

Whatever the precise origin of the races and varieties of maize cultivated by the Tepehuan of southern Chihuahua and however they evolved, the assemblage bespeaks ancient and widespread Mexican corns. Modern corns are strikingly like western Mexican corns in their general characteristics in that the ears are cylindrical—or nearly so—with tight husks, narrow and tough shanks supporting the ears, and no enlarged portions at the bases of the ears.[37]

The antiquity of maize among northern pre-Columbian and colonial Tepehuan is demonstrated by significant findings in the La Cueva de Los Muertos Chiquitos site on the Río Zape near El Zape and Zape Chico in the state of Durango; this site is certainly in what was aboriginal Tepehuan country, and it has been dated at about 600 A.D.[38] More than a dozen small cobs have been identified as *chapalote* (an Ancient Indigenous race) or as *reventador* (a Prehistoric Mestizo race). A few cobs of *harinoso de ocho* were found; this race belongs to the Pre-Columbian Exotic races as defined by Wellhausen and his associates. Several cobs from recent deposits are representative of the race *cónico norteño*, which belongs to the Modern Incipient group. Two representatives of the Poorly Defined races appeared in the Río Zape site, *onaveño* and *cristalina de Chihuahua*; most of the cobs and kernels belong to the latter strain. In addition, there are several cobs that resemble Pima-Papago strains in the American Southwest. Two cobs of Toluca popcorn were also recovered. Some of the cobs were very strongly contaminated with teosinte (*Euchlaena mexicana*) or with tripsacum, a related grass.

Archeological evidence concerning maize cultivated by the Tepehuan demonstrates that at least three and perhaps four of the modern strains were anciently grown. Present-day Pima-Papago strains, *cónico norteño* and *cristalina de Chihuahua*, appear to be analogous to those once cultivated near the Zape site. The more ancient *chapalote* or *reventador*[39] may constitute an analogue of today's crude *chapalote*. The evidence further suggests that three strains once grown by the northern Tepehuan—*onaveño*, Toluca popcorn, and *harinoso de ocho*—have been abandoned.[40]

There is little in the historical record concerning maize cultivated by the Tepehuan. The seventeenth-century account by Pérez de Ribas states that the Tepehuan ate foods similar to those eaten by neighboring tribes.[41] That maize was grown by most of the Indians seems certain since Pérez de Ribas remarked that all of the Indians labored at agriculture.

Wheat (a variety of *Triticum aestivum*) is subordinate to corn as a foodstuff, but its cultivation is characteristic of both upland and canyon Tepehuan.[42] Winter wheat is planted in the uplands, usually on land considered unsuitable for maize cultivation; spring wheat is planted in the canyons, where the fields are invariably irrigated since they are located along streams.

There are apparently no historical references to cultivation of wheat by the Tepehuan of southern Chihuahua, but it seems certain that wheat was important rather early among the Tepehuan of what is now northern Durango. The Jesuit report for 1604 refers to introduction of wheat and other seeds then unknown to the Tepehuan and specifically notes that, in that year, wheat was grown in abundance in the valley of Santiago Papasquiaro.[43]

Upland Tepehuan occasionally grow avena (a variety of *Avena sativa*) as a fodder plant. Small patches of this grain are frequently found in fields, particularly along trails leading from the west coast to the interior, as in the Arroyo de Milpillas. There, the Tepehuan state that the plants are pulled, bundled, and dried, and then stored for use as *pastura*—always a valuable asset whether for use as food for the few animals owned by the Indians or for sale to outsiders passing through the Tepehuan country.

Amaranthaceae. Approximately 65 percent of the canyon and upland Tepehuan families commonly plant seeds of an esteemed *quelite* (*Amaranthus leucocarpus*), which is known among the mestizos as *okiti* or *guatle* and among the Indians as *giági*. Canyon Tepehuan sow the seeds of this important food plant in irrigated fields, whereas the upland Indians sow them in corrals about the time of the spring rains. It is obvious that some stands of this amaranth are escapes, for the plants appear in well-watered areas in arroyos not far from Tepehuan fields; and in times of seed scarcity, the Indians gather the "wild" seeds for planting. Escaped stands are referred to as *plantas silvestres*.

Cucurbitaceae. Several varieties of squash (*ímai*) that are known to be relatively ancient in Mexico are cultivated by the Tepehuan; these squashes are grown in the fields along with corn. By far the most common is *Cucurbita pepo*, a summer squash that is frost-sensitive but which tolerates the upland coolness at Baborigame, Llano Grande, and the Mesa de Milpillas. *Cucurbita pepo* grows at elevations intermediate between the uplands and the warm canyons but does not appear in the canyon bottoms. A winter squash, *Cucurbita mixta*, is less frequently cultivated and is more an upland crop than it is a canyon one. This squash is known to be intolerant of cold weather and is somewhat sensitive to frost. Chilacayote (*Cucurbita ficifolia*), a hardy squash that withstands both frost and cool temperatures, is cultivated by the upland Tepehuan either in corn fields or in separate "plots." These separate plots do not qualify as true gardens. It is said that chilacayote "grows best" when cultivated apart from corn. According to older Indians, this fig-leaf gourd is not cultivated as much as it was about sixty years ago. *Cucurbita ficifolia* is not grown in the canyons; there, the people cultivate the *calabaza sehualca*, or *mumuimara* (*C. moschata*), a squash that is sensitive to both frost and cool temperatures.

Gourds of one type or another are indispensable among the Tepehuan for their use as dippers, storage containers, and rattles. The most common source for these objects is the white-flowered gourd (*Lagenaria siceraria*) that is represented by several varieties.[44] Known respectively as *vákoi*, *vákoi upúligami*, *vaúkamui*, and *awúpudami*, this gourd is cultivated only in the canyons, and its fruits are traded or sold to upland Tepehuan.

The antiquity of utilization of cucurbits (domesticated and wild) among the northern Tepehuan is attested to by remains of Cucurbitaceae recovered from the La Cueva de Los Muertos site on the Río Zape. The oldest horizon, which is at least 1,300 years old, contained evidence of wild species of *Cucurbita*, peduncles and seeds of *C. pepo*, and shell or rind fragments of *Lagenaria siceraria*; species of *Apodanthera* were found in several levels of the cave, and the condition of the seeds suggested to Brooks that they had served as food.[45]

Leguminosae. Field legumes (Table II) are grown by about 80 percent of the Tepehuan families.[46] There are at least fifteen varieties of legumes that may certainly be ascribed to *Phaseolus vulgaris*, one variety that is referable to *P. coccineus* (the scarlet runner bean), one variety that is a native or an indigenous bean belonging to the genus *Phaseolus* but yet of an undetermined species, and the Old World cowpea (*Vigna sinénsis*).[47]

Of the fifteen varieties of *Phaseolus vulgaris*, a common Mexican pink bean (*frijol vayo*) is the most widespread, being cultivated both in uplands and in hot canyons. Statements made by the Tepehuan living near Chinatú, Santa Rosa, Llano Grande, Milpillas, and Baborigame indicate that it is grown throughout the entire extent of Tepehuan country. The second most widely distributed bean is apparently another common Mexican bean, a pinto (*garrapata*), that is also grown in both uplands and canyons. Tepehuan who live at or near Llano Grande cultivate several varieties of *Phaseolus* that are distinctly similar to beans common to the United States: Great Northern, Black Turtle Soup, Oregon Giant, and Scotia. Appearance of these beans in the vicinity of Llano Grande and the subsequent appearance of their characteristics in beans cultivated by the Tepehuan can be easily explained. The Indians say that these beans were obtained from the local schoolmaster within the past twenty-five years.[48] The occurrences of the Red Mexican variety (similar to a United States bean) at Chinatú and the Well's Red Kidney at Santa Rosa may be explained by personal contacts between the Llano Grande schoolmaster and the people living at Santa Rosa and Chinatú. Moreover, the Jesuit mission at Chinatú has been instrumental in introducing new types of beans into the Tepehuan country, and there may have been introductions of new types by way of the lumber camp at Guachochic just north of the Río Verde. The origin of the five questionable types of *Phaseolus* cultivated at Llano Grande is not determined; however, the Indians state that all of these beans are "old" with respect to the history of their cultivation.

A *frijol silvestre del monte* (*tupuli*) is cultivated by a number of Indian

II— CHIHUAHUA TEPEHUAN FIELD LEGUMES

	Locale				
	Chinatú	Santa Rosa	Baborigame	Llano Grande	Milpillas
Phaseolus vulgaris varieties					
Pinto (*garrapata*)	x	x	x		
Vayo (a pink bean)	x	x	x	x	x
Similar to Great Northern	x				
Similar to Red Mexican				x	
Similar to Black Turtle Soup (a small black bean)				x	
Similar to Oregon Giant				x	
Similar to Well's Red Kidney		x			
Similar to Scotia (cream "ground" color suffused with brown; brown longitudinal stripes)				x	
Similar to a Hopi variety (a black or very dark blue bean)			x		
? variety (light "ground" color suffused with purple and black; black flecks tending toward stripes)	x			x	
? variety (a brown bean)			x	x	
? variety (a sulfur-yellow bean)				x	
? variety (a white bean with black eye and black mottle)				x	
? variety (a pink bean strongly suffused with purple)				x	
? variety (an orange-brown bean)				x	
P. species		x			
P. coccineus (highly variable in size and color; a white bean suffused with violet or strong purple, or a self-colored violet)		x			
Vigna sinénsis		x			

families in irrigated fields at Santa Rosa, the seeds having been originally collected at higher elevations. *Phaseolus coccineus* (the scarlet runner bean) is an old Mexican bean common to northern Mexico and is grown by approximately 30 percent of the Tepehuan families.

The Old World *Vigna sinénsis*,[49] which is known either as *frijol yurimun* or as *šúviuli*, appears only at Santa Rosa, where it is cultivated by about 50 percent of the Indian families; the Santa Rosa Tepehuan state that the cowpea was brought in long ago from the west. Upland Tepehuan state that it was obtained from the Cocoyome who occupied the uplands prior to the arrival of Tepehuan in southern Chihuahua.

When referring to beans, the Tepehuan rarely use the specific or varietal terms, usually preferring *bávi* (bean) or *babávi* (beans). There are exceptions, however, in that staked beans are invariably called *úšan* (derived from *úši*, which means *palo* or *árbol*) *bávi* (*frijol*) and *Phaseolus coccineus* is always called *tukámuli*.

Lawrence Kaplan believes that, on the whole, the beans cultivated today by the northern Tepehuan represent a post-Conquest assemblage,[50] and he offers the following reasons: of the fifteen known cultivated varieties, at least nine are self-colored and five are variegated. The higher proportion of self-colored to variegated beans is in a characteristic ratio that maintains for the whole of present-day Mexico. In contrast, prehistoric Southwestern beans demonstrate that, at least within the Southwest, about as many variegated varieties occurred as self-colored varieties prior to extensive introduction of beans from Mexico. Furthermore, only four of the fifteen types cultivated by the Tepehuan are identifiable with Southwestern prehistoric beans; the pinto and *vayo* beans, although the most frequent of the Tepehuan assemblage, are very restricted in their prehistoric occurrence, having been found in only a few sites and then not in abundance.

More than 500 uncharred seeds and a few fragments of bean pods have been recovered from the La Cueva de Los Muertos site on the Río Zape in Durango.[51] However, there is little in this evidence from the site that may be definitely related to the beans being cultivated by the Chihuahua Tepehuan. Two species and eight types of *Phaseolus vulgaris*, hitherto not recorded in archeological sites within the greater Southwest, were recovered. A most unusual find was the remains of the round-seeded, Carib lima bean (*Phaseolus lunatus*) which thus far had not been identified in archeological material from either northwestern Mexico or the American Southwest, and which is apparently not being cultivated by any of the Indians living in the greater Southwest. Only the remains of the scarlet runner bean (*Phaseolus coccineus*) can definitely be related to the present bean assemblage of the Chihuahua Tepehuan, although one variety of *P. vulgaris* does resemble the cultivar Red Mexican.

Malvaceae. It is almost certain that pre-Columbian Tepehuan of northern Durango cultivated a species of cotton. The Jesuit *anua* of 1596 refers to *vestidos de algodón* worn by the Tepehuan,[52] and Pérez de Ribas was rather explicit in noting that the Tepehuan (those who lived north of Durango City) wore a manta made of cotton or pita;[53] the Indians cultivated cotton and secured pita from plants growing in the uplands. Alegre states that seventeenth-century Tepehuan wore clothing made from cotton,[54] and an eighteenth-century account of Indé records the use of cotton blankets made by Tepehuan women.[55] Apparently, the sole historical reference to what may have been the aboriginal Tepehuan name for cotton is found in Rinaldini's dictionary: in the eighteenth century, the word for cotton was *toqqui* (properly, *tokui*).[56] The same word is still used today.

Cotton cloth was not found in the Río Zape site excavated by Brooks and his associates, but loose cotton string was recovered from "later strata."[57] This evidence and the very explicit references cited previously suggest that at least some of the northern Tepehuan were cultivating cotton in pre-Columbian times.

LOCATION OF FIELDS

Perhaps 50 percent of the upland Indian corn fields are located on the edges of the mesas, a term which, in much of Chihuahua south of the Río Verde, refers to features that are actually remnants of a former extensive plateau surface. These remnants have been separated from the plateau proper by erosion. Soil of the inner portions of the mesas is apparently as fertile as that along the margins, but springs are more plentiful along the edges of the mesas. Because the streams meandering about on the upland surfaces sometimes dry up, the Indians tend to construct their habitations and to develop their fields as near to permanent water sources as possible. Corn fields are also located in the many arroyos that trench the mesas of the rolling uplands. Some of these arroyos, such as those that mark the northern and eastern margins of the Mesa de Milpillas, are quite long and broad with easily tilled floodplains. Corn fields are located also on flatter portions of mesa spurs that project into the canyon country. Some of the upland Tepehuan prefer relatively inaccessible spots for their habitation sites and their corn fields—such spots as the flatter portions of ridges that determine the watershed system in the broken country between the Río Verde and Llano Grande. Except from the air, homes and fields are generally not discernible; often, smoke is the only indication to travelers on land that there are habitations on the ridges above the arroyos which wind in and about the broken country immediately south of the Río Verde. On the llanos, where villages such as Nabogame and Baborigame are situated, corn fields are often located on streamway floodplains that are characteristic of these upland depressions.

Canyon corn fields are invariably associated with flatter land along streams that are tributary to the main streams. Principal streams of the Tepehuan country are generally bordered by wide expanses of boulders and gravels that make tillage impossible; these gravel banks reach almost to the edge of the valleys, from which point the canyon walls usually rise abruptly. Even where relatively good soil is available, the danger of flooding precludes much utilization of major streamway floodplains for agriculture. It is only where water may be lifted by gravity flow to once-extensive alluvial terraces that agriculture is important in the principal canyons.

The upland Tepehuan appear to prefer newly cleared land for cultivation of beans, and after three or four years, flatter plots are given over to corn. Where the slope is too great for easy tillage with oxen and plow, the plots are generally abandoned and allowed to revert to scrub or pine vegetation. Bean fields should undoubtedly be termed "patches" since their acreages are hardly large enough to be considered fields. However, acreages used for beans are invariably larger than the garden plots. The patches are always located near habitations and are commonly developed on long and, often, steep slopes. The Indians seem not to understand that plowing across the slope is preferable to plowing up and down the slope. A significant amount of soil removal is the usual result. However, since bean patches are used only for several years, there is a minimum of damage from soil loss. The patches are sometimes located on alluvial land, particularly near the bends of streams, where the Indians state that overflow damage is minimal. Alluvial soil is believed to be excellent for the cultivation of beans; but generally such land must be used for corn, which is considered a more important foodstuff than beans.

In the canyons, beans are commonly planted in corn fields in the same holes as the kernels of corn. However, one legume, the Old World *Vigna sinénsis*, is planted apart from other legumes, generally in plots located among corn fields or in places where the streamway floodplain abuts upon the steep canyon slopes.

Fields (*išikami*) are located upon great rock-supported terraces found on both north and south slopes of the Río Verde Canyon particularly at lower elevations. These transverse terraces, whose outer walls are constructed in an exceedingly crude arrangement of large stones, appear to have long been in use.

However, there are numerous, relatively new, small stone terraces (Fig. 1) near Lagotera, Palos Muertos, La Ciénega, and Llano Grande that were needed to stem further denudation of the interior and margin of the Mesa de Milpillas—marked in some places by gullies fifteen feet deep.

1– Rock-supported terrace typical of the rolling terrain near Lagotera, Chihuahua.

Acreages utilized by the Tepehuan as field plots are not extensive in size, and apparently never have been although the introduction of oxen and plow some centuries ago might have stimulated development of larger areas. At Llano Grande in 1960, there were forty-seven families holding 290 hectares (716.5 acres) of ejido land for which the Indians paid $148.00 (pesos) in taxes for that year.[58] The sole early reference concerning the amount of land cultivated by the Tepehuan is apparently that of Pérez de Ribas, who noted in the seventeenth century that the Indians cultivated small acreages.[59] This statement is consistent with the fact that pre-Columbian Tepehuan could hardly have cultivated large acreages; the tools they possessed were not adequate for anything more than breaking the surface of the floodplains along which they lived.

Today the Indians are generally free to develop new field plots as they choose unless the land is held by others, Indians or mestizos, or is subject to the somewhat relaxed regulations concerning ejido lands in Southern Chihuahua.

Easy access to new land for tillage may be somewhat restricted in the next few decades. Pine land hitherto subject to opening by Indian and mestizo has been protected by the great canyon of the Río Verde against encroachment by lumber folk and by the fact that, until recently, trucks could not reach the pine country of the Mesa de Milpillas. However, during the past several years, a truck road has been built from a point west of Chinatú to Guadalupe y Calvo, and it is only a matter of time until a road is constructed over the rough and rolling terrain of the Mesa de Milpillas north to Baborigame at least. It is true that the pine stands of extreme-southern Chihuahua are not as valuable as those north of the Verde in the vicinity of Guachochic, but the southern stands are of some worth and will be very much so when the more northerly stands are depleted.

PREPARATION OF FIELDS

No data are available for the historical period concerning preparation of field plots by the Tepehuan, but the process of clearing land in the pre-Conquest period and during the colonial period must have been rather like that followed by men and youths of today even with some slight differences in tools. If the land destined for tillage today is covered with trees, the larger species are girdled with a metal axe and left to dry for a year, at which time these trees are burned along with smaller trees that have previously been cut down. If the land is covered with brush, as is frequently the case in canyons, the growth is cut and left to dry for a season before being burned.

The older Tepehuan recall having used stone axes for girdling trees, and examples of such axes (Fig. 2) may still be seen here and there in Tepehuan settlements. The axe heads are about eight inches long and about three and one-half inches wide at both ends; the grooved portion of the axe is about three inches wide. Anciently, the stone axe head was wedged into a forked oak branch and anchored with ixtle fiber or hide thongs.

The metal axe used today for clearing land of vegetation is called *tupúrai* and has a wooden handle prepared from easily worked timber, usually branches of the following trees: *Quercus rugosa*, which is known as *tupúrai* (*hacha*) *úsaraga* (*cabo de hacha*); *Q. bolanyosensis*; and a *fresno* (*Fraxinus velutina*), which is called *pítai*. Eighteenth-century Tepehuan referred to the axe (*hacha*) as *tupure*,[60] which is certainly the same as the twentieth-century term for this important tool. The axes are kept sharp by use of an *amoladera* (*moikári*), a crude whetstone obtained from an arroyo stream bed.

The Indians state that southern Chihuahua soils are relatively infertile; hence, new plots must be cleared every few years, particularly at elevations

2— The stone axe is typical of those found in uplands and canyons; fragments of what is said to have once been a war club appear only in western canyons. Knife for scale.

intermediate between higher uplands and deeper canyons. Burning of vegetation prior to planting (*mïïdi yókomiši* or *múmudaraga*, literally, "to burn a field for planting") may be a relatively ancient custom, for it is practiced by almost all the Indians. The month of May, just prior to the beginning of the spring rains, is marked in the Indian country by great clouds of smoke from burning vegetation.[61]

The Tepehuan plow (Fig. 3) is called *giíkai* or *šikianakaroi*[62] and is fashioned of oak and pine. The main body of the plow is made from any hard species of oak, such as *Quercus viminea*, which is known as *áli* (*chiquito*) *káli* (*saucillo*); *Q. coccolobaefolia*; and *Q. chihuahuensis*. There are variations in construction of this wooden plow, but the instrument described herein may be considered typical of the Tepehuan country. A portion of an oak tree trunk with a limb projecting at almost right angles from the trunk is smoothed and shaped with an axe so that the limb serves as a plow handle and the lower portion of the front end of the trunk as a plow point. This point is sometimes grooved for the insertion of a wooden share that is anchored in place by pegs. Some Indians prefer to burn a hole in the lower end of the plow point for inser-

3— The Tepehuan plow (*giɨkai*).

tion of a hard wooden or iron share that is held in by wedges. The block of the plow is notched near the base of the handle for insertion of the butt end of the tongue, which is invariably a carefully smoothed pine log. A hole is cut in the tongue about twelve inches from where the notch holds the butt end, and a matching hole is cut in the block of the plow; wedges are then driven through the tongue into the block so that tongue and plow are tightly held together. The tongue is usually about ten or twelve feet long. A small pole inserted through a hole at the front end of the tongue and secured with pegs serves as an anchor for the thongs of hide or rope that are used to tie the yoke to the tongue of the plow (Fig. 4). The yoke is fashioned of hard wood, with the end pieces carved into gentle convex arcs and shaped so the device will fit easily onto the horns of the oxen. Leather thongs are used to bind the yoke to the horns. Plows are invariably soaked before being used.

Almost all of the Tepehuan families own a plow, but few oxen are owned by the Indians. There were twenty-four working animals at Llano Grande in 1960 and only two of these were Tepehuan owned. Oxen are usually borrowed from mestizos with the promise of a stated amount of maize at harvest time. No

4– Oxen typical of those owned by Tepehuan at Llano Grande, Chihuahua.

data are available concerning the percentage of corn yield given to mestizos in return for the use of oxen for plowing, but when an Indian obtains oxen and seed corn from another Indian, the owner of the oxen and seed commonly receives one half of the total yield.[63]

Initial plowing of a newly cleared plot is followed by repeated use of a drag that serves to break up clods; the drag is made by squaring a very long pine log. Oxen are hitched to it, and it is pulled, first in one direction and then in another, across the field.

Historical data concerning the Tepehuan are singularly lacking in references to cattle, but oxen were probably not common among the Chihuahua Tepehuan until after the beginning of the eighteenth century and perhaps not even then. We know that only a few Tarahumar possessed cattle in the 1680's,[64] and these Indians were along the Río Conchos, far from the Tepehuan country. There is some slight evidence that oxen were still not common among the Chihuahua Tepehuan even seventy-five years ago. Sotero Montijo of Santa Rosa notes that oxen became a familiar sight at that place barely sixty years ago. Prior to that time, digging sticks were used to prepare plots on the floodplain of the stream at Santa Rosa. Lumholtz says little about agricultural practices among the Tepehuan, but he makes clear the importance of tillage at certain locales on the Mesa de Milpillas and at Nabogame.[65] It is possible that Tepehuan lands on the Mesa de Milpillas were cultivated in Lumholtz' time without oxen (or at least without much use of oxen), for the Indian holdings were usually located in broad, shallow arroyos where the soil could be tilled with just a digging stick. Oxen and plow were not necessary in these arroyos that trench the margins of the great mesa. Today at Nabogame, only the large floodplain is tilled; this floodplain could also be utilized for planting without oxen or plow—a dibble would serve nicely in making holes for planting the seeds.

Whenever and however the development of extensive use of oxen and plow came to be, it is clear that both have made it possible for the Tepehuan to move farther afield for tillage. They are no longer restricted to the narrow streamway floodplains as they certainly were in pre-Columbian times.

SEED AVAILABILITY AND SELECTION

There can be no doubt about the frequent lack of seeds (*ištuk*, *ištúkai*, *ištókai*) for planting among the Tepehuan of southern Chihuahua. Both Indian and mestizo refer to this problem which involves their major crops: corn, beans, squash, and wheat. Lack of seeds can be due to a complete or partial crop failure, the inability to store seeds because they are needed for food, or (in the case of corn) a great and depleting emphasis on the brewing of *tesgüino*.

Some Tepehuan claim that no particular attention is given to the selection of seeds for planting except in the case of corn where the larger grains are preferred for seeding. These same Indians claim that mixed (different-colored) grains are sowed together in one field but that grains from the tips of the ears are not planted at all. Other Indians note that different-colored grains *are* separated and that like colors are planted together. It is rather obvious that at least some care is given to selecting seeds for planting. The several distinct varieties of *Lagenaria siceraria* have maintained their individaul characteristics; and the collection of corn made among the Tepehuan in 1960 reflects, according to Anderson and Cutler, a considerable pride among growers in their crop.[66] Characteristics of the collection indicated more than a little attention to the selection of seed stock.

PLANTING AND HARVESTING SEASONS

The rather sharp contrast between upland and canyon environments is illustrated by the fact that in the uplands there is only one season for growing crops, which is during the summer months and is *temporal* (dry farming) in nature since there are no streams suitable for irrigation activities; whereas in the canyons there are actually two growing periods for crops, one extending from November until May or June, the other from July to November. Winter crops are irrigated if there is sufficient water, and summer crops are nourished by seasonal rainfall supplemented by irrigation water when there is an ample streamflow.

SEED PLANTING

Corn fields are plowed three times before planting, the second and third plowing being at right angles to the first and second respectively. During the last plowing, the plowman is careful to maintain an exact distance between each furrow; this is accomplished by thrusting a stick of the desired width through the wooden plow to serve as a guide. Plowing is commonly done by the men; but among the Tepehuan (unlike the Tarahumar to the north), women sometimes perform this necessary chore. Women usually work in pairs, one woman holding the plow and the other prodding the oxen with a long stick that is always carried into the fields.

Maize (*úúnui*) may be planted by men, women, and children, but it is generally done by men or youths who carry the grains of corn in a small basket or cloth. The basket is held in the hand, but the cloth is wrapped around the waist in such a fashion that the grain is suspended in front of the person. Usually, two men working together do the planting, and they follow the furrows made during the third plowing of the corn field. The lead man punches holes about two feet apart in the furrow with the sharp end of a dibble. The dibble, or digging stick, is known as *giíkai*,[67] which is also one of the terms used for the plow. Digging sticks are fashioned of oak and are from three to six feet long with one end sharpened to a fine point. The second man, or planter (*ušádami* or *ušádamoi*), drops several grains of corn in the hole, and as he moves forward he covers the corn with a movement of his foot. For some reason, the uplands are invariably characterized by this two-man arrangement for seeding corn fields, whereas a one-man operation is typical in the canyons. There, the planter carries his seed corn in a cloth at the waist, using his right hand to grasp the digging stick and his left to plant the corn. The hole is covered with a foot movement as he moves forward.

In the uplands, corn is sometimes planted during the third plowing of the corn field. Two plowmen and two planters operate in the field; as one plowman opens a furrow, his planter follows and drops a few grains of corn in the furrow, each set of grains being about two feet apart. The second plowman covers the grains as he moves forward, parallel to the seeded furrow. He is followed by a planter, and this seeded furrow is covered by the first plowman as he opens a new furrow.

A few Indians plant beans and corn together in the same fields, with both seeds placed in the same holes. However, most Tepehuan plant their bean plots apart from the corn. Beans are planted in much the same manner as corn; the seeder carries his beans in a basket or in a cloth affixed to his waist.

Varieties of *Lagenaria siceraria* (*vákoi*, *vákoi upúligami*, *vaúkamui*, and *awúpudami*) that supply the indispensable gourds are planted in corrals, on trash heaps, in fields, or on ant hills called *momosali*. (The ant that inhabits the hill is also known by this term.) Calabazas (*Cucurbita pepo*, *C. mixta*, *C. ficifolia*, and *C. moschata*) are planted in fields near habitations after the soil has been plowed several times. A digging stick is used for making holes in which the seeds are planted, but care is taken to see that the holes are not punched too deeply into the soil.

Wheat fields are plowed three times in crisscross fashion. The seeds are carried by the planter in a basket, an olla, or a small cloth bag. After the grains are broadcast, they are covered with earth by means of a crude wooden drag that is moved by men or animals across the field.

The Tepehuan highlight both planting and harvesting seasons with ceremonies.[68] However, these ceremonies are apparently more typical of canyon than of upland Indians. Near Santa Rosa, the planter-of-corn places a cross on the hill adjacent to the corn field on the day before planting is scheduled. He makes offerings before this cross that are usually small portions of the important corn foods (*túíšapi*, *momoiti*, *vakúlti* or *vákuli*, *doakámuli*, and *tátaskali*). Incense (*kobímadali*) prepared from the bark of a *Coutarea pterosperma*, that is known among the mestizos as *copalquín* and among the Indians as *čivúkali*,[69] is burned before the cross; and, always, a small olla of *tesgüino* is placed near the cross. When the field has been seeded, two men are tied up with their hands across their chests and with *huacales* (*vakáli*) filled with corn anchored to their backs. These two men, along with women and children, go up the hill to the cross; there, the cross is uprooted, and a procession is formed to take the cross to the center of the corn field. During the trip to and from the top of the hill, rattles (*marka*, *sásamuidakali*, or *sásamuidakaroi*) are shaken; drums (*tugúrai*) are beaten; and, if available, dynamite caps are exploded. After the cross has been moved to the center of the field, the two bound men make speeches, promising that they will rob the corn field if there is a good crop. These men are then unbound and presented with an olla of *tesgüino* as payment for their assistance in the ceremony. The cross is removed to a spot near the house of the owner of the corn field and placed behind a crude altar that consists of a board elevated upon stones or logs. A great feast is held, and a circle dance called *naidaga* is performed during the night. Any number of people, of either sex, may participate in the dance. The men form the outer circle, and each man usually carries a stick or a racket-making device. At a given signal, the dance begins with the circles moving in opposite directions, each participant hopping or skipping as he goes around. After about an hour, the participants move faster and faster as the accompanying music of drum, fiddle, or guitar becomes more frenzied. The dance ends as the sticks are broken into pieces. There is a short rest, and another such dance is held, until a total of nine dances concludes the ceremony.

The planting ceremony just described is apparently more typical of younger Indians than of the older Tepehuan; the older Indians commonly say prayers and sing songs in the field while planting takes place.

Indians who live in deep canyons west of Santa Rosa tell of their use of a *ratón del monte* during the planting ceremony. The blood of this rodent is let into a container, taken to the place where corn grains are being collected for planting, and sprinkled upon the grains. The rat is then buried in the center of the newly prepared corn field, and a cross is erected over the grave. According to older Tepehuan, an infant was used in this ceremony not long ago. The child's blood was sprinkled upon the grains of corn, and then its body was wrapped in maguey leaves and placed on the side of the corn field "upon which the sun rose." When the corn was planted, the child's body was roasted and eaten.

The antiquity of planting ceremonies cannot be determined with certainty since there are no precise comments concerning such customs in the historical material. However, two aspects of planting ceremonies appear to be relatively ancient. Dances among the Tepehuan are certainly an aboriginal custom; Pérez de Ribas referred to Tepehuan dances in the early part of the seventeenth century.[70] The relative antiquity of child sacrifice for one reason or another is also established by Pérez de Ribas who wrote that a child served as a sacrificial agent when a plague began, that children were thrown into flooding streams in order to make the water subside, and that they were also cast into streams in order to cure sick people.[71]

CARE AND PROTECTION OF GROWING CROPS

Temporal (dry-farming) agriculture characterizes the uplands wherever there is insufficient water for irrigating the crops; dry farming and irrigating are characteristic in canyons except during very wet years, when there is little effort made to irrigate crops along the streamways. Water is let onto canyon fields by gravity flow, the water being channeled into canals at some distance from the fields. There is apparently little friction among the Indians concerning water; allocation is made on the basis of previous use of the water by Indians living along the stream.[72]

With respect to work in the fields once the corn is up, Tepehuan tillage (*šikúanaraga*) practices vary from place to place, but there appears to be one rather distinct pattern: upland Indians generally prefer to plow rather than hill their corn, whereas canyon Indians tend to hill theirs. However, the upland plowman hills his corn in a sense; a stick is anchored to the plow share and drawn up in the form of a short bow, the two ends being held together by a piece of hide or fiber rope. This device rather effectively throws the soil up from the furrow and onto the roots of the corn plants.

A hoe, known as *azadón* or *sárui*, is used for hilling the corn after rains in the uplands or after irrigation in the canyons. It is also used in weeding the corn. On the whole, there seems to be little attention given to weeding the fields; however, when weeding is done it is accomplished by men, women, and children who use either their hands or a metal or wooden hoe. Metal hoes are rather common in the uplands but rare in the canyons; however, both canyon and upland Indians use a crude wooden hoe fashioned of oak. A branching limb or one that has a large knot at one end, either of which may be modified slightly with a metal axe, is used as a hoe.

Antiquity of the wooden hoe used today for the weeding and hilling of corn cannot be determined.[73] However, the term *sárui*, used in reference to an implement for hilling corn, is relatively ancient; Rinaldini recorded *zaroe* for the hoe (*azadón*) in the eighteenth century.[74]

Fences are not really typical of the uplands but are occasionally constructed. One type is the common rail or log fence with each section resting at about a forty-five degree angle from an adjoining section. In constructing this type of fence, the Indians use very heavy logs or split rails so that supports are not necessary. The second type is rather uneven in design: log ends are wedged between two upright posts anchored in the ground at the point where one section joins another. This type of fence is commonly constructed of slender saplings and is easily built around the upland bean fields that are located on slopes too steep for construction of the usual rail or log fence. Sometimes the bean fields are protected from stock depredation by brush fences.

Fences are more common in canyons than in uplands for a very good reason: mestizo families in both uplands and canyons commonly let their stock roam free in the canyons, where water and forage are generally available. Split-rail fences of the canyons are similar to those built in the uplands. Stone fences, which are rarely encountered in the uplands, appear in the canyons. Forked rail fences are constructed in this fashion: forked branches are anchored as posts in the ground, and logs are placed in the forks. Certain canyon trees and shrubs serve in the building of fences. Branches of *Lysiloma Watsoni*, which is known as *tepeguaje* or *gïdo* (*grande*) *sákoi* (*tepeguaje*), are anchored in the earth close together and entwined with brush; saplings of *palo dulce* (*Eysenhardtia amorphoides*), which is known among the Tepehuan as *áli* (*chiquito*) *sákoi* (*tepeguaje*), are utilized in the same manner. *Fouquieria fasciculata*(?), known among the Indians as *torote, ocotillo*, or *tarákovara*, is another canyon plant so used; sometimes the branches of this plant are placed very close together and tied to one another with pliable branches. Brush fences appear in the canyons near Santa Rosa, particularly on sides of fields that do not abut upon steep slopes. The Indians state that cattle are little inclined to cross brush fences but that they tend to knock down those constructed from saplings of *Lysiloma Watsoni* and *Eysenhardtia amorphoides*.

Newly sprouted bean plants are protected for a time by rocks that are arranged so that light may easily reach the plants. Women and children are responsible for seeing that chickens and goats do not disturb the bean plants. Some protection from chickens is achieved by the staking of certain bean plants (Fig. 5), particularly *tukámuli* (*Phaseolus coccineus*) which is often cultivated quite near habitations instead of in distant patches. Sprouting potato plants are also protected from chickens by rocks arranged for the admission of light.

A great number of animals and several birds are considered predators by the Tepehuan. The cottontail (*toči, toši,* or *toóši*) is reported to do much damage in wheat and corn fields. Two small ground squirrels (*suliki* and *tuúkuli*) prey upon the grain fields immediately after seeding; however, the large ground squirrel (*vúáma bobókoši*) is said to cause little damage in corn fields. A mole or gopher (*tuvoki*) preys upon sprouting corn. The ring-tailed cat (*kuítoli*), raccoon (*vavóïkai*), and coati are known to eat *elote* corn stalks. The bear (*voji*) and coyote (*bánai*) are both noted for eating young corn stalks. The gray fox (*kašío*) is said to eat young corn stalks blown over by high winds. Canyon Indians state that small bands of *jabalíes* or peccaries (*taíšoli*) topple corn stalks in order to reach the ears. White-tailed deer (*suímali*) appear in both canyon and upland corn fields and cause much damage. The crow (*kokóñi*) raids the corn fields immediately after seeding. A terrestrial owl (*tapómai*) damages newly sprouted corn while grubbing for insects.

Sóóyi is a grasshopper that does much damage to newly sprouted corn. Locusts, which are called *bávi mamáradaï* (literally, "the children of beans"), are known as scourges of bean plots. Indians at Llano Grande report that in recent years a winged creature appeared in the corn fields for the first time; this

5— Staked beans (*Phaseolus coccineus*).

"fly" ate down into the center of corn plants when the stalks were about three inches high. The *gusano de maíz* is well known in the Tepehuan country and appears every three or four years at Santa Rosa and Llano Grande.

Scarecrows are a favorite means for protecting field crops against birds. Llano Grande Tepehuan plant supple stakes that are about five or six feet high in the ground, scattering them about in one hectare of corn. Ixtle fibers are then attached to the stakes, and because of high winds in the uplands, the fibers are almost always in motion. This device is claimed to be rather effective in frightening crows away when corn is planted and when it sprouts. Canyon Tepehuan construct similar scarecrows. Sometimes a dead bird may be anchored to a pole planted in the middle of a corn field. The Indians state that this is another particularly effective device.

Seeds of the canyon *higuerilla* or *mukúkuli* (*Ricinus communis*), an Old World plant,[75] are crushed and added to *nixtamal* which is put on rocks in the fields as a poison for the rats, squirrels, and coyotes that prey upon young corn stalks. Tepehuan who live near Santa Rosa kill large field rats by preparing a poison from a plant called *yerba de la cucuracha* and adding it to *nixtamal*; the mixture is then used in the manner just described. Traps used to bring down animal predators are discussed in Chapter 5.

Corrals in which goats or larger stock are kept at night are commonly located in the fields, particularly in the uplands. Throughout the year, the corrals are moved from place to place—a custom that insures a certain amount of fertilization (Fig. 6) with a minimum of effort on the part of the Indians. The Tepehuan who live near Llano Grande report that they have occasionally collected

6— Corrals are moved from place to place in fields in order to facilitate fertilization.

guano from nearby caves for use as fertilizer in bean patches and garden plots; this guano is deposited by a long-eared bat known as *naakámuli*. The Indians state that the use of this fertilizer was suggested by the schoolmaster at Llano Grande.

For protection against damage to crops in the uplands from drought or hail, the Tepehuan practice what must be ancient customs to either promote rainfall or prevent damage by hailstones that sometimes average more than one-half inch in diameter. The Indians throw a bit of salt into the air during hailstorms to protect the crops from damage.[76] When drought or hail threatens the crops, older Indians gather in the field for prayers and singing, usually before a wooden cross that is supported by a heap of stones. Mason wrote of ceremonial meetings held when drought or hail threatened crops.[77] His comments about songs being sung by a shaman at these gatherings are consistent with those made by Lumholtz concerning efforts of the Tepehuan to prevent drought in southern Chihuahua.[78] The Indian shamans gathered at "medicine lodges," located in remote areas in the forest, in order to perform certain rites designed to promote rainfall. Eagle feathers, three cigarettes, and three jars of *tesgüino* were placed before a cross in these ceremonies.

Little information concerning care and protection of crops by colonial Tepehuan is available in the historical record. There is a specific reference to the introduction of irrigation techniques by Padre Juan Fonte to the Tepehuan who lived at San Pablo Balleza in the first decade of the seventeenth century;[79] we may assume, therefore, that the most northerly Tepehuan did not practice irrigation in pre-Columbian times. The practice of making offerings to spirits is undoubtedly a very ancient custom among the Tepehuan; Pérez de Ribas remarks that in one town the Tepehuan placed bows, arrows, animal bones, and beads at the base of a stone idol located near the townsite.[80] Whether these offerings were prompted by an effort to discourage hail or to promote precipitation is not known.

HARVESTING AND STORAGE OF FIELD CROPS

Harvest ceremonies are apparently more common in canyons than in uplands. Almost always the harvest season is opened by placing offerings before the cross that was put near the house of the owner of the corn field at planting time. When there is a particularly good crop, a special harvest dance known as *nato* (*terminar*) *yóvaragai* (*collectar, cosechar*) is held. Two people, usually a man and his wife, are the most important figures in this dance. Their hands are tied behind their backs with a *faja* (*givúrai*), round or conical-shaped baskets are anchored to their shoulders, and the baskets are filled with maize. Children and visitors dance about this couple, first in the field and then near the cross that was erected at seeding time. Rattles are shaken and violins and guitars are played during the dance. A cow or an ox may be killed to provide food for a feast.

Lumholtz recorded a Tepehuan harvest custom that had been adopted by the Mexicans (mestizos) in the 1890's: ". . . after the harvesting is over, the owner or his son is tied on a horse, and has to carry a cross made from three ears of corn. The horse is led to the house, and is received with rifle shots; and the men tell the women in the house that the man on the horse has stolen the corn, and they will not let him go unless they are given tesvino and a ball."[81] Lumholtz commented that this demand was always acceded to and that a dance accompanied by drum and violin music was held. Lumholtz also recorded a harvest custom that is apparently not practiced today. Prior to harvesting time, the Indians selected ears of corn from plants distinguished by at least three or four ears. The kernels of corn were stripped from the ears and used in preparing *tesgüino*. Stalks of the plant from which the ears were stripped were strewn upon the ground, along with squash plants, at the harvesting feast. Then a special dance called *kuvála* was performed over the plant material.[82]

After the corn is harvested in canyons west of Santa Rosa, those Indians who have buried a *ratón del monte* beneath a cross in the center of the corn field (see section on planting ceremonies in this chapter) dig up the rat. A shaman prays as he spreads out the bones, builds a fire over the bones, and later spreads the ashes over the field.

Many of the upland Tepehuan celebrate the harvesting of crops with a fiesta (*siádudagai*) distinguished by much drinking of *tesgüino*. Also in the uplands, very important Indian leaders conduct a specific kind of harvest ceremony, from which mestizos are apparently excluded. In the late evening a small fire is built, and the men sit about with bowed heads. The most important official talks as if he were God, discussing any subject he may care to. The fire is permitted to burn down, and the leader then slips away in the darkness. Those participating in such a ceremony refer to the session as a conference with God.

Men and women gather corn after it has dried on the stalks in the fields. A bone husking peg (Fig. 7), known as *yovákaroi* or *yovákali*, is used to pry ears of corn from the stalk; this instrument is made from the ankle bone of a deer, goat, or cow and is anchored to the user's fingers by ixtle fiber or leather thongs run through two holes that have been made in the instrument. Shucks are removed from the ears before they are tossed into burden baskets carried by the men and women on their shoulders by straps. There is apparently one exception to the common custom of drying corn in the fields that occurs in areas where animals owned by mestizos or Indians frequent the vicinity of unfenced fields. Corn from such fields is piled for drying near a habitation.

Ripe wheat is pulled up by the roots, tied into sheaves with *palmilla* fibers, and laid for drying against a small sapling anchored between two forked branches which are about eighteen inches high (Fig. 8). Dried wheat is usually threshed with a flail, a branch called *guitapakarai*, on an elevated platform (Fig. 9) that is constructed as follows: four good-sized saplings, marked at intervals by stubs of projecting branches, are anchored in the ground to form a square; additional, smaller saplings are affixed to this frame so as to form a platform at a point about four feet from the ground; spaces are left between the platform saplings to permit the passage of wheat grains; other saplings are affixed to the

7 – The *yovákaroi*, a bone instrument used
by upland and canyon Tepehuan for removing ears of corn from stalks.

8 – Mode of drying wheat in western canyons.

posts on three sides of the structure above the platform; and brush is entwined in the upper saplings. The dried wheat is caught on a fiber mat or a goat skin that is placed beneath the platform. Dried bundles of wheat are sometimes threshed on ground that has been swept clean with the Tepehuan broom (*vopóíšikaroi*); they are also threshed on a petate (*máíñi*). Whatever the mode of threshing, wheat is winnowed by being tossed in a basket (*asárai*) before being stored.

Beans are invariably dried in the fields or bean patches and are threshed on platforms constructed in the same fashion as those used for wheat.

9— Platform for threshing dried wheat.

Most of the Tepehuan use the Spanish word *troje* to designate cribs that are for the storage of corn, beans, and wheat regardless of whether such cribs are an integral part of the log dwellings built by the Indians (see Chapter 9) or are constructed apart from the habitations.

Round and square storage huts made from stone and mortar and topped by a conical frame covered with brush are built by the Tepehuan who live immediately south of the great canyon of the Río Verde. This type of hut apparently does not appear south of the northern portion of the Mesa de Milpillas nor does it appear in the western canyons.

The Tepehuan who live near Palos Muertos, La Ciénega, Lagotera, and Llano Grande construct beautifully made log structures (Fig. 10) for storing corn. The logs are carefully smoothed and notched in such a fashion that the four walls fit tightly together. Spaces between the logs in the floor are chinked with mud mortar as are spaces between the wall logs for a distance of about three feet from the ground. Logs serve to support the roof, which is slanted, one side supported on the edge of the main portion of the structure, the other supported by a crisscross arrangement of very short logs fashioned at two corners of the structure. This type of roof makes possible a crawlspace between

10— Log storage crib built by upland Tepehuan.

the roof of the crib itself and the shingled roof which sheds precipitation and which is held in position by stones. Entry into this structure is from the top; two or three logs are pulled aside for easy access. The ladder used in reaching an opening in a high storage crib or a chicken coop is known as *tusádikaroi*. (Figure 11 illustrates a crude *troje* that is used for storing fodder.)

Older Tepehuan note that the proper Tepehuan term for the storage crib (*troje*) is *bakámai* and that, anciently, the crib was circular in shape and made of saplings planted close to one another in the ground around a stone platform. The diametric size of the *bakámai* was determined by the amount of crop yield,

but the height of the walls was commonly about two and one-half meters. Of
some interest is the fact that a *parra silvestre*, or *uva cimarróna* (*Vitis arizonica*
and *V. rupestris*), is known among the Tepehuan as *bakámai* (*troje*) *bišáparagai*
(*envolver*), and according to older Indians, both of the *Vitis* species were used
to lash the saplings of the *troje* together after they had been anchored in the
ground around the stone platform. The top of this circular structure was covered by an inverted funnel-shaped frame of sticks covered with grass, with the
edges of the top extending over the edges of the crib. Entry into the structure
was via a small side opening that was usually covered with a few sticks. It is
claimed that this type of storage crib was still common about seventy-five years
ago in the canyons west of Baborigame.

11— Crudely constructed *troje* used for storage of fodder.

It may be that a climbing vine (*Lonicera involucrata*), which is known
among the Tepehuan as *madre selva del monte* or *bakambišpára*, was also used
to lash saplings together around the stone platform, for there is a relationship
between *bakámai* (*troje*) and the name of this vine.

Present-day Tepehuan speak of storage cribs built in the faces of cliffs in some of the western canyons and state that these cribs were never used by the Tepehuan. Rather, they were built and utilized by the Cocoyome.

The historical record does not indicate precisely what was used by aboriginal Tepehuan of the north to designate a storage crib; apparently, the sole historical reference to Tepehuan terms for storage huts is that of Rinaldini, who gives *jun tojare*, *jun butequere*, and *viajare* (*troge de maíz*) as eighteenth-century names for the cribs.[83] Of these terms, only the second might conceivably be related to *bakámai*.

The manner of storing foodstuffs in the cribs is about the same everywhere in the Tepehuan country. Shucked corn is piled in one corner; beans and wheat are placed in large baskets, large ollas, or wooden boxes before being put in the crib. Garden seeds are stored in several types of containers: small baskets, *guajes* with corncob stoppers, cloth bags suspended from the ceilings of storage cribs, and whole corn shucks which are also hung from the ceiling.

Ripe squash may be kept from one to two months in the storage cribs or under the gabled roofs that distinguish the Tepehuan dwellings. However, squash are commonly prepared for storage in this fashion: the rind is removed, and the squash is cut into two equal portions that are dried in the sun; the meat is then cut into circular strips about one and one-half inches wide; these strips are wound into balls and suspended from the roof of the dwelling until needed, or the strips are wound upon the end of a stick which is then thrust into a crack in the roof of a dwelling until the squash is desired as food.

CROP YIELD

No long-term data are available concerning crop yield among the Tepehuan; however, a survey made at Llano Grande in 1960 yielded data concerning acreage under cultivation, average yield per hectare, and the adequacy of the yield as food. In 1960, the Llando Grande Tepehuan were cultivating 158 hectares (415.1 acres) of maize, 43 hectares (106.2 acres) of beans, and 62 hectares (153.2 acres) of wheat. Relying on previous experience, the Indians believed that the maize yield would total about 45,000 kilograms, or an average of about 278 kilograms per hectare; the bean yield would total about 6,400 kilograms, or an average of about 148 kilograms per hectare; and the wheat yield would total about 9,000 kilograms, or an average of 145 kilograms per hectare.

Mestizos at Llano Grande were cultivating 186 hectares (465.6 acres) of maize, 56 hectares (138.3 acres) of beans, and 45 hectares (103.6 acres) of wheat. It was expected that the yield in corn would be approximately 58,100 kilograms, an average of about 315 kilograms per hectare. The beans were expected to yield about 8,200 kilograms, or about 146 kilograms per hectare. The yield in wheat was expected to be about 8,400 kilograms, or approximately 186 kilograms per hectare. Thus, the anticipated yield among the mestizos in corn, beans, and wheat was much higher than among the Tepehuan; this reflects better care of the land by mestizos, better equipment, and better care of crops.

According to responsible mestizos and Indians at Llano Grande, the following amounts of corn, beans, and wheat are necessary for the well-being of each person in the community per year: 245 kilograms of corn, 73 kilograms (about 150 pounds) of beans, and 73 kilograms of wheat.

There were 229 Tepehuan living at Llano Grande in 1960; therefore it is obvious that the expected yield of corn, about 45,000 kilograms, would be inadequate since it would total only about 196 kilograms per capita in that year—far short of the estimate as to minimum requirements of corn per year. The Indians expected to produce about 6,400 kilograms of beans; therefore there would be available about 27 kilograms per person per year, which is again short of the estimate as to what was essential.

If the estimates for the amount of beans and maize needed per year are reasonable and if the expected yields of 1960 are average, then it is obvious that there is much hunger among the Tepehuan of southern Chihuahua. Indians actually reported hunger and a lack of seeds for planting in 1960 and 1965. Understandably, there is less corn available for planting than is commonly realized because the corn is used for preparing the popular fermented beverage, *tesgüino* (*naváítai*).

It seems clear that the mestizos are better off than the Tepehuan in terms of food availability. There were 213 mestizos living at or near Llano Grande in 1960. Based on the expected yields in corn and beans, there would have been about 267 kilograms of corn per person that year from a total of 58,100 kilograms, and there would have been about 38 kilograms of beans per person from a total of about 8,200 kilograms. Thus, the individual shares of corn among mestizos was in excess of the 245 kilograms considered to be the minimum amount needed per capita per year, but less in the case of beans where 73 kilograms are considered a minimum per capita requirement each year. The deficiency in beans would be unimportant, however, since they could dispose of their excess corn by selling it to Indians or mestizos with money or by bartering the corn for beans from the Indians. Also, most mestizos own stock, a portion of which is sold each year to buyers who enter southern Chihuahua from

Chihuahua City and Parral; the money thus obtained could be used for the purchase of beans.

Partial crop failures are infrequent at Llano Grande, but they can result from droughts that sometimes persist for seven years or from "plagues" that appear every three or four years, such as the dreaded *gusano de maíz*. There is without doubt much suffering among the Indians when partial or whole crop failures occur.

Precise data concerning yield of corn and beans among canyon Tepehuan are not available; however, the canyon Indians report that their yields are somewhat higher, in terms of per unit of land cultivated, than in the uplands. This higher yield is due, undoubtedly, to better soil and to a relatively adequate supply of water for irrigation.

CHAPTER 2 NOTES

1— During the summer of 1965, mestizos paid the Indians five liters of maize per day for cutting and gathering fuel, for building fences, for plowing, and for "rough work." Ten pesos per day were paid for building a habitation of either logs or adobe bricks. The Indians maintained that the lumber camp operators paid only five pesos per day for stacking timber.

2— A survey of the thirty-four mestizo and forty-seven Tepehuan families living on an ejido on the Mesa de Milpillas in 1960 disclosed that all mestizo families and all but two Tepehuan families grew maize; the two Indian families that did not grow maize were without offspring, and both families were employed by mestizos who provided sustenance.

3— Wellhausen et al. (1952).

4— 1743: Rinaldini (1743), 85.

5— Wellhausen et al. (1952), 56.

6— MacNeish (1964), 34.

7— Wellhausen et al. (1952), 56.

8— Ibid., 62, 78-80.

9— Ibid., 79.

10— Ibid., 80, 84, 86.

11— Ibid., 89.

12— Anderson and Cutler [1960].

13— Wellhausen et al. (1952), 97-105.

14— Ibid., 99.

15— Ibid., 159.

16— Ibid., 111, 159.

17— Ibid., 155-57.

18— Ibid., 84, 150, 161, 165.

19— Ibid., 164.

20— Anderson and Cutler [1960].

21— Wellhausen et al. (1952), 150.

22— Anderson and Cutler [1960].

23— Wellhausen et al. (1952), 179-80.

24— Ibid., 189.

25— Ibid., 56-57, 69-70, 196-98.

26— Ibid., 196.

27— Ibid., 198.

28— Ibid., 69-70.

29— Brooks et al. (1962), 366.

30— Anderson and Cutler [1960].

31— Ibid.

32— Ibid.

33— Carter and Anderson (1945), 316.

34— Determination of *kokóñi ušidï* as *Euchlaena mexicana* was made by Hugh Cutler [1960b].

35— Lumholtz (1902), II, 429.

36— Cutler [1966].

37— Anderson and Cutler [1960].

38— Brooks et al. (1962), 356-57, 365-67.

39— *Chapalote* is considered to be an Ancient Indigenous race, whereas *reventador* is assigned to the Prehistoric Mestizo group [Wellhausen et al. (1952), 56-58, 90-97]. However, the two are very closely related [Ibid., 94; Brooks et al. (1962), 365].

40— I believe that data collections of corn made among the Tepehuan in 1960 and 1965 are representative; but I may be incorrect in assuming that *onaveño* and *harinoso de ocho* are not cultivated. These strains are grown by the Tarahumar who live to the north of the Río Verde [Pennington (1963)b, 40, 42].

41— 1645: Pérez de Ribas (1944), III, 137.

42— Out of forty-seven Tepehuan families living in the uplands near Llano Grande, thirty-one were cultivating wheat in 1960; a greater percentage of Indian families were growing it at Santa Rosa in the canyon country.

43— 1604: Carta Anua.

44— Thomas W. Whitaker [1960] states

that "there is a greater variability among the *Lagenaria* seeds than from any collection I have examined heretofore."

45— Brooks et al. (1962), 356-57, 367.

46— This percentage is about the same as among mestizo groups; some twenty-eight out of thirty-four mestizo families at Llano Grande were growing beans in 1960.

47— Gray (1950), 937.

48— This gentleman has lived in or near the Tepehuan country for most of his life, and after having been educated at Guadalupe y Calvo, Chihuahua, taught school at Santa Rosa, Chihuahua, where he married a woman of Tepehuan extraction. He later moved to the *rancheria Llano Grande* (located on the east side of the Mesa de Milpillas), where in 1960 he maintained the only school available to Tepehuan children at government expense since the school at Baborigame had been abandoned several years previously.

49— Gray (1950), 937.

50— Kaplan [1961].

51— Brooks et al. (1962), 359-65.

52— 1596: Carta Anua.

53— 1645: Pérez de Ribas (1944), III, 137.

54— 1780: Alegre (1956), I, 468.

55— 1777: Relación de Indé.

56— 1743: Rinaldini (1743), 8.

57— Brooks et al. (1962), 359-60.

58— In 1960 there were thirty-four mestizo families living on 319 hectares (778.2 acres) at Llano Grande; the users paid $148.25 (pesos) in taxes during that year.

59— 1645: Pérez de Ribas (1944), III, 137.

60— 1743: Rinaldini (1743), 67.

61— It is certain that a great amount of valuable timber is destroyed because of these fires. While traveling between Santa Rosa (canyon country on the west) and Baborigame (upland country) in May of 1960, I rode for about four hours through stands of pine and oak that had been partially destroyed, having been set on fire by sparks from nearby burning milpas. The land cleared by accidental burning could not possibly have been used for tillage.

62— *Giɨ́kai* seems properly to refer to the digging stick. Rinaldini gives *scicunanaxare* as the Tepehuan for *arado* and indicates that the term has the same meaning as *guiqui* [1743: Rinaldini (1743), 11], which is clearly related to the present-day name of the dibble.

63— Friction between Indians and mestizos is heightened by the fact that Indians frequently will not honor their "contracts" regarding work animals.

64— 1682: Letter of Joseph Neumann, February 20.

65— Lumholtz (1902), I, 422-36.

66— Anderson and Cutler [1960].

67— Some of the Tepehuan refer to the dibble as *wiká*, by which term the tool is known among the Tarahumar.

68— Mason [(1952), 47] states that there are no set ceremonies held by the Tepehuan at planting and harvesting seasons. This is incorrect, but it must be remembered that Mason collected data on the Tepehuan only at Baborigame where they rarely celebrate planting with any kind of ceremony. Mason did not visit the canyons to the west and southwest.

69— *Coutarea pterosperma* should not be confused with another *čivúkali* (*Phytolacca icosandra*), the roots of which are used in lieu of soap and whose leaves are eaten as a *quelite*.

70— 1645: Pérez de Ribas (1944), III, 155.

71— Ibid., 149, 212.

72— My impression is that, for one reason or another, mestizo families who irrigate along the canyon streamways obtain more water than do the Indian families; certainly, mestizo wheat fields in the canyons tend to be more luxuriant than Indian wheat fields. This was so in 1960 and 1965. However, the more luxuriant fields may represent better care rather than more water.

73— Beals [(1932), 163] states that the Tepehuan used hoes or mattocks to cultivate the soil and suggests that the wooden forms may be aboriginal. However, his data are taken from the Franciscan Fathers' Report (1778: Descripción topográfica . . .), a source that is suspect regarding the Tepehuan since most of the data clearly relate to the Tarahumar.

74— 1743: Rinaldini (1743), 3, 13.

75— Willis (1931), 568.

76— I am indebted to Dr. Burton Bascom of Baborigame for this information.

77— Mason (1952), 47.

78— Lumholtz (1902), I, 432-34.

79— 1645: Pérez de Ribas (1944), III, 159.

80— Ibid., 153.

81— Lumholtz (1902), I, 431.

82— Ibid., 215.

83— 1743: Rinaldini (1743), 137.

3
HORTICULTURE

The crops that require more careful attention and protection than the field crops are cultivated in garden plots which are located quite near habitations in the uplands and either away from or near to habitations in the canyons. Location of canyon gardens depends upon whether or not irrigation is practiced. Upland garden plots are always small in area except where former corral sites are utilized. The average upland garden rarely includes more than 120 square feet. Canyon gardens are invariably greater in extent than upland gardens.

Upland Tepehuan commonly protect their gardens from marauding stock by enclosing the plots with a fence of smoothed saplings or split stakes (Fig. 12) or with a low stone wall about two feet high (Fig. 13). Lowland Indians enclose their gardens with brush, rail, or stone fences or with closely staked stalks of *torote* or *ocotillo* (*Fouquieria fasciculata*?), which is known among the Indians as *tarákovara*. These stalks are anchored in the ground and bound together with fiber cordage so that the fence will not blow over. Some small plots in uplands and canyons are not fenced, but these are always located quite near habitations. Generally, young children or old people guard such plots against the predators that are known to damage field or garden crops (see Chapter 2).

Upland Tepehuan occasionally utilize former corral sites as garden plots, a practice that is not followed by canyon Indians, who do not customarily keep stock in corrals, preferring to let the stock roam the canyons in search of pasture. According to all informants, there is no effort made to transport fertilizer to garden plots from corral sites in the uplands, from the few cattle pens in the lowlands, or from places where cattle tend to congregate in canyons along the well-watered streamways. There is a minor utilization of guano taken from caves located near Llano Grande that are inhabited by the long-eared bat, *naakámuli*.

Upland plots are rarely irrigated and then only by women who transport water from a spring or stream in ollas. Lowland plots located near habitations away from streams may be similarly irrigated in time of extreme drought; lowland gardens located near streamways are always irrigated and in the same fashion as fields (see Chapter 2).

12— An upland garden plot protected by a stake fence.

13— Low stone walls are built around some upland garden plots.

Garden plots in both uplands and lowlands are plowed before being seeded, but apparently only the smaller plots are weeded. This chore is done by men, women, and children.

THE GARDEN CROPS

Gramineae. Three varieties of sorghum are cultivated by lowland Tepehuan, generally in large garden plots near streams. In some instances, however, small patches of sorghum are cultivated near habitations. One of the sorghum varieties is known as *maizana* among mestizos and as *momoiti* among the Tepehuan. The seeds, which are planted in June or July, are sowed by a man or woman who drops the seeds into a furrow made by a plowman. As the second furrow is made, the seeds are covered. This sorghum is harvested in November, and the seeds are much valued for use in preparing pinole (*túíšapi*), *esquiate* (*momoiti*), and tortillas (*tátaskali*). In addition, the fresh stalks or sprouts of *momoiti* are favored for use in preparing *tesgüino* (*naváítai*). A second variety of sorghum, that is sowed the same as *momoiti* and known as *maíz caña*, is said to be especially valued (because of its sweetness) in the preparation of *tesgüino*. It is rarely used for preparing pinole, *esquiate*, or tortillas. A third variety is known as *malo maíz* or *sorgo* and is planted somewhat differently from *momoiti* and *maíz caña*. Furrows in which *malo maíz* is sowed are more widely separated than those for *momoiti* and *maíz caña*. Hence, the seeds are not covered by the second furrow. They are covered only lightly by a man or woman who follows the plowman and the sower, brushing a bit of earth over the seeds with a branch. Seeds of *malo maíz* are used in preparing pinole, *esquiate*, tortillas, and atole (*vákuli* or *vakúlti*). Fresh stalks or sprouted seeds of this third variety of sorghum are used in preparing *tesgüino*.

It appears that these three cultivated varieties of *Sorghum vulgare* (identified as Shallu, Chinese Amber, and Hegari) are well integrated with the economy of canyon Tepehuan, particularly those who live at or near Santa Rosa. The importance of these varieties of sorghum is of interest because of their history. According to Vinall and his associates,[1] *momoiti*, or Shallu, was introduced into the United States by the Louisiana Experiment Station about 1890. After 1905, it was reported as being grown in Texas and Oklahoma, but the manner in which it reached the Tepehuan or exactly when it reached Mexico is not known. *Maíz caña*, or Chinese Amber, was introduced into the United States from China via France in 1853. It apparently reached Texas in 1857, when seeds were sent to the Brazos and Comanche Indian reservations in Throckmorton and Young counties by the United States Indian service;[2,3] but just how or when Chinese Amber reached the Tepehuan is also not determined.

Malo maíz, or Hegari, was introduced into the United States from Khartoum in March of 1908. The seeds were first planted at the United States Experimental Station at Chillicothe, Texas, eventually to become widely distributed in west Texas.[4] The Tepehuan state that this sorgo reached Santa Rosa by way of Sinaloa within recent years. This statement is consistent with the fact that Hegari is the most important variety of sorghum currently cultivated in Sinaloa.[5] Of these three varieties of sorghum, only Hegari has reached the upland Tepehuan country, where it is grown to a limited extent (in the Arroyo de Milpillas) in a milder environment than that characteristic of most of the uplands.

A variety of *Saccharum officinarum* is cultivated by the lowland Tepehuan in small garden plots located near habitations. Fresh stalks or sprouted seeds are utilized in preparing the fermented drink *naváítai*. Many of the Indians state that they enjoy chewing portions of the stalk of this sugar cane.

Liliaceae. Upland Tepehuan who live near Llano Grande collect seeds of a wild leek (*Allium Ampeloprasum*), presumably an introduction from Europe,[6] for sowing in corrals before the spring rains. Both upland and canyon Indians cultivate the common onion (*Allium Cepa*), which is also an introduction from Europe,[7] in garden plots located near habitations. Lowland Tepehuan plant it in February; the upland Indians plant it somewhat later in the year. Onions produced in the uplands are generally smaller than those harvested in the low country.

Cruciferae. Upland and lowland Tepehuan cultivate an introduced mustard (*Brassica campestris*)[8] in small garden plots; lowland Indians sow the seeds in February, and upland Indians sow them prior to the spring rains. Seeds of this plant serve as a condiment, especially liked for seasoning beans. The appearance of *Brassica campestris* in plowed fields of the uplands clearly indicates that it has, in part, escaped from cultivation; the Indians gather seeds from these "wild" plants each year. The more sophisticated Tepehuan who live in the western canyons cultivate the cabbage (*Brassica oleracea*), another introduction from Europe,[9] but it appears unlikely that this *repolla* will become a common food among the Indians since so many of them note that they do not care for its taste.

Leguminosae. The *chícharo* (*Pisum sativum*), or garden pea, is another introduction from Europe[10] and, without doubt, the most important garden plant cultivated by the Tepehuan; the plant occasionally is cultivated in fields. Lowland Indians cultivate it in irrigated plots, planting the seeds in December or January and harvesting the crop in June; the upland Indians plant the seeds in January or February and harvest in June. Older Indians state that this pea has long been a staple food among the Tepehuan. The introduced garbanzo, or chickpea (*Cicer arietinum*),[11] is cultivated by both upland and lowland Indians but is relatively unimportant as a source of food. Barely 5 percent of the upland Indians cultivate the chickpea, and older Indians state that it was rarely grown during the early years of this century. A vetchling (*Lathyrus vernus*), another European introduction,[12] is cultivated by the lowland Tepehuan; seeds of this *haba* are planted in December or January, and the crop is harvested in May or June. Western canyon Tepehuan occasionally cultivate the horsebean (*Vicia faba*), still another European introduction.[13]

Umbelliferae. The introduced *cilantro* (*Coriandrum sativum*)[14] is cultivated to a limited extent by both upland and lowland Indians. Leaves of the plant serve as a condiment and as a *quelite*. Lowland Indians sow the seeds in non-irrigated plots in February and utilize the leaves in June.

Cactaceae. Two species of *Opuntia*, both of which are recognized as bearing a superior fruit, are occasionally grown by both upland and lowland Indians in garden plots or at any suitable spot near habitations.

Solanaceae. The domesticated *papa* (*Solanum tuberosum*) is grown only by upland Indians, in or near garden plots. (In spite of its suitability as an upland plant, the potato is not generally cultivated). Lowland Indians cultivate a variety of *Lycopersicon esculentum* which is started in a seed bed. The small tomato plants are transplanted to a garden plot that is invariably fenced in some fashion for protecting the ripening fruit from poultry. The domesticated chile, *Capsicum annuum*, is known among the Tepehuan as *kóókoli* and as *chile caribe* among mestizos. Only the lowland Tepehuan cultivate this plant; the seeds are sprouted in a "small hole," which is actually a crude seed bed, and when the plants are about four inches high, they are transplanted to a garden plot or to any suitable and convenient spot near a habitation. These plants grow for many years, and their fruits serve as an esteemed condiment that is added to beans or boiled meat. Lowland Tepehuan also cultivate a chile plant (*Capsicum* sp.) known as *chile verde*.

The cultivated tobacco plant, *vívai* (*Nicotiana tabacum*), is grown by both upland and lowland Tepehuan. Seeds are planted in a germinating bed (Fig. 14) located where it will receive much sunshine. The earth is loosened and thoroughly soaked before the seeds are sown and lightly covered with earth. The bed is kept well watered until after the seeds germinate and sprout. When the plants are from fifteen to twenty days old, they are transplanted either to gardens or to larger plots which have been prepared for growing tobacco. These plots are usually areas from which timber or brush had been cleared the previous year. Whether in gardens or plots, the transplanted tobacco is carefully irrigated by the women, who carry water from a spring or stream in an olla. Planting takes place in June, and harvesting is done in October. Leaves are stripped from the plants and placed in a covered basket or a fiber bag for four or

14— Seed bed utilized for starting tobacco plants.

five days. The leaves are then cleaned of dirt by hand and sunned for several days, after which time they are stored in an olla until desired for smoking. As part of the harvest, stalks that contain the seed pods are bound up and hung to dry until the next planting season.

Lowland Indians supplement their usually meager supply of *Nicotiana tabacum* with the leaves of two wild species common to the canyons, *N. trigonophylla* and *N. glauca*; upland Tepehuan display little interest in gathering or utilizing the leaves of these two wild tobaccos.

Almost all adult males smoke when tobacco is available, but older males state that about seventy-five years ago, the young men were not permitted to smoke. Today, from among the females, only very old women are permitted to smoke. Pipes are not used by the Tepehuan of southern Chihuahua, and the older Indians state they never have been. Corn husks (*ovatuki* or *úúnurídaga*) serve as cigarette wrappers. Today, smoking among the Tepehuan is usually associated with the drinking of *tesgüino*.

The antiquity of smoking among the northern Tepehuan cannot be established with certainty, but the custom is certainly as old as the eighteenth century. Rinaldini gives no Tepehuan equivalent for *fumar*, but he refers to a *chupador de tabaco* as *dunicudamue*.[15]

Cucurbitaceae. Canyon Tepehuan cultivate the watermelon (*Citrullus vulgaris*), which is presumably an introduction from Africa by way of Europe.[16] Watermelon seeds are planted in field or garden plots, and the sprouting plants are hilled with a wooden hoe. Upland Indians rarely attempt to cultivate watermelons; however, some few plants appear along the Río Nabogame in warmer tributary canyons.

Compositae. Santa Rosa Tepehuan cultivate a lettuce, or *lechuga* (*Lactuca sativa*), another introduction from Eurasia,[17] in garden plots.

There is little in the record concerning cultivation of either native or introduced garden plants. A comment made by Lumholtz is apparently the sole reference to use of tobacco by the Tepehuan in the nineteenth century; in the 1890's, three cigarettes were placed before a cross during ceremonies held to promote rainfall.[18] The previously cited reference to *chupador de tabaco* found in Rinaldini's dictionary and his use of the term *vive* for *tabaco*[19] (a term that is clearly related to the current Tepehuan term for tobacco) make clear that tobacco was certainly known and probably used by the Tepehuan in the middle of the eighteenth century.

The Franciscan Fathers' report of 1778 records cultivation of sugar cane at Tohayana, Dolores, and Baborigame;[20] however, sugar cane could not possibly have been cultivated at the village of Baborigame. The cane referred to must have been cultivated in the warm canyons immediately to the west of Baborigame where sugar cane is cultivated today. The Franciscans erected a sugar mill at Nabogame shortly after they assumed charge of the former Jesuit missions following expulsion of the Jesuits from Mexico in 1767.[21] The available evidence suggests that sugar cane was introduced among the Chihuahua Tepehuan at some time early in the eighteenth century.

Watermelons (*sandias*) of an inferior sort were cultivated by the Tepehuan at Tohayana and Dolores in the eighteenth century.[22]

Whether chile was cultivated by aboriginal Tepehuan cannot be determined with certainty; however, there is a bit of evidence that it was cultivated by, or at least known to, aboriginal Tepehuan. Pérez de Ribas refers to the application of chile to fire-arrows that were used in battle by seventeenth-century Tepehuan.[23]

FRUIT TREES

Older Tepehuan state that domesticated fruit trees were rather uncommon among the Indians some seventy-five years ago. Today, however, apple and peach trees are maintained throughout the uplands and in the canyons. Out of forty-seven Indian families at Llano Grande, thirty-nine possessed a total of

447 apple trees in 1960; of these, 203 trees were producing. Thirty-one Indian families owned a total of 449 peach trees, with 227 trees in production. Out of thirty-four mestizo families, twenty-eight possessed apple trees, with 175 trees in production. Twenty-four mestizo families owned a total of 831 peach trees, with 603 in production. It is clear that upland Indians have more success in growing peach than apple trees. No data are available concerning the total number of apple or peach trees claimed by any one community of Indian families in the canyons, but it is certain that these trees are not as numerous in canyons as in uplands.

Within the uplands, fruit trees are grown by mestizos in what may properly be termed orchards. Indians, however, cultivate fruit trees in a distinctly haphazard fashion, planting the trees at random about their habitations or near the edge of timbered land, where resident trees must be removed in order to make possible the admission of ample sunshine for the young fruit trees. In canyons, fruit trees are planted as individuals near habitations and in clusters apart from the habitations, particularly along the edges of fields. Young fruit trees are vulnerable to marauding stock; therefore most trees are protected by a small log corral (Fig. 15). Indians and mestizos apparently respect and recog-

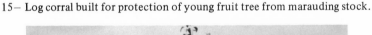

15— Log corral built for protection of young fruit tree from marauding stock.

nize ownership of fruit trees; when people abandon ejido land for any reason, the fruit from trees on that land is regularly gathered by the former holders.

Moraceae. The domesticated fig (*Ficus carica*), an introduction from Europe,[24] is cultivated by the Tepehuan who live in warmer canyons near Llano Grande and is reported to be grown throughout the Tepehuan country except in very hot canyons to the west.

Lauraceae. The canyon Tepehuan who live near Santa Rosa occasionally grow the aguacate tree (*Persea americana*), which is known as *laurelillo* or *gúru-duši*; the fruits of this tree are of an inferior quality.

Punicaceae. A pomegranate (*Punica granatum*), an introduction from Eurasia,[25] is occasionally cultivated by canyon Indians; the tree is propagated by seed or cutting.

Rosaceae. The peach tree (*Prunus Persica*), also a Eurasian introduction,[26] is widely distributed in the uplands, less so in the warm canyons. The pear (*Pyrus communis*), another introduction from Eurasia,[27] is cultivated only by upland Tepehuan. Two species of apple trees, *Malus baccata* and *M. sylvestris*, both of which are introductions from Eurasia,[28] are cultivated; the former, the crab apple, is known as *manzana de San Juan*, the latter as *manzana de San Miguel*. Both species are more common to uplands than to canyons. The quince (*Cydonia oblonga*), which is also an introduced species,[29] is restricted to the warmer canyons and arroyos that cut the flanks of the great Mesa de Milpillas; it does not appear in the uplands or in very hot canyons.

Rutaceae. An orange tree (*Citrus aurantium* var.), introduced by way of Europe,[30] is rather commonly cultivated in western and southeastern canyons. Older Indians state that oranges were rarely cultivated about seventy-five years ago. The introduced lemon (*Citrus limonium* var.)[31] appears in irrigated fields and gardens of western canyons. Several specimens of grapefruit trees (*Citrus decumana* var.) appear in canyon gardens near Santa Rosa.

All of these fruits, other than the lemon, are eaten when ripe; apples and peaches are also dried and stored in ollas that are placed in storage cribs. The apples are quartered and dried in the sun until ready for storage, and peaches are cut in half to dry. Apples are also stored in beautifully constructed log bins (Fig. 16); the Indians claim that if these bins are properly constructed, stored fruit may be kept from October until May or June. Those Tepehuan who possess significant numbers of fruit trees frequently sell fruit to mestizos.

There are apparently very few references in the early literature concerning cultivation of fruit trees by the Tepehuan. The only specific reference is found in the Franciscan Fathers' report of 1778,[32] in which it is stated that lemon and orange trees were grown at Tohayana and Dolores and in the Misión de Nabo-

16— Log bin constructed for storage of apples.

game. This early reference negates the statement made by present-day Indians that oranges were not commonly grown until about seventy-five years ago. Orange trees may not have been common at Santa Rosa seventy-five years ago, but the fruits certainly were known to the Tepehuan by the middle of the eighteenth century, undoubtedly having been introduced by Jesuits prior to their expulsion from northwestern Mexico in 1767.

CHAPTER 3 NOTES

1— Vinall, Stephens, and Martin (1936), 61.

2— Ibid., 66.

3— Quinby [1960].

4— Vinall, Stephens, and Martin (1936), 48.

5— Quinby [1960].

6— Gray (1950), 431.

7— Ibid.

8— Ibid., 707.

9— Ibid., 708.

10— Ibid., 936.

11— Ibid., 932.

12— Darlington and Janaki Ammal (1945), 159.

13— Ibid., 157.

14— Gray (1950), 1093.

15— 1743: Rinaldini (1743), 27.

16— Darlington and Janaki Ammal (1945), 115.

17— Gray (1950), 1555.

18— Lumholtz (1902), I, 433.

19— 1743: Rinaldini (1743), 131.

20— 1778: Descripción topográfica. . . .

21— Ibid.

22— Ibid.

23— 1645: Pérez de Ribas (1944), III, 168.

24— Darlington and Janaki Ammal (1945), 183.

25— Bailey and Bailey (1941), 607.

26— Ibid., 602.

27— Ibid., 609.

28— Ibid., 456-57.

29— Ibid., 613.

30— Ibid., 180.

31— Ibid.

32— 1778: Descripción topográfica. . . .

4
FOOD PREPARATION

FIELD AND GARDEN PRODUCTS

MAIZE FOODS

Maize is the principal foodstuff among the Tepehuan, and a number of distinct dishes are prepared from this grain. Some variety in the corn menu is obtained by the addition (when in season) of condiments, legumes, and *quelites*.

Pinole. The most common food (*kuádagai* or *koadaga*) among the Tepehuan is prepared by mixing ground, toasted maize with water (*súdagi* or *suudági*). Some Indians refer to the ground maize as *úúntui*, but generally, pinole (*túíšapi*) is the term used for this ingredient as well as the prepared food. Any available variety of maize may be used in preparing *túíšapi*, but soft corns are preferred since they burst open more readily when toasted than do the hard corns. Grains of corn are removed from the cob with the hands or by rubbing two ears of corn together. The grains are toasted, either in a special olla called *akíkali* or on the comal (*ákurai*), for about one-half hour. If the grains are toasted in an olla, a handful of sand (*órai*) is added to distribute the heat evenly among the grains of corn. Burst grains are separated from the sand by shaking them in a loosely woven basket (*asárai*). They are then ground to a fine state on the metate (*maútuli* or *móúturai*), and that portion of the pinole not used immediately is stored in an olla. Travelers carry it in a cloth bag or a gourd sealed with a stopper made from a corncob. Pinole is eaten three times daily: in the early morning, at midday, and late in the afternoon. The Indians state that it is almost never eaten after darkness sets in.

Most of the Tepehuan add a bit of salt (*ónai*) to pinole before it is eaten. The salt is obtained in lump form from mestizos who come from the west or from Hidalgo del Parral to trade with the Tepehuan or from local mestizos who bring in goods to trade or sell to the Indians. The salt is ground several times on a metate before it is used.

Of more importance than salt in giving flavor to pinole is the addition of leaves from one or several of the wild plants found within the Tepehuan habitat and the seeds of at least one of the grain sorghums. The following plants are known to supply leaves that are utilized almost everywhere as condiments added to pinole: *alisárapai* (*Tauschia nudicaulis*); the piquant *naváítai* (*tesgüino*) *biñáragadï* (*fermenter*), or *Chimaphila umbellata*; a wild mint (*Mentha canadensis*), known as *yerba buena* or *poléo*; the sow thistle, or *šiñaipuli* (*Sonchus oleraceus*), a European introduction;[1] and an orégano (*Lippia Berlandieri*). The roots and leaves of a false garlic (*Nothoscordum bivalve*), known among the Tepehuan as *cebollín del monte*, are also ground on a metate and added to pinole. Several of these plants are restricted in occurrence, some being available in the canyons and some in the uplands. However, the Indians will travel rather far to gather sufficient amounts of fresh leaves to flavor the prepared pinole; both men and women do this chore. Seeds of *maizana* or *momoiti* (Shallu, a variety of *Sorghum vulgare*) are toasted and ground before being added to pinole.

Esquiate. Only slightly less important than *túíšapi* as a food is *esquiate*, or *momoiti*, which is made more palatable than pinole by adding a variety of plant leaves, seeds from the three grain sorghums, and fruits from domesticated and wild chiles; all of these additions are to be found in the Indian habitat. It is enjoyed as a warm weather food and is eaten very frequently when supplies of corn are diminishing.

The initial procedure for preparing *esquiate* is similar to that for pinole. After the grains of corn have been toasted in the olla and separated from the sand, they are mashed—not ground—on a metate. A small amount of water is added during this process. The resulting mixture is a paste, the basic ingredient of *esquiate*. The dish itself is prepared by stirring the paste thoroughly into a small amount of water.

All of the following plants are sought after for use as condiments in *esquiate*: leaves of a *mostaza silvestre* (*Brassica Kaber*) and the introduced sow thistle (*Sonchus oleraceus*) are favorite seasonings, as well as the piquant leaves of *alisárapai* (*Tauschia nudicaulis*). Another favorite is obtained from *amapola*, or *bitúši*, a small-flowered variety of *Oenothera rosea*. Small amounts of the fruits of the chickpea, or garbanzo (*Cicer arietinum*), a European introduction,[2] are crushed on a metate and added as a "thickening agent." Fruits of the domesticated *chile caribe*, or *kóókoli* (*Capsicum annuum*), and the wild *chile piquín*, or *čívuli* (*C. baccatum*), are crushed and added whenever available. The Tepehuan who live near Santa Rosa collect leaves from an unidentified *trompillo* for use. Seeds of the three grain sorghums (Shallu, Chinese Amber, and Hegari) are toasted on a comal and ground on a metate before being added. Three species of *Opuntia* supply leaves that are peeled, cooked, and added to the dish just before it is eaten. These species include a very large cactus distinguished by handsome yellow flowers and edible fruit found in canyons near Llano Grande, an upland cactus called *nakíši*, and a yellow-flowered cactus known as *šikóraka* (*redonda* or *circulo*) *návoi* (*nopal*). The leaves of a tiny arroyo plant, *šiñáka* (*Cirsium mexicanum*), that is common to gravel bars along streamways in the Tepehuan country, are singed of their spiny borders and crushed before being added. Baked mescal is crushed on a metate until the fibrous matter may be easily separated from the edible portion that is then added to the dish.

Atole. According to all reports, soft corns are preferred in preparing atole (*vákuli* or *vakúlti*), a crude mush. An olla of boiling water is removed from the fire, and several handfuls of soft maize are put into the hot water for softening. After the grains are softened, the contents of the olla are poured into a loosely woven basket strainer (*šišikarai*) through which most of the water passes. The softened maize is then placed on a metate and mashed; a small amount of hot water is added during the process. This mush is made more palatable by the addition of salt, fresh or dried fruits of the domesticated chile (*Capsicum annuum*), fresh or dried fruits of the wild chile (*C. baccatum*), leaves of a canyon plant called *kokówali*, leaves of *bitúši* (*Oenothera rosea*), mashed fruits of the introduced chickpea (*Cicer arietinum*), cooked leaves of the same three species of *Opuntia* that were mentioned in the preparation of *esquiate*, toasted and ground seeds of the three grain sorghums (Shallu, Chinese Amber, and Hegari), and leaves of *Tauschia nudicaulis*. The grain sorghums are cultivated for the most part only in canyons, and their seeds are not readily available to upland Indians; however, the upland Tepehuan frequently barter for small amounts of sorghum seeds, which are particularly liked as an additive in atole.

Yoríki. This food resembles the atole gruels in appearance and taste but is prepared in a somewhat different fashion. Soft maize is ground on a metate several times, and the meal that results is added to water and boiled for several hours. *Yoríki*, or *idórai* as the food is commonly called among the Tepehuan, is made very palatable by adding the cooked leaves of several species of *Opuntia*; leaves of an *amapola* (*Oenothera rosea*), *amapola grande* (*O. triloba* and *O. grandis*), and *pato de cuervo* (*Phacelia teucriifolia*); fresh or dried fruits of *Capsicum annuum* and *C. baccatum*; and a grub (*kakéduñi*), which is removed from a cocoon that appears upon *Arbutus glandulosa* and *A. arizonica*. Canyon Tepehuan also add the leaves of *kokówali*. Dried and crushed plumes of young maize plants are frequently added to the dish. The Tepehuan use the shoots of a small upland plant called *muradágai* (*espiga de maíz*) *vóíšikai* (*limpiar*) for use in cleaning dust from the maize plumes; these small shoots are pushed back and forth through the plumes.

Pozole. Another food that resembles the atole gruels is *pozole*, or *doakámuli*. The hard corns that are generally used in preparing this dish must be softened; the processing agent is either oak ash (*mátai*) or lime (*ojomátai*) obtained from limestone rock. For *mátai*, green branches from any of the many species of oak in the uplands are cut up and burned in a depression in the ground; the ashes are then winnowed before being stored in an olla. Limestone rock that occurs on ledges along canyon streams where small amounts of lime have been precipitated is the source for *ojomátai*; small amounts of this rock are placed in a pit lined with green oak or dried animal dung (*víítai*). The chunks are covered with coals that are renewed repeatedly over a period of twenty-four hours. After the limestone has cooled, it is removed from the pit and crushed on a metate or flat stone. The crushed material is then winnowed by being tossed up and down in a basket. If wood ashes are used to soften the hard corn grains, the ashes are placed in a basket which is held over an olla containing the corn, and water is poured through this basket into the olla. A bit of fresh water is added to the olla, and the grains are boiled until softened. *Ojomátai* is always used when the corn grains are particularly hard. The lime is placed in the olla containing the corn, and after the grains are boiled for a time, they are removed from the olla and washed carefully, either in a stream or in an olla, until water poured over the grains runs clear. Little attention is given to the washing of corn boiled in water that was poured through wood ashes.

The softened corn is called *nixtamal*, or *matáimidi*, and is added to boiling water and cooked for a short time before being eaten. *Pozole* is made more palatable by adding the leaves of orégano (*Lippia Berlandieri*), *bitúši* (*Oenothera rosea*), *amapola grande* (*O. triloba*), *pato de cuervo* (*Phacelia teucriifolia*), *poléo* (*Mentha canadensis*), and the introduced sow thistle. Beans (*babávi*), cooked meat (*babáídi*), and *menudo* (*vókadi*) are also added to the dish.

Tortillas. The *matáimidi* used for *pozole* is also used in preparing tortillas, one of the foods most commonly eaten by the Tepehuan. *Matáimidi* is thoroughly mashed on a metate several times, and during the process, the following may be added: toasted and ground seeds of two sorghums (Shallu and Hegari); the flower stem of a *palma de San Pedro*, or *óyi* (*Yucca decipiens*); cooked, washed, and crushed acorns from *tupáratui* (*Quercus arizonica*); and dried maize plumes (*murádagai*). Tortillas (*tátaskali*), shaped from a small pat of the mashed corn, are cooked on a comal.

Tamales. There is no evidence that tamales (*tútumaiti*) constitute an important foodstuff among the Tepehuan, but both upland and lowland Indians know and occasionally prepare this food. Dried corn is made into *nixtamal*, which is then made more palatable by adding bits of meat (*babáídi*), leaves of any of the plants utilized as condiments in preparing corn dishes, fresh or dried fruits of the domesticated and wild chiles (*Capsicum annuum* and *C. baccatum*), toasted and crushed seeds of *ukavoli* (*Persea Liebmanni*), and onions when available. The resulting mixture is formed into elongated pats that are wrapped in corn shucks (*ovatuki* or *úúnurídaga*) and boiled for an hour.

Esquite. Occasionally, the Tepehuan eat corn that has been parched on a comal (*ákurai*) or in an olla that contains sand; this roasted corn is known as *esquite* or *ááki*.

Miscellaneous Corn Foods. *Elote* (*kaibíadi*) ears of corn are shucked (*úlipai, desojar elotes*) and placed against a hot stone or on a bed of embers for roasting. Fresh corn is often removed from the ears with a knife and boiled for a short time. However, boiled and roasted corn dishes are not customarily prepared by the Tepehuan.

The juice in a corn stalk (*voúgadï*) is a minor food item among canyon Tepehuan. When the corn does not fruit, the stalks are chewed or they are mashed with a stone on a metate to extract the juice, which is cooked and eaten after a bit of honey is added. This food is called *úúnbauga*.

WHEAT FOODS

Wheat dishes are of much importance in the diet of canyon Tepehuan but are of limited significance among the upland Indians. The variety of wheat dishes is not as great as those prepared from corn, and condiments are rarely added to these dishes.

Pinole prepared from wheat is a common food in the lowlands. Threshed wheat is removed from its storage place and winnowed by being poured from one basket into another. The wheat is then toasted in an olla or on a comal. Sand is not put in the olla to distribute the heat evenly as is the case when corn pinole is prepared. The toasted wheat is ground at least three times on a metate and then mixed with water or milk. Occasionally, *siñáka* leaves (*Cirsium mexicanum*) are singed and crushed and then added to wheat pinole immediately before it is eaten.

For the preparation of *esquiate* from wheat, the grains are toasted (as for pinole) and mashed on a metate. The crushed grains are then stirred into water. Wheat *esquiate* is seasoned by adding salt (*ónai*) or the crushed leaves of *Cirsium mexicanum*.

Wheat used in preparing tortillas is ground on a metate several times, and during each grinding, a bit of water is added. The paste that results is formed into pats that are flattened out and cooked on a comal.

For wheat tamales, the grains are toasted in an olla, ground on a metate several times, and then moistened so that the mass can be shaped into elongated pats. These are wrapped in corn shucks and boiled for a short time.

Santa Rosa Tepehuan construct crude ovens of stone and mortar near their habitations for baking a crude and almost tasteless "wheat bread."

SQUASH FOODS

Squash foods constitute a favorite item in the Indian diet; they are prepared from fresh or dried portions of *mumuimara* (*Cucurbita moschata*), chilacayote (*C. ficifolia*), and *ímai* (*C. mixta* and *C. pepo*).

Fresh green squash is a particularly esteemed food; the unpeeled squash is cut into slices and fried on a comal or cut into squares and boiled until tender. Portions of dried, green or ripe squash are soaked several hours before being boiled until palatable.

Ripe squash is boiled or roasted; but regardless of the cooking process, the squash is cut in half, the seeds are removed, and it is boiled or roasted on coals according to personal taste. When ripe squash is roasted, the halved portion of the fruit is placed, rind down, on the coals. This roasted squash is commonly eaten with a bit of the cooked, hardened rind used as a spoon.

The squash seeds (*káídi* or *káítukai*) that are removed from the ripe fruit prior to cooking are dried in the sun; or, the interior pulp of the squash is spitted and anchored to the ceiling of a dwelling until the seeds are dry. As a food, squash seeds are considered a delicacy; they are roasted on a comal and peeled before being eaten. They are only eaten occasionally since the seeds must be husbanded for planting.

Squash blossoms are another food enjoyed by the Tepehuan; the flowers are washed, boiled for a short time, flavored with a bit of grease or suet, and eaten with meat. The flowers are also occasionally fried.

BEAN AND PEA FOODS

Tepehuan methods for preparing foods from beans and peas are relatively simple. Dried beans are apparently never soaked; rather, they are boiled until soft enough to eat. Boiled beans are sometimes mashed on a metate and fried for a few minutes on a comal, with or without meat. Fried beans are occasionally used as a "stuffing" for tortillas. Fresh string-bean pods are cleaned of dirt and washed before being broken up and boiled.

Whatever the fashion of preparing bean foods, the Indians add one or several of the following condiments when in season: seeds of an introduced *mostaza* (*Brassica campestris*);[3] fruits of the domesticated and wild chiles (*Capsicum annuum* and *C. baccatum*); leaves of *patúsai* (*Chenopodium ambrosioides* var.), *ipasote* (*C. Fremontii*), *Chimaphila umbellata*, *Oxalis albicans*, an introduced *mostaza silvestre* (*Raphanus Raphanistrum*)—which is really a wild radish—and an introduced *cilantro* (*Coriandrum sativum*).[4]

The Old World chickpea (*Cicer arietinum*) and *chícharo* (*Pisum sativum*)[5] are usually prepared in the green state; the peas are hulled and cooked until most of the water in the cooking pot is evaporated. The mixture is then mashed with a wooden spoon and eaten. The introduced horsebean (*Vicia faba*)[6] is either prepared for eating in the same manner as string beans or the pods are baked in ashes, after which the beans are removed and salted before being eaten. The Old World cowpea (*Vigna sinénsis*)[7] is prepared in the same fashion as the native legumes.

MISCELLANEOUS FOODS

The potato (*Solanum tuberosum*) is baked in ashes or is cut up without being peeled for boiling. Any of the condiments added to other foods may be added to boiled potatoes, as are pieces of meat when available. *Brassica oleracea*, an introduction from the Old World,[8] is boiled and salted before being eaten; apparently, condiments are not added to this cabbage dish. Another Old World plant, the *lechuga*, or lettuce (*Lactuca sativa*),[9] is eaten raw.

The cultigen *Amaranthus leucocarpus*, known among the Tepehuan as *giági* and among the mestizos as *okiti* or *guatle*, is cultivated by canyon Indians in fields and by upland Indians in former corrals as a valued *quelite*; its leaves are boiled and lightly salted before serving as a food.

BEVERAGES

The Tepehuan utilize domesticated and wild plants as sources of ingredients for preparing both crude, fermented drinks designed to stimulate and beverages taken as a light refreshment. These plants fall within two categories: those that supply the basic ingredients and those that serve as catalysts.

MAIZE DRINKS

Maize (*úúnui*) is, without doubt, the most significant source of an ingredient used in preparing the all-important fermented drink, *naváitai* or *tesgüino*. The juice that serves as the basis for this drink is extracted from sprouted maize or from stalks of *elote* corn. Among the Tepehuan, *naváitai* is the term commonly used for the drink when it is prepared from sprouted corn, whereas *voúgadïnaváitai* is the term used for the one prepared from *elote* stalks.

The Tepehuan prefer *tesgüino* prepared from sprouted corn. Grains of corn are soaked for several days, then seeded in a place away from the sun's rays. If the weather is warm, a small depression is scratched out in a corner of the house; if the weather is cool, a small depression is made in a shaded area out-of-doors. In either case, pine needles from *Pinus durangensis*, known among the Indians as *vakákali* (*hoja acicalar del pino*) *úkui* (*pino*), are placed in the shallow pit. The needles are thoroughly wetted, and the grains of corn are placed on top of them. Additional pine needles are added as a covering layer over the grains and watered a bit each day for seven or eight days. The sprouted corn is then removed and mashed on what can only be termed an unfinished metate (*maútuli* or *móúturai*) since it is only partially hollowed out. During the mashing process, one or several catalysts are added. The catalysts known to and used by both upland and canyon Indians include the following: seeds and plumes of three different plants known as *lebadura* or *vasmónai* (*Bromus arizonicus, B. molliformis,* and *B.* sp.), bark of an *encino* known simply as *túái* (*Quercus crassifolia*) among the Tepehuan, a small herb (*Chimaphila umbellata*) the Indians call *naváítai* (*tesgüino*) *biñáragadï* (*fermenter*), another small herb (*C. maculata*) known as *encinilla*, and roots of an unidentified herb (*espadaña*) known among the Indians as *maka* (*espadaña*) *vásoi* (*zacate*).

Bark utilized as a catalyst is removed from the tree trunk with a knife, sharp stone, or metal axe and pounded on a metate or any conveniently situated stone before it is added to the crushed corn sprouts. Catalytic stems and plumes from the *Bromus* species are used in the green or dry state and are crushed on a metate before being added to the corn sprouts. Herbs are mashed a bit before being added.

The choice of catalysts used is apparently determined by personal preference or by the availability of any particular one. However, many of the catalysts mentioned above are readily available within the Tepehuan habitat.

The crushed ingredients (sprouts and catalysts) are added to water and boiled for about twenty-four hours over a slow-burning fire. During this boiling period, the mixture is removed from the olla several times, and each time, the liquid is strained into another olla through a *cedazo* known among the Indians as *šišikarai*. This strainer is manufactured from pliable leaves of any one of the small palmas found in the Tepehuan country and is round or square in shape. After this initial preparation, the *tesgüino* is poured into a larger olla and set aside to ferment, which usually requires three days during the summer and from four to five days during the winter. The fermenting jar is called *naváítakaro* and ranges in size from an olla that may hold only four or five quarts to a very large one that may be five feet in height and about two and one-half feet in diameter with a partially closed upper portion (Fig. 17).

When available, flowers from *inditas* (*Bouvardia ternifolia*) are gathered and affixed in some fashion to the upper portion of an olla that contains fermenting *tesgüino*.

Although sprouted corn *tesgüino* is usually prepared from soft corns, the hard corns are sometimes used. They are soaked in lime water for several hours before being washed thoroughly and placed in the pine-needle seed bed to sprout. Sometimes, they are used without being sprouted. The soaked grains are washed, ground on a metate, cooked for several hours, then added to water and set aside for several days to ferment. Catalysts are not added to this type of *tesgüino*.[10]

17— An olla used for fermentation of *tesgüino*.

In preparing *voúgadï naváítai*, the fresh corn stalks are stripped and piled in a large, hollowed-out pine log called a *canoa*. The stalks are beaten with a thick stick or a crudely shaped club, and the juice is collected with a dipper made from halving a dried fruit from a species of *guaje* (any one of the culti-vated varieties of *Lagenaria siceraria*). The juice is then strained into an olla through a loosely woven basket or strainer, added to water, and boiled for about twenty-four hours before being placed in an olla or a hollowed-out log (Fig. 18) to ferment. Any one or several of the catalysts available to the Tepe-huan are added during the boiling process.

The antiquity of *tesgüino* brewing by the Tepehuan cannot be established

18– Hollowed-out log that serves for fermentation of *elote* cornstalk *tesgüino*.

with certainty. The Indians state that maize *tesgüino*, their most important beverage today, was not at all common about seventy or eighty years ago. It is certain, however, that the preparation of some kind of intoxicating beverage is very ancient among the Tepehuan. The theme of drunkenness appears repeatedly in the historical documents, although it is impossible to determine exactly what sort of beverage was involved. A very early account, published in 1611, refers to excessive drinking among the Oclotani,[11] those Tepehuan who lived northwest of Durango and northeast of the Acaxee. Pérez de Ribas noted that the Tepehuan of the seventeenth century were very prone to drunkenness, particularly at fiestas; intoxicating drinks were prepared from mescal and other wild fruits.[12] Gerónimo de Figueroa wrote in 1662 of intoxicating beverages made by Indians at San Pablo (the present-day Balleza, Chihuahua) where there were both Tepehuan and Tarahumar. He noted a "vino que hacen de maíz (este es más ordinario y se hace como Cerveza de Flandes, con sú raíz) ó de maguey ó mescale (y este es fuertísimo). . . ."[13] Therefore, it seems certain that at least some of the seventeenth-century Tepehuan prepared *tesgüino* from maize. Relative antiquity for the present-day Tepehuan term, *naváitai*, is found in Rinaldini's eighteenth-century dictionary which gives *nabaiti* as the Indian term for *vino*, *nabaiti maitpuqquetadajamoe* for *vino sin fuerza*, *nabaitemora mabaitani* for *hacer vino*, and *nabayti zaddaguibumujamoe* for *vino aguardo*;[14] there is nothing in these terms to suggest that maize was an ingredient in the beverage. However, the Indian term for *vino sin fuerza* must, in some fashion, refer to a drink prepared from mescal since the present northern Tepehuan word for mescal (*mái*) forms a portion of the Indian term for this weak beverage. Bruman refers to a letter written by the Bishop of Durango to the viceroy in 1790 in which the Bishop details drunkenness among the Tepehuan;[15] the reference was mostly to distilled mescal and there was no mention of *tesgüino*. For the late nineteenth century there is the comment made by Lumholtz concerning the use of *tesgüino* in ceremonies held to promote rainfall.[16] In Lumholtz' time, the Tepehuan believed that if *tesgüino* were not made throughout the year, then the world would come to an end.

AMARYLLIDACEAE DRINKS

A fermented beverage is prepared from four species of *Agave* that are common to the Tepehuan country: *čawé* (*ájurai*), maguey or mescal (*mái*), *mescalillo* (*guvúkai*), and *lecheguilla* (*jápari*). Hearts or crowns of these plants are baked in an earth oven (See Chapter 5), crushed on a rock, and then added to an olla of water and boiled for several hours before being set aside to ferment for about eight days. Any available catalyst is added during either the boiling process or the fermenting stage, but two are claimed to be most effective in making this beverage "strong": the crushed bark of *túái* (*Quercus crassifolia*) and seeds and plumes of the *lebadura* or *vasmónai* (*Bromus arizonicus, B. molli-formis, B*. sp.).

What is termed a *vino* is prepared from *jápari*, one of the *Agave* species just mentioned. Crowns of the plant are baked in an earth oven and then crushed on a rock with a wooden club. The juice is collected and placed in an olla contain-ing several quarts of water. This mixture is boiled for several hours and strained through a basket into a hollowed-out log in which it is cooled for twenty-four hours. The strained liquid is then boiled for several hours before being set aside to ferment. Many of the Tepehuan state that catalysts are not added to this beverage and insist that the drink is distinct from *tesgüino*. Older Tepehuan state that it was not made at all about seventy or eighty years ago.[17]

The antiquity of maguey and mescal drinks among the Tepehuan is attest-ed to in the just-cited comments by Gerónimo de Figueroa, Pérez de Ribas, and the Bishop of Durango. Lumholtz noted in the 1890's that the Tepehuan were often "deprived" of their property "through the agency of mescal, for which they have an unfortunate weakness."[18] He also wrote of an intoxicating bever-age made from an agave called *tschawí* (properly, *čawé*) that might well be the agave which is known today as *ájurai* by the Tepehuan. According to Lum-holtz, the Indians "put much importance on this brew, and say that the plant is so sensitive that if one passes a jar in which it is being boiled the liquid will not ferment."[19]

LILIACEAE DRINKS

Hearts of *šúšida kúrui* (*Dasylirion Wheeleri*) are baked in an earth oven and pounded with a stick or a stone to extract the juice, which is mixed with water and boiled for several hours. The mixture is then strained through a basket into an olla and set aside to ferment for several days. Any available catalyst is added to this *tesgüino*.

FRUIT DRINKS

The Indians who live near Santa Rosa collect fruits of a *savóči* (*Randia laevigata*) for use in preparing a refreshing drink. The fruits are mashed on the metate and added to cool water. The Old World peach (*Prunus Persica*)[20] is utilized in preparing a *vino*; the fruit is mashed, put in an olla of water and boiled over a slow fire for twenty-four hours. After the fruit mash is cool, the juice is strained into another olla and put aside to ferment for two days. Catalysts are not added to this drink.

MISCELLANEOUS DRINKS

Upland and canyon Tepehuan are fond of preparing a *tesgüino* from the Old World wheat (a variety of *Triticum aestivum*), but they utilize only the sprouted seeds that are started in pine-needle seed beds exactly like those used in sprouting the corn for maize *tesgüino*. The same catalysts used in the corn drink are also used in the wheat beverage.

The canyon Indians near Santa Rosa utilize a variety of the introduced sugar cane (*Saccharum officinarum*) in preparing a popular fermented drink; the seeds are sprouted in the pine-needle seed bed, and the sprouts are processed precisely the same as the sprouted corn and wheat. The boiling and fermentation periods are also the same.

Canyon Tepehuan also prepare a *tesgüino* from sprouts or stalks of the Old World varieties of grain sorghums that have been introduced into the canyon country, *maizana* (*momoiti*), *maíz caña*, and *malo maíz*, or sorgo. Techniques followed in preparing sprouted sorghum *tesgüino* are the same as those for the fermented beverages from sprouted corn, wheat, and sugar cane; and the same catalysts are used. There is no essential difference between methods of processing grain-sorghum stalks for *tesgüino* and those for making it from corn stalks.

The Indians living near Santa Rosa collect seeds of the *cupilla* or *ukavoli* (*Persea Liebmanni*) for use in making a "coffee." The seeds are peeled, soaked for twenty-four hours, toasted, and mashed before being added to water and boiled for a short time; it is drunk as a very refreshing drink.

Bark of the handsome *aliso* or *sojárai* (*Platanus Wrightii*) that appears along well-watered arroyos in the canyon country is used in preparing a tea taken as a refreshing drink.

Canyon Tepehuan crush the stems of a lowland grass (*té límon*) on a metate which are then added to a small amount of water and boiled for a few minutes. The result is a stimulating drink.

CHAPTER 4 NOTES

1– Gray (1950), 1554.

2– Ibid., 932.

3– Ibid., 708.

4– Ibid., 706, 1083.

5– Ibid., 932, 936.

6– Darlington and Janaki Ammal (1945), 159.

7– Ibid., 171.

8– Gray (1950), 708.

9– Ibid., 1555.

10– Indians offered no rational explanation of why catalysts are not used in the preparation of this type of corn beer.

11– 1611: Dabertzhofer (1611).

12– 1645: Pérez de Ribas (1944), III, 137, 139.

13– 1662: Figueroa. "Puntos de Anua . . . ," in *Doc.* (1857), 4th series, III, 219.

14– 1743: Rinaldini (1743), 14.

15– Bruman (1940), 57.

16– Lumholtz (1902), I, 433-34.

17– It is probable that the Tepehuan learned, by some means, that a *vino*, or *sotol*, may be prepared from species of plants belonging to the families Amaryllidaceae and Liliaceae and have since prepared this crude, fermented drink even though they lacked some details, particularly distillation techniques, of the process.

18– Lumholtz (1902), I, 424.

19– Ibid., 256.

20– Bailey and Bailey (1941), 602.

5
HUNTING, GATHERING, AND FISHING

The Chihuahua Tepehuan are essentially a sedentary agricultural folk; but, as among other native peoples of northwestern Mexico, the products of hunting, gathering, and fishing are significant supplements to the basic diet of corn, beans, and squash. Southern Chihuahua is distinguished by a relative abundance of wildlife (particularly valuable in time of crop failure) that is hunted and killed by techniques which, for the most part, must be quite ancient among the Tepehuan. Certain species of birds are sought because of their usefulness as food and as medicine. Wild vegetable food products, especially the *quelites* are eagerly sought during the early spring, for by that time, foodstuffs stored the previous year are about used up. When in season, wild fruits and nuts provide variety in the basic corn diet. And, fishing is today a source of food as it must have been in the past.

FOWLING

A wild turkey common to the pine-clad and the pine and oak uplands of the Tepehuan country is known as *oidígana* (*silvestre*) *tova* (*cócono*);[1] this large bird appears only occasionally in upper portions of the canyons and hardly ever in the very warm, western canyons. The Indians who possess rifles have no difficulty in bringing down turkeys, but since rifles are relatively uncommon among the Tepehuan, most of the turkeys that serve as food are trapped. The common trap consists of a square fruit crate measuring about twenty-four inches on each side and about twelve inches in depth. This crate is constructed from carefully smoothed and notched wooden sticks bound together with maguey-fiber cordage or leather thongs. The sticks are made from any one of the easily worked, soft woods of southern Chihuahua. The crate is inverted, and one edge is raised and supported by a stick about eighteen inches in height that is grooved about one and one-half inches from the ground. One end of a string is attached to this groove, and the other end is affixed to the opposite side of the inverted crate and made taut. A few grains of corn are placed on the ground in the center of the trap. The turkey is lured by the bait, and in moving about the spot where the grains are scattered, it trips the string, causing the supporting stick to collapse. Older Indians refer to the construction of a small, conical brush trap in which a few grains of corn were placed. When a turkey entered such a trap and began to eat the corn grains, it was clubbed to death by someone who had hidden nearby. Small turkeys are frequently run down, and sometimes they are maintained as domestic fowl until large enough to be eaten. Turkeys are easily trapped in the vicinity of a *palo verde* (*Ilex rubra*), known among the Indians as *tïdogidava úši* (literally, a "green tree"), because they frequently feed on the fruits of this tree. They are also treed and shot down with arrows. The wild turkey is an esteemed food when, after having been defeathered and eviscerated, it is boiled in an olla or roasted on a spit.

A noisy brush bird known as *chachalaca*[2] appears in thickets of arroyos west of Baborigame throughout the year; this fowl is killed with stones and boiled or roasted on a spit.

Each of several long-tailed, multicolored birds is known as *faisán* among the mestizos and as *tarágai* among the Tepehuan; these birds are brought down with rifles or bows and arrows when they are found perched on the limbs of low shrubs or trees. The *tarágai* is said to be so swift that it is difficult to shoot down when on the run. The bows and arrows used to bring it down are somewhat smaller than those used on large game. Moreover, the arrows are cross-tipped or have a corncob tip. (In using a blunt-tipped arrow to knock down and stun smaller game, the hunter is able to salvage more of the meat than if he uses an arrow with a sharp point.) After being plucked and cleaned, the *tarágai* are boiled in an olla or roasted on a spit.

The Tepehuan who live along well-watered streamways in the southwest bring down a *martín pescador* (*baivukali*) during the winter months with an expertly thrown stone. This kingfisher is described as having a white belly and a blue back[3] and is eaten after being roasted on a spit; it is carefully defeathered and eviscerated before being prepared as a foodstuff.

The Indians who live near the Río Verde report a conspicuously marked bird that appears along the river during the winter months. Marked with a curved bill that is depressed toward the tip, this bird must be a whimbrel.[4] When defeathered, eviscerated, and cooked on a spit, the flesh of this bird is a favored dish. Two other water birds are repeatedly mentioned by the Tepehuan. One of these is the *vakóñi*, a large heron (*garza*)[5] that appears along upland streams and the Río Verde; it is brought down with stones or a rifle. Commonly, it is roasted on a spit, but on occasion, the rather "tough meat" is boiled with beans. *Vakági*, the other water bird, is a dark brown or black loon that appears in the uplands during the *tiempo de las aguas*.[6] This bird is hunted with a rifle or with a bow and arrow and is prepared for eating the same as the *vakóñi*.

The crow (*kokóñi*)[7] rarely appears in the pine-clad Tepehuan country except at seeding time, but it is abundant in better-watered stream valleys of the canyon country on the west. The Indians make every effort to kill this glossy black bird because of the damage it inflicts upon corn fields immediately after planting. The *kokóñi* is brought down with rocks or a bow and arrow or caught in a steel trap baited with grains of corn. After being defeathered and cleaned, crows are roasted on spits.

A handsome red-tailed hawk (*vujíbi*)[8] is quite common in the pine and oak country fringing the uplands as well as in the upper portions of the canyons. It is particularly disliked because it preys on chickens. The rifle is the most effective weapon for bringing down this hawk, but an Indian armed only with a bow and arrow or a rock will sit quietly for hours watching for one to fly to a relatively open limb and light facing away from him. Occasionally, when some of these hawks are known to be in the vicinity, a few chickens are permitted to roam unprotected in open spaces as bait. Once killed, the hawk is defeathered, eviscerated, and boiled or roasted; its feathers are used in the manufacture of arrows.

Yet another hawk, *šišikamuli* or *čičikamuli*, distinguished by a reddish tail and back,[9] also preys upon chickens, but it is rarely brought down except with a rifle. This red-tailed hawk is claimed to be more common in the uplands than in the canyons. When it is killed, it is plucked and cleaned, then boiled in an olla or roasted on a spit; its feathers are also used on arrows. Two other hawks are sought because their handsome feathers are desired for use on arrows. They are the *pipíkoli*, that is known to prey upon doves in the uplands, and the *tobavi*, a *gavilán de la tierra*, that preys upon chickens.

A *tecolote* (*tukúrai*) marked by tufts and grayish feathers[10] is sought by upland Indians when it calls at night; it is killed with a rock or a bow and arrow and, after being defeathered and eviscerated, is boiled or roasted. The long-legged owl, *kukúvuli* or *lechuza*,[11] distinguished by a white heart-shaped face, is sought in hollow trees and is brought down with a rock, a bow and arrow, or a rifle. This particular owl is always boiled before being eaten.[12] The largest of the tufted owls in southern Chihuahua is the *kokoájo* (*buho*) and is rather easily located after it makes its distinctive call or hoot.[13] This owl is boiled or roasted after being plucked and cleaned.

Three woodpeckers common to the pine and oak country of southern Chihuahua are eaten by the Tepehuan after being defeathered, eviscerated, and roasted on a spit. Apparently, the most widely distributed of these woodpeckers is the *kúratu*, which is distinguished by a conspicuous red head.[14] This bird is brought down with a rock, a bow and arrow, or a rifle; or—failing with these weapons—the Indians may fell a tree containing the nest. Both adult and young birds are eaten and are generally roasted on a spit after being properly prepared. The *vïpïgi* (*rojas*) *kúratu* (*carpintero*) is another woodpecker common to the pine and oak country and is very conspicuous because of its spotted chest that has black spots predominating on a white background.[15] This bird is brought down and prepared as a foodstuff in the same fashion as the common *kúratu*. By far the most common woodpecker at lower elevations is the *čikúrurui* (*pájaro carpintero*), distinguished by white patches on its wings and by a reddish breast and a yellow belly.[16] This bird is easily located because of its habit of making numerous holes in one tree, and the Indians state that it is readily brought down with a rock, a bow and arrow, or a rifle. After being defeathered and cleaned, it is spitted and roasted.

A meadow lark, known as *saiyana* (*zacate*) *úrugi* (*ave*), appears in profusion in grassy areas of the pine-clad uplands, particularly where the pine stand has been cleared and grass has appeared. It is marked by a yellowish belly with a conspicuous black "v."[17] It is brought down with an expertly thrown stone and is esteemed as a food when roasted on a spit or boiled in an olla. A white-winged dove,[18] known as *oríga* (*paloma torcáz*), appears in conspicuous numbers near watering places in southern Chihuahua especially at lower elevations. It is killed with a rifle, a bow and arrow, or with a well-thrown stone and, among all birds sought as food, is probably the most favored. Commonly, doves are spitted and roasted after having been plucked and drawn. A *paloma del monte* (*túgu*) is a large bird with a white band on top of its tail;[19] it appears in great numbers in oak country when acorns ripen and is brought down with a thrown stone, a bow and arrow, or a rifle. Older Indians maintain that it was once trapped in a tiny brush hut, but details of how this was accomplished are lacking. The *túgu* is a tasty foodstuff when roasted on a spit, and its eggs (*nonodï*) are perhaps the most favored of all that are sought as food; they are eaten raw. Nests (*kósa*) of the *túgu* are frequently robbed of newly hatched birds, which are eaten without any preparation whatever.

The Tepehuan describe several species of quail, all known as *váívoli*. These species include the following: a gray quail with a white head, common to dry canyons of the southwest; a gray quail with a black or brown crest, associated with chaparral vegetation in southwestern canyons; a gray-chested bird with a reddish tuft, also common to dry southwestern canyons; a gray quail which is undoubtedly the bobwhite,[20] well known because of its distinctive call; and a much spotted quail, the *codorniz pinto*. The bobwhite and the *codorniz pinto* are apparently the only species common to the uplands. Quail are flushed by accident or by design; when the birds light in a relatively open spot, they are killed with rocks, bows and arrows, or rifles. As a favorite source of food, the birds are plucked, drawn, and boiled in an olla or roasted on a spit. Quail eggs are often hunted by children, who eat them raw.

Upland Tepehuan tell of a large bird, called *akitusdali*, that is distinguished by a short bill, a long tail and neck, and a streaked breast.[21] An expertly thrown rock is used to bring down this bird as it perches on a rock or a fence.

A hummingbird (*vipíši*) is occasionally taken by an Indian who stands patiently with a branch near a flowering shrub known to be frequented by this tiny creature. Should the hunter be successful in getting one with a swat of the branch, its head is pulled off and discarded, the feathers are removed, and it is added to a pot of beans.

Several birds of southern Chihuahua are sought because of their supposed value in preparing medicinal agents. The conspicuous, white-tipped tail feathers of the squirrel cuckoo[22] are thought to be of value in aiding childbirth; the feathers are singed and then sniffed during parturition. The handsome ivory-billed woodpecker, known as *kúratu*,[23] is occasionally killed because its feathers are believed to be an effective cure for earache. The feathers are placed over the afflicted ear and held there by a rag. The flesh of this *kúratu* is never eaten, for to do so would prevent the birth (conception?) of male children. The Turkey buzzard (*nuí*)[24] that appears in the uplands and canyons is frequently shot with a rifle or a bow and arrow as it perches on a tree branch. The viscera is removed but not the feathers; the carcass is then mashed on a metate and added to water to be drunk as a certain cure for gonorrhea. The *pipídamuli* is a *golondrina* common to the uplands,[25] where it nests in the loft areas of habitations or storage huts; this small swallow is marked by a blue back and a black wing and tail. It is not killed to be eaten as food but, rather, to be used as a medicinal potion given to children who have not learned to talk. The bird is defeathered, cleaned, and boiled for a short time before being thoroughly mashed on a metate and fed to the afflicted child.

Comments by older Tepehuan and practices followed by the younger Indians suggest that certain birds have been held in superstitious regard for a long time. Although several woodpeckers are eaten (*kúratu*, *vipígi kúratu*, and *čikúrurui*), a very common one of the pine and oak country is not eaten even though it is occasionally killed in sport. It is distinguished by a black crown, a whitish breast and belly, and white outer tail feathers as opposed to the black inner feathers.[26] It is believed that to eat this bird would prevent the birth (conception?) of male children, who are so important in helping with agricultural activities or would cause the death of male children already born.[27]

A similar superstition is held regarding other common birds in the Tepehuan country, particularly the following: *vavai torúši*, a long-billed water bird common to canyons with permanent streams that is sometimes caught when very young and kept as a pet but never eaten; *mar (hijo) mukí (muerto)*, a meadow bird with red, black, and white feathers; *úši (palo or árbol) komíuli* (*subir*), a common *pájaro del bosque*; *mavaítuši*, a white-breasted, large-billed bird that commonly appears near what are locally called (at least in the uplands) lagoons (*váíkirï*); the blue jay (*šišívikami*); a *quelele* (*kušimuli*); and what must be the hairy woodpecker (*šikirïli*).

Many of the Indians believe that the appearance of a *saltapared* (*mavítuši*) over a dwelling indicates arrival of a visitor in the near future. It is also believed that when the *kukúvuli* (*lechuza*) and the *túkurai* (*tecolote*) "sing," sickness will develop.

Certain predators are killed whenever possible because of the damage they do to crops and to small domestic fowl or animals. Among the most common predators are the *báágai*, a turkey-sized eagle that reportedly preys upon small pigs and chickens and, occasionally, upon young children; the *šikóranui* (*sopilote*), a black vulture[28] that preys unceasingly upon chickens; and the *tapómai* (*pica metate*), a terrestrial owl[29] that appears in open uplands near Llano Grande, where it is reported to do much damage in the corn fields while grubbing for insects near newly sprouted corn. The eagle is shot down with a rifle or caught in a steel trap baited with a small chicken, the black vulture is killed with a rifle, and the owl is brought down with an expertly thrown stone.

Birds (*úrugi*) are sometimes maintained as pets while they are young and, apparently, are never caged. Quail (*váívoli*), the *paloma del monte* (*túgu*), the crow (*kokóñi*), and the *tapómai* (*pica metate*) are the ones usually chosen as pets, but all of them, except the *tapómai* and the *kokóñi*, are permitted to fly away when grown. These two are killed since they are known to damage corn fields.

That the ancient Tepehuan held birds in superstitious regard seems certain since Pérez de Ribas remarked in the seventeenth century that the Indians trained owls and brought them to the houses of Spaniards, where the birds sang "sad cooings" which were supposed to frighten the Spaniards away.[30] More recent evidence concerning superstitions associated with birds is found in comments made by Lumholtz and by Mason. Lumholtz referred to the use of eagle feathers in ceremonies held to promote rainfall, and he also noted that the Tepehuan believed that doves might once have been larvae on *madroño* trees.[31] Mason commented that some Tepehuan believed illness to be related to the singing of birds.[32]

Wild fowl must have constituted an important source of food in ancient times. Pérez de Ribas noted that seventeenth-century Tepehuan had access to plenty of wild fowl.[33] Eighteenth-century documents refer to the use of quail, doves, cranes,[34] and turkeys (*pavos silvestres*) as food.[35]

Pérez de Ribas also gives evidence of the ancient use of feathers to make headdresses worn at celebrations. One specific reference is to a very elaborate feather headdress designed for an Indian leader who lived near Guadiana.[36]

HUNTING AND TRAPPING

Hunting and trapping fulfill a twofold function among the Tepehuan: not only are they means of supplementing the meager diet of corn, beans, and squash, they are also sports much enjoyed by the participants. Today, the Tepehuan apparently do not hold ceremonies before hunting begins, but about seventy-five or eighty years ago, according to older Indians, there was a twenty-four hour period of dancing before a hunting expedition departed. One tradition that is still followed as it was in the past, according to informants, is a tendency for hunters to remain within a somewhat restricted area. Upland Indians rarely hunt in the canyons, and canyon Indians seldom hunt in the uplands.

Deer and squirrels are apparently the most important game animals sought today, but other game found in the Tepehuan country are equally valued as food. Dogs constitute an important element in individual or communal hunting, and good hunting dogs are highly prized. The fact that they are frequently wagered as bets preceding the kickball race is an indication of their considered worth.

The common modes of hunting game include use of the figure-four release trap, bow and arrow, lance, stake trap, snare, dog, and rifle. The figure-four release rock trap (Fig. 19) is known as *tútudï* (*trampa*) *ódai* (*piedra*) and is constructed in a simple fashion. A rock is propped up with one stick arranged so that it will fall away when the bait that is attached to another, the trigger stick, is disturbed. The vertical stick is notched about two inches from the ground so that the trigger stick may be wedged into a horizontal position between the lower portion of the tilted rock and the notch in the upright stick. A few grains of corn (*vájomi*)[37] are attached to the trigger stick with a spring; when these grains are disturbed, the supporting stick collapses, and the prey is crushed by the falling rock. Fruit crates are also used in a figure-four release trap; however, the top of the crate is generally weighted with a stone so that an animal, such as the gray fox, whose skin is coveted for making a quiver will not be injured but yet will not escape.

Present-day Tepehuan utilize bows (*gaágatoi*) of three sizes: a large bow about forty-eight inches in length when unstrung, a smaller bow about thirty inches in unstrung length, and a diminutive bow about seventeen inches long (Fig. 20). The two larger bows are used for hunting game animals and birds at long range, whereas the diminutive bow is used for birds and fish at close range.

19— The figure-four release trap used by the Tepehuan.

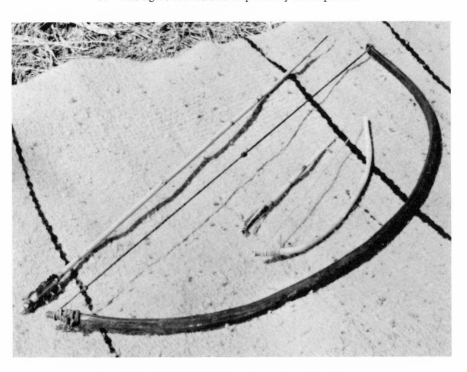

20— The Tepehuan bow (*gaátoi*) and arrow (*úyi*).
The large and diminutive types are displayed on a Tepehuan woven blanket.

All three sizes are commonly made from the following woods: *Morus micro-phylla*, which is known as *mora* or *kóji*; *Haematoxylon brasiletto*, the brazil of southwestern Tepehuan country; *palo amarillo* (*Tecoma stans*); and *guázima* (*Guazuma ulmifolia*). Branches used in the manufacture of bows are cut in the green state and smoothed with a sharpened stone or knife after the bark (*kómi*) has been removed. When *Morus microphylla* is used, the ends of the green bow are heated and thrust into a crack in wood or rock so that they may be bent slightly. Most bows are wrapped with animal skin or green bark at a point not far from the notched ends of the bow to prevent breakage when it is strung. One end is notched on only one side, the other end is notched on both sides.

Among the Tepehuan, the bow string is known as *giáragai*. For large bows, the strings (*gígiaragai*) are made of sinew taken from the back of a deer, leather strips, or ixtle-fiber thongs; the diminutive bow may be strung with any one of the three or with a cord made by twisting hair from a cow's tail on the *tarabilla* (see Chapter 8 for a discussion of this tool). Whatever the source of material used for the bow string, it is twisted when the bow is strung.

The arrows (*úyi*) most commonly used by the upland Indians are prepared from the easily worked wood of a *fresno* (*Fraxinus velutina*), known as *pítai*; a *koomági* (*gris*) *účigai* (*morado*); a *palo verde* (*Garrya laurifolia*); a *membrillo* (*Ceanothus azureus*); and the *Mahonia fascicularis*, known as *palo amarillo* or *vúáma* (*amarillo*) *bopotai* (*puntas de las flechas*). Lowland Tepehuan also uti-lize these woods in the manufacture of arrows but, in addition, use the follow-ing reed grasses: *Phragmites communis*, the *kóókoli* (*chile caribe*) *bopotai* (*puntas de las flechas*) of the canyons; *vapákai*, a common *carrizo* of the can-yons; and *utútali*, a wild grass found along streamways. *Phragmites communis* and *vapákai* are the most commonly used for both the reed arrows and the shafts of composite arrows that have wooden foreshafts and points. *Utútali* serves mostly for the making of toy arrows used by children.

In the construction of composite arrows, a foreshaft made from one of the following woods is forced into the reed shaft: *Berberis Fremontii*, generally known as *palo amarillo* or *vúáma* (*amarillo*) *úši* (*palo* or *árbol*); *Garrya lauri-folia*, the *čivo* (*amargo*) *bopotai* (*puntas de las flechas*); *G. ovata*; and *Ipomoea arborescens*, known as *palo cabra* or *šivátu* (*cabra*) *úši* (*palo* or *árbol*).

The wooden arrows, as well as the composite ones with foreshafts, average about thirty-two inches in length, and both types are used with the large bows. The cane, or reed, portions of the foreshafted arrows comprise between eigh-teen and twenty inches of the total length. The wooden arrow used with the diminutive bow is only about eleven inches long. When a composite arrow is used with this bow, the cane portion is from seven to eight inches long.

With the exception of very short arrows of cane or wood that are used for killing birds or fish at close range, all arrows are feathered. One end of the wooden or cane arrow is split, and three halved feathers (*áàña*) are inserted. The feathers are anchored with *usábai*, a gum from a species of pine, and tied in place with sinew from a deer's back, with gut, or with vegetable fiber. Older Tepehuan state that canyon Indians used to fletch their arrows with two split feathers rather than three. The most favored source of feathers is the red-tailed hawk (*šišikamuli* or *čičikamuli*), but the feathers from another red-tailed hawk (*vujíbi*) are a close second choice.

Although there is no evidence that flint or stone is used today in the manufacture of arrowheads, older Tepehuan maintain that both flint and stone arrowheads were once used. Wood is now the most common material from which arrowheads are manufactured. Rather well-made arrowheads (*bopotai*), fashioned from any of the hardwoods used in arrow shafts, are inserted into the ends of the long, wooden or foreshafted arrows and tied in place with vegetable-fiber cordage or with gut. Arrowheads are rarely put on the small, wooden or composite arrows designed to bring down game at close range. Occasionally, projectile points are made from tiny bits of iron by the Indians who have contacts with mestizos fortunate enough to have pieces of the metal.

According to older Indians, a stone arrow-straightener was used about seventy-five or eighty years ago; today, a small piece of broken pottery serves this purpose. The potsherd, in which a v-shaped cut has been made, is heated before being used as an arrow wrench.

Arrows and bows are invariably colored with *útai* (*almagre*), which is prepared by crushing a reddish rock obtainable near Llano Grande, in the Arroyo de Milpillas, near Baborigame and Nabogame, and on upper portions of the canyon slopes.

The Tepehuan bowman (*mïmïdamui* or *muwaukudami*) wears a guard (*pulcera*) called *kavalai* on his wrist (*jubiši*). This guard, which is always worn on the left wrist, is made from dressed deer hide. The bow is held vertically if the target is at a great distance, horizontally if it is nearby. The arrow is placed on the left of a vertically held bow and on top of a horizontally held bow. The arrow is initially gripped between the index and next fingers, but when the bow string is pulled back and the arrow is ready for release, the index finger is removed from the top of the arrow.

The quiver (*aljaba*) used by the Tepehuan is called *vogusai* and is made from the skin of a *kašío*, the common *zorra gris* of the Tepehuan country. Mason refers to a quiver of deer skin but gives no details for its preparation.[38] Either of two methods may be followed in manufacturing a quiver from the fox pelt. One method involves splitting the carcass down the middle; removing head, legs, and tail; and sewing together the cut edges of the carcass with leather thongs. The body cavity is then filled with earth that is left inside the carcass for several days. The other method involves cutting a small strip of skin from the neck of the fox and easing the carcass out through the hole in the skin. Once the entire skin is free, the holes in it (from the removal of legs and tail) are closed up, and the scalp part of the hide is cut off. The skin is then stuffed with earth as above. The quiver is carried over the left shoulder and held there by a leather strap. Older Indians state that, not long ago, all men who went far from home carried a bow and five or six arrows—the bow in the left hand and the arrows in a quiver.

Canyon Indians drive wounded animals from caves with a wooden lance (*itatari*) fashioned by sharpening one end of a smoothed sapling. Short clubs prepared from any easily worked wood are often used to dispatch wounded animals. Older Indians refer to a former use of stone clubs or axes in killing animals or humans. Remnants of the stone clubs (war clubs?) found here and there in the Tepehuan country (see Fig. 2, page 62), particularly in the canyons, suggest that the clubs averaged about one and one-sixth inches in diameter, were beautifully rounded and smoothed, and were characterized by a narrow groove at one end. According to older Tepehuan, an ixtle-fiber cord or a leather thong was attached to the club. These stone clubs may be the *sandro sonanicucumicarude* (*hachas de armas*) referred to in the eighteenth-century Tepehuan dictionary compiled by Rinaldini.[39]

The rifle is the most desired weapon for hunting, but few Tepehuan possess the means for obtaining this weapon, much less the means for acquiring shells. Furthermore, it is clear that the mestizos who hold authority in the Tepehuan country discourage the posssession of rifles and pistols by the Indians.[40] The lack of rifles among the Tepehuan undoubtedly explains their dependence upon the bow and arrow, the steel trap, and other means of bringing down game.[41]

The cottontail (*toči, toši,* or *toóši*) of the Indian country is much disliked because of the damage it inflicts upon young corn and wheat. The weapons used on the cottontail are the rifle, a bow and arrow, or an expertly thrown stone (either cast by hand or from a sling). Once killed, the cottontail becomes a valued foodstuff when, after being skinned and drawn, it is roasted on a spit or boiled. An arrow is sometimes used to force a rabbit from its burrow; or, as among the upland Tepehuan, a large pointed stick is used to impale the rabbit as it hides in its burrow. One method used for hunting rabbits is to track them down in the snow. Hunting the cottontail is a source of great sport among the Tepehuan; when a *toči* is spotted, men and youths form a line and run toward the animal, gradually converging in a circle that becomes smaller and smaller until, at last, the hapless creature is encircled and either clubbed to death or caught by hand and strangled.

The Tepehuan hunt five species of squirrels that are killed either because they are edible or because they prey upon newly planted corn fields. Squirrels constitute perhaps the most important game animal that serves as a foodstuff. The *suliki* is a small ground squirrel with a long bushy tail that is taken with the rifle, a bow and arrow, or with the rock or basket trap. As with other species of squirrel, the *suliki* is much esteemed as food and is skinned, drawn, and then roasted on a spit or on coals. *Tuúkuli*, or the *ardilla del campo*, marked by a non-bushy tail, is a small and spotted ground squirrel that is reportedly the most harmful of all the types of squirrels common to southern Chihuahua; it does a great deal of damage in grain fields immediately after planting. As food, the *tuúkuli* is prepared in the same way as other squirrels. A large yellow-brown squirrel, common to pine and oak country but sometimes found among stands of *madroño* (*Arbutus arizonica*) in the upper portions of canyon slopes, is known as *vúáma bobókoši*. This species is said to cause little damage in corn fields, but it is hunted anyway because of its value as a foodstuff. It is usually killed with a rock, but sometimes a tree is felled if one is hiding in the branches. The common gray squirrel of the pine and oak country is called *kooma bobókoši*. Marked by a white belly and a very bushy tail, this squirrel is claimed not to do much damage to grain fields, but as a desired food item, it is brought down with an expertly thrown stone, with a bow and arrow, or by a stone cast from a sling. [The Tepehuan sling is manufactured by affixing strings of hide or ixtle fiber to a cowhide pouch or to a net prepared from leaves of the *kúrui* (*Dasylirion simplex*) or the *šúšida kúrui* (*D. Wheeleri*).] The *makuaši*, or *ardilla voladora*, is a small gray squirrel that is apparently restricted to lower elevations in southwestern canyons, where the Indians state that it does not ordinarily damage corn. However, it is killed for its food value with a bow and arrow, a rifle, or a rock as it tries to escape from a felled tree.

The Tepehuan who live on the middle portions of southwestern canyon slopes hunt the armadillo (*alívuli*) because of the quality of its meat. Dogs are used to track the animal to its burrow, but all Indians note that it is often difficult to dig it out of hiding.[42] When an armadillo is captured, it is beaten to death from its underside with a club.[43] Armadillo meat is spitted and roasted.

Tuvoki is a term applied indiscriminately to a small black mole (*topo*) and to a large gray gopher (*tuza*), both of which prey upon the roots of corn plants when they sprout. Moreover, when the corn has matured, both animals may topple corn stalks and drag ears of corn to their burrows. At Santa Rosa, the *tuvoki* frequently eats the bark and roots of young orange trees and does much damage to *chícharo* (*Pisum sativum*) plants. The young plants are cut down and dragged into the tunnels constructed by these small creatures. They also are known to damage small fruit trees in the uplands. Gophers and moles are caught in steel traps (borrowed or traded from the mestizos), or when found in the open, they are killed with bows and arrows. However, the Indians state that there is little opportunity for surprising gophers or moles in the open since the animals can detect the scent of human beings for some twenty or thirty feet. Once killed, they are skinned, drawn, and roasted on a spit or boiled with scraps of any other meat that may be available.

Vošïkai is the generic name for rodents common to the fields; several species are trapped by the Tepehuan and eaten after having been skinned, drawn, and roasted on a spit or over coals. The *kivïšali* is a small mouse that enters storage houses in search of seeds. The *dïgi* is a bushy-tailed woodrat also known to raid storage houses. Either of these rodents may be readily trapped with an inverted and tilted *cajete* (*ásokoli* or *ajáskoli*, a flattish earthenware bowl) supported by a figure-four release mechanism and baited with a few grains of corn or wheat.

Uúpai is the term used for any of the striped, hognose, and spotted skunks, all of which appear in the Tepehuan country. They are particularly disliked because they prey upon chickens. Some Indians maintain that skunks serve as a starvation food. If one is to be eaten, it is carefully skinned, drawn, and washed thoroughly in running water prior to being roasted on a spit.

The bobcat (*gato montés*) of the Tepehuan country is known as *áli* (*chiquito*) *mavídai* (*león*)[44] and is frequently encountered in upper portions of the canyon slopes. Indians hunt the bobcat because it preys upon small domestic animals and poultry and because its skin is useful; it is brought down with a rifle, a bow and arrow, or by means of a very large rock trap that is supported by a substantially constructed, figure-four release mechanism and baited with a live chicken. The skin is cured, then sold or traded to mestizos or utilized in the manufacture of sandals.

A puma[45] that is known among the Tepehuan as *mavídai* (*león*) appears frequently in the pine and oak country but only rarely in the hot canyon country to the west and southwest. It is claimed to be particularly destructive to goats and pigs. When such predation becomes widespread, the Tepehuan attempt to hunt down the animal with a rifle or a bow and arrow. Lacking a rifle, an Indian will seek the assistance of a mestizo who possesses such a weapon and who has quite as much interest as the Indian in removing this predator from the scene. Puma skins serve as sleeping mats.

The Tepehuan who live in southwestern canyons describe a *tigre* or jaguar, a large predatory animal marked by dark spots on a tan background, that inflicts much damage upon wandering pigs and goats. When a *tigre*[46] is reported as roaming a specific area, the Tepehuan attempt to locate the animal and hold it at bay with dogs until assistance can be obtained from someone who owns or has access to a rifle. The bow and arrow is said to be ineffective in bringing down this predator. Pelts of the *tigre* are valued for use as sleeping mats.

The jaguarundi[47] of the canyons is known as either *onza* or *león* and is feared for its predatory ways with domestic fowl; it is claimed to be very difficult to bring down with a bow and arrow, and as in the case of the *tigre*, the Indians seek help from anyone possessing a rifle. Jaguarundi skins are occasionally tacked to house support posts as trophies. The Tepehuan deny that the pelt is traded or sold to mestizos, and they note that the meat serves only as a starvation food.

Flesh of the spotted ocelot[48] is boiled and eaten, and its skin is highly prized for use as a sleeping mat. These cats are reported to inflict much damage upon poultry and goats.

One of the most handsome of the wild creatures found in southern Chihuahua is the nutria, common to most of the upland streams. This otter,[49] distinguished by a brown pelt, is sometimes killed with stones, but more commonly it is clubbed to death after being smoked from its stream-bank den or nest. Otter skins are rarely utilized by the Tepehuan but are traded or sold to the mestizos instead; the meat, however, is considered good to eat when roasted on a spit.

Kuítoli, the ring-tailed cat,[50] is a nocturnal animal common to the pine and oak country and, to a degree, the upper portions of canyons. This creature is intensely disliked because it preys upon chickens and *elote* corn and, occasionally, upon young pigs. It is frequently spotted on moonlit nights near elevated chicken coops and is then dispatched with a rifle, bow and arrow, or an expertly thrown stone. Dogs sometimes corner one but have difficulty in killing this animal which is described as *muy bravo*. When dogs tree a *kuítoli*, the Indians use stones to bring the creature down. There is no evidence that the meat is eaten, but the pelts are occasionally hung on house supports as ornamental decorations.

The raccoon (*vavóïkai*),[51] which appears in the Tepehuan country wherever there are perennial streams, is disliked because of the damage it inflicts upon corn fields. Indians state that the raccoon damages not only the young corn plants but also the mature plants; the animals are known to stand up on their hind legs in order to reach the ears of corn. Killed with dogs, a rifle, a bow and arrow, or the rock trap, the animal is skinned, drawn, and roasted; or the carcass is prepared for eating the same way as that of the wild pig (see below). Raccoon skins are used as sleeping mats and as pads for saddles.

The *cholugo* or coati,[52] known as *tukávoli*, is rather common along the borders of the pine and oak country and plentiful at lower elevations in the southwest and west. All of the Indians note that the coati inflicts much damage in maturing corn fields, especially during the early evening when the animal appears with its young. Adult animals are brought down with rifles, and the young are often killed by dogs. Only the young coati is eaten after having been skinned, drawn, and roasted on a spit.

Kašío, the common gray fox (*zorra gris*)[53] of southern Chihuahua, is known to prey upon chickens and to eat fresh corn on stalks that have been blown over by the wind. It is brought down with a rifle, a bow and arrow, or by means of the large rock trap. A large fruit crate also may be used to trap the gray fox, and it is weighted down with stones so that the animal cannot escape when the trap is sprung. Both traps are invariably baited with a small chicken. Fox skins are valued because of their usefulness in preparing quivers and in manufacturing sandals.

The Tepehuan who live in the canyons are well acquainted with the habits of the coyote (*bánai*),[54] a hated predator since it preys upon chickens and eats young corn stalks. Coyotes (*baábanai*) are killed with rifles, bows and arrows, or by poisoning; or they are trapped in a pit about the size and shape of a grave (see accompanying diagram) constructed as follows: a log or sapling (A) is

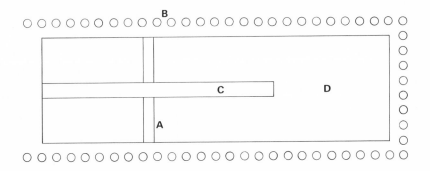

placed across the pit at a point about one-third of the length of the pit; the pit is surrounded on three sides by upright saplings planted in the ground (B); a plank (C) is placed so that it extends from the edge of the pit to a point far beyond the cross-piece (A); and a live chicken is tied to the ground at the end of the trap (at D). When the coyote attempts to reach the chicken by moving along the plank, it topples, and he falls into the pit. Coyote meat is apparently not eaten, but the skins are often used as sleeping mats or made into saddle bags.

The wolf (*lobo*),[55] known among the Tepehuan as *sǘi*, is much hated because of the damage it inflicts upon goats; *el lobo* is found everywhere in the Tepehuan country except in pine-clad terrain. This animal is killed with a rifle, trapped in a pit constructed the same as that used for coyotes but with a young

kid as bait, or poisoned with a commercial substance (obtainable from mestizos) that is applied to a dead kid.

A peccary (*jabalí*), known among the southern Chihuahua Tepehuan as
taíšoli,[56] appears commonly in western and southwestern canyons at lower elevations; it occasionally roams into the pine and oak country to feed on acorns.
The Indians state that a band of them can cause much damage to an unguarded
corn field. The stalks are toppled by these wild pigs to reach the ears of corn.
Peccaries are killed with rifles, bows and arrows, or with a very sharp wooden
lance when one of them is cornered in a cave small enough to prevent the animal from maneuvering. Older Tepehuan state that, not long ago, peccaries were
smothered with smoke from burning pine branches if cornered in a cave and
that sometimes they were driven over cliffs. The skins are apparently held in
little regard, but the meat is much esteemed. The carcass is cleaned, impaled on
a stake planted in a shallow pit, and surrounded by stones upon which a fire is
maintained for several hours or longer depending upon the size of the
peccary.[57]

The Tepehuan who live near Santa Rosa state that a black bear (*voji*)[58]
occasionally wanders into the canyons from the uplands and wreaks much
havoc in the corn fields. Upland Indians refer to depredations by bears in the
fields, but no Indian could cite a recent incident in which a bear had actually
been seen. Dogs are used to locate bears but are of no value in killing the creatures. When a bear appears in the canyon country, the Indians seek the assistance of mestizos who possess guns. The meat is cut up into large pieces and
pit-roasted the same as peccary meat; the skins are highly prized as sleeping
mats, just as they were in the not-too-remote past according to older Indians.

The white-tailed deer (*suímali*)[59] is apparently the only species of deer
hunted by the Tepehuan.[60] *Súsuimali* are sought as a food source and also because their hides are used in the manufacture of bags and sleeping mats and
because the animals inflict damage upon the corn fields. Deer are hunted by
individuals and by groups, and there is a tendency for the hunter or hunters to
stay within certain boundaries. When groups of men are planning a deer hunt,
the best hunter is sent out to find signs of the animals.

Apparently, no ceremonies are held today before or after deer hunts, but
according to older Tepehuan, dances were once held both before and after such
hunts. The older upland Indians speak of an *espíritu del monte* (*kúkuduli*), an
old man who appears in the fog and who is the spirit of the deer. Long ago, a
hunter who wished to kill a deer was expected to go out into the mists and ask
this spirit for permission to hunt. If the spirit should forbid the hunt and if the
hunter refused to comply, then a wrestling match between the man and the
kúkuduli determined the issue. Winning of the match by the hunter automati-

cally guaranteed success in his hunt. (This tradition was also recorded by Lumholtz in the 1890's. See below.) Within the memory of living Tepehuan, offerings of *tesgüino* were put out in the fog for this spirit of the mountains. Mason commented that the Tepehuan believed deer hunts were unsuccessful when *kúkuduli* was riding his deer; therefore a small olla of *tesgüino* must be put out for him. Mason also wrote that "women should not eat meat from the back of the deer; if they do, they will be very ill for many days with aching backs."[61]

The Tepehuan hunt for deer near stands of *Viguiera montana*, a browse plant known to be favored by deer. The Indians who live near Llano Grande and Lagotera look for deer where stands of a *yerba del venado* (*Zexmenia* sp.) are known to be common.

Deer are brought down with bows and arrows and rifles as well as by techniques that are undoubtedly rather ancient among the Tepehuan. A hunter frequently stands near a trail or a water hole or close to converging fences erected along trails and waits for the deer to appear. The animals are sometimes chased over cliffs; and in the rather smooth terrain of some portions of the uplands, deer are run down by men and dogs. Sharp-pointed saplings are often planted in the ground along deer trails, particularly at a point where the animals must jump some obstruction such as a boulder. The Indians note that when fields are surrounded by brush fences, the deer tend to jump the fences always at the same point to get into the fields. Therefore, stakes are put in a field, beyond the fence, so that a deer will be impaled when it jumps the fence. Santa Rosa Tepehuan report that a snare is used to capture a deer. It is constructed in a simple fashion: a hole is dug in a well-known deer trail, and a noose is made at the end of a long ixtle-fiber cord and coiled within the hole; the cord is then attached to a sapling which has been bent down and anchored by another, but much shorter, cord to a stick in the center of the hole; the hole is then filled with leaves. As the deer steps into the hole, the shorter cord is released, and the sapling springs back, drawing the noose tightly about the deer's legs.

Canyon Indians report two traps for deer that involve building corrals in August when bean plants are available as bait. For one of the traps, a small corral is built in an area known to attract deer; inside the enclosure and about three feet from the entryway, a pointed stake is anchored at an angle in the ground, the sharpened end pointing toward the entrance. Bean plants are placed in the corral each day until the deer has become accustomed to finding them there. Then, one day, as the deer is just within the entryway, a waiting observer makes a noise so that the deer leaps and is impaled on the stake. For the other trap, a larger corral is built of *encino* saplings, their branches entwined. Many *mecates de palma* are then entwined loosely about the sapling walls of this corral. Deer are enticed through a small opening by a bait of fresh bean plants that is replaced daily for some five or six days. A hidden observer may "frighten" the deer so that it tries to leap the wall and is entangled in the *mecates de palma*.

According to the canyon Tepehuan, deer were hunted with a decoy not long ago; the hunter wore a deer skin, the head of the deer secured to the hunter's head and the skin wrapped around the hunter's body. During the rutting season, a hunter may imitate the cry of a fawn to attract a male deer. Some Indians wear a red handkerchief about their necks when hunting deer and claim that the sight of the red cloth causes the deer to "freeze," thereby presenting the hunter with an easy target. If a deer is not brought down when shot with an arrow, it is chased until it falls from exhaustion; it is then dispatched with a knife.

Deer meat is roasted on a spit (*gaíkaroi*); or it is cut into slices, salted, and then suspended from the rafters of a dwelling until desired as food. Blood (*ïrai* or *uradï*) from the deer is mixed with leaves of a plant called *uvákoči* (*Salvia* sp.) and boiled until it thickens. This is a favorite dish. The vertebrae (*upidï ódï*) are crushed, boiled, and eaten. Bone marrow (*ovagadï*) is much esteemed as a foodstuff. There are apparently some regulations concerning the disposition of certain portions of the deer's body. The spine is always given to the one who killed the deer, and the shin bone is presented to a man over forty years of age. With certain exceptions, the remainder of the animal can be eaten by anyone. A woman over forty years of age may eat any portion of the deer, but women under forty are forbidden to eat the marrow. Apparently, the present-day Tepehuan make no use of the *tripa* from deer as food, but older Indians state that, in their youth, the guts were cleaned and boiled. Deer sinew serves today as a material for manufacturing bow strings and strings for violins. Deer gut is also sometimes used for the latter.

Archeological and historical records suggest a long history of certain animals being an important source of food among the northern Tepehuan. Evidence in the Río Zape site of northern Durango indicates that deer, coyotes, jackrabbits, squirrels, mice, rats, and other small animals were hunted in pre-Columbian times.[62] The historical significance of hunting and the importance of certain weapons among the Tepehuan are found in the seventeenth-century account of Pérez de Ribas, who noted that hunting was a means of livelihood among the Indians.[63] The Tepehuan bow was made of a long branch tied up at both ends to form an arc. It was described as being very light (*ligero*) in weight, and according to Pérez de Ribas, the Tepehuan rarely went about without bows and arrows.[64] It is probable that the Tepehuan were accustomed to using fire-arrows in battle, for he also refers to the use of arrows and fire in an Indian attack on the Spaniards in the early seventeenth century: "comenzaron luego la batalla con bárbara algazara y baldones y con tal ímpetu de flechas, piedras y fuego que pegaron a la casa, rompiéndola por varios portillos y por lo alto de la aztoea y arrojando por ellos adentro fuegos encendidos con chile, que en España llaman pimientos. . . ."[65] Antiquity of the bow and arrow among the northern Tepehuan is indicated by stone arrowheads and fire-hardened arrow foreshafts found in the Río Zape site by Brooks and his associates.[66] There are repeated references to the use of a club (*macana*), pike (*chuzo de brasil*), *lanza*, and an axe (a stone axe?) in Pérez de Ribas' account of battles between Indians and Spaniards.[67] Rinaldini records a wooden lance (*usci cugguer*) that was used by the eighteenth-century Tepehuan.[68] Pre-Columbian utilization of the lance or spear among the northern Tepehuan is demonstrated by the recovery of a seven-inch-long obsidian blade and a six-inch-long chert spear or lance head from the Río Zape site.[69] The antiquity of the sling (*honda*) cannot be determined with certainty, but this weapon was used during the eighteenth century. According to Rinaldini, the eighteenth-century term for the sling was *bagguivinajare*.[70] Another eighteenth-century account[71] indicates that the weapons referred to by Pérez de Ribas in the seventeenth century were still commonly used.

Evidence concerning superstitions relative to some of the animals in the Tepehuan country is found in Lumholtz' account of the Indians in the 1890's. *Cúcuduri* (properly, *kúkuduli*), the name for the master of the deer, was a small, thickset man who rode a deer over the mountain tops in foggy weather. If there was a great amount of fog and rain, a Tepehuan went into the forest to engage in a wrestling match with *Cúcuduri*, and although *Cúcuduri* was very strong, the Indian often won the bout. If the Indian did win, it meant he would find a deer nearby and shoot it. Lumholtz commented that unmarried women were not permitted to eat meat from the spinal column of the deer since women who ate such meat developed spinal curvature. The Tepehuan also believed that if a man stepped "over a man, the latter will not be able to kill another deer in his life." However, women could be passed in this fashion without such a result. The Indians informed Lumholtz that one kind of a squirrel changed into a bat, another kind into a parrot, and the ground squirrel sometimes became a snake.[72] Additional evidence of ancient superstitions regarding animal life among the Tepehuan is found in a remark made by Pérez de Ribas in the seventeenth century: the Indians used bats, mice, lizards, and other animals in ceremonies designed to bring chaos to great or small nations.[73]

Relative antiquity for deer disguises among the Tepehuan is certain. Pérez de Ribas noted that, at fiestas, the Indians adorned themselves with greenery and foliage and, with horns of deer in their hands appeared as wild beasts of the mountains.[74]

THE FISH RESOURCE

The fish resource of southern Chihuahua does not supply a significant portion of Tepehuan foodstuffs, but it does offer variety in the diet. And fish must be viewed as a rather important source of protein. Fishing is practiced throughout the year, particularly by the canyon Tepehuan who live near permanently flowing streams. Upland Indians apparently are not as much concerned with fishing as lowland Indians are.

Scant information is available regarding the species of fish (*vatopa*) common to streams of southern Chihuahua, but those reported by Lumholtz and by Almada undoubtedly are to be found also in the streams south of the Río Verde. In Lumholtz' time, three species of overgrown minnows were common to western Chihuahua: *Cyprinodon eximius*, a squaw-fish (*Ptychocheilus lucius*), and a dace (*Leuciscus niger*). Lumholtz also recorded a mountain sucker (*Pantosteus plebeius*) and a bullhead catfish (*Ameiurus dugèsi*).[75] According to Almada, an eel (*Anguilla rostrata*), a skatelike fish (*Mugil cephalus*), a sardine-like fish (*Clupea sardina*), a carp (*Cyprinus carpio*), a blue-nose fish (*Opaledus olivaris*), a black bass (*Micropterus salmoides*), and a bagre (*Ictalurus dugèsi*) appear in Chihuahua streams.[76] The fish remains that have been recovered from the Río Zape site in northern Durango belong to at least three families of fishes: catfishes (Ictaluridae), suckers (Catostomidae), and minnows (Cyprinidae).[77]

The Tepehuan of southern Chihuahua speak of fishing for *sardinas*, *matalotes*, and *bagres*. Preferred catches are *mukui* (*puntiagudo*) *úšui* (*boca de animal*), a *sardina* found in streams near Santa Rosa; *doakámuli* (*pozole*) *úšui* (*boca de animal*), a *matalote* common to streams near Santa Rosa and in the Arroyo de Los Tarahumares; and *ááši*, or *ááči*, which refers to any of several catfish species common to streams of southwestern Chihuahua.

Important fishing techniques include the use of hook and line, dynamite caps, and stupefying agents. Fish stupefaction is induced by putting toxic-bearing plants into stone corrals constructed in the center or along the edges of fish-bearing streams or into slowly moving water behind a crude, stone and earthen dam in shallow streams. Short arrows are sometimes used to kill fish in clear water, and a basket is used to gather fish that have become trapped between converging stone walls by a weir across the narrow part of the walls. The weir is constructed from the branches of a *túbuli* (*Salix Gooddingii*) or a *jarilla del río*.

Canyon Tepehuan make a fishhook (*babaidakari*) by bending a piece of wire into the desired shape; the hook is baited with a worm and attached to a line that is made by rolling ixtle fibers on the thigh (*káhi*). The Indians deny making use of a fishing pole. Instead, the fisherman (*kokodakari*) prefers to sit on the bank, holding the line in such a fashion that the baited hook will drift downstream a bit rather than to the bottom of the stream. Some canyon Indians state that a thorn (*hoí*) is sometimes used as a fishhook.

The Indians near La Ciénega utilize seeds and leaves of the *tolache* (*Datura meteloides*) in hook-and-line fishing. The crushed seeds and leaves are rubbed onto the lower portion of the ixtle-fiber line to which a large wire hook is attached. The line is then dropped into a pool where fish are known to be. When fish have gathered near the line, the fisherman jerks it up and a fish is garnered. It is claimed that, formerly, a bone fishhook was similarly used.

Dynamite caps are difficult to obtain, but when they are available, the Indians gather to clean and roast the abundant catch; the caps are used only in streams where there are many fish.

The most prevalent method of fishing is that of stupefaction effected by adding toxic-bearing substances to relatively quiet water. The stupefaction of fish is never practiced when streams are in high water. During the dry season, the southwestern canyon streams are characterized by numerous pools in which fish are entrapped. Fish can also be found in many of the shallow streams that flow throughout the year. It is in these pools and shallow streams that fish stupefaction becomes feasible. Semicircular stone corrals are built near rocks located in pools of water, or similar corrals may be constructed near large rocks that project into the pools. Toxic-bearing plant materials are either dumped into the stone corrals or placed in a basket and doused in the corral several times; within a short time, the fish can be removed from the trap by hand or with a basket. To take fish from a stream, piles of crushed toxic-bearing plant materials are thrown into the slowly moving water behind crudely constructed stone and earthen dams.

The toxic plant material used to stupefy or to kill fish is obtained from species belonging to seven different families and from several unidentified species. All of these are flowering plants and are found within the Tepehuan habitat.

Amaryllidaceae. Three species of agave, known collectively as *bíñivai* or *amole*, appear on rocky slopes almost everywhere in the canyon country; the leaves of these species of cacti are crushed on a rock and thrown into a corral constructed in a fish-bearing stream or wherever fish have been trapped behind a weir of some type. Fish appear on the surface about fifteen minutes after the crushed material is put in the water.[78]

Juglandaceae. The Indians living near Santa Rosa collect leaves of a nogal (*Juglans major*) for use during the early spring as a stupefying agent. Great quantities of the leaves are placed on a smooth rock and beaten for a short time with a wooden mallet. This agent is claimed to be most effective when thrown into dammed areas in creeks.[79]

Papaveraceae. Upland and canyon Tepehuan gather and crush large amounts of the leaves and stems of a poppy (*Argemone ochroleuca* subsp. *ochroleuca*), known as *cardo*, for use as a fish-stupefying agent.[80]

Rosaceae. Four species of Rosaceae are sources of piscicides used by canyon and upland Tepehuan: *Prunus virens*, known as *capulín* or *úvagi*; *P. serotina*, known as *úvagi* or *capulín grande*; *P. capuli*, known as *capulín pequeña* or *túkuši*; and *Licania retifolia*, also known as *capulín* or *túkuši*. The bark and leaves are gathered in great amounts, crushed on a flat rock with a wooden mallet or club, and then dumped into a stone corral or behind a stone and earthen dam.[81]

Leguminosae. *Tephrosia nicaraguensis*, known as *yerba del piojo*, is a favored fish-stupefying agent in use near Santa Rosa. Several plants are crushed and placed in a basket which is sloshed about in the water within a stone corral or behind a crudely constructed stone dam. Both *Tephrosia Thurberi*[82] and a *yerba del pescado* (*Lupinus* sp.) that appears quite commonly along streams in the uplands are similarly used.[83] Another *yerba del pescado* (*Phaseolus salicifolius?*) and a species of *Brongniartia* are also handled the same way.

Euphorbiaceae. Indians living in canyons use the bark of *tescalama* (*Hura crepitans*), known as *bokuripi*, in fish stupefaction. The bark, which is claimed to "sting" when improperly handled, is stripped from the tree and crushed on a stone before being thrown into a stone corral constructed where the water is relatively quiet. This agent is rarely used on fish that are trapped behind weirs or dams, where the flow of water is greater than in a corral.[84]

Compositae. Roots of a *peonía* (*Zexmenia podocephala*), which is known as *gogóši* (*perro*) *viítai* (*excremento*), are collected by canyon Tepehuan for stupefying fish. The roots are crushed and thrown into rock corrals. Upland Tepehuan know this plant but apparently utilize it only as a medicinal plant.

Unidentified Specimens. Canyon Tepehuan collect the whole of a yellow-flowered plant called *yerba del piojo de los puercos* for use in fish stupefaction; the entire plant is crushed and thrown into the circular stone trap. Lowland Tepehuan also report a *yerba del pescado* and a *yerba loca* that serve as piscicides. Upland Tepehuan utilize the crushed roots of a *frijolillo* (*bavísuri*) in fish stupefaction.

Generally, fish are eaten immediately after being caught. Heads are rarely removed, and the fish are roasted on coals after having been split down the middle and cleaned of their *tripa*. Some Tepehuan note that fish are occasionally salted and dried for storage.

As previously mentioned, the fish remains found in the Río Zape site of northern Durango suggest a pre-Columbian utilization of fish by peoples in that area at least as early as 600 A.D.[85] The historical record offers little concerning the use of fish by the Tepehuan. Pérez de Ribas commented in the seventeenth century that there were plenty of fish in a stream that ran through Santiago Papasquiaro but made no mention of whether these fish were sought by the Tepehuan.[86] Lumholtz refers to fishing by the Tepehuan and notes that the Indians made an offering to *Cúcuduri* (properly, *kúkuduli*), the "master of the fish," in order to secure a catch. As a sacrifice, three small fish were thrown into the water; if this were not done, the "master of the fish" would drive the fish away and throw stones at the fishermen. Lumholtz also commented that the Indians believed that catfish turned into otters.[87]

The sole early reference to fish stupefaction for an area inhabited at least in part by the Tepehuan is in a late eighteenth-century document that tells of San Miguel de Las Bocas; the author of this report referred to the use of a plant called *barbasco* in fish poisoning.[88]

FRUITS AND NUTS

Pinaceae. Piñon nuts are important to all Tepehuan, but only the upland Indians emphasize the gathering of this foodstuff; the canyon Tepehuan state that too much effort is required to journey to areas where pine nuts may be gathered in quantity. The important pines that supply nuts include the following: *pipíkami* (*muchas espinas*) *úkui* (*pino*), which is *Pinus ayacahuite*, one of the most common upland pines; *úbišdali* (*P. Engelmanni*), another rather common upland pine; and *P. leiophylla*. Generally, piñon nuts are collected from the ground in the fall, but if desired earlier, the green cones are heated and pounded against a rock to extract the nuts. They are apparently not stored, and before being eaten, they are always roasted.

Liliaceae. Canyon and upland Tepehuan eat the fruits of a *palma de San Pedro* (*Yucca decipiens*) known as *óyi*. This yucca appears in great numbers on middle canyon slopes.

Juglandaceae. Lowland Tepehuan eagerly hunt for the nuts of a nogal (*Juglans major*) that grows near stream courses almost everywhere in the canyon country; the tree also grows in arroyos and washes that trench the borders of the uplands, where children collect the nuts in the fall.

Fagaceae. Ten species of oaks supply acorns, a favorite food among the Tepehuan. These trees appear everywhere in the Tepehuan country but are more common on the great benches of the canyons and in the flattish areas where the uplands break away to the canyon country. Acorns are gathered from the following oaks: *Quercus durifolia*; *káli* (*Q. albocincta*); *túái* (*Q. chihuahuensis*); *popuišoli* (*Q. Endlichiana*); *encino rosillo*, or *áli* (*chiquito*) *úbotai*, which is *Q. hypoleucoides*; *alíága* (*hoja chiquita*) *kútuai* (*encino*), which is *Q. omissa*; *Q. rugosa*, known as *tupúrai* (*hacha*) *úsaraga* (*caba de hacha*); and two kinds of *tupáratui* (*Q. arizonica* and *Q.* sp.). Acorns are eaten without much preparation; they are toasted on a *cajete* or on a comal. However, when *Quercus arizonica* acorns are to be used as an ingredient for tortillas, they are cooked, washed, and then crushed.

Moraceae. Fruits of the ubiquitous *mora*, or *kóji* (*Morus microphylla*), are eaten *crudo* or are mashed and added to gruels.

Loranthaceae. Three parasitic species, known collectively as *bulíkadali*, appear in profusion on oaks in the Tepehuan country. These species are *Struthanthus diversifolius*, *Phoradendron scaberrimum*, and *P.* sp. Their fruits are eaten in the spring.

Lauraceae. Fruits of the *Persea Liebmanni*, which is known everywhere as *cupilla* or *ukavoli*, are eagerly sought by upland Tepehuan.

Rosaceae. Upland and canyon Indians favor the edible berries (*ivókoli*) that are obtained from three widely distributed species of Rosaceae: *zarza mora*, or *ivókoli*[89] (*Rubus* sp.); *mora colorada* (*R.* sp.), known as *vipígi* (*rojas*) *ivókoli* (*mora*); and *fresa*, or *ibíši* (*Fragaria vesca*). An important canyon tree that supplies edible berries is *tejocote*, or *vuamášuli* (*Crataegus* sp. af. *mexicana*). Upland Tepehuan favor the fruits of a *capulín*, or *túkuši* (*Licania retifolia*), a rather common arroyo tree. Three species of *Prunus* are undoubtedly the most widespread source of edible fruits: *P. serotina* is known as *úvagi* or *capulín grande*, *P. virens* is called *capulín* or *úvagi*, and *P. capuli* is designated *túkuši* or *capulín pequeña*.

Rhamnaceae. The fruits of a *cacachila* (*Karwinskia Humboldtiana*), a common tree in canyons near Santa Rosa, serve as a starvation food. Upland Tepehuan collect the fruits of a *duraznillo*, or *tupurúši* (*Rhamnus serrata?*).

Vitaceae. Three species of wild grapes are important as sources of edible fruits: *Vitis arizonica*, known as *uva cimarróna*, *parra silvestre*, or *bakámai* (*troje*) *bišáparagai* (*envolver*); *V. rupestris*, or *bakámai*; and *V. bourgaeana*, known as *uva cimarróna* or *avo* (*liviano*) *úši* (*palo* or *árbol*).

Cactaceae. Apparently only one species of tall cactus, *Pachycereus pecten-aboriginum*, known as *pitahaya* or *aasáñi*, appears in significant numbers in the Tepehuan country and then only in the west at lower elevations.

One such locale is the canyon country near Santa Rosa, where the plants flower in late February and fruit in early June. The fruit has spines that drop off when it ripens. Ripe fruits are plucked from the tall, curving branches of this cactus with a long *caña* pole or a trimmed sapling that has a two-pronged fork at one end made of wire or wood; the fork is anchored to the pole with vegetable-fiber cordage. Immature fruits are also gathered because they serve as hairbrushes when dry. Fruits from several species of *Opuntia* are esteemed as food. Two small cacti plants associated with rocky promontories along streamways, *Echinocereus* sp. var. *triglochidiatus*(?) and *E.* sp. af. *Reichenbachii*(?), both known as *súduli*, supply edible fruits in July.

Myrtaceae. Canyon Tepehuan collect the fruits of the guava tree (*Psidium guajava*), which is apparently restricted in occurrence to warmer canyons.

Ericaceae. Heath species appear in much of the Tepehuan country; they are found as thinly scattered growths in pine stands and as thick growths in cutover pine and oak country, but they are rarely found in canyon country below the middle portions of canyon slopes. The following species appear to be the most widely distributed: *Arbutus glandulosa*, known as *madroño pequeño* or *áli (chiquito) opíndali (madroño)*; *A. arizonica*, known as *madroño grande* or *opíndali*; and *A. xalapensis*, the *madroño del barranca*. *Arctostaphylos pungens*, known either as *yóli* or as *manzanilla*, appears in thin colonies on drier slopes everywhere in western Tepehuan country but is rare in the north and in pine country. The fruits of all of these heath species are much sought by the Indians and are eaten raw or used in the preparation of gruels. The fruits of a *manzana del monte* (*Gaultheria* sp.) are gathered in the uplands. *Vaccinium confertum*, which is known as *áli (chiquito) yóli (manzanilla)* near Llano Grande, supplies a favorite edible fruit.

Sapotaceae. A zapote (*Achras zapota*), known among the Indians as *jobi-yi*, appears occasionally along canyon margins near Santa Rosa; the fruits (*óvidi*) of this tree serve, for the most part, as a starvation food.

Asclepiadaceae. Tepehuan children spend much time seeking the tiny fruits of the *pico de cuervo* (*Asclepias sordida*). Fruits of the *talayote* (*Asclepias strictiflora*) are eaten in September.

Solanaceae. In June, the Tepehuan living near Llano Grande collect the fruits of a *Saracha jaltomata*, which is known as *tomatillo del monte* or *oidígana* (*del monte* or *silvestre*) *popóskuli* (*tomatillo*). In September, upland Tepehuan seek the fruits of a *suímali* (*venado*) *vuji* (*ojo*), a species of *Physalis*. Fruits of the *Physalis viscosa* (*tomatillo*) are claimed to be very sweet. An edible fruit is obtained by upland Indians from a *chichiquelite* (*Solanum nigrum*), presumably an introduction from Europe.[90] The fruits of another *chichiquelite* (*Solanum gracile*) are eaten by canyon Indians; however, they are said to be very bitter. Fruits of a *jaltomate*, or *totúkuli* (*Chamaesaracha* sp.), are collected by upland Indians in October.

Rubiaceae. Two southwestern canyon trees, *Randia echinocarpa* and *R. laevigata*, both of which are known as *papache* or *savóči*, are important sources of edible fruits. Canyon Indians collect the fruits of *Rubus trivialis*.

Caprifoliaceae. Indians living near Llano Grande enjoy the fruits of a *madre selva del monte* (*Lonicera involucrata*), known as *bakambišpára*. *Lonicera pilosa*, another upland plant, supplies what is considered to be one of the best wild fruits gathered by the Tepehuan.

Unidentified Specimens. Canyon Indians eagerly seek the fruits of two species of tuna: *tuna colorada*, which flowers in May and fruits in July, and *nakíši*, which flowers in June and fruits in late July. Another canyon nopal that supplies an esteemed fruit is *kasti návoi*. Canyon Indians collect the green fruits of *chapote* (an unidentified herb) and bury them in sand for ripening.

The long-time importance of collected fruits among the Tepehuan is attested to by archeological material and by statements made during the colonial period. In the seventeenth century, Pérez de Ribas remarked that when the Indians lacked seeds (corn), they ate wild fruits.[91] The remains of the fruit and leaves of an *Opuntia*, black walnuts, juniper berries, piñon nuts, and acorns have been recovered from the Río Zape cave excavated by Brooks and his associates.[92] Some of these remnants were associated with burials, and it is assumed that the items were left as food for the dead. What is considered to be food for the dead can also be interpreted as food for the living.

COLLECTED HERBAGE

Collected greens (*ívagi*) serve as an important element in the Tepehuan diet during the rainy season and, to a lesser extent, at other times. Canyon *quelites* are more or less restricted to arroyos and disturbed ground, but greens are widely distributed in the uplands, in moist spots in the pine-clad country, in plowed fields, along the borders of fields, along arroyos, and in gardens.

Moraceae. Leaves of the widespread *mora*, or *kóji* (*Morus microphylla*), are gathered in both canyons and uplands for use as a valuable *quelite*; the leaves are boiled for a short time and lightly salted before being eaten.

Polygonaceae. Perhaps the most important *quelite* utilized by canyon Tepehuan is a *lengua de vaca*, or *čiwáwa* (*Rumex altissimus*), which appears in profusion along borders of plowed fields, particularly along rock fences. Before serving as a food item, the leaves are boiled and salted, or they are drained and fried after being boiled. Another species, *Rumex crispus*, also known as *čiwáwa* or *lengua de vaca*, is similarly used, as is the introduced *R. pulcher*,[93] or *quelite de Chihuahua*. Leaves of an *Eriogonum* species are boiled, drained, and lightly salted before serving as a favorite *quelite*.

Chenopodiaceae. *Chenopodium album* and a variety of *C. ambrosioides* appear in both uplands and canyons. These species are known as *patúsai* or *ipasote*. The leaves are washed, boiled, and drained before being eaten. Upland Tepehuan particularly like the leaves of *Chenopodium Berlandieri* and *C. Berlandieri* var. *sinuatum*(?) as *quelites*. The Tepehuan who live near the Mesa de Milpillas know *Chenopodium incanum*(?) as *koomági* (*gris*) *ívagi* (*quelite*) and they prepare the leaves as a green potherb by washing, boiling, and draining them.

Amaranthaceae. One of the favored Amaranthaceae utilized as a *quelite* is a cultigen, *Amaranthus leucocarpus*, known among the Indians as *giági* and among the mestizos as *okiti* or *guatle*. It is cultivated by canyon Indians in fields and by upland Indians in former corrals (see Chapter 2), but it also appears as an escape in stands near cultivated fields in canyons. The leaves are boiled, drained, and lightly salted before being eaten. *Amaranthus Palmeri*(?) appears in well-watered arroyos in the uplands, where it is known as *quelite de las aguas*. Yet another upland amaranth is *Amaranthus Powellii*, known as *momomai* or *quelite de las aguas*. Leaves from these two amaranths are prepared as a foodstuff the same as *giági*.

Phytolaccaceae. Canyon and upland Tepehuan collect the leaves of a tiny herb called *čivúkali* (*Phytolacca icosandra*)[94] for use as a potherb; they are boiled and drained before being salted.

Portulacaceae. A purslane, *Portulaca oleracea*, presumably an introduction from Europe,[95] grows in profusion on moist canyon slopes near Santa Rosa. The Tepehuan know it as *vošïkai* (*ratón*) *naáka* (*oreja*), and the mestizos know it as *verdolaga*; the entire plant is boiled before being lightly salted.

Cruciferae. A *berro* (*Nasturtium officinale*), another introduction from Europe,[96] appears in brooks and along streamways in the uplands, where it is known as *mura* (*mula*) *súúsaka* (*herradura*) by the Indians; the leaves are eaten raw, or they are boiled, drained, and fried. An introduced *mostaza* (*Brassica campestris*)[97] is similarly prepared as a *quelite*. Upland Tepehuan enjoy the leaves of *Descurainia pinnata*, known as *ívagi* or *suavoli*, when they are boiled, drained, and fried. Leaves of the *tuámuši* (*Roripa islandica*) serve as an important *quelite*.

Oxalidaceae. The piquant leaves of a wood sorrel (*Oxalis albicans*), known as *socoyole* or *áli* (*chiquito*) *ïko* (*agrio*), are boiled, drained, and salted. *Oxalis stricta* (*limoncillo*) grows in profusion along the borders of fields; its leaves are prepared as a potherb, as are those from *O. albicans*.

Onagraceae. Leaves of a *bitúši* (*Oenothera rosea*), an *amapola* of southern Chihuahua, are collected by upland and canyon Indians for use as an esteemed *quelite* eaten with beans or meat; the leaves of this plant are boiled and drained before being lightly salted.

Umbelliferae. Leaves of the *alisárapai* (*Tauschia nudicaulis*) are collected by Santa Rosa Tepehuan during the rainy season; they are boiled, drained, and fried on a comal. Leaves of the *sarápai* (*Osmorhiza radicans*) are similarly prepared. The introduced *cilantro* (*Coriandrum sativum*),[98] which is cultivated in tiny gardens maintained by upland Indians, serves not only as a source of leaves used as a condiment but also as a potherb that is boiled and lightly salted.

Oleaceae. Leaves of a *Fraxinus velutina*, the *pítai* of the Tepehuan, are boiled, drained, and lightly salted before serving as a *quelite*.

Hydrophyllaceae. Indians living near Llano Grande seek the leaves of a *Phacelia congesta*(?) for use as a potherb. Leaves of this *porra* are boiled and lightly salted, as are the leaves of a *pico de cuervo* (*Phacelia teucriifolia*).

Solanaceae. *Solanum nigrum* is presumably an introduction from Europe[99] and grows in profusion along the borders of plowed fields. Leaves of this *chichiquelite* are washed, boiled, and drained before being salted.

Scrophulariaceae. *Mimulus guttatus*, known among the Indians as *suudági* (*agua*) *mamaradï* (*crece en el agua*), appears in brooks and very moist meadows. Its leaves are cooked and drained to serve as a foodstuff.

Plantaginaceae. A *lantén* (*Plantago* sp.), known among the Tepehuan as *šiñakali*, is much favored as a source of leaves eaten as a *quelite* at locales west of Chinatú.

Compositae. *Cirsium mexicanum* appears in gravel along streamways throughout the Tepehuan country; the leaves of this *šiñáka* are singed to remove the thorns and then boiled and lightly salted. A sow thistle (*Sonchus oleraceus*), introduced from Europe,[100] is widely distributed around the borders of upland meadows; leaves of this *šiñaipuli* are prepared as a foodstuff the same as other *quelites*.

Unidentified Specimens. Upland Tepehuan make much use of a *kuči* and an *okata* (*abajo del pino*) *ívagi* (*quelite*) as sources of leaves; they are boiled, drained, and fried.

ROOTS

The roots (*táka*) of wild plants play a minor role in the basic diet of the Tepehuan. It is clear that canyon Indians utilize this source of food more than upland people do; the upland Indians are familiar with and occasionally eat the roots to be found in the canyons, but on the whole, they make no great effort to journey to the canyons to secure them.

Liliaceae. Two Liliaceae species supply roots that are gathered by canyon Tepehuan, particularly in times of food shortages: *Dasylirion Wheeleri* and *Yucca decipiens*. The former is known as *sotol* or *palma* and by its Indian name, *šúšida kúrui*; the latter is known as *óyi* or *palma de San Pedro*. A considerable number of roots are collected and removed to a pit, known as *maíkaro* or *tuba-majaroi*, that is about three feet in depth, several feet in diameter, and lined with wood and stones. The wood is fired, and when it is almost burned away, the roots are arranged on the hot stones. A layer of *madroño* wood (*Arbutus arizonica*, *A. glandulosa*, and *A. xalapensis*) is placed on the roots and covered with loose earth. A fire is built and maintained on the earth covering for several days, and then the dirt and branches are removed. The cooked roots are either eaten immediately, or they are sliced and dried for storage. When dried portions of the roots are prepared as a foodstuff, they are boiled for several hours; but whether the roots are eaten fresh or dried, only the non-fibrous portion of the cooked root is eaten. Canyon Indians note that neither the roots nor the crowns of these two Liliaceae species are as desirable as the roots of Amaryllidaceae species.

Amaryllidaceae. Four *Agave* species supply roots much sought by canyon Tepehuan: *ájurai*, known among the mestizos as *čawé*;[101] *mái*, known among the mestizos as *maguey* or *mescal*; *jápari*, or *lecheguilla*; and *guvúkai*, or *mescalillo*. The roots and crowns of these species are pit-baked in the same fashion as Liliaceae roots. The cooked crowns contain much indigestible matter; therefore they are chewed until the digestible portion is separated from the fibrous material, which is rejected. Occasionally, cooked roots of Amaryllidaceae or Liliaceae are pounded on a metate with a wooden mallet until the fibrous material is separated from the edible part. This part is eaten immediately, or it is shaped into small cakes that are dried and stored; the cakes are soaked before being eaten. *Nardo* (*Bravoa* sp.) roots, collected in damp meadows near Baborigame and Nabogame, are eaten raw.

Bombacaceae. Specimens of *javómali*, or the pochote tree (*Ceiba acuminata*), occasionally appear along canyon margins near Santa Rosa and in the Short-tree Forest country on middle canyon slopes. The large, fleshy roots of this tree are eaten raw in the green stage; more mature roots are either peeled, crushed, and cooked about thirty minutes or baked whole in ashes or coals.

Convolvulaceae. Roots of a climbing vine (*Exogonium bracteatum*) that grows in southwestern canyons are roasted over coals.

Solanaceae. Roots of the *Solanum cardiophyllum*, a plant apparently restricted to the uplands, are collected and boiled. Another species of *Solanum*, known as *jícama* or *čičávoli*, supplies a root that is eaten raw. Roots of a *papa del monte* (*Solanum* sp.) are collected in August and September by upland Indians, who bake them in ashes.

Valerianaceae. A species of *Valeriana* supplies a root much esteemed when baked in ashes.

Unidentified Specimen. The Tepehuan who live in the canyons near Llano Grande diligently seek the roots of a *békoči* (*contra yerba*); they are washed and eaten raw.

The antiquity of utilization of the agave, yucca, and opuntia as food items is attested to by the chewed, fibrous remains of these plants recovered from the Río Zape cave site by Brooks and his associates.[102]

MISCELLANEOUS COLLECTED FOODS

The Tepehuan who live west of Chinatú collect the stalks of an arroyo plant called *šiñaka* (*Cirsium mexicanum*) for use as a foodstuff; the stalks are scraped with a sharp stone or knife before being eaten raw. Flower stalks of the following *Agave* species are roasted on coals: *mái, jápari, guvúkai,* and *ájurai.* The flower stalk of a yucca called *óyi* (*Yucca decipiens*) is similarly prepared as a foodstuff. The pads of two cacti species common to rocky terrain along arroyos, *súduli,* or *pitahaya* (*Echinocereus* sp. var. *triglochidiatus*?); and *ibávoli,* or *biznaga* (*Ferocactus* sp.), are de-spined, sliced, and boiled as a foodstuff during the spring.

Many classes of mushrooms (*yóra*) appear in the high country south of the Río Verde; some of them are known to be exceedingly poisonous, particularly the *hongo de la víbora* and the *hongo del sapo.* Of the edible mushrooms, *hongo de la tierra* (a reddish mushroom), *hongo del pino* (a white one), and *hongo del encino* (another white one) are the best known.

The antiquity of mushrooms utilized as a foodstuff is suggested by their numerous fragments recovered from the Río Zape cave site in northern Durango.[103]

The Indians living near Llano Grande value the toasted seeds of a *samuidá-karoi* (*Crotalaria incana*). They are sometimes added to pinole, as are the cooked flowers of *Lupinus Havardii*, a widely distributed plant near Llano Grande. Children eat the flowers of an arroyo plant called *tamúši.* Another food item in the Tepehuan diet is the pithy interior of a *bolita* that appears on *Quercus crassifolia* in the spring.

INSECTS AND REPTILES

Several types of insects supply honey (*vapaigari*) for the Tepehuan. The *mosco de enjambre*, or *sáívoli*, is said to be a medium-sized bee, common to canyons and uplands, that builds a hive (*papaiga*) in a cave or a tree trunk. When the hive is located in a tree, the tree is cut down, and the bees are smoked out. The hive in a cave is knocked to the floor after the bees have been smoked out. The honey, which is gathered in May, is eaten *puro* or with pinole. A *sáívoli* is described as being essentially *prieto* (blackish) in aspect but marked, however, by a bit of yellow.

The *mosco de enjambre chiquito*, or *alïdo*, is a somewhat smaller bee and is the introduced European honey bee (*Apis mellifera*).[104] These yellow bees build their small hives in oak or pine trees in the *monte*, and the honey is said to be an esteemed additive to pinole.

The *dávurai*, or *dáburi*, is a yellow insect that builds an underground nest in the *monte*. The nest is opened with a stick, and smoke is used to drive away the larger insects. Smaller ones are removed from the hive and toasted on coals. The *dávurai* is sought throughout the year.

The *jicotera*, or *úragai*, is a bumble bee (*Bombus formosus*) that builds an elongated underground hive with round cells. Hives are dug up from May until July. Older bees are driven away with smoke, and the "honey," which tastes not unlike stale walnut meats, is eaten with pinole or as a sweet.

The *mïmiïvai* is a wasp (*Polybia diguetana*) that builds its nest in a cave or in a tree; the nest, which may range in size from a large softball to that of a large watermelon, is sometimes removed to a tree located near an Indian habitation and anchored in it with pliable branches. The "honey" in the nest is taken out in October.

Antiquity of the use of honey by the Tepehuan, whether that produced by escaped domestic bees (undoubtedly introduced by the Spanish settlers who reached northwestern Mexico in the late sixteenth and early seventeenth centuries) or by bumble bees or wasps, cannot be determined with certainty. Rinaldini referred to *avejas de la miel chica* (*sáívoli dúdude*), *avejas de la colmena grande* (*gugur sáívoli dúdude*), *avejas de panales* (*mumuve dúdude*), *avejones de baja de la tierra* (*dabure*), and *avejones de otra fuerte* (*juraga*) in the eighteenth century.[105] Three of these references are clearly related to present-day Tepehuan terms for insects that produce a sweet substance utilized as a foodstuff. *Dabure* is without doubt *dávurai*, *juraga* is the *úragai* (*Bombus formosus*), and *mumuve dúdude* is the *mïmiïvai* (*Polybia diguetana*). Rinaldini's clear references to the bumble bee and the wasp suggest that the use of "honey" from the nests of these insects represents an aboriginal custom, perhaps of great antiquity.

Upland and canyon Tepehuan esteem a grub (*kakéduñi*) taken from a cocoon that is found on *Arbutus arizonica*, *A. glandulosa*, and *A. xalapensis*; this grub is added to the corn dish *yoríki*.

Snakes (*kói*) play no significant role in the lives of the Tepehuan. However, at least nine types of snakes are known to the Indians, and two of these are eaten. Types of snakes include the following: a deadly *coralillo*, known as *túki-ši*; a harmless coral snake; the *pichiquate*, known as *bidágai*; a small rattlesnake, known as *áli* (*chiquito*) *ádagai* (*cascabel*); a larger rattlesnake, known simply as *ádagai*; the *víbora negra*, called *bakúšuli*; the *mamarai*, known either as *víbora sorda* or as *víbora caseta*; the *tudokoi*, or *víbora chicatera*; and a very poisonous "gray" snake, called *maimokami*.

Rattlesnake meat is eaten. The rattles (*šigíkarodï*) and the head of the snake are cut off, and the skin is removed; the meat is cooked for about an hour in an olla.

The data concerning hunting, gathering, and fishing presented herein are not in agreement with Mason's statement that "wild fowl is of slight importance at present . . . there are many deer in the mountains, but they are seldom hunted today. Traps are made for coyotes and foxes but none for deer."[106] It is true that deer are seldom hunted near Baborigame, that portion of the Tepehuan habitat best-known to Mason. The numerous mestizos at Baborigame with rifles have practically eliminated deer in their area. However, deer are much hunted near Llano Grande, Santa Rosalia, and Santa Rosa; and, as previously indicated, several types of traps are constructed for deer. Moreover, it is apparent that fish are certainly caught by means other than "by hand nets of cloth."[107]

On the whole, it is rather clear that wild food is of much importance. Were it not available, the Indians would suffer more than they do because of lack of seeds for planting and because of crop failure.

CHAPTER 5 NOTES

1– Undoubtedly *Meleagris gallopavo* described by Leopold [(1959), 268-75].

2– Probably *Ortalis vetula* described by Blake [(1953), 102].

3– Undoubtedly *Ceryle alcyon caurina*, which is known to range Baja California and western Mexico south to Sinaloa and Durango (Ibid., 275).

4– Probably *Numenius phaeopus hudsonicus* (Ibid., 138-39).

5– Probably *Ardea herodias* (Ibid., 27).

6– Without doubt, *vakági* is *Gavia immer elasson* (Ibid., 4).

7– Probably *Corvus ossifragus imparatus* (Ibid., 376).

8– Undoubtedly one of the races of *Buteo jamaicensis* (Ibid., 79).

9– This is undoubtedly the sparrow-hawk, *Falco sparverius* (Ibid., 99-100). Indians of the uplands refer to this hawk as *šišikamuli*, whereas the canyon Indians call the bird *čičikamuli*.

10– Probably one of the races of *Otus asio* (Ibid., 211-12).

11– Undoubtedly *Tyto alba pratincola* (Ibid., 208).

12– The Tepehuan offer no rational explanation for this general exception in preparing owls as food.

13– This *kokoájo* is undoubtedly one of the races of *Bubo virginianus* described by Blake [(1953), 215].

14– Probably the acorn woodpecker *Melanerpes formicivorus* (Ibid., 294).

15– Probably *Colaptes cafer* (Ibid., 288-89).

16– *Čikúrurui* is, without doubt, one of the races of *Sphyrapicus varius* (Ibid., 298-99).

17– Probably the *Sturnella magna* (Ibid., 520).

18– No doubt the *Zenaida asiatica* described by Leopold [(1959), 183-84].

19– Undoubtedly *Columba fasciata* (Ibid., 180-81).

20– Probably *Colinus virginianus* described by Leopold [(1959), 245-50] and Blake [(1953), 112-13].

21– Probably the upland plover (*Bartramia longicauda*) described by Blake [(1953), 137].

22– Without doubt the *Piaya cayana* (Ibid., 204-205).

23– Undoubtedly *Campephilus imperialis* (Ibid., 304).

24– Perhaps *Cathartes aura* (Ibid., 63-64).

25– Probably the barn swallow *Hirundo rustica erythrogaster* (Ibid., 371).

26– Undoubtedly one of the races of *Dendrocopos villosus* (Ibid., 300).

27– I could obtain no rational explanation of why certain other woodpeckers were safe to eat while this one was not.

28– Undoubtedly *Coragyps atratus* described by Blake [(1953), 62].

29– Probably *Speotyto cunicularia* (Ibid., 217-18).

30– 1645: Pérez de Ribas (1944), III, 213.

31– Lumholtz (1902), I, 433, 436.

32– Mason (1952), 48.

33– 1645: Pérez de Ribas (1944), III, 137.

34– 1777: Relación de Indé.

35– 1777: Relación de Nabogame.

36– 1645: Pérez de Ribas (1944), III, 155, 190.

37– *Vájomi* here refers to several grains of corn, but it also may refer to the *mazorca de maíz*.

38– Mason (1952), 45.

39— 1743: Rinaldini (1743), 67.

40— Field work among the Tepehuan during the summers of 1960 and 1965 indicated that animosity of some proportion does exist between mestizos and Indians but hardly to the point of armed conflict. The carrying of pistols by mestizos, in spite of a depistolization program fostered by the central and state governments, appears to be largely a matter of prestige.

41— Mason [(1952), 43] states that bows and arrows survive only as symbols and toys. This may be so for the country immediately adjacent to Baborigame, but it is not accurate for more remote areas.

42— Interestingly enough, the Tepehuan apparently do not realize that armadillos construct escape burrows.

43— According to Leopold [(1959), 339-43], there is only one North American species of armadillo in Mexico, the nine-banded armadillo (*Dasypus novemcinctus*). However, the Indians of southern Chihuahua insist that *alívuli* refers to both of two distinct classes of armadillos.

44— Probably *Lynx rufus* described by Leopold [(1959), 484-87].

45— Perhaps *Felis concolor* (Ibid., 476-82).

46— Undoubtedly *Felis onca* (Ibid., 464-70).

47— Perhaps *Felis yagouaroundi* (Ibid., 482-84).

48— Probably *Felis pardalis* (Ibid., 470-73).

49— Undoubtedly *Lutra canadensis* or a related species (Ibid., 461-64).

50— Probably *Brassariscus astutus* or a related species (Ibid., 424-28).

51— Undoubtedly *Procyon lotor* (Ibid., 428-32).

52— Probably *Nasua narica* (Ibid., 432-37).

53— Probably *Urocyon cinereoargenteus* (Ibid., 408-11).

54— Perhaps *Canis latrans* (Ibid., 394-99).

55— Undoubtedly *Canis lupus* (Ibid., 399-405).

56— Probably *Pecari tajacu* (Ibid., 493-97).

57— Of some interest is a tale told by a canyon Indian concerning two small peccaries that he retrieved after their mother had been killed in a cave. The two animals were raised with dogs and goats and, when grown, served as better "watchdogs" than did the dogs.

58— Undoubtedly *Ursus americanus* described by Leopold [(1959), 411-16].

59— Probably *Odocoileus virginianus* (Ibid., 507-13).

60— The Tepehuan are familiar with the mule deer, which is rather common in the Tarahumar country north of the Río Verde, but state that it does not appear in extreme-southern Chihuahua.

61— Mason (1952), 47-48.

62— Brooks et al. (1962), 356.

63— 1645: Pérez de Ribas (1944), III, 137.

64— Ibid., 143, 156.

65— Ibid., 168.

66— Brooks et al. (1962), 358.

67— 1645: Pérez de Ribas (1944), III, 137, 170, 175.

68— 1743: Rinaldini (1743), 78.

69— Brooks et al. (1962), 358.

70— 1743: Rinaldini (1743), 91.

71— 1777: Relación de Indé.

72— Lumholtz (1902), I, 434-36.

73— 1645: Pérez de Ribas (1944), III, 146.

74— Ibid., 139.

75— Bean (1898), 165-68.

76— Almada (1945), 46.

77— Brooks et al. (1962), 356.

78— Precise identification of these species of agave was impossible; hence, we cannot state what toxic properties might be involved. However, recent studies [Wall et al.

(1957), 655-59] have demonstrated that sapogenins are present in a number of Mexican species of *Agave*. For example, chlorogenin and tigogenin have been isolated from *Agave Schottii*, which appears in the Tarahumar country immediately north of the Tepehuan habitat. Muenscher [(1947), 55] records a toxic substance in *Agave lecheguilla*, another rather common agave within the Tarahumar country.

79— Nothing is known of the precise toxic agent in *Juglans major*, but flavanoids and tannins have been isolated from a related species, *J. nigra* [Wall et al. (1959), 708], and resins and tannins have been isolated from *J. cinerea*, another related species [Claus (1956), 221]. Any or all of these toxic elements may be present in *Juglans major*.

80— This plant is known to contain the alkaloids protopine and allocriptopine (Seine [1960]); small doses of protopine have a narcotic effect on frogs, and large doses inhibit their reflex action. Undoubtedly, a similar action is exerted on fish.

81— Standley [(1920-1926), 341] notes that the toxic elements in *Prunus capuli* are probably cyanogenic glucosides, for the bark, leaves, and seeds of this tree, upon hydrolysis, yield such elements. Claus [(1956), 159-60] states that the bark of *Prunus serotina* is known to contain a cyanogenetic glucoside that acts as a sedative and pectoral. Wall et al. [(1957), 679] have demonstrated the presence of tannins and flavonoids in *Prunus serotina*.

82— I have no data concerning the precise toxic substance in *Tephrosia nicaraguensis* and *T. Thurberi*, but species of *Tephrosia* are widely used in fish poisoning throughout the world [Pammel (1911), 833].

83— Various species of *Lupinus* are known for their alkaloid content [Claus (1956), 519; Pammel (1911), 548-49].

84— Presumably, *Hura crepitans* is characterized by properties common to *H. poly-*

andra, the bark of which is used in fish stupefaction on the west coast of Mexico [Standley (1920-1926), 646].

85— Brooks et al. (1962), 356.

86— 1645: Pérez de Ribas (1944), III, 143.

87— Lumholtz (1902), I, 435-36.

88— 1777: Relación de San Miguel de Las Bocas.

89— The Tepehuan commonly identify fruit and tree with the same term; for example, *ïvókoli* refers not only to the *zarza mora* (*Rubus* sp.) but to the berries from this plant as well.

90— Gray (1950), 1253.

91— 1645: Pérez de Ribas (1944), III, 137.

92— Brooks et al. (1962), 357.

93— Gray (1950), 570.

94— This *čivúkali* should not be confused with another *čivúkali* (*Coutarea pterosperma*) from which incense is prepared.

95— Gray (1950), 609.

96— Ibid., 716.

97— Ibid., 708.

98— Ibid., 1093.

99— Ibid., 1253.

100— Ibid., 1554.

101— *Čawé* is, I believe, a Tarahumar word.

102— Brooks et al. (1962), 357, 360-62.

103— Ibid., 360.

104— Professor Charles D. Michener of the Department of Entomology, University of Kansas, Lawrence, Kansas, was kind enough to identify some of the insects that supply honey in southern Chihuahua.

105— 1743: Rinaldini (1743), 1.

106— Mason (1952), 43.

107— Ibid.

6
ANIMAL HUSBANDRY

The Tepehuan of southern Chihuahua are familiar with and know how to utilize stock of one kind or another, but with the exception of goats, domestic animals are not commonly owned by the Indians. Moreover, the distribution of stock among the Tepehuan is very uneven.

CATTLE

The scarcity of work cattle owned by Tepehuan is well illustrated by the situation that obtained in 1960 at Llano Grande, where only two out of forty-seven Indian families owned oxen (*vóíši*). There was a total of two animals. Ten out of thirty-two mestizo families owned a total of twenty-one working oxen. Twenty-three mestizo families owned a total of 137 milk cows, whereas sixteen Tepehuan families owned a total of 40 cows. However, the ownership of these forty cows was not well distributed since seven Indian families owned a total of twenty-one of them.[1]

The Indian's difficulties with primitive methods at plowing time are compounded because the Tepehuan are extremely reluctant to use horses, burros, or mules as draft animals even when they are available.

When they do own oxen or cows or, for that matter, any animal, the Indians are frequently faced with the necessity of having to sell the creatures in order to buy corn for food or for the preparation of *tesgüino*. The high value of animals is such that the Indians find it difficult to resist the price they bring from mestizos or itinerant cattle buyers. In 1960 and 1965, a working animal was valued at between 800 and 1,000 pesos ($64.00 to $80.00) at Llano Grande and nearby La Ciénega. A milk cow was valued at about 500 pesos ($40.00). When crops fail, the Indians must sell whatever they can in order to obtain money for purchasing food, and stock constitutes the most valuable asset. At Llano Grande in 1960, four Tepehuan reported that they had been compelled to dispose of work stock the previous year because of a crop failure.[2]

Because of their potential value, young cattle, sheep, and goats must be protected against such predators as the bobcat, puma, jaguar, jaguarundi, wolf, black bear, and coyote. Young stock are kept at night in substantially built corrals which are square or octagonal in design and about fifty square feet in area. In constructing these enclosures, the Indians make every effort to fashion them so that the stock cannot dislodge the poles (*kuparadi*). For square corrals, this is accomplished by using rather large heavy poles or by notching the ends of the logs so that they interlock. Octagonal corrals are made fast by firmly planting two upright poles against the walls at each of the corners. Sheep and goats are commonly maintained at night in square corrals that are covered with heavy logs (Fig. 21). Occasionally, more sophisticated Tepehuan construct what might be termed a crude barn for sheltering stock. This is particularly true near Lagotera, Palos Muertos, and La Ciénega. Such shelters are built of logs, and include a "stall" and a small covered opening just outside the "stall." The whole structure is covered over either with shingles weighted down with stones (Fig. 22) or with hollowed-out logs (*canoas*).

Precise data as to when stock was introduced among the northern Tepehuan are not available, but the date was undoubtedly early. Pérez de Ribas refers to the removal of much stock from central Durango by Indians who swept into the Guadiana site (now, Durango City) during the great rebellion of 1616.[3] A portion of this stock was killed, but many animals were transported to Indian settlements. Cattle may have spread into extreme-southern Chihuahua after Jesuits introduced significant numbers of stock into Tarahumar missions located north of the Río Verde in the late seventeenth century.[4] However, it appears that the general use of oxen by the Tepehuan of southern Chihuahua developed rather late; older Indians in the western canyons maintain that oxen were very uncommon about seventy-five or eighty years ago (see Chapter 2).

SHEEP AND GOATS

The distribution of sheep and goats among the Tepehuan and mestizos at Llano Grande in 1960 was somewhat better than that of oxen and cows. In that year, fourteen out of thirty-four mestizo families maintained a total of 130 sheep, whereas eighteen out of forty-seven Indian families owned a total of 107 sheep; twenty-four mestizo families owned a total of 434 goats, and twenty-eight Tepehuan families maintained 331 goats. Precise data concerning sheep and goats owned by canyon Indians are lacking, but most of the canyon Tepehuan were herding goats in the spring of 1960.

Tepehuan women and children have little to do with the herding of sheep (*kañiro*, a corruption of the Spanish word *carnero*) and goats (*šivátu*, a corruption of the Spanish word *chiva*); instead, dogs are trained to do the herding.

21 – The Tepehuan goat pen and chicken coop.

22 – A Tepehuan barn located near Lagotera, Chihuahua.

Under the care of one adult male or a youth, the dog keeps the animals out of the fields and assists in directing the flocks toward suitable pasture. The sheep and goats are kept at night in corrals built near habitations and are driven out each day to graze. If pasture sites are located far from the Indian habitation, the creatures are penned at night in a cave which may be blocked in some fashion to discourage predators.

Sheep and goats are valued as a source of wool used in the manufacture of blankets and sashes and also as a source of foodstuffs served at celebrations.

No data are available concerning the introduction of sheep and goats into southern Chihuahua, but these animals were numerous in the Tarahumar country near Cárichic and Sisoguichic in 1682;[5,6] hence, there was the opportunity for diffusion of the animals into the country south of the Río Verde prior to the end of the seventeenth century.

HORSES, BURROS, AND MULES

Horses are commonly maintained by mestizos in the Tepehuan country, but they rarely appear among the Indians. Twenty-one out of thirty-four mestizo families at Llano Grande owned a total of sixty-five horses in 1960, whereas only six out of forty-seven Indian families owned eight.

The ownership of horses by Indians not only gives much prestige to the owners, but it also makes easier many of the Indians' tasks, such as transporting fuel to their habitations when the surrounding timber has been removed. Moreover, to own a horse makes it possible for the Indian to obtain money occasionally by using or renting it as a pack animal. Horses are not penned but are permitted to roam at will; sometimes, several days are required for the Indians to locate their animals that have wandered into the canyons in search of pasture not available in certain areas of the uplands.

Most of the mestizo families living at Llano Grande in 1960 owned burros. There was a total of 196 animals possessed by twenty-four out of thirty-four mestizo families. Only nine out of forty-seven Indian families owned burros.

As with the ownership of horses, possessing burros (*ašnitu*) enables the Indians to obtain cash by renting them as pack animals and to perform certain chores with ease. The Indians state that all Tepehuan strive to own a burro, but the cost of one (about 100 pesos) at Llano Grande in 1960 precluded purchase except under the most unusual circumstances.

The crude pack saddle used by the Tepehuan is fashioned in a simple manner: two pieces of board are anchored to leather thongs that are used to strap blankets or hides onto the burro, and the material to be transported is anchored to the boards with rope or strips of leather. The wooden crates that serve as traps on occasion are anchored to the wooden pack saddle for transporting corn or other goods.

Burros are permitted to roam at will. Since each Indian seems to know his animal, there is little need for branding or marking these animals in any way.

Out of thirty-four mestizo families, eighteen owned a total of forty-nine mules at Llano Grande in 1960, whereas two Indian families owned two. The Indians do not use mules in the field but employ them as pack animals. Unless there is a shortage of oxen, mestizos do not ordinarily use mules in the fields either, but they do favor them as riding animals. In 1960, the value of adult mules (about 600 pesos each) precluded their general ownership by the Tepehuan.

It is not clear whether the Tepehuan of the north made use of horses before enough Spaniards arrived in northern Durango to make the animals more available. The first reference to horses among the Tepehuan is apparently that of Pérez de Ribas, who remarked in the seventeenth century that when the Tepehuan came into direct contact with the Spaniards, the Indians learned how to ride well and became proficient pikesmen.[7]

SWINE

As with other domestic animals, the mestizos at Llano Grande in 1960 owned more pigs (*taĭšoli*) than did the Tepehuan. There was a total of ninety-two pigs owned by twenty-one of the thirty-four mestizo families. In contrast, fifteen out of forty-seven Indian families owned a total of twenty-eight pigs; however, their distribution among the Tepehuan families was rather good, with only one family owning as many as seven. The average number of pigs per family among the Indians was two.

In 1960, young swine could be purchased for as little as thirty pesos, and an adult pig cost seventy to eighty pesos. Unfortunately, the Indians can rarely muster sufficient money to purchase an adult pig, and young pigs are frequently sold to obtain money for the purchase of essentials such as cotton cloth or salt, or they are traded for corn or beans.

Generally, pigs are permitted to run wild, and they are marked in some fashion, usually by a slit in one ear, to indicate ownership. If the corn crop is particularly good, pigs are penned for fattening in a small log corral constructed near habitations.

DOGS AND CATS

Most of the Indians maintain dogs because the animals are prized as watchdogs around the habitations and as protectors of sheep and goats from predators. They are especially valuable if trained to herd sheep and goats. The dogs (*góógoši*) are small and scrawny, and males are frequently castrated, at any age, if they are to serve as watchdogs around habitations. The Tepehuan believe that being castrated makes a dog *muy bravo*. Dogs are often given the names of other animals, such as *tuvoki* (*tuza* or *topo*). They are fed from a small *canoa* or a hollowed-out rock; the common dog foods are *nixtamal*, pinole and water, and meal drippings from the metate.

There is no evidence that dogs are eaten, nor are they buried at death; rather, they are left as food for the *sopilote*, the black vulture.

Few Tepehuan keep cats (*mǐšitu*); but those who do, prize these pets as killers of the rats that are common around dwellings.

There is little in the available record to indicate the antiquity of the dog among the Tepehuan. However, we do know that, at one time, the Tepehuan named people after animals, and the dog was no exception to this rule. One of the great Tepehuan leaders in the rebellion of 1616 was named Gogoxito,[8] which certainly is related to the present word for dog (*gogóši*).

POULTRY

In 1960, twenty-five out of thirty-four mestizo families at Llano Grande owned a total of 475 chickens (*takúku*), whereas thirty-six out of forty-seven Tepehuan families owned a total of 252. Chickens are rarely eaten; they seem to be valued primarily because their eggs can be traded to the mestizos for corn and beans. Very little attention is given to fowl, with almost no attempt to provide nests. Chickens are watched in order to learn where they have located their nests. Upland Indians can keep more chickens than the canyon Indians apparently because, in the canyons, bird predators kill any small chickens that are not being watched. Generally, chickens are carefully watched during the day because of the danger of attack by hawks and owls. At night, poultry is penned in elevated chicken coops built of logs (Fig. 21, page 151); these structures resemble crude miniature log cabins and are roofed with shingles held down with large stones. The chickens go to roost by means of a notched log that is removed after the coop is closed. The Indians state that only an elevated construction prevents raids by quadrapeds on the coops at night.

Nothing is known of exactly when chickens became common among the Tepehuan; they must have been brought into Chihuahua in the early seventeenth century by the Tepehuan who moved northward after the rebellion of 1616, but chickens could have reached southern Chihuahua by way of the Jesuit missionaries at Nabogame and Baborigame. It is certain that they were kept by the Tarahumar in the eastern missions during the 1680's.[9] There is some slight evidence that the Tepehuan displayed little interest in chickens in the eighteenth century. An account of a visit made in 1715 by Francisco Javier

Díaz to Tepehuan pueblos in northern Durango notes that the Indians were exhorted to forbid Negroes and mulattoes from entering their towns; to sleep on high beds; to place crosses upon their doors; to avoid drunkenness; and to raise chickens, cats, and dogs.[10]

BEES

Nine out of thirty-four mestizo families at Llano Grande maintained bees in 1960, whereas only two out of forty-seven Indian families kept them. It is clear that bees are not commonly kept by upland Indians, and no canyon Indians admitted to keeping them. Upland Indians state that certain birds prey upon the insects and make the keeping of bees exceedingly difficult.[11]

No definite data concerning the introduction of domesticated bees among the Tepehuan are available, but the date must have been rather early. Bees could have been started either by people who brought them to early mining communities in northwestern Mexico or by deliberate introduction by the Jesuits. The first specific reference to bees among the northern Tepehuan is apparently that of Rinaldini, who made a distinction in the mid-eighteenth century between wild and domestic insects that provided honey.[12] A late eighteenth-century reference to Nabogame states that the Indians (Tepehuan) raised bees, but with little success or care.[13]

DOMESTIC ANIMALS AS FOOD

Cows or oxen are killed in connection with fiestas (*šíádudagai*) held in celebration of planting and harvesting, burials, and the election of officials. There is no evidence that animals are killed at the celebration of the one religious festival in which some Tepehuan participate, that one held on *Sábado de Gloria* (the Saturday before Easter).

Officials are elected on two dates, January 6 and October 24, the former date being the more important election day. The senior government officials are always elected in January, the lesser officials are chosen in October. Six animals are killed in January and five in October.[14] The beasts are always penned in a corral near the scheduled election site for a night or two before the fiesta begins. Killing of the animals is either accomplished quickly, or it is a drawn-out affair. The animal may be thrown, tied up, and killed immediately by being clubbed between the ears or by repeated thrusts of a long knife into the chest cavity. The club can be either a single-bladed axe or a large stone anchored in the fork of an oak branch. When dances accompany the killing, the animals are not dispatched immediately. Each animal is thrown and tied with ropes. The dancers advance first to the left and then to the right of the animals, parading in a circle about the helpless creatures. Occasionally, a dancer steps out of the circle and jumps up and down on one of the beasts. Violin and guitar music may accompany the dance, which lasts for something more than an hour. The animals are eventually dispatched with random knife thrusts into the chest cavities.

The blood (*ïrai* or *uradï*) is caught in a *cajete* (*ajáskoli*) and cooked for a short time before being put in another container together with the heart, which has been cut into very small pieces. This mass is cooked until it thickens. When available, onions and leeks (the introduced *Allium Cepa* and *A. Ampeloprasum*);[15] leaves of the European *cilantro* (*Coriandrum sativum*);[16] orégano leaves (*Lippia Berlandieri*); fruits of the *kóókoli*, or *chile caribe* (*Capsicum annuum*), and the *čívuli* (*C. baccatum*); and leaves of the *uvákoči* (*Salvia* sp.) and the *Chimaphila umbellata*, known as *naváítai* (*tesgüino*) *biñáragadï* (*fermenter*), are added to the dish. This food is commonly eaten with tortillas. The brains (*ovadï*) of the animals are fried on a comal, and the lungs and intestines (*íhi*) are cut up and boiled until palatable. Generally, the meat is cut up and prepared as a stew, or it is spitted and roasted. There is apparently no attempt to prepare the meat for storage. The Tepehuan claim that salt is not added to the meat foods that are prepared as a part of the fiestas associated with the election of officials. Usually, the owner of each slain beast gives about one-fourth of the meat to a friend, who must then kill an animal at the following festival.

The Tepehuan dispose of their dead by inhumation; the bodies (*mukíadï, tukúga* or *tuukúga*) are buried in crudely constructed wooden boxes or in blankets. Immediately after death (*mukí* or *mukígami*), close relatives are advised about the time scheduled for the procession toward the place of burial. Only persons with close family connections attend the burial. Shortly after the funeral, the personal property of the deceased, excluding certain items such as stock for example, is collected in a specific place and local Indian authorities preside over disposition of the property. The fiesta in honor of the deceased is held exactly one year after the burial. At this fiesta, an animal is killed, and emphasis is given to preparing foods known to have been favored by the deceased. Friends of the deceased dance through the night and then eat the food that has been prepared.

Those Tepehuan who live in rather close association with mestizos use cow's milk (*vïíbai*) for general human consumption, whereas those Indians who live in remote areas use milk only in the preparation of cheese. Some Tepehuan trade corn or beans for milk to be used in cheese-making. To curdle the milk, a portion of the stomach of a cow, goat, or deer is boiled for a short time, then lightly salted and dried and put in the milk. After about two hours, the curdling agent is removed from the milk, which is stirred until it begins to thicken The thickened milk is squeezed in a loosely woven basket or in a piece of cotton cloth to remove most of the whey. The curd is then mashed with the hands on a stone until all of the whey is expelled. Salt is added, and the cheese is pressed into a circular wooden mold prepared from any easily worked wood.

The Tepehuan state that sheep and goats are killed for very important festival occasions and also at the funeral fiestas held some time after the burial of an important person in the community. Skins of these slain animals are prized as sleeping or sitting mats. Sheep or goat meat is boiled as a stew or spitted and roasted. The lungs, kidneys, and heart are cut up and boiled, as are the intestines which are an esteemed addition to *pozole*. The testicles (*oliadï* or *jolïši*) of sheep and goats are boiled as a foodstuff. Stews prepared from the meat of cows, sheep, or goats are made more palatable by the addition of condiments (see Chapter 4).

Swine are slaughtered in a very crude fashion. The animal is held down by several men, and the heart is located by holding the front legs of the creature against its chest. A knife or sharpened stake is thrust into the body until the heart is pierced. The blood is caught in a *cajete* and prepared as a foodstuff in exactly the same fashion as the blood of a cow. Kidneys and lungs are boiled and salted before they are eaten. The skin is made into *chicharrones* by removing the fat and cutting up the skin and boiling it in a large container. Stew prepared from the meat (*babáïdi*) is seasoned by the addition of any condiment that is available. Some of the Tepehuan prepare a food known as *menudo* (*vó-kadi*) among the mestizos. The pig's large intestine is cleaned in running water and cooked for several hours before being stuffed with ground corn that has been seasoned with various condiments. The intestine is then cooked for about another hour. *Menudo* is frequently added to *pozole*.

Generally, the intestines of all domestic animals killed for food are given to those more sophisticated Tepehuan who know how to prepare soap (see Chapter 9).

There is no evidence that the Tepehuan eat horse or burro flesh when these animals die.

PASTURAGE PLANTS

Tepehuan herders and their dogs drive the flocks of sheep and goats to places where certain types of forage may be found. The flocks are taken to graze either along the edges of the great mesas, where the uplands break away to the lower country, or they are taken to the upper slopes of the canyons. The canyon-bottom streamways are not particularly well endowed with forage. The

Indians know well the specific areas where grazing is good and insist that no damage has been done to the forage by overgrazing.

Listed below are specific plants that the Indians claim are of value as forage. Some of the plants are restricted in their distribution because of ecological factors, but all are apparently known to both upland and canyon Indians.

Gramineae
    Panicum plenum (*zacate de bola*)
    P. texanum
    Trisetum sp.
Commelinaceae
    Tradescantia angustifolia (*palma*)
Cyperaceae
    Carex sp. (*baliómadagai*)
Juncaceae
    Juncus sp.
Liliaceae
    Smilax sp. (*kováiboli*)
Polygonaceae
    Polygonum hydropiperoides
Ranunculaceae
    Aquilegia Skinneri (*madre selva* or *uvióši*)
    Ranunculus micranthus
Cruciferae
    Descurainia pinnata (*suavoli*)
Crassulaceae
    Echeveria sp.
Rosaceae
    Potentilla sp. af. *exsul* (*fresa* or *ibíši*)
[This *ibíši* should not be confused with *fresa cimarróna* (*Fragaria vesca*), which is also known as *ibíši*.]
Leguminosae
    Calliandra herbacea (*áli sákoi*)
(Not to be confused with *Eysenhardtia amorphoides*, which is known as *áli sákoi* or *tepeguaje chiquito*).
    Cassia leptadenia
    Cologania angustifolia (*frijolillo*)
    C. obovata (*patos*)
    Dalea Gentryi (*íkoi*)
    Desmanthus sp.
    Desmodium sp. (*amorescos* or *arásadajami*)
    Indigofera sp. (*acetilla*)

Lotus sp.
Lupinus sp. (*chicharillos*)
Phaseolus sp. (*frijol del monte*)
Trifolium sp. (*socoyole del arroyo*)
Geraniaceae
    Geranium chihuahuense
Euphorbiaceae
    Manihot sp. (*pato de gallo*)
Rhamnaceae
    Colubrina glomerata (*espino* or *úparai*)
    C. Greggii
Violaceae
    Viola sp. (*ukuvuli*)
    V. sp. (*kokuvuli*)
Primulaceae
    Anagallis arvensis
Asclepiadaceae
    Asclepias amplifolia (*yerba de la mula*)
Scrophulariaceae
    Castilleja sp.
    Pentstemon sp. (*yerba morada*)
Rubiaceae
    Bouvardia bouvardioides (*vipíši úšidï*)
    Hedyotis sp.
Compositae
    Arnica zygomeris (*chicharillo*)
    Aster subulatus
    Bidens sp. (*acetilla*)
    B. sp. (*espiga de escoba*)
    Cosmos sp.
    Eupatorium sp. (*escalera* or *tusádikaroi*)
    Galinsoga parviflora
    Haplopappus stoloniferus (*áli vúáma yoošígai*)
    Tithonia fruticosa
Unidentified Specimens
    carricillo (*áli tótoikami*)
    mučípali

SWINE FORAGE

The Indians commonly turn their pigs out to forage in areas where certain food plants are known to be plentiful. Little is said concerning specific plants associated with the keeping of pigs, but it is stated that acorns from the following oaks are particularly good as food for swine: *encino grande* (*Quercus Urbanii*), known among the Indians as *kokorákami*; *Q. rugosa*, known as *tupúrai* (*hacha*) *úsaraga* (*cabo de hacha*); *Q. coccolobaefolia*; and *ívotai* (*Q. candicans*). Swine herders watch for places where *Panicum bulbosum*, known as *koomági* (*gris*) *yorádagai*, is found in abundance; the roots of this plant are said to be a favorite of pigs. They also eat the tiny bulblike roots of another *yorádagai*.

According to both upland and canyon Indians, availability of pasturage plants for their animals constitutes a year-round problem, particularly in the rolling uplands where pines dominate.

CHAPTER 6 NOTES

1— These figures include only oxen and cows maintained in 1960 near Llano Grande on the Mesa de Milpillas; the mestizos there owned large numbers of stock that they let run in the canyons and that were sold twice yearly when cattle buyers entered southern Chihuahua from the west or the east.

2— The summer of 1965 was marked by a great number of severe hail storms at La Ciénega, located to the south of Baborigame. Indians living near La Ciénega maintained there would be such a shortage of corn that much stock would have to be sold in order to procure corn for the winter of 1965/66.

3— 1645: Pérez de Ribas (1944), III, 206.

4— The Jesuit record is rather explicit concerning cattle among the upland Tarahumar. In 1682, only a few of them possessed cattle at Sisoguichic (1682: Letter of Joseph Neumann, February 20), and in the following year, about 2,500 head of cattle were collected in Sonora at Cucurpe, Arizpe, Oposura, Sahuaripa, Aribechi, and Guazavas for movement into the interior to the Tarahumar missions (1683: Letter of Juan Bautista Ancieta, March 20). By 1725, there were more than 10,000 head of stock held by the Tarahumar upland missions [1725: "Carta del Padre San Juan de Guen-

dulain . . . ," in *Doc.* (1857), 4th series, IV, 22-33].

5— 1682: Letter of Joseph Neumann, February 20.

6— 1683: Ratkay. An account of the Tarahumar missions. . . .

7— 1645: Pérez de Ribas (1944), III, 137, 206.

8— Ibid., 205.

9— 1683: Ratkay. An account of the Tarahumar missions. . . . Ratkay wrote that many chickens were maintained at Cárichic; these fowl were not eaten but were kept for sale to the Spaniards.

10— 1715: Actas de la visita. . . .

11— A more rational explanation for the lack of bees among the Indians seems to be ignorance of, or lack of attention to, beekeeping techniques.

12— 1743: Rinaldini (1743), 1, 28.

13— 1777: Relación de Nabogame.

14— No rational explanation was given for the number of animals killed.

15— Gray (1950), 431.

16— Ibid., 1093.

7
CEREMONIES, GAMES, AND DRUGS

Many species of plant life common to southern Chihuahua are utilized in the manufacture of various objects (batons for Indian officials, flutes, rasping sticks, rattles, drums, and violins) that fulfill various functions in Tepehuan ceremonies and games. In addition, the plant resource supplies a large number of species used in the preparation of medicinal compounds.

CEREMONIES AND PLANTS

Batons of the Officials. The Tepehuan "pueblos" are governed by an elaborate hierarchy of officials (*duukámi*) whose designation, position, and duties undoubtedly reflect a blending of aboriginal and colonial customs. The more important officials include the following: *gobernador* (*kaigi*), *general* (*moiyi*), *suplentes* (*sonurakakami kaigi*), *capitanes* (*katañi*), *sargento* (*sonurakakami katañi*), *cabo* (*sonurakakami katañi*), *justicia* (*surikami*), *fiscale* (*fiskari*), and *fiestero* (*maduma*). There are five sets of officials for the "governments" at Baborigame, Cinco Llagas, Santa Rosa, Nabogame, and Dolores. With the exception of the *fiscales* and the *fiesteros*, who are appointed to office, all of these officials are elected by vote.

Responsible Indians in each "pueblo" gather on December 25 and decide among themselves the names of candidates for offices. A great crowd of Indians gathers on January 6 and chooses the *gobernador* by voice vote; only men get to vote. Usually, three men have been suggested for the office. An elderly Indian who has much prestige presides at the vote, which is not a ballot as such; people in the crowd scream the name of the man they desire as *gobernador*. The final decision is left to the man designated to preside at the election. Governors are elected for one year, but custom decrees that these officials be re-elected many times. Death while in office results in an immediate special election. The important duty of the *gobernador* is apparently that of presiding at courts (*umpadaragai*) which settle all manner of problems, particularly those difficulties caused by gossipers, thieves, and murderers. If *gobernadores* do not perform their duties according to custom, they may be ousted, and according to older

Tepehuan, ousted governors were whipped and forbidden to participate in government affairs of any sort. They might also be banished from their home community.

The *general* is elected in the same fashion as the governor and works with him in presiding at court and meting out punishment. For example, if an Indian murders his wife, he is usually imprisoned locally until he can be sent to the federal authorities at Guadalupe y Calvo; the *general* attends to such matters as transporting the accused person to the federal prison. He also commonly represents the governor in handling land squabbles, those between mestizos and Indians, which must be settled in Chihuahua City. *Generales* may hold office for many years, being re-elected every January 6.

Suplentes, usually six in number, are elected in the same fashion as *gobernadores* and *generales*, and they function as foremen for the senior officials and as investigators of complaints within the jurisdiction of each governor. Commonly, they hold office until a new governor is elected.

Capitanes are elected by voice vote at the same time the governor and the general are elected. Each *capitán* may select twelve men who are expected to assist him in his duties. The twelve assistants may bring squabbling men to a designated spot, where the *capitán* either settles the argument or presents the matter to a higher authority. *Capitanes* generally hold office for a longer time than *gobernadores* and *generales*.

Sargentos, *cabos*, and *justicias* are elected by voice vote the same as the higher officials and remain in office as long as they display "good behavior." A *sargento* has jurisdiction over a small number of *ranchos* that are usually widely scattered; a *cabo* has jurisdiction over a closely grouped number of *ranchos*; and a *justicia* commonly exercises jurisdiction over a group of families, those living on a *rancho*. By custom, *sargentos*, *cabos*, and *justicias* serve as local authorities who may order trouble-makers or accused persons into court.

Fiscales serve as janitors responsible for the cleaning of churches or chapels and the home of the Indian governor. *Fiesteros* generally prepare the alters, maintain the candles, and ready the church or chapel for the infrequent visits of priests to Chihuahua south of the Río Verde.

Upon election to office, all officials, except the *fiestero* and the *fiscale*, are presented with badges of authority in the form of canes (*úpasai*) made of brazilwood (*Haematoxylon brasiletto*). This polished cane is about four feet in length and resembles a broomstick; it is carried only when an official is on duty. The importance of these badges of authority is demonstrated by the fact that the *gobernador* is not obeyed unless he is carrying his baton. This situation obtains particularly if he is presiding at court (*umpadaragai*), which is held every other Sunday before the most conveniently located church or chapel.

For the most part, these courts concern themselves with accusations of rape, murder, or theft. Land squabbles are generally settled by the local ejido director, who is usually a mestizo closely linked with the Indians by family ties.

Evidence for a great antiquity in the use of a badge of authority among the Tepehuan is lacking.

Musical Instruments. The Tepehuan flute (*kukuitusajaroi*) is fashioned from a section of the *vajáji* stalk (*Arundo donax*), an introduction from Europe[1] that is readily available in western canyons. A joint of the cane is tapered at one end, and a convex piece of reed is attached with fiber cord. A slit is cut below the mouthpiece, and from one to four tiny holes are fashioned as stops. Mason described a flute used by the Tepehuan near Baborigame as follows: "the simple flute is a short section of cane with two modifying finger-holes and an attached mouthpiece leading the breath over a third hole."[2] Reed flutes are used mostly by children today, but older Tepehuan state that, not long ago, they were much used by Indian men when alone in a canyon. The men of today play reed flutes only at festivals associated with religious activities. There is almost nothing in the historical record, and certainly nothing in the archeological record, to indicate that aboriginal Tepehuan played reed flutes. However, some type of musical reed instrument may once have been used to send or convey messages among the Tepehuan. Pérez de Ribas commented that prior to the attack on Guadiana in 1616, the Indians held a fiesta and that, during the celebration, trumpeters made certain sounds to indicate an attack was to take place.[3] The use of a metal *trompeta* (an instrument obtained from the Spaniards) for such a purpose may mean that the aboriginal Tepehuan made a similar use of a reed flute. However, the call to battle by the Indians in 1616 may represent an outright borrowing of a Spanish custom. Rinaldini notes *cucuitujarjare* as a specific Tepehuan term for the *flauta* in the eighteenth century.[4] This suggests that the flute was known to and used by northern colonial Tepehuan, among whom Rinaldini lived for most of the time he was an active missionary.

The rasping stick is made from brazilwood (*Haematoxylon brasiletto*) available in western canyons. The instrument is comprised of a stick about eighteen inches long that is notched slightly on one side; another stick of brazilwood is rubbed back and forth over the notches. Canyon Indians note that this instrument was used a great deal in ceremonies about seventy-five years ago.

The ordinary hunting bow serves as a crude musical instrument and is played in this fashion: the bow string is tightened, one end of the bow is held in the mouth, and the string is struck lightly with an arrow.

Drums are called *tugúrai*. The typical instrument is a wooden drum, fifteen to twenty-four inches long and covered at both ends with skin. A suitable pine log (about eighteen inches in width) is cut to the desired length, and the interior is burned out with coals—altogether a tedious process. The interior is then carefully scraped with a sharp knife or stone. The bark is removed, and untreated deer or goat skins (scraped clean of hair) are stretched over the ends of the drum and laced together tightly with rawhide; the skins are always wetted before being affixed to the drum. Pliable strips of wood are then cut to the proper length and fastened around the ends of the drum by means of tiny pegs that are inserted through the circular strips and into the drum; these strips are not flush with the ends of the drum, and they serve to hold the skins in

23— The Tepehuan drum (*tugúrai*).

place. Two other strips of wood, somewhat wider than the first ones, are affixed at the outer edges of the first strips. Holes made in these wider strips, which project beyond the drum head, are used for rawhide laces that are wetted before being inserted. The first set of laces used to hold the skin tightly in place are removed, and a hole is cut in one side of the drum (Fig. 23). Most Tepehuan drums are decorated with *útai*, a reddish rock that is available nearly everywhere in the Tepehuan country; it is crushed and moistened before being used.

Nothing is known of the use of a drum by aboriginal Tepehuan. Apparently, the oldest reference to drums is that of Lumholtz, who recorded their use by the Indians in the 1890's in connection with planting and harvesting ceremonies.[5] Drums are similarly used today.

Violins (Fig.24) are fashioned everywhere in the Tepehuan country. The boxes of these instruments are fashioned from the wood of *Pinus reflexa*; *pino prieto*, or *tukúkui* (*P. chihuahuana*); *verako*, or *taíšoli* (*marrano*) *oliadï* (*testiculos*), which is a species of *Thevetia*; and an unidentified wood, *vogusai* (*aljaba*) *muíšuli* (*quemado*). Parts of the boxes are carved with a knife and, after being carefully scraped, are glued together with a compound prepared from roots of the *Nolina matapensis*, which is known among the Indians as *daapáka* (*liso*) *kúrui* (*palma*). The roots of the plant are crushed and added to a bit of water and boiled for several hours. Wet leather thongs are used to tie the box

24— The Tepehuan violin.

tightly together until the glue is firmly set. The neck of the violin is fashioned from the wood of *pítai* (*Fraxinus velutina*) or from *yóli*, the *manzanilla* (*Arctostaphylos pungens*) which is generally available throughout the Tepehuan country at middle elevations. Violin bows are fashioned from three widely distributed hard woods: *šivátu* (*cabra*) *úši* (*palo* or *árbol*), which is *Garrya ovata*; *G. laurifolia*, that is known among the Indians as *čivo* (*amargo*) *bopotai* (*puntas de las flechas*); and *Ipomoea arborescens*, also known as *šivátu* (*cabra*) *úši* (*palo* or *árbol*).[6] The bow string (*giáragai*) is prepared from deer gut or from horsehair, and the violin strings are prepared from gut, horsehair, or wire obtained from mestizos. Violins are tinted with a dye prepared from the scrapings of a *tapókai* (*Alnus oblongifolia*), which is known among mestizos as *carnero*.

No data are available concerning the introduction of the violin among the Tepehuan. However, the instruments were recorded among these Indians by Lumholtz in the 1890's.[7]

Not a single guitar was noted among the Tepehuan during the spring and summer of 1960 and 1965, but the Indians insist that this instrument is used and that it is manufactured by the canyon Indians. Certainly, the skill of the Indians in fashioning violin parts suggests that they could manufacture a guitar as well.

Rattles are known among the Tepehuan by the mestizo term (*sonajas*) or by Indian terms (*maraka*, *sásamuidakali*, or *sásamuidakaroi*); these instruments serve as noise-making devices during almost all Tepehuan celebrations, such as church festivals and planting and harvesting ceremonies. Occasionally, they are used on birthdays. There is disagreement among the Tepehuan concerning the sources of rattles used today. Some Indians insist that rattles are brought in from the Tarahumar country to the north or from Culiacán, whereas other Indians maintain that rattles are manufactured locally from the fruits of *Cucurbita foetidissima*, which is widely distributed in western canyons. Fruits from this plant are reportedly dried in the sun, holes are punched in both ends of the gourds, the interior pith is removed with a sharp stick, a few tiny pebbles are inserted in the gourds, and sticks are then wedged into and through the fruits (Fig. 25).

There are apparently no historical references to rattles among the Tepehuan except for a comment by Rinaldini, who recorded *sonajas* as *sommoidajare* in the eighteenth century.[8]

GAMES AND PLANTS

The Tepehuan display a great fondness for games (*tutubi*) and, with the exception of church ceremonies and funerals, play them on almost any occasion when people congregate. There are games of chance and games of dexterity. The historical record suggests that the northern Tepehuan once played a rubber-ball game not unlike one that was once played in southern Mexico. The antiquity of games among the Tepehuan is demonstrated in the Jesuit annual report of 1595 in which there is a reference to games played at celebrations.[9] However, these games are not described.

By far the most important game today among the Chihuahua Tepehuan is kickball, which is played throughout the year whenever a few or more people are so inclined.[10] The Tepehuan call this game *utúinaragai*. A wooden ball (*oró-ši*) about three inches in diameter is carved from any of the following woods:

25— The Tepehuan rattle (*maraka, sásamuidakali* or *sásamuidakaroi*)
and pine-cone comb (*gašíúvikaroi*) displayed on a skin used as a sleeping mat.

Arbutus xalapensis, the *madroño del barranca* or *madroño pequeño*, known among the Indians as *áli* (*chiquito*) *opíndali* (*madroño*); *A. arizonica*, known either as *madroño grande* or as *opíndali; palo verde* (*Garrya laurifolia*); *Guazuma ulmifolia*, a common *guásima* of the canyons; aguacate, or *laurelillo* (*Persea americana*), known as *gúruduši*; a canyon tree (*Thevetia* sp.), known as *verako* or *taíšoli* (*marrano silvestre*) *oliadï* (*testiculos*); *palo rojo* (*Wimmeria* sp.), which is characteristic of canyons near Santa Rosa; and *palo verde*, an unidentified species common to arroyos near Santa Rosa.

The ball is painted either with a red pigment (*almagre*) prepared from crushed and moistened *útai* or with a green pigment prepared by crushing the leaves of *Juglans major, Persea americana*, or a species of *Opuntia*; balls are decorated with stripes or dots so that each team may recognize its ball during the race.

There are two teams in kickball, ranging in number usually from one to three people, but there may be as many as twenty to a team for a big race—one between "villages," or "pueblos," or between members of the two social groups recognized among the Tepehuan, the *Arribeño* and the *Bajeño*. The number of men on each team depends largely upon the importance of the occasion. Two men may run a kickball race to provide personal or local amusement. The Tepehuan refer to a runner as *utúisdami*.

There is no evidence that the Tepehuan train in any fashion for even an important race, but there are some restrictions placed upon the runners during the twenty-four hours preceding the race. For a really big race, each team spends the night before the race in a special place, usually an abandoned house or hut. *Tesgüino* and *jápari* (a fermented beverage made from the juice of an agave species) are forbidden to runners for twenty-four hours before a race. If team members remain in their homes the night before a race, they must refrain from sexual activity.

The racecourse (*mïrikarui*) may be straight or circuitous in design; however, straight courses are generally laid out upon mesas or upon streamway floodplains, whereas circuits invariably involve terrain of both mesas and canyons. Some courses are so long and so difficult that seven or eight hours are required to complete the number of circuits established for the race. This is consistent with Lumholtz' remark that races occasionally lasted from midday until about eight in the evening.[11]

Each team has a leader or captain, and at a given signal, the leaders lift their balls with one foot and toss them forward. Members of each team dash forward, and the person who first reaches his team's ball lifts it with his foot and tosses it ahead. The ball cannot be touched with the hands except when necessary to remove it from cracks in the rocks or when it is lodged in the brush or some roots. (Roots are often exposed by erosional activity in the uplands and canyons and, hence, constitute a hazard.) Each team captain may have one or more assistants who search for the ball, but they may not touch it when it is found. Runners are always barefooted and usually stripped to the waist while running important races. For the really important races held as a competition between two communities, the legs of team members may be painted with red or white pigments.

Judges (*nokadákami* or *kóími*) are stationed where the race begins and at the turning point or points of the course to discourage cheating. If members of one team kick the ball of the opposing team, the race is forfeited. Judges are required to make sure that if a man stops to rest, he can continue in the game only if he follows the set course of the race and makes up any laps he may have missed.

Important races are accompanied by violin music and drums.[12]

The taking of stimulants is permitted during the game, and men and women are stationed along the racecourse to give *tesgüino*, pinole, and *esquiate* to the runners. Thorny branches of an *algarroba* (*Acacia pennatula*), known among the Indians as *úparai*, are used to switch the runners' legs (*kajidï*) during important races; a flow of blood presumably causes the participants to try for greater speed. A species of *Carex*, known as *baliómadagai*, is used in the preparation of a wash that is applied to the runners' legs before the race begins. The lotion is said to increase the running capacity of the men. Peyote (*íkuli*) is traded from the neighboring Tarahumar for use in preparing another lotion that is rubbed on the legs of runners to promote strength and to make them fleet of foot.[13] The Tepehuan state that, occasionally, runners chew the leaves of a poisonous herb and then blow their breath into their opponents' faces in order to "slow them down."[14]

There is much betting of dogs, goats, firewood, blankets, maize, and beans on the outcome of the kickball race. Bets (*tukai* or *toki*) are piled in a specific place, called *tukaidarágui* or *tokidarágui*, located near the beginning point of the race. Mason recorded betting on the kickball race among Baborigame Tepehuan but noted that the bets were for small stakes.[15]

No one can state with certainty that aboriginal Tepehuan played kickball or that the game was played in the early colonial period. It is true that comments by Rinaldini suggest that the game was played in the eighteenth century.[16] However, his reference to a *juego de la bola* may be to the rough shinny described below, and his reference to the *bocosoli* (*bola*) might mean the ball used in shinny even though *bocosoli* is clearly related to the present-day term *oróši* (*bola*). Rinaldini referred to the *corredor* (runner) as *mulidagaxamue*, whereas the Tepehuan term is now *utúisdami*. That betting is an ancient custom seems certain, for he also recorded *apuesta* as *á tucaraga* and *iuquidaraga*. The verb *apostar* (to bet) was recorded as *tutuquidi*, *tuquidianta*, and *tuquidani*. However, there is nothing in this record to suggest that the betting referred to wagers on the kickball game.

It seems likely that the game of kickball is a post-Columbian element in northern Tepehuan culture essentially because there are no known references to the game for the Indians living east of the Sierra Madre Occidental prior to the eighteenth century.[17]

There is evidence in Rinaldini's dictionary that Tepehuan of the eighteenth century played a rubber-ball game (*juego de la ulāma*) known as *ulé* or *ulāma*.[18] Rinaldini gives *tuliafe*, *tuliafanta*, and *tuliafani* as the Indian terms meaning "to play *ulé*" (*al ulé jugar*). The Tepehuan name for the game was either *tuliagaraga* or *oli*, and the playing court was called *tuliagaraequer* (*lugares adonde juegan al ulé*). The Tepehuan of today know nothing of this rubber-ball game, so presumably it disappeared from the Indian culture in the eighteenth century.

Tepehuan women favor a running game that is known among the Indians as *šibúbaruai* (literally, a "circle of wood") and as *ariweta* among mestizos. A wooden hoop about five inches in diameter is made from any one of a number of woods readily available within upland or canyon country: *áli* (*chiquito*) *opíndali* (*madroño*), which is either *Arbutus xalapensis* or *A. glandulosa*; *opín-dali* (*A. arizonica*); *Ficus petiolaris*; *Pinus leiophylla*; *kóji* (*Morus microphylla*); *tarákovara* (*Fouquieria fasciculata?*); and *túbuli* (*Salix Gooddingii*). Occasionally, the hoop is fashioned from thick plaits of leaves from *óyi* (*Yucca decipiens*); *šúšida kúrui* (*Dasylirion Wheeleri*); *kúru* (*D. simplex*); and *daapáka* (*liso*) *kúrui* (*palma*), which is either *Nolina matapensis* or *N. durangensis*. Mason noted that the hoop used in this game was "a small ring of grass wound with yucca leaves."[19] A straight stick about twenty-eight inches long is used to throw the hoop forward; the Indians claim that a hooked stick is never used. The racecourse is laid out on mesas or within rough arroyos or canyons, but the straight or circuitous course is by no means as long as that laid out for the kick-ball game. Commonly, only two women play the game; it is only on very special occasions that several members make up a team. Judges are placed along the racecourse to insure that cheating does not take place. There is much betting on this game.

Dadáíši is another game played by women on a course that may be straight or circuitous; when the course is circuitous, it is always run in a clockwise fashion. Two teams participate, the number on each team depending upon the size and importance of the gathering. In the race, each woman has a stick with which she picks up and throws forward two three-inch sticks that have been anchored together with leather thongs or ixtle fiber. The game is marked by much betting and, as with the other races, is won by the player or team that first returns the playing object to the starting point.

An important game of chance played by the Tepehuan is *quince*, a game that resembles *patole*. There are two participants who play with four bamboo sticks about twelve inches long, each one decorated with a different geometric design on one side. The four designs indicate values of *quince, catorce, quatro*, and *seis*. Upland Indians generally use whole cane sticks, whereas canyon Tepehuan prefer slit segments. The cane used for these sticks is called *otati* and is readily available in warmer canyons. Black and red tints are used to accent the carving on each stick. This dice game is played on a square court that may vary considerably in width from a few feet to as many as seven feet. The playing court is outlined by nine holes at each of the four corners, with one hole at the corner and four rather evenly spaced holes on each side of the corner hole. Five additional holes arranged in a curve or a straight line extending outward from two diagonally opposite corners serve as tails or goals. Each player has a pawn, or marker, which is usually a small stone. The objective in the game is for a player to move his pawn from the end of his tail goal completely around the square before his opponent can do the same; the opponent's tail goal is not counted as part of the square. The number of moves per play is determined by the value of the geometric designs that show when the cane dice are dropped.

The dice are held vertically in the player's fist and dropped into the middle of the court, or they are struck against a stone at the side of the court. At Santa Rosa in 1960, the following scoring method was used:

Quince up and three canes down	15 points
Catorce up and three canes down	14 points
Quatro up and three canes down	4 points
Seis up and three canes down	6 points
All canes up	5 points
All canes down	10 points
Two canes up and two canes down	2 points
Three canes up and one cane down	3 points

There are certain restrictions in the playing rules. If a player moves his pawn into a hole occupied by the marker of his opponent, the opponent must begin anew. If a pawn is between certain points on the square and its player makes fourteen points with his throw, it may be advanced only one hole. Restriction to a two- or three-point count is common when a marker is being moved within a certain portion of the court. In the final stretch of the game, only one, two, or three counts may move a pawn. *Catorce* may be valued at fourteen points or at one point according to the whim of the players. Players must move their markers around the court in opposite directions, but they are not obligated to move them into an opponent's tail goal.

The Tepehuan of Chihuahua refer to *quince* as *suligari*, which is undoubtedly an old term for the game whatever the antiquity of the game itself among the Tepehuan. *Quince* certainly dates back to the eighteenth century, for Rinaldini refers to *suligarague* as the name of a *juego de los patoles* and gives the name of the gaming place (*lugares adonde juegan al patole*) as *suligaragaquer*. Also, there must have been some kind of solitaire *patole* played in the eighteenth century since Rinaldini refers to *patoles solos* as *jutascare*.[20] The names applied to *quince* by both twentieth- and eighteenth-century Tepehuan are clearly related to the term used by the Nabogame Tepehuan in the late nineteenth century as reported by Lumholtz: *intuvigai zuli gairagai* ("game straight throwing").[21] At that time, the die sticks were fashioned from ash, walnut, or from pine.

Another dice game, known as *taba*, requires two players, who accumulate points according to the position in which a knuckle bone of a deer falls to the ground after being tossed in the air. The four sides of the bone are assigned the following values: one-half point, one point, two points, and zero points. If the bone stands up on end when it lands, a total of twelve points is made—the winning score. There is no evidence of betting on either of the two dice games as played today by the Tepehuan.

The Chihuahua Tepehuan enjoy *cuatro*, or quoits, a game usually played by two men. Two holes (*dïga*) are dug in the ground about twenty-five feet apart, and two stone disks (*jolïši*)[22] are used by each player. The stones are marked in some fashion so that each player may readily identify his stones. Points are awarded according to the following chance arrangement of the stones as they are thrown from one hole to the other:

One stone in the hole	4 points
One stone near the hole	1 point
Two stones near the hole	2 points
One stone covering another stone in the hole	0 points
Two stones on top of one stone in the hole	4 points

A score of twelve points constitutes the game. *Cuatro* is said to have been learned from the Cocoyome, and the Chihuahua Tepehuan claim that the Cocoyome used their women as bets. There is no evidence that the Tepehuan bet on this game as it is played today.

There is much betting among the Indians on an archery game that involves shooting arrows either at a line drawn on the ground some distance from the players or at a hat placed on the ground some distance away. Present-day Tepehuan call this game *vupadami*, which is clearly related to the eighteenth-century terms, *vupi* and *vuparaga*, given by Rinaldini as the Indian terms for a *juego de las flechas*. The gaming place (*lugares adonde juegan á las flechas*) was called *vupadaragaquer*.[23] Therefore, it is likely that the archery game, or a variant of it, is relatively ancient among the Tepehuan.

Tepehuan children play with a wooden top carved from any easily worked, local wood. An ixtle-fiber string serves as a cord. A relatively recent introduction for the top is suggested by statements from older Indians that the top was unknown in southern Chihuahua during their childhood. Moreover, Lumholtz did not mention tops in the 1890's. The first reference seems to be that of Mason, who recorded them among the Tepehuan at Baborigame in the early 1950's.[24]

Rinaldini referred to a sport called *tocca'idaraga* (*juego de la bola*) that apparently was played only by women, who utilized a stick called *toccare, toccalianta,* or *toccarudani* (*al palo de las mujeres*). The playing field was called *toccarudaragaquer* (*lugares adonde juegan á la bola*). A wooden ball must have been used in this game, for Rinaldini noted that *anean capisciate* and *boscoli an guve* were the Tepehuan equivalents for *á la pelota*.[25] The references are not precise, but the Tepehuan terms for the playing stick, *toccare, toccalianta,* and *toccarudani,* suggest the name of a very rough game, *tákuari,* played today by southern Chihuahua Tepehuan. In this game, two teams drive a wooden ball back and forth on a large playing field. Both men and women play the game, and the participants may come from one or several communities. Really important games of *tákuari* are played by teams representing the two social groups among the Tepehuan, the *Arribeño* and *Bajeño*. There are six to ten players on each team, and each team member has a playing stick (*toyi*) which is about one yard in length with a spoonlike device at one end. The playing court is established in an open field with definite goal-line markers at each end of the court. The ball is thrown into the air by one of the team captains, who is standing in the center of the court at the start of the game. All participants rush toward the ball, and each player strives to be the first to "toss" it to the end of the court assigned to the opposing team, whose members then try to toss the ball back from the goal line. The game is won by the team that first accumulates a stated number of points by tossing the ball across the goal line defended by the opposing team.

MEDICINAL PLANTS

As might be expected, disease (*kokóida* or *šúšigai*) of one kind or another plagues both mestizo and Indian in southern Chihuahua. A great variety and number of plants from at least fifty-six plant families provide roots, leaves (*áága*), stems, and (occasionally) seeds (*ištuk*, *ištúkai*, *ištókai*) and flowers (*yo-ošígai* or *yoočígai*) that are used by the Tepehuan in preparing poultices, infusions, and teas that serve as medicines. Many unidentified specimens are also used as remedies for various ailments. Medicinal plants are utilized frequently without the assistance or knowledge of the herb doctor, known as *matúkami*, who enjoys a certain prestige in the Tepehuan world. However, he is usually consulted when there is serious illness and, always, when the illness is severe enough to warrant the taking of several types of medicinal preparations. Medicines are prepared by the *matúkami* in private. He uses a particular olla which is a small, handled container known as *naakásoli*, a name derived from *naáka* (*oreja*) and *sóli* (a canyon plant, the root of which is scraped and used in preparing a tea taken as a febrifuge).

Respiratory infections are the most dreaded and, indeed, the most prevalent of diseases among the Tepehuan, who make a rather sharp distinction between the treatments used for what is considered to be influenza (*catarro*), pneumonia (*pulmonía*), and the common cold. Contraction of these illnesses is related to exposure, particularly in the cold and damp uplands. *Pulmonía* is held in great fear, and the Indians note that treatment with even their most effective native medicines is rarely helpful in relieving the "tightness" of the chest (that is, the inability to expel phlegm) associated with this illness. *Catarro* is treated with a variety of medicines, and the Indians invariably recover unless they are old and very feeble. Certain medicinal teas are considered efficacious in promoting the coughing up of phlegm associated with *catarro*. The common cold is accepted as something that is inevitable and it is rarely treated. Fever is recognized as a symptom and is commonly associated with both *catarro* and *pulmonía*. The various teas given to reduce the fever are believed to cure most cases of *catarro* eventually, but not *pulmonía*.

Two types of measles (*sarampión*) are recognized and, in fact, appear in epidemic form in both canyons and uplands, often with fatal results for very young people afflicted with the more severe type. Medicinal teas prepared from many plants are given to reduce the fever associated with measles.

A modified form of smallpox (*varioloide*) is reported as an occasional occurrence among the canyon Tepehuan. The true smallpox has not appeared during recent years apparently because of widespread vaccination by government doctors in the early 1920's and because the schoolmaster at Santa Rosa vaccinated or revaccinated many young Indians about twenty-five years ago. *Varioloide* among the canyon Indians is probably the result of contacts between west coast people, who enter the Tepehuan country as traders or visitors, and the Indians. The seemingly high incidence of venereal disease in the western canyons may possibly be explained in the same fashion. The Tepehuan apparently make no distinction between gonorrhea and syphilis regarding the medicinal preparations used as treatments.

A number of canyon Indians to the west, especially those near Santa Rosa, have enlarged masses on the sides or fronts of their necks, but whether these goitrous conditions reflect heredity or an iodine deficiency is not known. An Indian will apply poultices made from various herbs to a newly developed goitre but will abandon treatment as the growth develops.

Numerous plants serve as a base for medicines to relieve the ever-recurring rheumatism and to assist in relieving discomforts associated with menstruation and childbirth.

Western canyons abound in snakes, among which are two species of rattlesnakes and a coral snake that are known to be poisonous. Rattlesnakes are rare in the uplands, but they do appear occasionally in rocky terrain along with the coral snake and the very deadly *maimokami*, a "gray" snake. The Indians rarely open snakebite wounds and depend upon the application of poultices, prepared from a variety of plants, to effect a cure. There seem to be relatively few deaths from rattlesnake bites, and the reason for this is obscure. Certainly, the leg of many an Indian is marked by a scar where infection from the bite of a rattler caused skin and flesh to slough off. The bite of the true coral snake is reported to result in death—always.

Indians living in the canyons apply lotions prepared from certain plants to portions of the body infected by scorpion stings, which in themselves are rarely fatal but are exceedingly painful. Infections (*vipitokori*) or inflammations that result from cuts (*íboidaga*), bruises, or scratches are treated with lotions or poultices, but mostly, with little success.

Toothache is a common complaint among the Indians, and various remedies are applied to relieve this particular discomfort. Of interest is that, on the whole, the Tepehuan do not lose their teeth even in old age; there is no evidence of deliberate attempts to remove diseased teeth.

During the winter season, a predominantly corn diet inevitably results in chronic constipation, and the Indians employ specific plants in preparing purgatives.

The Tepehuan set broken legs and arms, but the results of these efforts are not entirely satisfactory. The arm or leg is encased in poorly fashioned wooden splints for several weeks, and poultices and lotions prepared from certain plants are applied after the splints are removed.

Polypodiaceae. Species of Polypodiaceae are sought by the upland Indians living near Llano Grande for preparing a tea taken by women just prior to and after parturition. *Asplenium monanthes* leaves are steeped in very hot water for about ten minutes; the concoction is then "cooked" for about ten minutes before it is drunk by the woman. Some Tepehuan know this plant as *calaguala* or *áli* (*chiquito*) *úpasai* (*calaguala*); others know it as *negrito* and insist that two different species are involved. However, both plants are *Asplenium monanthes*, the difference between the two being that *negrito*, in its physical characteristics, reflects growth in a shady environment under pines, whereas the *calaguala* reflects growth in a sunny environment. *Asplenium monanthes* tea is also taken to alleviate severe rheumatic pains. The roots of *Dryopteris pilosa*, known among the Tepehuan as *vavíki* (*en la ciénega*) *kokóñi* (*cuervo*) *tara* (*pié* or *pata*), are crushed and decocted into a drink that is believed to be effective in stemming the flow of blood (*írai* or *uradï*) at parturition or in alleviating menstrual pains. A tea prepared by steeping the roots of a *pato de cuervo* (*Pteridium aquilinum* var. *pubescens*) is taken by women during childbirth.

Equisetaceae. Well-watered stream courses in the Tepehuan country are marked by large stands of a *cola de caballo* (*Equisetum laevigatum*), the stems of which are used in preparing a tea taken to relieve stomach (*voóka*) cramps.[26]

Pinaceae. The budding cones of *úkui* (*Pinus arizonica*), a very common pine in the higher uplands, are crushed on a rock and used in preparing a tea taken to reduce fever or to alleviate coughing spells. The fresh stems (*wadï*) of *úbišdali* (*Pinus Engelmanni*), yet another widely distributed pine in the uplands, are cooked and eaten as a cure for influenza (*catarro*).[27] Gum from the *Pinus ayacahuite*, known as *pipíkami* (*muchas espinas*) *úkui* (*pino*), is used as a poultice applied to wounds on the feet. A gum from the bark of *Pinus leiophylla* is valued as a treatment applied to sores of all kinds.

Cupressaceae. A *táscate* (*Juniperus* sp.) that is known as *áli* (*chiquito*) *gáyi* (*táscate*) supplies branches used in preparing a crude sweat bath. The branches are piled in the sleeping quarters of a house and fired. Water is thrown on the burning branches, and a blanket is used to "drive" smoke toward an ill or infirm person, who is then covered with a blanket until he sweats.

Gramineae. Upland Indians cook all portions of a plant called *yerba del paisano* (*Eleusine indica*) in preparing a tea taken to relieve acute stomach distress. Canyon Tepehuan value the roots of *otatillo* (*Mühlenbergia dumosa*), or *áli* (*chiquito*) *tótoikami* (*carrizo* or *garrocha*), for its use in preparing a tea taken to relieve stomach cramps.

Commelinaceae. The seeds of *yerba de la borrego* (*Commelina erecta*) and a species of *Tradescantia* are placed under badly swollen eyelids.

Liliaceae. Seeds of the *óyi*, or *palma de San Pedro* (*Yucca decipiens*), are mashed, added to warm water, and drunk as a purgative. A medicinal tea prepared by boiling a plant called *zacate de burro* (*Hypoxis hirsuta*) is taken for stomach disorders.

Amaryllidaceae. Fresh leaves of a *funcus* (*Amaryllis* sp.) are crushed and placed on the forehead (*kóva*) to relieve headache; the leaves are held in place with a pliable branch or a strip of cloth. The handsome yellow flowers of *sabila* (*Agave bovicornuta*), that grows abundantly on canyon slopes, are crushed and added to sap extracted from the crushed leaves of this plant for application as a poultice to sores on animals afflicted by worms. Sap from the leaves of *sabila* is also used for alleviating toothache by being placed on the cheek and held there by a rag for a few minutes.

Orchidaceae. The stems of a *Malaxis* species are used in preparing a very strong tea that is taken to alleviate stomach cramps caused by overindulgence in eating.

Salicaceae. White bark from an *alamillo* (*Populus tremuloides*) is used in a tea taken by women to alleviate menstrual pains, to stimulate parturition, or as a tonic immediately after parturition.

Fagaceae. The bark from a mature oak, *popuišoli* (*Quercus Endlichiana*), a common tree almost everywhere in the uplands and on higher canyon slopes, is boiled to make a refreshing mouthwash. Scrapings from the bark of another oak, *túái* (*Quercus crassifolia*), are much esteemed as a poultice for aching gums; the scrapings are held between the outer gum and the cheek for about thirty minutes.

Loranthaceae. *Struthanthus diversifolius* is a parasitic plant that appears in abundance on oaks of the middle canyon slopes near Santa Rosa. Mestizos know this plant as *toji* or *muérdago*, whereas the Tepehuan refer to it as *bulíka-dali* (*ammarar*); its leaves are much used in preparing a tea taken by women experiencing difficulties at childbirth.

Chenopodiaceae. *Ipasote*, or *patúsai*, is a variety of *Chenopodium ambrosioides* that appears in thick growths along the margins of well-watered arroyos in canyons, in areas of good soil along canyon streamways, and occasionally in warmer arroyos of the uplands. The Tepehuan use the leaves of this chenopod in a tea taken by women to facilitate parturition. It is also taken by anyone afflicted with intestinal worms.

Amaranthaceae. A tea for the relief of stomach disorders is prepared from the leaves of a *tiánguis*, or *kijoso* (*Alternanthera repens*). The roots are crushed and decocted into a drink taken to reduce fever.

Nyctaginaceae. The Tepehuan who live near Santa Rosa value the *saranda* (*Boerhaavia mirabilis*) as a source of leaves used in preparing a very strong tea taken as a febrifuge.

Caryophyllaceae. Leaves of a *yerba de la víbora de la sierra* (*Stellaria* sp.) are crushed and steeped in a decoction taken to induce sweating. A plant called *ancillo* (*Silene* sp.) is boiled in preparing a drink taken to stimulate the passage of urine.

Ranunculaceae. A strong tea prepared by boiling the leaves and stems of a *paloma consulta* (*Thalictrum Fendleri*), a plant that grows abundantly in pine-clad uplands near Baborigame, is taken to relieve stomach cramps or as a febrifuge. Canyon Indians seek this plant in the uplands for use in preparing a lotion that is said to be valuable in reducing fever. The patient is bathed repeatedly with this lotion. Upland Indians favor a *taatámu* (*diente* or *muela*) *doadígami* (*remedio*), a species of *Ranunculus*, as a source of roots which are mashed on the metate and placed on aching gums. Stems of a *yerba de la muela* (*Ranunculus Forreri*) are used in curing toothaches by pushing the tiny stems into caries.

Magnoliaceae. Flowers from a handsome magnolia tree (*Magnolia Schiedeana*) that frequently grows along well-watered arroyos on middle canyon slopes are used in preparing a tea taken to alleviate stomach pains.

Lauraceae. The aguacate (*Persea americana*) is cultivated to some extent by sophisticated Tepehuan in the canyons, but for the most part, this tree appears in the wild state. Mestizos know the aguacate as *laurelillo*, whereas the Tepehuan invariably refer to it as *gúruduši*. Seeds of the immature fruits are crushed and used in preparing a medicinal tea taken to alleviate diarrhea. The seeds are also used in preparing a poultice which is placed between the cheek and aching gums for about ten minutes; it is also applied to a goitre. To make the poultice, the seeds are crushed on the metate and mixed with *manteca* (*giígi*). Pulp from the immature fruits is mashed and applied to wounds or inflammations.

Papaveraceae. The mestizos and Tepehuan living in canyons near Llano

Grande know a prickly poppy (*Argemone ochroleuca* subsp. *ochroleuca*) as *cardo*; this plant grows in profusion in sandy stretches along streams. A milky excrescence from the stalk serves as a lotion for killing fleas (*tatápiši*) or lice (*átïï* or *ivapatï*) on humans and animals. The seeds are crushed, added to warm water, and taken as a purgative. Leaves of a *palo del diablo* (*Bocconia arborea*), common to canyons near Llano Grande, are moistened and crushed for use as a poultice on sores, wounds, and goitres; the crushed leaves are also held against the forehead to relieve headache. Scrapings from the bark of this tree are used in a tea taken to relieve stomach upsets. The scrapings may also be used as a poultice for styes. A field poppy (*Papaver Rhoeas*), which is undoubtedly an introduction from Eurasia,[28] appears in cultivated fields near Santa Rosa and supplies flowers that are boiled to make a tea given to quiet fever-stricken people.

Cruciferae. The Tepehuan living near Llano Grande use seeds of the cultivated *mostaza* (*Brassica campestris*), another introduction from Eurasia,[29] in preparing a tea taken as a febrifuge. Seeds of a common peppergrass (*Lepidium virginicum*) that grows profusely in fields near Santa Rosa are used in preparing an atole given to very ill people. Some Indians note that a tea made from stems of this *lentajilla* is valuable as a febrifuge. A common watercress (*Nasturtium officinale*), presumably an introduction from Europe,[30] is known among mestizos as *berro* and among Indians as *mura* (*mula*) *súúsaka* (*herradura*) and is used in the preparation of a medicinal tea taken for influenza.

Crassulaceae. A *siempreviva* (*Echeveria simulans*), known everywhere among the Indians as *áli* (*chiquito*) *mái* (*mescalito*) because its small waxy leaves resemble those of a tiny mescal plant, is crushed, heated, and used as a poultice for goitres and inflammations.

Hydrangeaceae. *Hydrangea Oerstedii*, a rather common shrub that grows in canyons throughout the Tepehuan country, is known by the mestizos as *yedra grande* or *yedra del monte* and by the Indians as *tumámara*; although its leaves are reported to be very poisonous when eaten by stock, a tea made by steeping the leaves is taken to relieve severe cases of *catarro*. The flowers and leaves of another species of *Hydrangea*, known as *yedra de la sierra* or as *tumámara*, are used in a tea taken for kidney disorders and as a purgative.

Rosaceae. The mestizos living near Llano Grande and Lagotera know *Potentilla Thurberi* as *clameria* or *yerba colorada*, whereas the Indians know the plant as *taatámu* (*diente* or *muela*) *šišimuli* (*á dormir*). The interior portion of the roots is crushed and placed between the cheek (*kaáma*) and aching gums, or the entire plant is crushed and used in a tea taken to relieve intestinal disorders. Leaves of *fresa*, or *ibíši* (*Potentilla* sp. af. *exsul*),[31] are used in a tea taken as a febrifuge. Another species of *Potentilla* is used in preparing a lotion applied to snakebites. Leaves of the widely distributed *capulín pequeña*, or *túkuši* (*Prunus capuli*), are crushed and placed on scratches, stings, or inflammations.

Leguminosae. Santa Rosa Tepehuan esteem a *vinola* (*Acacia cochliacantha*), commonly known as *šúšigai* (*dolor*) *doadígami* (*remedio*), as a source for leaves that are used in a tea taken to relieve chest pains or when urinating is difficult. Occasionally, crushed leaves of a *lecheguilla de la sierra* (*Senecio* sp.) are added to make this tea more effective. Santa Rosa Tepehuan favor the bark (*kómi*) from an *algarroba* (*Acacia pennatula*) in preparing a decoction taken to ease discomfort caused by venereal disease; bark from the side of the tree upon which the sun rises is preferred. *Cassia leptadenia* is a plant that grows in profusion among stands of oak in the vicinity of Santa Rosa, and a medicinal tea taken as a febrifuge is prepared by boiling the entire plant for a few minutes. Santa Rosa Tepehuan use the leaves of a *yerba de la pulga* (*Dalea* sp.) in preparing a poultice to counteract fleas on humans. A handsome flowering legume (*Erythrina flabelliformis*) appears in conspicuous growths on rocky canyon slopes almost everywhere in the Tepehuan habitat. It is known as *colorín* or *chilicote*, and its seeds are used—in very small amounts however—in preparing a purgative. *Lathyrus vernus*, a vetchling which is an introduction from Europe,[32] is known among Indians as *mišitu* (*gato*) *naáka* (*oreja*) and among mestizos as *oreja del gato*. The entire plant is crushed and applied as a poultice to infected areas or to wounds. The widely distributed *Lysiloma Watsoni*, known as *tepeguaje* or *gïdo* (*grande*) *sákoi* (*tepeguaje*), is a favored source for bark that is used in preparing a wash applied to sore gums; water in which scrapings of the bark have been boiled is cooled and then held in the mouth for a few minutes. A sweet-smelling *trébol* (*Melilotus indica*), presumably an introduction from Europe,[33] is found along canyon streams everywhere. This plant is frequently used in preparing a tea taken as a febrifuge, and its leaves are often used as a remedy for headache. The leaves are dampened and held on the forehead for a short time. *Psoralea pentaphylla* is known by upland and canyon Indians as *contra yerba*, and its leaves are much used for making a tea taken for the relief of a fever. Another *contra yerba* (*Psoralea* sp.), apparently restricted to the upland environment, is similarly used. *Ojo de chanate* (*Rhynchosia pyramidalis*) is known among the Indians as *áraiši* (*chanate*) *vuvúji* (*ojos*); its black and white seeds are crushed upon a metate, added to water, and drunk to alleviate internal injuries resulting from falls. The seeds and roots are also crushed, moistened, and used as a poultice to cure inflammations. A *yerba del piojo* (*Tephrosia nicaraguensis*) is much utilized by the upland Indians in a lotion for animals and humans afflicted with fleas; it is prepared by soaking the plant for a short time. The leaves of *Tephrosia Thurberi* and a species of *Brongniartia* are similarly used. A *yerba de la víbora* (*Zornia diphylla*), or *kói* (*víbora*) *vasógadï* (*yerba*), is esteemed by Llano Grande Tepehuan because the entire plant is believed to be valuable for making a tea taken to relieve pains caused by the grippe. A medicinal tea prepared by boiling the leaves and stems of *Cologania angustifolia* is taken for a fever. An acid stomach is relieved by a tea steeped from the flowers of *Lupinus Havardii*. All of a *Desmodium* species plant is used in preparing a decoction taken to reduce fever.

Oxalidaceae. A tiny wood sorrel (*Oxalis albicans*), called *socoyole* by the mestizos and *áli* (*chiquito*) *íko* (*agrio*) by the Indians, is boiled to make a tea that is drunk as a febrifuge. A tea prepared from the crushed *socoyole morado* (*Oxalis sordida*) is taken after an extended period of drinking *tesgüino*. The leaves of *Oxalis Dillenii* (*íkuli*)[34] are crushed and rubbed on aching or swollen gums. Another species of *Oxalis* is utilized in a tea taken for upset stomach.

Polygalaceae. The entire plant of a *Polygala* species is boiled in preparing a tea taken for stomach disorders. Upland Indians crush all of a *yerba del piojo* (*Monnina* sp.) for a poultice designed to remove fleas from humans or animals.

Euphorbiaceae. A *yerba de la golondrina* (*Euphorbia maculata*) is esteemed by canyon Tepehuan because of its value in preparing a lotion for aching feet and for cleansing sores, wounds, and inflammations. The whole of this plant is boiled in an olla of water for ten or fifteen minutes; the water is then set aside to cool before being used. A tea prepared from another *yerba de la golondrina* (*Euphorbia trichocardia*) is taken for colic, and an excretion from the leaves of this plant is used as a poultice for festering wounds. *Hura crepitans*, the *bokuripi* or *tescalama* of the canyons, supplies a gum much used for preparing a poultice to relieve pains from internal injuries or from stings; it is also applied to a budding goitre. The gum is further used in preparing a purgative—in small amounts however. A bit of the gum is added to warm water and taken immediately. Upland Indians collect a *contra yerba* (*Poinsettia radicans*) for use in making a tea taken as a febrifuge. The castor bean (*Ricinus communis*), an introduced plant,[35] appears conspicuously along the streams of deeper canyons in the western Tepehuan country. The upland Indians gather the leaves of this *higuerilla*, or *mukúkuli*, for use as a poultice for goitres and inflammations. The canyon Indians not only utilize the leaves in a similar fashion but, in addition, crush the seeds for use as a purgative. An *ortiguilla*, or *vijuli* (*Tragia nepetaefolia*), is esteemed for its usefulness in preparing a lotion which is applied to the body of a person suffering from fever; the lotion presumably induces sweating.

Rhamnaceae. Canyon Tepehuan utilize the bark of a *cacachile* (*Karwinskia Humboldtiana*) in making a tea taken to reduce fever; the bark is boiled in about a quart of water for several hours, and the tea is taken hot or cold.

Vitaceae. Throughout the Tepehuan country, the leaves of *uva cimar-*

róna (*Vitis arizonica* and *V. rupestris*), or *bakámai* (*troje*) *bišáparagai* (*envolver*), are used in preparing a poultice for deep scratches.

Malvaceae. A malva (*Malva rotundifolia*), which is apparently an introduction from Europe,[36] grows copiously in fields near Santa Rosa. The entire plant is used in preparing a febrifuge. Upland Tepehuan utilize *Malvaviscus aboreus* in a similar fashion. Yet another malva (*Sida cordifolia*), that grows in profusion along the borders of cultivated fields near Santa Rosa, is valued for its use in a strong tea taken as a purgative.

Sterculiaceae. Santa Rosa Tepehuan boil the bark of a *guásima* (*Guazuma ulmifolia*) in preparing a drink taken to relieve shortness of breath. *Yerba del pasmo* (*Waltheria americana*?) is a common plant along water courses near Santa Rosa; the whole of this plant is boiled in an olla of water for about an hour, and after being cooled, the water serves as a lotion that is used on wounds or inflammations.

Fouquieriaceae. The mestizos who live in the canyons know *Fouquieria fasciculata*(?) as *torote* or *ocotillo*, whereas the Indians refer to this shrub as *tarákovara*. Seeds of the plant are much esteemed because of their usefulness in preparing a poultice for aching gums that is placed between the cheek and gums. The flowers are eaten to cure throat disorders.

Onagraceae. A large-flowered variety of *Oenothera rosea* is known by the mestizos as *amapola* or *yerba del golpe* and by the Tepehuan as *bitúši* (*amapola*) *úlidï* (*abuelo*).[37] The entire plant is used for preparing a tea taken to relieve stomach upsets or to reduce fever. A medicinal tea prepared from *Epilobium glandulosum* is also taken to reduce fever.

Umbelliferae. Canyon Tepehuan utilize the leaves of a *yerba del sapo* (*Eryngium Hemsleyanum*), or *babádai* (*sapo*) *vasógadï* (*yerba*), in a tea taken to alleviate stomach pains. The tiny *Eryngium Rosei*, or *kokoida* (*espíritu*) *šivoradï* (*desilachado*), is much sought for preparing a tea taken to relieve heart palpatations. The flowers of *Eryngium humile* are thought to be efficacious for colic when cooked and eaten. The seeds and stems of *Eryngium yuccaefolium* are also cooked and eaten to alleviate colic. A species of *Conium* called *yerba del oso* is sought because its seeds are valued as an ingredient in a violent cathartic preparation.

Pyrolaceae. Upland Indians collect an *encinilla* (*Chimaphila maculata*) for use in a medicine taken for liver disorders; the entire plant is cooked and the potion is set aside for a night. It is always taken immediately upon arising in the morning.

Ericaceae. A *manzanilla* (*Arctostaphylos pungens*) grows profusely in eastern and southeastern Tepehuan country, but only sparsely in the vicinity of Nabogame and Baborigame, and very rarely in the western canyons. However, the leaves of this plant are widely traded throughout the Indian country as they are much esteemed for preparing a tea taken to relieve discomfort resulting from colds. The tea is also claimed to be a stimulating beverage.

Primulaceae. The scarlet pimpernel (*Anagallis arvensis*), presumably an introduction from Europe,[38] grows in profusion in plowed fields near Santa Rosa and is valued because of its use in the preparation of a tea taken for the relief of *catarro*.

Loganiaceae. A butterfly bush (*Buddleia sessiliflora*), known as *teposán*, is much esteemed because its leaves and bark are believed to be of value in making a tea taken by women to alleviate menstrual pains. The Tepehuan who live near Llano Grande use the leaves, bark, and roots in preparing a decoction taken to relieve stomach disorders. The crushed and moistened leaves are used as a poultice for wounds. The *palo cenizo* (*Buddleia tomentella*), common throughout much of the Tepehuan country and known among the Indians as *koomági* (*gris*) *úši* (*palo* or *árbol*), supplies leaves used in making a tea taken to relieve discomfort caused by diarrhea.

Apocynaceae. The leaves and stems of *San Juanito* (*Macrosiphonia* sp.) are boiled to make a drink taken to alleviate stomach disorders. Latex from a *verako* (*Stemmadenia Palmeri*) serves as a lotion that is applied to warts and ringworm.

Asclepiadaceae. The Indians living near Santa Rosa know *Asclepias hypoleuca*, a rather widely distributed milkweed, as *suímali* (*venado*) *nanáaka* (*orejas*); the entire plant is used in preparing a weak tea taken to relieve discomfort from overeating. A very strong tea prepared by soaking the leaves in cold water for about twenty-four hours serves as a purgative. Another milkweed, *Asclepias Linaria*, known as *áli* (*chiquito*) *okága* (*se paracen a las hojas de los pinos*), appears in great numbers in the poor and rocky soils of the higher pine-clad country, particularly between Llano Grande and Baborigame. The plant is very poisonous according to all reports, but a few of its leaves are utilized in preparing a tea taken to induce vomiting when someone is afflicted with severe stomach cramps. Greater amounts of the leaves are used in a very strong purgative. Some Tepehuan note that the crushed leaves are effective when used as a poultice for headache; the leaves are placed on the temples and held there by a cloth band. The leaves and stems of an *oreja del venado* (*Asclepias atropurpurea*) are crushed and used as a poultice applied to an aching back. A *contra yerba de la sierra* (*Asclepias* sp. af. *quinquedentata*) serves in preparing a febrifuge. A medicinal tea made from an *inmortal* (*Asclepias* sp.) is taken to alleviate throat discomforts attendant upon the common cold. The dried roots are sniffed to help clear nasal passages.

Polemoniaceae. The upland Tepehuan living near Baborigame prepare a favorite febrifuge from the leaves of a *yerba del coyote* (*Leptodactylon* sp.). A very strong tea taken to alleviate chest pains or to arrest fever is made by both canyon and upland Indians from the leaves of a *guachichile* (*Loeselia* sp.). The fresh leaves of this *totósadamali* are often moistened with hot water and placed on the back of a woman who has difficulty in providing milk for her infant.

Boraginaceae. A tea made from the leaves of *Lithospermum incisum* is taken to reduce fever and to alleviate stomach upsets.

Verbenaceae. Canyon Tepehuan gather the leaves of a common verbena (*Verbena ciliata*) for use in preparing a weak tea taken as a febrifuge. The Indians everywhere prepare a tea from another verbena (*Verbena elegans* var. *asperata*), or *alfombrillo* as it is sometimes called, as a remedy for stomach disorders and *catarro*. Lowland Indians use a poultice made from the crushed leaves of *Verbena elegans* as a certain cure for cuts that will not heal. This species is also crushed, salted, and eaten to relieve severe stomach cramps.

Labiatae. *Mentha canadensis* is a wild mint that grows conspicuously along upland streams. The plant is known everywhere as *poléo*, and a tea prepared from its crushed leaves is taken to alleviate stomach cramps. The leaves of *acete mexicana* (*Mentha rotundifolia*) are used in preparing a tea taken for headache; they are also placed within the ear for earache. A lotion applied to sore and bleeding gums is prepared from a *yerba de la muela* (*Prunella vulgaris*), an introduced Eurasian plant.[39] Flowers and leaves of a *moradilla* (*Salvia azurea*) are used in making a tea taken to alleviate stomach disorders. Another tea taken to reduce fever is prepared from a *salvia del monte* (*Salvia* sp.).

Solanaceae. The common Jimson weed is known among the mestizos as *tolache* (*Datura stramonium*) and among the Tepehuan as *tokórakai*; its leaves are much esteemed for use in preparing a poultice applied to the forehead to relieve headache. The leaves are also heated and placed on inflammations. Older Indians maintain that, not long ago, its leaves were used in preparing a decoction taken to relieve diarrhea. A warm-country *saca manteca* (*Solanum madrense*) is much used in preparing a poultice applied to inflammations. The leaves of this plant are also utilized in making a lotion applied to scorpion bites. *Solanum nigrum*, presumably of European origin,[40] is known generally as *chichiquelite*; its leaves are used in the spring of the year for brewing a strong tea taken by anyone suffering from intestinal worms. A lotion made by soaking the leaves is applied to worm sores on animals or humans. Another *chichiquelite* (*Solanum podiflorum*) is similarly used. The Tepehuan who live in and near the Arroyo de Milpillas frequently collect the leaves of a species of *Solanum* that is considered to be extremely effective in curing toothache; the fresh leaves are crushed and placed between the cheek and gum. A tea prepared from this plant serves as a febrifuge.

Scrophulariaceae. Both mestizos and Tepehuan know a species of *Castilleja* as *chupón* and frequently collect the plant for use in a tea taken to stimulate urination. Branches of *Castilleja indivisa* are crushed and used as a poultice on festering wounds. All of this plant may be used in preparing a tea that serves as a violent purgative. A tea made from the stems and leaves of *Pentstemon barbatus* is drunk for severe stomach cramps. *Mimulus guttatus* is a common plant in the Tepehuan country, growing in shallow water and in damp meadows; it is known as *berro* or *suudági (agua) mamaradï (crece en el agua)*. A tea prepared by boiling the entire plant in a small amount of water for a few minutes is an esteemed febrifuge.

Plantaginaceae. The Tepehuan who live immediately west of Chinatú collect the roots of a *lantén* (*Plantago* sp.), commonly known as *šiñakali*, for use in a favorite remedy for fever; the roots are crushed on a metate and boiled in a small amount of water for about ten minutes. The water is then strained through a basket and drunk while warm. Another *lantén* (*Plantago* sp.) is utilized in preparing a potion taken to relieve stomach cramps.

Rubiaceae. *Coutarea pterosperma*, a rather common *copalquín* in western canyons, is known among the Tepehuan as *čivúkali*;[41] its bark is valued because of its use in a tea for reducing fever and for the relief of influenza as well. The tea serves also as a lotion for cleansing wounds resulting from snakebites. Upland Tepehuan seek a *yerba del coyote* (*Galium aparine*) for preparing a lotion applied to aching limbs. A tea made from the *yerba del coyote de la barranca* (*Galium triflorum*) is taken for colic, and it also serves as a lotion for aching limbs. Another *Galium* species supplies leaves for preparing a tea taken to relieve stomach disorders. A tea made from the entire plant of a *Hedyotis* species is taken to relieve dysentery.

Caprifoliaceae. *Saúco* (*Sambucus caerulea*) is a small tree distinguished by very handsome yellow flowers that are much used in preparing a tea taken as a febrifuge; the tea is also believed to cure "heart trouble." The crushed, young leaves are utilized in a poultice for cuts. The flowers of another *saúco* (*Sambucus canadensis*) are made into a tea for the relief of severe coughing. A tea prepared by using the entire plant of a *Lonicera* species is taken for stomach disorders.

Lobeliaceae. *Guadalupe* (*Lobelia laxiflora*) is a common arroyo plant in the uplands; its leaves are collected and placed between the cheek and gum to relieve toothache.

Compositae. *Artemisia mexicana*, known simply as *alcanfor*, appears in relatively open areas amidst the pine forests of the uplands. The entire plant is utilized in a tea taken to ease discomfort caused by colds. Upland Tepehuan make much use of a *yerba del pasmo* (*Aster intricatus*) in preparing a poultice for bruises and wounds. An *estafiate* (*Artemisia dracunculoides*) is used in preparing a tea taken to relieve colic pains. A tea made from the leaves of a *manzanilla del Castilla* (*Astranthium mexicanum*) is taken by women at childbirth. A *coronilla* (*Berlandiera* sp.) is widely utilized by the Tepehuan living near Baborigame in preparing a decoction taken to relieve stomach disorders; its roots are crushed and boiled in a small amount of water for about fifteen minutes. A common upland meadow plant, *Bidens ferulaefolia*(?), known everywhere as *té*, is favored because of its value in preparing a tea taken to relieve stomach cramps. Roots of a *bavisa* (*Bidens aquatica*) are mashed and made into a tea taken for stomach disorders. The whole of an upland *yerba del pasmo de la sierra* (*Brickellia laciniata*) is crushed on a stone and used as a poultice to reduce swelling.

Roots of a *Cacalia* species are crushed and used in preparing a tea taken for rheumatism. *Chromolepis heterophylla* is a small arroyo plant known as *íkuli* (*peyotl*) *vópoi* (*lana*). The root of this plant is characterized by small "buttons" that resemble a peyote plant; they are used in preparing a poultice applied to a child's navel when his umbilical cord (*ikodi*) is cut. The Tepehuan who live westward of Chinatú esteem a *šiñáka* (*Cirsium mexicanum*), the roots of which are crushed and boiled for a short time to prepare a drink taken to reduce fever or to relieve chest pains. All portions of a *yerba de la Juanita* (*Erigeron* sp.) are used in the preparation of a decoction taken to relieve headache.

Franseria acanthicarpa, common to uplands and canyons, is known as *estafiate* among the mestizos and as *tuavuši* among the Tepehuan. A tea made from the leaves is taken to relieve stomach upsets. The leaves are also crushed and applied as a poultice to inflammations. The entire plant is sometimes heated near the fire and is then sat upon by a person suffering from diarrhea. Women who are experiencing difficulty in parturition drink a tea made from the leaves of *chícura* or *čikuli* (*Franseria* sp.),[42] a widely distributed shrub in the canyons near Santa Rosa. Tea made from the leaves of an *acetilla* (*Galinsoga ciliata*) is taken to relieve severe stomach cramps. For their value in preparing a tea taken to relieve heart pains as well as coughing spells, the upland Tepehuan favor the leaves of a *manzanilla del río*, or *gordolobo* (*Gnaphalium Macounii*), which is also known by its Indian name, *avo* (*liviano*) *yoošígai* (*flor*). Canyon Tepehuan utilize the leaves of another *manzanilla del río* (*Gnaphalium* sp.) in preparing a decoction to relieve stomach disorders or dysentery.

A tiny herb, *Hieracium Fendleri*, known either as *oreja del gato* or as *míšitu* (*gato*) *naáka* (*oreja*), is crushed and used as a poultice applied to infected areas and wounds. Leaves of a *manzanilla bollona* (*Hieracium* sp.) are used in a tea taken to relieve headache or stomach disorders. The crushed leaves of yet another *Hieracium* species are applied as a poultice to wounds.

The flowers of a *clavel* (*Pinaropappus roseus*) are used in the preparation of a tea taken to relieve headache. The upland Tepehuan who live near Baborigame brew a medicinal tea taken as a heart stimulant from the leaves of a *lecheguilla* (*Senecio* sp. af. *actinella*). All parts of a *manzanilla de la piedra* (*Senecio* sp.) are boiled to make a tea taken to relieve kidney discomfort. A lotion prepared from another *Senecio* species is used to bathe sick persons. The stems and leaves of a *Silphium* species are crushed and applied as a poultice on wounds or bruises. The Indians living near Llano Grande know *Stevia stenophylla* as *yerba de la virgen* or as *hïvai* (*hielo*) *vasógadï* (*yerba*), and they use the plant in a poultice that is applied to broken bones. A tea taken to relieve stomach disorders is made by Santa Rosa Tepehuan from the entire plant of *Tagetes jaliscana*, a small herb that grows in conspicuous numbers on canyon slopes.

A *yerba del aire* (*Trixis* sp. af. *radialis*) is known among the Tepehuan as *ïvïli* (*aire*) *yoošígai* (*flor*); its roots are used in preparing a poultice for broken bones, and its crushed flowers are placed in the ear to alleviate earache. *Zexmenia podocephala* is known either as *peonía* or as *gogóši* (*perro*) *vïïtai* (*excremento*) because the bulbous roots resemble dog dung. Although the roots are claimed to be poisonous when used—even in small amounts—Indians who live near Llano Grande crush and add them to warm water to be taken as a purgative.

Usneaceae. The upland Tepehuan know a common lichen (*Parmelia reticulata*) as *ódai* (*piedra*) *yoošígai* (*flor*); the mestizos know it as *flor de piedra*. Both Indians and mestizos utilize the lichen in preparing a tea taken to relieve discomfort from kidney disorders or venereal disease. The tea is commonly prepared in the late afternoon and is set aside for one night before being drunk.

Unidentified Specimens. Canyon Tepehuan prepare a medicinal tea taken as a stimulant from the stems and leaves of an *alióvali*. The stems of a lowland cane known as *carricillo* or *áli* (*chiquito*) *tótoikami* (*carrizo* or *garrocha*) are used in a tea to be taken by women at childbirth. Upland Indians prepare a tea taken to reduce fever from *chupón*, a tiny arroyo herb. A lotion applied to snakebites is prepared from a small herb called *doadígami* (*remedio*). Baborigame and Nabogame Tepehuan esteem the roots of an *esconcionera* because of their usefulness in making a strong tea taken to relieve stomach cramps. A medicinal tea taken for fever is prepared from *espadaña* (*maka*), a rather common grass that appears in upland meadows. Yet another tea taken by the upland Indians is brewed from a small plant known as *guachichile* or *totósadamali* (*espumosa*). A poultice for cuts and bruises is prepared from the whole of a plant called *íboidaga* (*llaga*) *doadígami* (*remedio*). The Indians living near Santa Rosa collect leaves from a *jarilla del río* for use in preparing a mixture given to cows that cannot calve; the leaves are cooked for a short time and then thrust down the throat of the animal. *Junco* is a small cactus found near Llano Grande; a tea made by boiling its stalk is taken to relieve stomach cramps. Near Llano Grande, a tea made from a *manzanilla bollona* is taken as a certain cure for diarrhea.

A favorite poultice for the relief of a headache is prepared from crushed and dampened leaves of *modï* (*cabeza*) *doadígami* (*remedio*). Lowland Indians use the white flowers of a *moigai* (*purgación*) *doadígami* (*remedio*) in preparing a tea taken to cure venereal disease. The flowers of a *moradilla*, or *arátupi* (*empacho*) *doadígami* (*remedio*), are crushed in water and then eaten to relieve the pain caused by stomach disorders. Roots of an *ógina*, or *ípušuli*, are gathered by Arroyo de Milpillas Tepehaun for use in a poultice for wounds and aching arms or legs; the roots are mashed on a metate and moistened before being used. Baborigame Tepehuan collect leaves from an *oreja del gato* for use in preparing a poultice for wounds and inflammations.

The roots of *palo baboso*, or *arámakïdï* (*baboso*) *úši* (*palo* or *árbol*), are crushed and added to water given to persons suffering from a high fever. A tea made from the leaves of a pungent *poléo* is esteemed as a remedy for *catarro* among the upland Indians. Another one, *poléo del monte*, is used for brewing a very strong tea taken to relieve coughing spells. Baborigame and Nabogame Tepehuan use the leaves of a *saranda* in making a weak tea taken as a febrifuge. The roots of a tiny plant called *sóli* are crushed and sniffed by a patient suffering from a cold or a high fever. This root is also used in preparing a tea taken to reduce fever. Llano Grande Tepehuan search diligently for a yellow-flowered herb called *yerba del piojo de los puercos*, a plant considered very efficacious in removing fleas from animals or humans if it is crushed and applied as a poultice. Everywhere, the Tepehuan utilize a *zacate de burro*, or *ašnitu* (*burro*) *vasogadï* (*yerba*), in preparing a tea taken for the relief of stomach upsets.

It is impossible to determine just how long the northern Tepehuan have made such an extensive utilization of plant material to be found within their environment in the preparation of medicines. Of the 157 positive identifications, nine specimens are clearly of European introduction and, therefore, were probably not used during the very early colonial period. But certainly, medicinal potions prepared from plants are an integral part of present-day Chihuahua Tepehuan culture, and this fact points to, or at least suggests, a long-time interest in the utilization of plants for medicinal purposes.

The eighteenth-century Tepehuan used a term which meant, according to Rinaldini, "to cure illness" (*enfermedad remediar*).[43] The term was *doadide*, or *doadiante*, and both terms are clearly related to the present term, *doadígami* (*remedio*), used by the Chihuahua Tepehuan in reference to medicinal preparations. Rinaldini also recorded a term for *curandero*: *mamatukami*,[44] which is certainly related to the present-day term *matúkami*, the name for the herb doctor. Apparently, the earliest specific reference to medicinal plants utilized by the Chihuahua Tepehuan is in a Franciscan account of 1777. It was stated that the Nabogame Tepehuan used various plants or their roots, such as the *chuchupasto*, *bavisa*, *inmortal*, *escorcionera*, and *pasmo*, in the preparation of medicines.[45]

A possible clue to dating the extensive development of medicinal plant use among the Tepehuan may be found in the plant names used by the Indians. Many of the plants are known by the common names used by mestizos or by terms that are literal translations of the mestizo terms into Tepehuan. This phenomenon may indicate that the Indians learned of the use of certain plants only rather recently; but on the other hand, it may indicate only that the Indians have become so integrated with the mestizo complex that the older Indian terms have been abandoned.

CHAPTER 7 NOTES

1— Perdue (1958), 370.

2— Mason (1952), 45.

3— 1645: Pérez de Ribas (1944), III, 190.

4— 1743: Rinaldini (1743), 62.

5— Lumholtz (1902), I, 431.

6— The Indians present no rational explanation for the use of the term *šivátu* (*cabra*) *uši* (*palo* or *árbol*) to designate two such different trees, *Garrya ovata* and *Ipomoea arborescens*.

7— Lumholtz (1902), I, 431.

8— 1743: Rinaldini (1743), 130. It should be noted that *sonajas* may be translated as "timbrels" and that *sonajero* is perhaps the more correct Spanish term for "rattle." However, the present-day northern Tepehuan use the term *sonaja* to designate their gourd rattle, and one of their Indian terms for rattles, *sásamuidakaroi*, is not unlike Rinaldini's *sommoidajare*.

9— 1595: Carta Anua.

10— Mason [(1952), 48] states that ball races are held only three times a year, one of the times at Easter. This is, I believe, an incorrect statement.

11— Lumholtz (1902), I, 362.

12— See also Mason [(1952), 49] on this point.

13— Mason [(1953), 46] states that the Tepehuan make no use of peyote at present. This may be true of some Tepehuan near Baborigame, but it is not correct for most of the Indians. Moreover, there seems to be a long history of its use by the Tepehuan. Arlegui, writing in the eighteenth century concerning Indians and customs within territory occupied by Franciscans, referred to *peyotl* as the "root" venerated most by the Indians. It was used in the preparation of a medicinal compound and was taken with water before battle [1737: Arlegui (1851), 154]. Although this reference to the use of peyote does not apply to the Tepehuan of Chihuahua (the Franciscans did not appear in the upland Chihuahua missions until after expulsion of the Jesuits from Mexico in the 1760's), the comment is valid. Franciscans labored among the Tepehuan of central Durango before Jesuits arrived in that area in the late sixteenth century [Dunne (1944), 16-18].

14— Could these leaves be from the *Calliandra humilis* var. *reticulata* which are chewed by cheaters in the Tarahumar kickball race [Pennington (1963)b, 170-71]?

15— Mason (1952), 49.

16— 1743: Rinaldini (1743), 11, 33, 77.

17— For a discussion of this problem see Pennington [(1963)b, 172-73].

18— 1743: Rinaldini (1743), 76-77.

19— Mason (1952), 49.

20— 1743: Rinaldini (1743), 77.

21— Culin (1907), 153-54.

22— Here, *jolíši* refers to small stones, but the term also means testicles.

23— 1743: Rinaldini (1743), 76.

24— Mason (1952), 45.

25— 1743: Rinaldini (1743), 76-77.

26— Pammel [(1911), 323-25] notes that several species of *Equisetum* are poisonous when eaten by animals, and Muenscher [(1947), 24-26] specifically notes that *E. laevigatum* contains poisonous properties.

27— Professor N. T. Mirov of the University of California informs me that these stems are an excellent source of vitamin C.

28— Gray (1950), 681.

29— Ibid., 708.

30— Ibid., 716.

31— Not to be confused with another *ibíši* which is *Fragaria vesca*.

32— Darlington and Janaki Ammal (1945), 159.

33— Gray (1950), 895.

34— *Oxalis Dillenii* is not to be confused with the peyote plant (*Lophophora Williamsii*) which is also known as *íkuli*.

35— Willis (1931), 568.

36— Gray (1950), 1001.

37— The Indians do not confuse this "grand-father" of the *amapola* with *bitúši*, a small-flowered variety of *Oenothera rosea* that serves as a condiment and as a *quelite*.

38— Gray (1950), 1142-43.

39— Ibid., 1225.

40— Ibid., 1253.

41— Not to be confused with another *čivú-kali* (*Phytolacca icosandra*), the leaves of which serve as a *quelite*, the roots as a source of saponin.

42— Not to be confused with another *chícura*, or *čikuli*, which is a *cebollín silvestre* that grows in the meadows at Baborigame.

43— 1743: Rinaldini (1743), 120.

44— Ibid., 46.

45— 1777: Relación de Nabogame.

8
LEATHER, FIBERS, TEXTILES, AND PERSONAL ADORNMENT

LEATHER GOODS

The Tepehuan of Chihuahua utilize the skins of cows, oxen, goats, and certain wild animals in the manufacture of sandals, sleeping and sitting mats, carrying baskets, the aprons used by arrieros, saddle bags, small bags used for carrying pinole or seeds, a bowman's wrist guard (*kavalai*) and quiver (*vogusai*), slings, quirts, and braided ropes.

Skins (*ulidaga* or *jógi*) from larger animals are staked out flat on the ground in a shady place and left to dry for one week; smaller skins are anchored with rocks. When thoroughly dried out, the skin is soaked for about two weeks in a hollowed-out log or a depression that has been made in a ledge of soft stone. The Indians commonly add lime (*ojomátai*) prepared from oak ashes or from limestone rock (see Chapter 4) to the water in which the skin is soaked.

A tanning agent is made from the bark of any of the following species of trees: *Quercus omissa*, known by the Tepehuan as *alíága* (*hoja chiquita*) *kútai* (*encino*); *káli* (*Q. albocincta*); *ívotai* (*Q. candicans* and *Q. coccolobaefolia*); *túái* (*Q. crassifolia* and *Q. chihuahuensis*); *tuápoli* (*Q. durifolia*); *popuíšoli* (*Q. Endlichiana*); *algarroba* or *úparai* (*Acacia pennatula*); and *palo rojo* (*Wimmeria* sp.?). The bark is removed from the tree or shrub with a knife or an axe. Then the outer portion of the bark is removed, and the remainder is placed in a hollowed-out rock and crushed with a wooden mallet. The crushed material is added to water in a hollowed-out log or rock that serves as a vat; the skin is put into the vat and soaked for about fifteen to twenty days. It is then wrung dry and spread on a large, clean rock. When available, the brains of a cow or any other "large" animal are smeared on the skin; sometimes, intestines are used for this part of the process. The softening agent is left on the skin for about three days. The hide is then carefully scraped and either laid out on a flat surface and rolled with a small, smoothed log or it is rolled up and worked back and forth on a flat surface. If brains or intestines are not available, the skin is dried thoroughly before being scraped and rolled.

When leather goods must be sewn, the Indians use a wooden needle about eight inches long. Holes are punched in the leather with a wooden awl called *mukakami* (*agudo*). Ixtle (*taídï*) fibers serve as thread in the sewing of small bags, whereas narrow leather thongs are utilized in sewing the aprons used by arrieros. Braided or twisted ropes made from strips of rawhide are used to anchor burdens to pack animals; the strips are soaked until pliable enough to be easily handled. Unprocessed skins are cut into narrow strips that are soaked before being made into the nets of carrying baskets. Tumplines for these carrying baskets are affixed with narrow leather thongs.

With the exception of the very few Tepehuan who wear leather shoes obtained in trade from the mestizos, the Indians invariably wear leather sandals not unlike those pictured in Lumholtz.[1] Canyon Indians occasionally make fiber sandals, and they also plait branches into sandals that are anchored to the foot in exactly the same fashion as the ones made from rawhide, processed leather, or pieces of rubber tires. This latter type of sandal has become an important element in the Tepehuan culture. Sandals made from rawhide or from processed leather are manufactured in a very simple fashion: the material is cut to the shape of the foot, and three holes—one in the front and two at the rear—are made with a wooden awl; the end of a long narrow thong is inserted into the front hole and knotted beneath the sole; the heel strap, a short thong, is inserted into the two rear holes and knotted at both ends beneath the sole; and a hole is then punched in the center of the heel strap. The wearer draws the front thong between the toes and across the instep; wraps it around the ankle, inserting it through the hole in the heel strap; and ties it at the instep.

Skins processed for use as sleeping mats are not cleaned of their hair (Fig. 25, page 169).

It is likely that the ancient Tepehuan made at least some use of processed hides in view of a seventeenth-century comment by Pérez de Ribas, who noted that the Indians rarely left their arms for a moment.[2] Their arrows must have been carried in a quiver which, today, is commonly prepared from the skin of a gray fox (see Chapter 5) or, according to Mason, from a deerskin.[3] It is certain that the ancient Tepehuan used skins in the manufacture of supernatural objects, for Pérez de Ribas wrote about an object used by a Tepehuan witch doctor that was about the size of an apple and was enveloped by several layers of skin. He commented that these layers of skin may have been from human scalps.[4]

Apparently, the sole early historical reference to footgear is found in Rinaldini's dictionary of 1743, but the reference is not a clear one. Eighteenth-century Tepehuan used the term *usci súsaxa* (properly, *uši súúsaka*) when referring to *abarca de madera*[5] (wooden sandals?). The reference is probably not to wooden clogs as such, but it may be to plaited sandals made with pliable branches like those made in the hot canyons today.

FIBERS

The important fiber plants utilized by modern-day Tepehuan of Chihuahua are *óyi*, or *palma de San Pedro* (*Yucca decipiens*); *daapáka* (*liso*) *kúrui* (*palma*), which is *Nolina matapensis* or *N. durangensis*; *kúrui*, or *palmilla* (*Dasylirion simplex*); and *šúšida kúrui*, or *sotol* (*D. Wheeleri*). The magueys were once important as a source of fibers for making thread used in sewing together the pita-fiber garments referred to in the early accounts of the Tepehuan.[6] The magueys are utilized today as a source of ixtle fiber which, like goat hair and hair from the tails of cows and horses, is processed into rope with the *tarabilla*. There is no evidence that the Tepehuan cultivate cotton today, but their ancient relatives who inhabited what is today northern Durango grew cotton in the late sixteenth century and used the fibers to make cotton thread which was woven into *vestidos*.[7] *Yucca* and *Nolina* species undoubtedly have maintained their importance because they are a source of materials for manufacturing the indispensable baskets and mats. These species do not grow in the pine-clad uplands but are generally available at the margins of the uplands (where the pine country gives way to the pine and oak complex) as well as in the canyons. Magueys are distributed everywhere in the Tepehuan country but are more common along the margins of the uplands and in the canyons.

Baskets. Most of the Liliaceae utilized in the manufacture of baskets (*ásarai*) are distinguished by leaves that have sharp spines which must be removed with a sharp stone or knife before weaving can begin. If the despined leaves are not used immediately, they become stiff. Therefore, if an article is not completed right away, it is discarded or, in some instances, soaked until the leaves become pliable again. Baskets are commonly woven by the women (Figs. 26 and 27), although the Tepehuan men are familiar with the weaving process and sometimes make baskets. Square and round baskets of the single- or double-twilled variety are made, some being tightly woven and others loosely woven. The latter are used for straining either *tesgüino* or *nixtamal*. Covers are rarely made. Very small baskets are used for the storage of seeds, and medium-sized baskets are used as carrying receptacles for grain at planting time.

The carrying basket, or *vakáli* (*huacal*), utilized by both upland and canyon Tepehuan is constructed from a variety of fibers: pliable branches (*úšmamaradï*) of any of the oaks common to the Tepehuan country; narrow strips of unprocessed hide; branches of the *suaz* or *chihuite* (*Salix Gooddingii*), known

26— Mode of weaving baskets.

27— Baskets typical of upland and canyon Tepehuan country.

28 – The Tepehuan carrying basket (*vakáli*).

by the Indians as *túbuli*; branches of the *torote* or *ocotillo* (*Fouquieria fascicu-lata*?), known as *tarákovara* among the Tepehuan; and ixtle fibers. This basket (Fig. 28) is carried on the back and held in place by either a tumpline or a strap passed over the shoulder; carrying baskets may also be tied to the sides of a pack animal. Two rather distinct types of frames are used in these baskets: a roundish frame and a conical one. The round basket frame consists of two pliable *encino* branches about forty-four inches long that are bound together at their midpoints by means of a leather thong, one branch at right angles to the other. The ends of the branches are notched and fitted into matching notches that have been cut in a circular frame of *encino* measuring about forty inches in circumference. The frame is covered by a net made of maguey fiber, unprocessed rawhide strips, or branches of *Fouquieria fasciculata* (?) or *Salix Gooddingii*. The tumpline (*mecapal*) is fashioned of leather, ixtle fiber, or wool. Occasionally, the Tepehuan *faja* (sash) serves as a tumpline. The conical carrying basket is made by bending three pieces of oak branches, each piece about five and one-half feet long, into circles and binding them together with rawhide or maguey fiber. Two of the circles are bound together at one point and then are spread apart and anchored with thongs or fiber to the third circle. The net is fashioned the same as that used in the round basket.

Carrying baskets are used solely by the men, and then apparently only for

transporting corn from the fields to storage huts. Of interest is that Indian
males are unwilling to carry by hand any item they may acquire while en route
from one place to another; Indian women seem not to have such an inhibition.
Whether this is an old trait or one acquired through association with mestizos is
not known. Most Tepehuan males wear a white rag tied about their waists or
looped over their shoulders which serves as a "pocket" for carrying small articles. If the Indians are caught without this rag and have occasion to carry some
small article, they will usually tuck the object away in a hiding place to be
picked up at a future time.[8] Tools, weapons, and firewood are the only objects
carried in the hand of an Indian male en route from one place to another.

The Tepehuan who live near Baborigame and Nabogame make "twig" baskets by weaving very thin and pliable branches of *túbuli* (*Salix Gooddingii*).

There are apparently no early historical references to baskets among the
Tepehuan. Relative antiquity may be assigned to the carrying baskets since
today's baskets are quite similar to those pictured in Lumholtz' account of his
visit to the Tepehuan in the 1890's.[9] It is clear that today's woven baskets
should be considered analogues of pre-Columbian baskets, for plaited basketry
remains have been recovered from the Río Zape site.[10] Although the Tepehuan
of today know nothing of a coiled basketry technique, pre-Columbian Tepehuan probably did; the Río Zape site has also yielded fragments of coiled basketry covered with pitch.

Sleeping and Sitting Mats. The petate (*máíñi*) is rarely seen in the uplands
and only occasionally in the canyons, where some Indians maintain that it is
not locally manufactured but is brought in as a trade item from the west. However, other Indians insist that petates are woven from the leaves of *šúšida kúrui*
(*Dasylirion Wheeleri* and *Arundo donax*).[11] There is no doubt about the antiquity of petates among the northern Tepehuan; Pérez de Ribas referred to a
mat (*estera*) that served to cover entryways into the crude *jacalillos* or *chozas*
constructed of branches (*ramas*) or straw (*paja*) by seventeenth-century Tepehuan north of Durango City.[12] Plaited matting associated with burials has been
recovered from the Río Zape site.[13]

Hats. Older Tepehuan men who live in the canyons wear fiber hats woven
by the women from leaves of *Nolina matapensis*, *N. durangensis*, and *Dasylirion simplex*; the two *Nolina* species are known as *daapáka* (*liso*) *kúrui* (*palma*)
among the Tepehuan, the *Dasylirion* species as *kúrui*. All of these species are
rather common on canyon slopes. Very young leaves are preferred for weaving
hats, but the small spines on these leaves must be carefully removed before
weaving begins. Little care is taken to insure that these simple, twilled hats fit.

Cordage. A rather useful cordage is manufactured from ixtle fiber obtained from three species of *Agave* common to the canyon country: *ájurai*, *mái*,
and *guvúkai*. Fresh leaves from these plants are anchored to a post, sapling, or
large tree in some fashion; and a scraper, made by wedging a knife blade or a

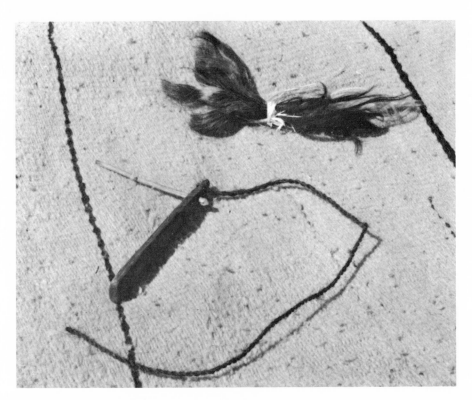

29— Tarabilla used in manufacturing cordage.

piece of iron or stone into a crude wooden handle, is used to remove the tough
outer portion of the leaves. The leaves are then scraped further with a knife or
sharp stone to obtain the fibers, which are washed and dried. Very thin cordage
is prepared by rolling some fibers on the thigh. Heavier cordage is manufactured on the *tarabilla* (Fig. 29), which is, without doubt, a device introduced by
the Spaniards. Several strands of fiber are piled up and rolled into a loose skein.
A loop of the fiber is attached to the *tarabilla*, which is turned by a person who
backs away from the person holding the fiber. If a larger rope is desired, the
completed rope is doubled, attached to the *tarabilla*, and twisted a second time.
Hair from a goat, from the tail of a cow, or from the mane and tail of a horse
may be turned into rope with the *tarabilla*. Cordage is also made by plaiting the
leaves of *óyi* (*Yucca decipiens*) and an unidentified *palma* called *sowali*. Un-
modified *óyi* leaves are frequently used as a tying cord, particularly in constructing the fruit crates that are made of sticks fashioned from easily worked
pine timber. Thin ixtle-fiber cordage is used in weaving nets for gourd canteens
(Figs. 37 and 38, page 212) and as tumplines.

The antiquity of cordage made from plant material in pre-Columbian
times is revealed by remnants of cotton string and fragments of agave leaves in
the Río Zape site of northern Durango.[14] However, the available archeological

30— Typical clothing for boys in the uplands.

evidence suggests that wild plants were the primary source of material used for manufacturing cordage. Cotton material represented only a small percentage of the items made from fibers that were found in the Río Zape site.

Sandals. Crude sandals (*súúsaka*) are made from *óyi* leaves (*Yucca decipiens*) and are usually double in thickness. Two leaves are twisted together in the center with their ends pointing in opposite directions. A number of these twisted sets are prepared and lashed together in the center with additional leaves; the leaves projecting from the center are plaited to the size of the sandal desired. The loose ends are turned back and twisted into the sandal. Very firm leaves are then woven back and forth between the two thicknesses. The sandal is held to the front portion of the foot by a transverse cord of fiber. Two other cords that are affixed to the heel of the sandal are looped about the wearer's ankle and then tied.

TEXTILES

Woolen and Cotton Clothing. Today, most adult Tepehuan males wear jeans or *calzones*, a ready-made shirt or one of the cotton-cloth shirts made by

31 – One-piece cotton dress typical of the uplands.

the women, sandals of leather or rubber, a headband of cotton cloth, a cotton-cloth or woolen sash, a blanket wrapped about the body in cold weather, and (frequently) a bandana about the neck. In remote areas, men wear only a breechclout made of cotton cloth, a cotton-cloth or woolen headband, and a crudely made cotton shirt with rather full sleeves and no collar. Young boys (Fig. 30) commonly wear a short-pants version of the *calzones* and a crudely made cotton shirt held in at the waist by a cotton-cloth sash or, in some instances, by a very narrow woolen sash. In remote areas, boys wear only a cotton breechclout and a cotton blouse or shirt.

Most adult Tepehuan women wear a bandana about the head, a cotton-cloth blouse, a short cotton skirt (*ïpurui* or *tuaraga*),[15] and (occasionally) a woolen or cotton-cloth belt or sash. Sandals are not commonly worn by women, and they rarely wrap themselves in a blanket even in the coldest weather; they prefer to wear an additional blouse or skirt. The adult women who live near Baborigame and Nabogame (Fig. 31) wear a one-piece dress that has two or three narrow ruffles at the bottom of the skirt and a pattern of tucks on the yoke portion of the dress front; the back of the dress is not tucked. Young girls dress as their mothers do, but their clothes generally are not as well made as those worn by the women.

The cotton cloth used in making shirts, blouses, *calzones*, headbands, and sashes is bought or bartered either from traders who enter the Tepehuan country or from stores maintained here and there in southern Chihuahua by mestizos.

Some data concerning the articles of clothing worn at the beginning of the twentieth century are available in comments made by very old Indians who were living near Santa Rosa (in the canyon country) in 1960. The adult male wore a sash (*givúrai*) about eight feet long and about two inches wide. It was decorated with red, yellow, white, and black motifs, the colors having been obtained from native vegetable dyes. A headband (*movudaragai*) was made of either wool or palm fiber. The woolen headband was rarely decorated in any fashion. Loincloths (*bakúli*) were fashioned from cotton cloth, woolen cloth, animal skin, or fiber. Hats were not worn, and *calzones* were worn only by those Indians in close contact with the mestizos. Shirts were not worn. Blankets (*sosóáyi*), worn in cold weather, were wrapped about the body. A woolen poncho-like garment was worn by the canyon Indians but not by those in the uplands. Sandals made of leather or palm fibers were generally worn.

Women wore headbands of about the same size as those worn by the men; they were made of wool or palm fiber. Blouses or shirts were not commonly worn by the women; most of them wore only a poncho-like cotton-cloth garment and a short cotton skirt that came to just below the knee. Blankets were sometimes worn as skirts. Skirts were held in by sashes, somewhat smaller in width and shorter in length than those worn by the men.

Weaving. Wool used in fashioning present-day blankets and sashes is called *vópoi*, a term commonly used to mean hair from any animal. Wool from sheep or goats is washed thoroughly in running water and then beaten with a stick before being dried in the sun. After the wool is dried, it is carded by hand and twisted into strands which are rolled into balls for storage. The rolled wool is spun into coarse thread on a wooden whorl (*vidíñajoroi*) made from any species of pine and *sákoi* (*Lysiloma Watsoni*). The stick, which is made of pine, is about thirty inches long; and the wheel, which is made of *sákoi* wood, is about six inches in diameter (Fig. 32). The whorl is usually held in the right hand, with the left hand guiding the strand as the thread is spun (Fig. 33). Blankets are woven by the women on a horizontal loom (Fig. 34), called *gitúki* (*telar*) or *sosáátajaroi* (literally, a "blanket-maker"), that is located in a shady place near the habitation. The end logs used in constructing this loom are called *kákavidajami*; the side logs are called *sašárajami*. The ball of thread is called *avójadi*, and the thread itself is referred to as *vídiñi*. Two shed sticks (*ikíštajaroi*) are used. The shuttle is called *áadajaroi*, and the beating stick is *šikiúmajaroi*.

32– The Tepehuan whorl (*vidíñajaroi*).

33– Mode of using whorl among the Tepehuan.

34— The Tepehuan loom (*gitúki* or *so sáátajaroi*).

Woolen blankets manufactured today (Fig. 20, page 120, and Fig. 35) by the Tepehuan women are apparently about the same size as those made in Lumholtz' time, but they are generally not as profusely decorated as were the earlier blankets. The ends of, and sometimes the centers of, present-day blankets are decorated with a few black, brown, or yellow strips of varying width, but those of Lumholtz' time were heavily marked with colored strips.[16] Some blankets are decorated today with a checked design (Fig. 35). There is no doubt that women once wove much finer blankets than those now commonly seen. A very old blanket, much like those photographed by Lumholtz, was displayed by an old woman who lived at the edge of the Mesa de Milpillas in 1960; this woman stated that she had made the blanket in her youth and that the article was typical of blankets made by all women not long ago. The blanket was distinguished by a much finer weave than the blankets of today, which can only be described as very heavy and coarsely woven.[17]

Most dyestuffs utilized by the Tepehuan of southern Chihuahua are obtained from traders. Only two native dye plants were reported by the Tepe-

35— An Indian blanket (*sosóáyi*) made in the uplands.

huan in 1960 and 1965, an *acetilla* and a *palo amarillo* (*Mahonia* sp.), from which a yellow dye was prepared. Flowers from both the plant and the tree were mashed and soaked in warm water for a short time. Additional water was added, and the wool was soaked in the mixture for several days; the Indians claimed that no setting agent was used.

The antiquity of both the loom and the use of pita and cotton fibers among the Tepehuan is indicated in very early historical accounts of the Tepehuan north of Durango. The Carta Anua of 1596 refers to *vestidos de algodón* worn by the Indians,[18] and the seventeenth-century account of Pérez de Ribas is very explicit concerning pita and cotton fibers.[19] The Tepehuan grew cotton and secured pita from plants growing in their uplands. The fibers were woven into mantas and *faldellines* (aprons or skirts) on a loom. This clothing must not have been very ample since Pérez de Ribas refers to the efforts of priests to obtain clothing for the nude Tepehuan.[20] Cotton blankets (and garments?) were recorded for eighteenth-century Tepehuan at Indé.[21] The early acceptance of wool and the resulting decline of pita fiber (and cotton fiber?) as a source of material for weaving clothes and blankets are indicated in the Jesuit report of 1596, which refers to *vestidos de lana* among the Tepehuan north of Durango.[22]

These historical data make clear that pita and cotton clothing were manufactured by the Tepehuan at the time of the Conquest. The archeological evidence suggests that, at least by 600 A.D., the Tepehuan of what is today northern Durango were utilizing pita fiber in the manufacture of fabrics and that, at some time before European contact, the Indians had begun to raise cotton. Yucca and agave leaf fragments have been recovered from almost all levels excavated at Zape; cotton string, however, appears only in relatively late pre-Columbian strata. Wooden objects found in the Zape site resemble shuttles and battens used in weaving. Fragments of cloth have also been recovered from this northern Durango pre-Columbian site, but whether the cloth is of pita or cotton fiber has not been determined.[23]

PERSONAL ADORNMENT

Tepehuan males generally wear their hair (*kúpai*) in what may conveniently be described as an abbreviated page-boy bob. A few men wear a moustache (*tiñivo*). Women wear their hair somewhat longer and frequently in braids (*ïtoši*) after the fashion of hair style among mestizo women. Older Indians at Santa Rosa insist that, not long ago, the hair was either worn long and brushed away from the forehead or cut in a page-boy bob. Lumholtz photographed men with their hair cut at about shoulder length, held back by gaily decorated woolen and cotton bands; some of the men appear to have worn caps.[24] Decorated woolen bands are rarely used today for binding the hair. Instead, a folded bandana or a cotton-cloth band is wound about the head for this purpose. Fiber headbands are worn by the canyon Indians.

The saponaceous qualities characteristic of certain plants are known and appreciated by the Tepehuan, who utilize the plants in washing their hair and their clothes. An amole known as *bíñivai* (*Agave* sp.), which is common to rocky promontories along streamways in southwestern Tepehuan country, supplies leaves that are crushed on a rock and rubbed on a water-soaked blanket. The blanket is resoaked in the quiet water of a stream for several hours and then rubbed on a rock before being rinsed and dried. *Sabila* (*Agave bovicornuta*), which appears frequently on higher portions of the slopes in southwestern canyons, has a sap in its leaves that is used as a soap for washing hair. *Phytolacca icosandra* is an herb known among the Indians as *čivúkali*;[25] its roots are crushed and used for washing blankets in the same manner as the amole leaves. The Indians living near Llano Grande, Lagotera, and Cascate use the seeds and

36— An *estiladera* used in making soap (*totósaga*) in the uplands.

fruits of a *gongora* (*Phytolacca americana*) as a source of soap. The seeds and fruits are crushed and applied to clothes before the clothes are soaked in stream water. Both are also used for cleaning hands. Gum from the *úbišdali* (*Pinus Englemanni*) is mixed with lard and used as a soap for cleaning blankets and clothes. Seeds of the *higuerilla* or *mukúkuli* (the Old World *Ricinus communis*),[26] are also used for cleaning blankets. The seeds are mashed and rubbed on thoroughly dampened articles, which are soaked and then rubbed vigorously on a rock before being rinsed and dried. Roots of the *óyi*, or *palma de San Pedro* (*Yucca decipiens*), are crushed and rubbed on thoroughly soaked blankets; the blankets are then resoaked in the quiet water of a stream and either beaten with a stick or rubbed on a rock before being rinsed and dried.

More sophisticated Tepehuan of the western canyons prepare soap (*totósaga*)[27] in this fashion: a pig is killed, and its stomach and some of the fat are boiled; an *estiladera* (Fig. 36), an inverted pyramidal-shaped lattice frame made from *torote* stalks (*Fouquieria fasciculata*?) and supported by four upright posts, is built; the frame is lined with grass, and ashes from a number of burned oak logs are placed inside; water (and occasionally urine) is poured over the ashes; the liquid (*liga*) is caught in a *cajete* placed beneath the *estiladera* and then boiled for a short time; the *tripa*, cooked stomach, and fat from the pig are added to the liquid and boiled for several hours. The mixture is then strained and put aside to cool; it is expected to harden into soap within forty-eight hours.

Necklaces (*baoáívukai*) are made by stringing grass seeds, the red seeds of a *colorín* (*Erythrina flabelliformis*), or small shells (brought in by traders from the west) on pita-fiber thread. It seems certain that necklaces of some sort were worn by Tepehuan at the time of European contact, for Pérez de Ribas commented that necklaces which the Tepehuan wore were placed before stone idols during ceremonies. He further stated that the Indians adorned themselves with feather headdresses.[28]

Additional evidence of the antiquity of necklaces of one sort or another among the Tepehuan of what is now northern Durango is found in archeological material from the Río Zape site, which has yielded beads of ground *Olivella* shells and clam-shell discs in association with human remains.[29]

Upland and canyon Indians commonly manufacture combs (*gašiúvuka-roi*) from pine cones by wetting the mature cones and removing the outer coverings. The antiquity of this custom is indicated by Rinaldini, who noted that the eighteenth-century Indian term for *peyne* (*peine*) was *gascibicare.*[30]

A *Senecio* species, known as *lecheguilla* or *koomági* (*gris*) *vásoi* (*zacate*), is believed to be of value in making the hair grow; the entire plant is boiled and drained, and the cooked plant material is rubbed on the hair.

CHAPTER 8 NOTES

1— Lumholtz (1902), I, 427.

2— 1645: Pérez de Ribas (1944), III, 143.

3— Mason (1952), 45.

4— 1645: Pérez de Ribas (1944), III, 146.

5— 1743: Rinaldini (1743), 1.

6— 1645: Pérez de Ribas (1944), III, 137.

7— 1596: Carta Anua.

8— In the spring of 1960, I gave a pair of khaki pants to a wandering Indian who immediately tucked the pants away in the crotch of a tree. When asked why he did not take the pants with him, he replied that he had "nothing to carry them in." He did, in fact, lack a white rag about his waist or over his shoulder.

9— Lumholtz (1902), I, 424.

10— Brooks et al. (1962), 358.

11— *Arundo donax* is an introduction from Eurasia [Perdue (1958), 370].

12— 1645: Pérez de Ribas (1944), III, 227.

13— Brooks et al. (1962), 358.

14— Ibid., 358-61.

15— Both of these terms are used today to designate the short cotton skirt worn by women. *Tuaraga* may be the more correct term since Rinaldini gives *tuadaraga* as the Tepehuan term for *falda de vestido* [1743: Rinaldini (1743), 61].

16— Lumholtz (1902), I, 427.

17— This observation is consistent with a comment made by Mason [(1952), 44] concerning blankets.

18— 1596: Carta Anua.

19— 1645: Pérez de Ribas (1944), III, 137.

20— Ibid., 237.

21— 1777: Relación de Indé.

22— 1596: Carta Anua. See also the report by Padre Ramírez who worked among the Tepehuan north of Durango prior to 1600 [1780: Alegre (1956), I, 468].

23— Brooks et al. (1962), 357-59.

24— Lumholtz (1902), I, 423, 427.

25— Not to be confused with another *čivúkali*: *Coutarea pterosperma*, or *copalquín*.

26— Willis (1931), 568.

27— *Totósaga* is a term applied to any substance that produces "foam" which assists in cleaning cloth items.

28— 1645: Pérez de Ribas (1944), III, 153, 155, 190.

29— Brooks et al. (1962), 358.

30— 1743: Rinaldini (1743), 106.

9
DWELLINGS

HOUSEHOLD ARTICLES

Gourd Utensils. The Chihuahua Tepehuan utilize gourds from at least six cultivated varieties of *Lagenaria siceraria* in the manufacture of canteens (*bokoši*), containers, and dippers. Four of these varieties are known as *vákoi, vákoi upúligami, vaúkamui,* and *awúpudami* respectively. *Lagenaria siceraria* is not cultivated by upland Indians, who must secure gourds in trade from canyon Indians. Very large gourds are made into canteens (Figs. 37 and 38) that are carried by Indians who go on long journeys. A hole is made in the neck end of the gourd, and the dried interior pith is removed with a sharpened stick. A carrying net is prepared from horsehair cordage, leather thongs, or ixtle fiber. These canteens, which usually have cob stoppers, are carried over the left shoulder. The Indians state that they are never anchored at the waist nor are they carried in the hand. Gourd canteens are usually utilized as water containers; however, *tesgüino* is sometimes carried on a journey and, if so, is transported in the gourd canteen.

Dippers and bowls (Fig. 39) are also manufactured from the *Lagenaria siceraria* gourds. They are split down the middle, and the pith is carefully removed before the utensils are dried in the sun. Cracked dippers and bowls are mended with a glue made from the roots of *Nolina matapensis*; the roots are boiled in a bit of water until most of the water is evaporated. A cracked dipper is held in the hand until the glue sets. Drinking vessels (*jicaras*) prepared from gourds are called *íkaroi*, an obvious corruption of the Spanish term for this article.

Pre-Columbian utilization of *Lagenaria siceraria* gourds by the northern Tepehuan is attested to by the finding of shell or rind fragments of this species in the La Cueva de Los Muertos site on the Río Zape.[1]

Ceramics. Clay (*bidái*) for making the indispensable pottery utilized by the Tepehuan is obtained from arroyos. The clay is ground on a large flat rock or on a metate. The ground particles are apparently never winnowed. If the clay must be tempered, the agent is sand or pulverized potsherds. The crushed mate-

37— Gourd canteens fashioned from varieties
of *Lagenaria siceraria* (*vákoi* and *vákoi upúligami*).

38— Gourd canteens fashioned from *vaúkamui*
and *awúpudami* (varieties of *Lagenaria siceraria*).

39— Gourd utensils prepared from varieties of *Lagenaria siceraria*, and wooden spoons carved from species of *madroño* (*Arbutus arizonica* and *A. xalapensis*).

rial is placed on a stone, on a shingle, or in a large batea and moistened and kneaded until it has the desired consistency. Upland Indians apparently prepare the bottom portion of an olla in a somewhat different fashion than do canyon Indians. The upland pottery-maker prepares a clay pat in the shape desired for the olla bottom and places it on a board, a rock, or a shingle (Figs. 40 and 41). Lowland Indians prepare a pat and roll it out with a round stick. The flattened clay is then molded over the bottom of an olla which is approximately the size and shape desired. A small concave depression is prepared in the ground, and the olla bottom is pressed gently into it. From this state until completion of the olla, upland and canyon Indians follow the same technique: pats of clay are rolled by hand into elongated pieces (Fig. 42); the first roll is affixed to the bottom of the olla (Fig. 43), and subsequent rolls are coiled on top of each other as the pot takes shape. The pottery-maker always has at hand an olla containing water. A smooth stick, a piece of *guaje*, or a broken potsherd is moistened and used to smooth the outside of the olla as each coil is added. The inside of the olla is smoothed with the fingers just before the rim is affixed (Fig. 44). The completed olla (Fig. 45) is carefully scraped with a sharp stone or potsherd. A handle may be added to one side, or stubby handles may be affixed to both sides. Ollas are dried either out in the sun or in shade for about an hour before being polished with a potsherd or with the bright red beans of a *colorín*

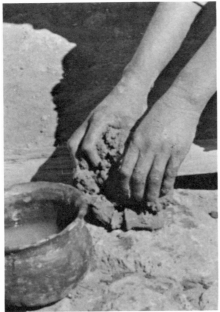

40– Pottery making: beginning stage.

41– Bottom of olla takes shape.

42– Shaping the roll of clay.

43– Coil being affixed.

44— Before rim is affixed. 45— Completed olla.

(*Erythrina flabelliformis*). *Animïdi áyi* means literally "to fire an olla," and this is accomplished in a shallow hole in the ground; three stones are arranged in the hole so that the olla (*áyi*) is supported by the stones. Oak branches are placed about the olla, and dung (*viítai*) is piled over the oak and ignited. Firing requires about an hour.

There is a considerable variety in the size and shape of ollas (*ájayi*) manufactured by the Tepehuan of today (Fig. 46); the sizes range from very small ollas used in storing seeds to large ollas (Fig. 17, page 107) used for fermenting *tesgüino*. Very large ollas are sometimes distinguished by a constricted middle, and smaller ollas are marked with slightly flaring rims, a characteristic that facilitates removal of the olla from the fire with two sticks. Comals (*ajákurai*) and bowls of various shapes (Figs. 47 and 48) have as much variety in their size and shape as the ollas.

Some types of pottery are known by rather distinct terms. A small, handled olla used in preparing teas taken for refreshment or for medicinal purposes is called *naakásoli*. The comal is known as *ákurai*, and *naváítakaro* is the term given to any large olla used for fermenting *tesgüino*. Any of the handled ollas may be referred to as *nanáakami áyi*. The flattish *cajete* is called *ásokoli* or *ajáskoli*.

Most Tepehuan dwellings have a cooking platform (Fig. 49), called *óroni*, which invariably is surmounted by at least one olla supported by several stones or sticks of wood and a comal supported by two stones.

The Tepehuan women always have available small pieces of bone referred to as *ódï* (*hueso*) *miïdadï* (*quemado*) for use in cleaning the comal so that tortillas will not stick. Since many of the upland Tepehuan habitations are located rather far from water, the very large ollas used as water containers are often placed in the cooking corner of the dwelling. They are always covered with an inverted basket. Water is transported from its source to these large containers in rather small flat-bottomed ollas that are frequently carried on the women's heads. The olla is supported by a *vičókoli*, which is a rag or branch wound about the head.

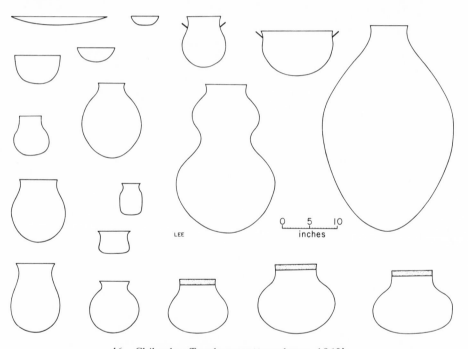

46 – Chihuahua Tepehuan pottery shapes, 1960's.

Broken ollas are mended with the glue prepared from *Nolina matapensis* roots. If the broken olla is small, the pieces are held together in the hand until the glue sets. If the broken olla is large, the pieces are held together by hand until the glue is partially set, and fiber cordage is then drawn tightly about the olla until it is thoroughly set.

There is no evidence that the Tepehuan decorate their pottery with pigments. Some ollas, however, are decorated with beading on the rim (Fig. 48).

47 – Pottery bowls manufactured by upland Tepehuan.

48 – Ollas (*ájayi*) manufactured by upland Tepehuan.

49— The Tepehuan cooking platform (*óroni*)
with a comal (*ákurai*) supported by two stones.

50— A metate that serves only for grinding clay used in pottery manufacture.

Pottery material recovered from the Río Zape site represents a "plain utility ware" for the most part, with only a few examples of sherds and pottery of "better made polished redware."[2] This evidence suggests that the pre-Columbian Tepehuan north of what became Durango City manufactured pottery, albeit of a crude type.

Stone Items. The legless metate used today by Tepehuan is known as *móúturai* or *maútuli*, and almost all habitations contain at least one of these stone articles. Some of the canyon homes have three metates: one used for grinding chile, another for grinding the corn used in the various corn dishes, and

51 – The Tepehuan metate (*móúturai*) which is occasionally supported by a crude stand.

another for the mashing of corn sprouts used in making *tesgüino*. Some canyon Indians have still another *móúturai* that is used exclusively for the grinding of clay in the manufacture of pottery (Fig. 50). Metates are shaped from the vesicular lava that appears in abundance in Tepehuan country. Most of them are anchored to the ground or placed on medium-sized rocks so that the grinder may kneel with comfort behind the metate. However, some of the more sophisticated Indians of the uplands, those who have been strongly influenced by the mestizos, manufacture a very crude metate stand (Fig. 51) that consists of a pine board about twenty-five inches long, about ten inches wide, and about three inches thick. A shallow bowl is carved at one end of the board. Three legs are inserted into the board, one at the rear of the metate stand and two at the front. The two forward legs are longer than the third leg and are affixed to the board so that they project forward, thus giving stability to the stand when it is in use. The metate is so arranged on the stand that its lip protrudes over the carved bowl.

Apparently, the Tepehuan make no attempt to manufacture the hand-held, upper grinding stone: the mano or *túpai*. Instead of making one, the Indians obtain a stone with the proper dimensions from a creek bed.

The stone axes once utilized by the Tepehuan have been described in connection with agricultural activities (see Chapter 2).

Little is known of the ancient utilization of stone by the northern Tepehuan. Stone objects found in the Río Zape site suggest that manos and metates were chosen from suitable river boulders and that no effort was made to shape the stones prior to their being used. Choppers and hammerstones were rather scarce, appearing only in the lowest cave deposits.[3]

The ancient Tepehuan "worshipped" stone idols according to numerous references in the late sixteenth and early seventeenth centuries, but whether the Tepehuan or another Indian group manufactured the idols is not known.[4] But, it is clear that at least some of the seventeenth-century Tepehuan venerated stone objects used by witch doctors. There is a specific reference in Pérez de Ribas to a stone artifact about the size of an apple and covered with skin. The *hechicero* who owned this object believed that it had the power to cause or remove illness and that whosoever possessed the idol had fortitude and would come out unscathed in battle. This stone idol also "told" the witch doctor of events that would transpire in the future.[5]

Wooden Items. The most important of household articles prepared from wood are spoons and bowls. These utensils are manufactured from *madroño grande*, or *opíndali* (*Arbutus arizonica*); *madroño pequeño*, *madroño de la barranca*, or *áli* (*chiquito*) *opíndali* (*madroño*), which is either *A. xalapensis* or *A. glandulosa*; and a *Salix* species known as *sauz*. Large knots on the *Arbutus* species serve well in the fashioning of bateas, which are carved out with a knife. Spoons (Fig. 39, page 213) vary in size from short-handled spoons about eight inches in length to long-handled ones about fifteen inches in length. Certain species of plant life are preferred as sources of wood used in the manufacturing of small spoons. These species include *verako*, or *taíšoli* (*marrano silvestre*) *oliadï* (*testiculos*), which is a *Thevetia* species, and an unidentified *palo carpintero*, known as *šipúndali* (*tronador*).

Stools are rarely manufactured by the canyon Tepehuan, and they are relatively rare in the uplands. The wooden stools used by upland Indians (Fig. 52) are about eighteen inches long, eight inches wide, and about two inches

52 – Wooden stools fashioned by upland Tepehuan.

thick; they are fashioned from any available pine timber. Three legs, about four inches long, are inserted into holes made in the underside of the pine slab. (Apparently, the Indians favor three legs as a supporting structure.) The trunk of an oak or a *madroño* tree with conveniently projecting branches may also be used in fashioning a stool. Some of the upland Indians make crude straight chairs, characterized by plaited hide seats, for use within or without habitations (Fig. 57, page 225). A few examples of wooden benches appear in the uplands. Chairs and benches are utilized for the most part by men.

Headrests (*móčikaroi*) are also fashioned of pine timber; these articles are about twelve inches long and four inches wide and are distinguished by a convex upper side. The relative antiquity of the headrest is indicated by Rinaldini's reference to *moscare* (clearly related to the present-day *móčikaroi*) as the Indian word for *almohada* in the eighteenth century.[6]

There are apparently no early references to wooden household items manufactured by the Tepehuan. Lumholtz commented that wooden spoons were brought into the Tepehuan country by Aztec and Otomi traders from southern Mexico.[7]

HABITATIONS

Today most of the Tepehuan dwellings are constructed of timber, but anciently, the Tepehuan who lived in what is today northern Durango built their habitations from wood and saplings (*madero y palos de monte*), stone and mud (*piedra y barro*), branches (*ramas*), or straw (*paja*). A grass mat (*estera*) closed the entrance opening of the straw hut, which was very small (*estrecho*) and poor in construction.[8]

Utilization of stone and mud as construction materials survives to a limited extent in the canyons of southwestern Chihuahua. Present-day Tepehuan use the term *vaki* in referring to houses built of stone (*ódai*) or of wood (*úši*); however, older Indians, especially those who live in the canyons, insist that *vaki* properly refers to the rush or grass huts that were still common in canyons at the beginning of the twentieth century. This statement is probably correct since Rinaldini wrote in the eighteenth century that the Indian term for *casa de zacate* was *baqui*, whereas the *casa de terrada* was called *biddavaqui*.[9] The huts constructed in the canyons at the beginning of the twentieth century must have been of the "jacal" type noted by Hewett, who made a pack trip down the eastern portion of the Sierra Madre Occidental in 1906. Hewett specifically referred to the use of vertical poles for walls, and at least one type of roof was made of thatch.[10]

Upland habitations are located either in the center of an ejido plot or near the edge of the plot next to the forest. Although the upland Indian prefers to locate his house near a permanent source of water, it is not always possible to do so since many of the upland streams dry up occasionally. If a specific location for a dwelling is preferred, the possibility of there being an occasional drought does not prevent its construction. During periods of water shortage, water is transported by olla from a brook, a spring, or an arroyo, all of which may be some distance from the dwelling.

Assistance in building a house is obtained by payment with corn, or the house-builder may readily secure help if he has sufficient corn to prepare a large quantity of *tesgüino*.

The builder selects a portion of the upland forest (*úšiga*) that contains a fairly large contiguous stand of the type of timber desired and, with a metal axe, fells and trims trees into logs which are left to dry for a season. The dried logs are then dragged to the house site with oxen or by human labor if oxen are not available. The logs are trimmed a second time and carefully smoothed before being notched some twelve to twenty inches from the ends.

Log structures built by the upland Tepehuan range in size and complexity from simple log dwellings about twelve feet square, seven or eight feet high, with open-ended gable roofs of logs covered with shingles held down by stones (Fig. 53) to large multiroomed structures with very high, gabled roofs that are centered over the entryways and extended to cover not only the rooms but also open spaces that may or may not be walled in with the shingles (Figs. 54, 55, and 56) so commonly used in Tepehuan country. Upland Indians occasionally construct what is essentially a shingle house (Fig. 57), which has a frame of carefully smoothed and notched logs upon which the shingles are placed.

Occasionally, a multiroomed dwelling is protected from rain by a sloping roof of logs supported by a ridgepole erected about six feet from the entrance

53– A crude log dwelling typical of uplands near the Mesa de Milpillas.

54– Multiroomed dwelling typical of country near Llano Grande, Chihuahua.

of a dwelling and slanted to the opposite side of the structure. The ridgepole is supported by forked branches anchored in the ground. Such a dwelling is pictured in Lumholtz' account of the Tepehuan.[11] Lumholtz believed that this type of structure was an old form among the Indians.

The typical multiroomed dwelling of the uplands usually contains three contiguous rooms. One of the end rooms serves as a cooking room which may contain the cooking platform called *óroni* (Fig. 49, page 218); this platform is

55 – Upland dwelling located in Arroyo de Milpillas.

56 – Beautifully constructed log dwelling near La Ciénega.

57– A "shingle house" constructed by upland Tepehuan at Lagotera, Chihuahua.

built of mud mortar and is about four by five feet in size and about two and one-half feet in height. Probably no more than 20 percent of the Tepehuan construct these platforms; most Indians prefer to cook on the ground. Except for one or two crude shelves made by thrusting shingles in between the logs that form the walls and for a few sticks that serve as hooks, there is generally nothing in the cooking room but the required utensils and an olla of water.

The center room is used for storage, and the logs that enclose this room are invariably chinked with mud mortar. Most of the Indian males fashion beautifully made planks for the floor of the storage room, the only room where plank floors are utilized. All of the rooms in multiroomed dwellings are fitted with door jambs, but except for the storage room, doors are not commonly made. Storeroom doors are made of planks, and some of them are fastened to the door jambs with intricate wooden locks.

Some of the upland Tepehuan construct storage rooms somewhat apart from their habitations (Fig. 54), particularly when the fields are characterized by high yields of corn.

The third room serves as a sleeping chamber, and the open doorway of this room is closed by a lattice made of pine shingles which is stood against the door frame at night to prevent dogs from entering the dwelling.

Cooking, storage, and sleeping rooms are generally ceiled with logs that are notched so they fit snugly on the four walls of each room.

It is clear that the northern Tepehuan have failed to heed certain advice given to them by Francisco Javier Diáz in the early eighteenth century;[12] Diáz admonished the Indians to "sleep upon high beds." However, bedsteads of any sort are exceedingly rare among the Tepehuan in spite of the fact that most of the men are expert in the use of axes. Occasionally, an Indian will construct what is clearly a "bunk" bed that extends the width of the house at one end of the sleeping room.

Generally, the family sleeps on the bare ground or on skins that are made more comfortable by placing certain materials between the skins and the

58– An upland dwelling in the Arroyo de Los Tarahumares.

ground. As a padding, upland and canyon Indians use fiber from the *pochote* tree (*Ceiba acuminata*), or *javómali*, as the tree is known among the Indians. A *zacate*, called *bakotadali*, and a *carrizo*, known as *okati* or *tótoitakami*, are similarly used. Upland Indians use pine needles to make their sleeping mats more comfortable.

For the most part, the Tepehuan seem disinterested in closing up the high gabled roofs (Fig. 55). Therefore, the open space above the rooms is used for storing articles not commonly kept in the storage room, such as ollas, plows, bows and arrows, drums, and seeds; the seeds are stored in containers (ollas and gourds) suspended from the ceiling. The open side of the dwelling may be closed in with a combination of planks thrust between two stakes or planted in the ground or with brush (Fig. 55). In some instances, the entire dwelling is enclosed with beautifully made pine shingles (Fig. 54). Porches of some of the upland dwellings are partially enclosed by logs (Fig. 58) wedged in between two upright poles that support the roof corners.

Some upland habitations are very poorly constructed apparently because they serve only as temporary dwellings during the season that fields must be protected from stock depredation. The low gabled roof is constructed in such a way that the storeroom at one end of the dwelling is covered (Fig. 59).

Shingles used in covering the roofs and sides of upland and canyon dwellings are made from any of the soft pine timber available in the uplands. The bark is removed from a dried or partially dried log, and the log is cut into pieces about forty inches long. A piece is then cut into two-inch-thick slabs with an

59– A crudely constructed upland dwelling on the Mesa de Milpillas.

axe. A machete, or *azuela* (*saikuanakaroi*), is then wedged into one end of the slab and worked through it. The shingles are stacked and left to dry where they are made (Fig. 60). However, before being used, shingles are soaked in a stream.

It is clear that only those Tepehuan who are closely associated with mestizos use nails made from pine for anchoring shingles to roofs. The shingles are affixed to wooden cross-pieces by means of the nails, about six to each piece. The strips of shingles are then anchored to the logs that constitute the roof frame with additional pine nails. The first piece is put on the roof at its lowest portion. Additional cross-pieces are added until the gable is reached.

Most Indians use rocks to hold shingles in place (Figs. 53, 58, and 59), and in such instances, the shingles are laid on the roof frame with one shingle overlapping another; a large stone is then used to anchor each set of shingles. Rocks are a favored means of keeping shingles in place—and for a good reason. Shingles weighted down with stones may easily be pulled from the roof in case of fire, a frequent occurrence since there are usually no flues. Sparks from fires in either the cooking room or the large, open or enclosed space to one side of the three contiguous rooms frequently ignite the shingles.

Almost everywhere in the uplands, a tiny wooden cross is anchored to the rooftop; this cross is fashioned from the wood of a *palo amarillo* (*Berberis Fremontii*), or *vúáma* (*amarilla*) *úši* (*palo* or *árbol*), as the tree is known among the

60— Stacks of freshly cut shingles left to dry at place where they were cut.

Indians. Incense (*kobímadali*) prepared from the bark of *copalquín* (*Coutarea pterosperma*), known everywhere as *čivúkali*,[13] is burned in a small olla placed before the cross. When the cross is first placed upon the rooftop, the family dances about the outside of the house while singing songs.

Windows are not fashioned by the Tepehuan, and only those Indians who live on culturally intimate terms with the mestizos build flues. However, regardless of the simplicity or the complexity of the dwelling, a fire is always maintained in a habitation that is occupied, either in the cooking area or in the enclosed portion of a multiroomed dwelling. This habit is consistent with a comment made by Pérez de Ribas, who noted in the seventeenth century that fires were maintained at the doors of Tepehuan huts during the night.[14]

Older Indians maintain that, not long ago, a fire was made by rubbing two sticks together; when the sticks were fired, they were poked into *yesca* (*javókali*), the root pith of oak timber. The fire is known as *tái*, which means light, as well. Flint (*ipídorai odaíjadi*) is commonly used in starting fires when matches are lacking.

No one can state with certainty how long the Tepehuan have constructed the crude log dwellings which are so common in the uplands today. The earliest reference to such dwellings is apparently that of Lumholtz, who referred to "commodious log-cabins, with interlocked corners . . . the roofs are gabled and often supported by piles of wood. They are covered with shingles, over which are placed rows of stones to keep them in place. The doors are furnished with jambs."[15]

Relative antiquity of the use of timber in construction is attested to by comments made by Pérez de Ribas, who noted in the seventeenth century that Tepehuan used timber not only to construct dwellings but also to build wooden ladders; there is a specific reference to *escaleras de palos* used by the Indians to get into places where the Spaniards could not easily reach, as for example, the upper portion of a steep ravine.[16] The stone axes (see Chapter 2), which undoubtedly were used in ancient times for girdling trees, must have served in preparing timber used for construction, just as they must have served in clearing timber and brush from streamway floodplains desired for tillage purposes.

At present, it is only in the canyons that the Tepehuan make significant use of stone as a building material and then only in combination with timber and, occasionally, with adobe bricks (Fig. 61). Most of the canyon dwellings are rude in design and simple in construction. A typical dwelling in the canyon (Fig. 62) is constructed as follows: two long, forked poles are planted in the ground about ten or twelve feet apart; two additional pairs of forked poles, somewhat shorter in length, are planted in the ground on opposite sides from the first pair so that a rectangle is formed; horizontal poles are set in the forks of the three sets of posts; and additional poles are anchored to these roof poles to make a supporting frame for the shingles which are held on the roof by stones. Side walls are rarely filled in completely; a stone or adobe wall is usually built about halfway up the height of the building on one or two sides, or the side walls may be partially closed with *torote* or *ocotillo* stalks (*Fouquieria fasciculata?*), the *tarákovara* of the canyons. These stalks are laced together with fiber thongs to form a lattice which is anchored to stakes placed along the wall. Multiroomed dwellings are rarely built in the canyons. A storage hut of logs—actually a miniature log cabin—is usually constructed under one end of, or in the corner of, the canyon dwellings.

Canyon Indians frequently construct very simple huts of shingles near the edges of fields (Fig. 63); they are occupied only during that period when crops must be guarded against predators.

Heavy winds characterize some of the western canyons; and, occasionally,

61— Canyon house in which stone,
adobe bricks, and pine shingles are utilized in construction.

62— A relatively open canyon dwelling
marked by partially closed walls of *ocotillo* (*Fouquieria fasciculata*?).

63— A "shingle house" utilized by canyon Tepehuan
who are responsible for protecting fields against predators.

the Indians transplant a *saúco* (*Sambucus caerulea*) from its natural habitat to a place on the windward side of a dwelling. This tree serves beautifully as a windbreak.

The Tepehuan habitations are swept several times daily with a broom (*vopóíšikaroi*) prepared from the stems of a tall, harsh grass, *Mühlenbergia Emersleyi*.

There is no evidence that the present-day Chihuahua Tepehuan abandon a dwelling following the death (*mukí* or *mukígami*) of one of its occupants, but older canyon Indians state that, in their youth, a hut was abandoned immediately after the death of its owner or a member of his family. This is, in part, consistent with a comment made by Pérez de Ribas, who noted that seventeenth-century Tepehuan were reluctant to enter a church after observing that a corpse had been taken through its doors.[17]

Apparently, the Tepehuan do not currently make use of caves (*tíhoi*) as habitations, but there is some slight evidence that some of the eighteenth-

century Indians lived in caves. Martín Peláez, in commenting on the distribution of the Indians north of Durango City, was very specific in stating that some
of the Tepehuan lived in caves.[18] The western canyons, particularly near Santa
Rosa, abound with caves which were unmistakably once used as habitations.
These are the caves which, according to present-day Tepehuan, were occupied
by the Cocoyome, a people who once inhabited the area in Chihuahua south of
the Río Verde at the time the Tepehuan reached the Sierra Madre of
Chihuahua.

CHAPTER 9 NOTES

1— Brooks et al. (1962), 367.

2— Ibid., 359.

3— Ibid.

4— See particularly an account by Pérez de Ribas which contains a résumé of many early references to stone idols by missionaries who entered the Tepehuan country of what is now northwestern Durango in the 1590's and early 1600's. One such idol was about forty inches in height and represented the head of a man on a stone column; this idol was located at the summit of a hill [1645: Pérez de Ribas (1944), III, 145-48, 153].

5— Ibid., 146-47.

6— 1743: Rinaldini (1743), 8.

7— Lumholtz (1902), I, 430.

8— 1645: Pérez de Ribas (1944), III, 137, 227.

9— 1743: Rinaldini (1743), 24.

10— Hewett (1936), 59.

11— Lumholtz (1902), I, 424.

12— 1715: Actas de la visita. . . .

13— This *čivúkali* should not be confused with another *čivúkali* (*Phytolacca icosandra*), the roots of which serve as soap and the leaves of which are eaten as a *quelite*.

14— 1645: Pérez de Ribas (1944), III, 156.

15— Lumholtz (1902), I, 424-25.

16— 1645: Pérez de Ribas (1944), III, 137, 204.

17— Ibid., 157.

18— 1605: Relación de Martín Peláez.

10

THE TEPEHUAN AND
THE TARAHUMAR

The concern of this monograph has been essentially that of presenting important elements of the Chihuahua Tepehuan material culture as it existed in the 1960's. However, where adequate historical and archeological data were available, they were utilized as indications of the approximate development in time of certain aspects of Tepehuan material culture, particularly those traits introduced by the Spaniards. The data presented suggest that the Chihuahua Tepehuan—like their Indian neighbors to the north, the Tarahumar—remain geopolitically and culturally isolated from the mainstream of Mexican life in spite of more than three hundred years of contact with Spaniard and mestizo.

The outward appearance of most Tepehuan habitations and plantations differs little from those of the mestizo population, which is clearly in the majority in Chihuahua south of the Río Verde. However, it is clear that the Tepehuan are distinct unto themselves not only with respect to language but also with respect to many of their customs. Like the Tarahumar, the Tepehuan have materially benefited from contact with outsiders, while at the same time, they have maintained their integrity as the surviving northern remnant of a group that, in immediate pre-Columbian times, once dominated the country between Nayarit and Jalisco on the south and the Río Verde on the north.

The Tepehuan insist that they should be considered Indians, and they emphatically deny mestizo connections which in many cases patently exist. What might be termed a distaste for the mestizo world is expressed by the Tepehuan in two very obvious ways. The Tepehuan, much unlike the Tarahumar, have been disinclined to associate with Roman Catholicism except in the most rudimentary fashion. Tepehuan antagonism toward the mestizo is also expressed in an attitude toward the few schools, government and Jesuit, found south of the Río Verde in Chihuahua; the Tepehuan rarely learn to read or write, noting that if they do, they will be relegated to the status of a mestizo.

Not only do the Chihuahua Tepehuan maintain themselves as a distinct entity amongst a large mestizo population, they also maintain themselves as a distinct Indian group as opposed to the far more numerous Tarahumar who dominate the country north of the Río Verde. It is true that, occasionally, renegades move either south or north of the Verde and that, on rare occasions, there are mixed marriages; but for the most part, the two major Indian groups still surviving in the northwestern Mexican highlands rarely mix.

No one knows exactly when the Tepehuan and the Tarahumar first came into significant contact with each other. The two groups were certainly marked by cultural associations earlier than the seventeenth century. The historical record indicates that seventeenth-century Jesuit missionaries encountered Tepehuan and Tarahumar living along the Río San Juan in southeastern Chihuahua in the "gateway" country between what was essentially Tepehuan land and what was essentially Tarahumar country. Also, there must have been contacts between the pre-seventeenth-century Tepehuan who lived south of the Río Verde and the Tarahumar who lived north of the river. Therefore, in pre-Columbian times there probably were ample opportunities for cultural exchanges between the northern Tepehuan and the Tarahumar. These opportunities were undoubtedly increased after the arrival of Jesuit missionaries in western and southern Chihuahua in the seventeenth and eighteenth centuries when the Indians were gathered together in mission centers without regard to tribal group.

Some years ago, Riley and Winters suggested that the Chihuahua Tepehuan had perhaps been "Tarahumarized."[1] The question of how much these northern Tepehuan have been influenced by the Tarahumar or how much the Tarahumar have been influenced by the Tepehuan cannot be answered with exactitude. The two groups have largely remained aloof from one another, and it is always difficult to determine the real influence of any group upon another when they are located close together. Another difficulty exists because many of the basic culture traits of the Tepehuan and the Tarahumar are so ancient that it is impossible to determine the origin of these traits.

Tables III through XXX[2] indicate not only the resemblances between Tepehuan and Tarahumar customs and material culture but also some of the major differences, several of which are difficult to explain. In this discussion of the possible influence of the Tepehuan and the Tarahumar upon each other, I have given attention only to contemporary, historical, and archeological materials that pertain directly to the two groups. The larger picture, with respect to culture traits within the greater Southwest, has been ignored.

AGRICULTURE

Anderson and Cutler[3,4] have identified thirty-three distinct types or varieties of maize (see Table III) now grown by the Tepehuan and the Tarahumar;

there are twenty-nine varieties or types common to the Tepehuan and seven common to the Tarahumar. Of these types or varieties, only two strains, Pima-Papago and Pueblo corns, are common to both Indian groups. Nine types or varieties have been found in what are presumably pre-Columbian Tepehuan or Tarahumar archeological sites; of these, eight types or varieties are common to the Tepehuan and three to the Tarahumar. Only *chapalote*, one of the oldest of Mexican corns, and the Pima-Papago corns are archeologically common to both groups. Whereas the Tepehuan corns represent a rather sophisticated complex having marked affinities with southern and western corns, the Tarahumar corns are cruder and seemingly more akin to corns of the American Southwest than to southern and western Mexican strains. That both Tepehuan and Tarahumar have long experimented with teosinte (*Euchlaena mexicana*) in their corn fields seems almost certain in view of documentation of the use of this plant in 1960 and Lumholtz' reference to *maizillo* or *maizmillo* near Nabogame in the 1890's.[5]

For the most part, beans cultivated by present-day Tepehuan and Tarahumar represent a post-Conquest assemblage that more closely resembles beans of the Mexican Plateau than those of the American Southwest. Representatives of *Phaseolus vulgaris* are the most numerous types among the Tepehuan and the Tarahumar; there are fifteen varieties among the former, seven among the latter. However, only one of the types, the pinto, is shared. Of the presumably old beans, only *Phaseolus coccineus* is cultivated by both groups, but only in the case of the Tepehuan is there archeological evidence for the antiquity of this scarlet runner legume. The tepary (*Phaseolus acutifolius* var. *latifolius*) is apparently cultivated only by the Tarahumar. *Phaseolus lunatus* was cultivated by northern Tepehuan in pre-Columbian times. The introduced cowpea is an important legume cultivated by both groups.

Four important edible cucurbits, *Cucurbita pepo, C. mixta, C. ficifolia*, and *C. moschata*, are cultivated by the Tepehuan; of these four species only *C. moschata* is not grown by the Tarahumar. Environmental conditions undoubtedly explain the absence of *Cucurbita moschata* among the Tarahumar. Archeological evidence of *Cucurbita pepo, C. mixta*, and *C. moschata* appears in the Tepehuan site at Zape, and there is archeological evidence that *C. mixta* was cultivated in pre-Columbian times by the Tarahumar.

Archeological and contemporary evidence suggests that both the Tepehuan and the Tarahumar have had a long acquaintance with the bottle gourd, *Lagenaria siceraria*. An Old World cucurbit, the watermelon (*Citrullus vulgaris*), is cultivated occasionally by the Tepehuan and the Tarahumar under favorable conditions.

III— FIELD CROPS*

	Tepehuan		Tarahumar		Sources
	Contemporary	Archeological	Contemporary	Archeological	other than Pennington
Gramineae					
Zea mays					
Ancient Indigenous races					
Chapalote	x	P?xxB		PxxC	Brooks et al. (1962); Cutler (1960)a
Pre-Columbian Exotic races					
Harinoso de ocho		PxxB	x		Brooks et al. (1962)
Elotes occidental			x		
Maíz dulce	x				
Prehistoric Mestizo races					
Cónico				xxW	Wellhausen et al. (1952)
Cónico and other corns	x				
Elote cónico	x				
Reventador		P?xxB			Brooks et al. (1962)
Tabloncillo					
Tabloncillo and other corns					
Maíz amarillo	x				
Maíz breve	x				
Maíz fofo	x				
Maíz pinto	x				
Tabloncillo perla	x				
Tabloncillo perla and other corns	x				
Vandeño	x				
Modern Incipient races					
Celaya			x		
Chalqueño	x				
Chalqueño and other corns					
Maíz canelo; maíz amarillo	x				
(cont'd)					

*For explanation of symbols used in Tables III through XXX see note 2, this chapter.

FIELD CROPS (cont'd)

	Tepehuan		Tarahumar		Sources
	Contemporary	Archeological	Contemporary	Archeological	other than Pennington
Chalqueño and other corns (cont'd)					
Maíz colorado	x				
Maíz pepitillo	x				
Maíz rojo	x				
Maíz viejo	x				
Cónico norteño	x	PxxB			Brooks et al. (1962)
Poorly Defined races					
Cristalina de Chihuahua	x	PxxB			Brooks et al. (1962)
Dulcillo del noroeste			x		
Maíz blando de Sonora	x			PxxC	Cutler (1960)a
Maíz blando de Sonora and other corns					
Maíz amarillo	x				
Maíz chino	x				
Maíz duro	x				
Onaveño		PxxB	x		Brooks et al. (1962)
Miscellaneous strains					
Central and western Mexican popcorns	x				
Elote corns	x				
Pima-Papago varieties	x	PxxB	x	PxxC	Brooks et al. (1962); Cutler (1960)a
Pueblo varieties	x		x		
Toluca popcorn		PxxB			Brooks et al. (1962)
Western Mexican yellow flint mixed with pointed popcorn	x				
Western Mexican pointed subdent	x				
(cont'd)					

FIELD CROPS (cont'd)

	Tepehuan		Tarahumar		Sources
	Contemporary	Archeological	Contemporary	Archeological	other than Pennington
Gramineae (cont'd)					
Avena sativa var.	x				
*Coix Lacryma-Jobi			x		
Euchlaena mexicana	x		xx?L		Lumholtz (1902)
*Hordeum vulgare var.			xxP		Plancarte (1954)
*Saccharum officinarum var.			x		
*Sorghum vulgare var.			x		
*Triticum aestivum var.	x		x		
Amaranthaceae					
Amaranthus leucocarpus	x				
Leguminosae					
Phaseolus acutifolius var. latifolius			x		
P. coccineus	x	PxxB	x		Brooks et al. (1962)
P. lunatus		PxxB			Brooks et al. (1962)
P. sp.	x				
P. vulgaris varieties Pinto	x	PxxB	x		Brooks et al. (1962)
Vayo	x				
Similar to Great Northern	x				
Similar to Red Mexican	x	PxxB			Brooks et al. (1962)
Similar to Black Turtle Soup	x				
Similar to Oregon Giant	x				
(cont'd)					

FIELD CROPS (cont'd)

	Tepehuan		Tarahumar		Sources
	Contemporary	Archeological	Contemporary	Archeological	other than Pennington
P. vulgaris varieties (cont'd)					
Similar to Well's Red Kidney	x	PxxB			Brooks et al. (1962)
Similar to Scotia	x				
Similar to a Hopi variety	x				
Similar to a *bolitas* variety			x		
Similar to commercial Black Valentine			x		
Similar to California Pink			x		
Similar to Jacob's Cattle or *vaqueta*			x		
Small Red Kidney			x		
Small white bean			x		
Miscellaneous variety				PxxZ	Zingg (1940)
Miscellaneous varieties (seven)		PxxB			Brooks et al. (1962)
Miscellaneous varieties (six)	x				
*Vigna sinénsis	x		x		
Malvaceae					
Gossypium sp.		PxxB			Brooks et al. (1962)
Convolvulaceae					
Ipomoea batatas			x		
Solanaceae					
Solanum sp.			x		
S. tuberosum	x		x		
(cont'd)					

FIELD CROPS (cont'd)

| | Tepehuan | | Tarahumar | | Sources |
	Contemporary	Archeological	Contemporary	Archeological	other than Pennington
Cucurbitaceae					
*Citrullus vulgaris	x		x		
Cucurbita ficifolia	x		x		
C. mixta	x	PxxB	x	PxxC	Brooks et al. (1962); Cutler (1960)a
C. moschata	x	PxxB			Brooks et al. (1962)
C. pepo	x	PxxB	x		Brooks et al. (1962)
Lagenaria siceraria	x	PxxB	x	PxxC	Brooks et al. (1962); Cutler (1960)a

Present-day Tepehuan cultivate one species of Amaranthaceae, *Amaranthus leucocarpus*, as their ancestors probably did in pre-Columbian times. This statement is consistent with what is known about widespread utilization of amaranths in pre-Hispanic Mexico and is also consistent with the assumption that aboriginal Tarahumar probably cultivated *Amaranthus blitoides*, *A. retroflexus*, and *A. Palmeri* (see Table IX, page 260). The historical record of the Tarahumar refers to the cultivation of a plant that must have been an amaranth; and, today, the Tarahumar gather seeds of the aforementioned species that appear as *plantas silvestres* within the Tarahumar habitat.

Both the Tepehuan and the Tarahumar cultivate *Solanum tuberosum*, albeit on a small scale. Only the Tarahumar grow the sweet potato (*Ipomoea batatas*).

At least four Old World grasses (wheat, oats, barley, and sugar cane) have apparently been known to both groups for more than two and one-half centuries. However, in spite of the efforts of early missionaries to promote widespread acceptance and utilization of these plants, the Indians generally have not cultivated the grains because the environment of upland Chihuahua is not suitable for their growth. The story of sorghum, another Old World grain, is not clear. Sorghum is rather important as a garden crop among the Tepehuan since it is an important ingredient in the preparation of several beverages and foods. However, even though a variety of sorghum appears in some Tarahumar field plots, the grain has not gained general acceptance among these Indians north of the Río Verde.

Whereas the Tarahumar emphasize cultivation of *Coix Lacryma-Jobi*, an Old World grass with an unknown New World entry date, the Tepehuan display no interest in the plant whatsoever. There is archeological and historical evidence that cotton was cultivated by the Tepehuan in pre-Columbian and immediate post-Columbian times.

Ethnological, archival, and archeological investigations among the Tepehuan and the Tarahumar of Chihuahua indicate that the basic foodstuffs have long been prepared from corn, beans, and squash (the plant complex that obtained in so much of what is today Mexico long before the arrival of Europeans). Grain amaranths may have contributed significantly to foodstuffs in pre-Columbian and immediate post-Columbian times. The white potato and the sweet potato apparently have never contributed significantly to the Tepehuan and Tarahumar diet.

The available evidence suggests that long ago, in pre-Columbian times, both groups cultivated corn, beans, and squash as their main food source. Among these foodstuffs today, however, only the edible squashes are common to both groups (except for *Cucurbita moschata*, which is apparently not grown by the Tarahumar). That edible squashes are common foodstuffs for both the Tepehuan and the Tarahumar indicates an ancient diffusion of these plants into northwestern Mexico. Hardly any varieties or types of corn and beans are common to both groups, a phenomenon difficult to explain since the Tepehuan and the Tarahumar have lived side by side for at least four or five centuries. The lack of duplication regarding these basic items (corn and beans) suggests that neither group has had—at least within recent centuries—much influence upon the other.

Additional evidence for a lack of influence between the two groups rests with the bottle gourd, *Coix Lacryma-Jobi*, sorghum, and cotton. If data collections of seeds made in the 1950's and 1960's are indeed representative, there are six distinct varieties of *Lagenaria siceraria* cultivated by the Tepehuan, but there is apparently only one variety cultivated by the Tarahumar. Whereas the Tepehuan pay no attention to cultivating *Coix Lacryma-Jobi*, the seeds of this plant are widely used by Tarahumar women in their necklaces. This seems strange since Tepehuan women are also interested in materials for necklaces. Why the Tarahumar have not adopted the three distinct varieties of sorghum (Shallu, Chinese Amber, and Hegari) used by the Tepehuan in making *tesgüino* is unanswerable. Absence of cultivated cotton among the Tarahumar in the colonial period is puzzling since there is nothing in the physical environment of southeastern Tarahumar country, particularly in the foothills, to preclude cotton-growing. And certainly, there were skilled weavers among the Tarahumar.[6]

As might be expected, there are few differences in field preparation techniques characteristic of the Tepehuan and the Tarahumar (Table IV). Brush and brambles are burned today as they were in the past; and trees are girdled today as they were in the past. However, whereas stone axes and, undoubtedly, sharp stones were once used for this task, metal axes serve today. The use of a digging stick for working in the ground seems to have been characteristic of both groups in pre-Columbian times. Terraced agriculture is practiced by both groups; however, the Tarahumar construct more sophisticated terraces than do the Tepehuan. Both groups manufacture the same type of plow, a type introduced into Mexico in early post-Columbian times by Europeans. Both groups utilize a drag for breaking the clods, and both make use of fertilizers. The major difference between Tarahumar and Tepehuan with respect to field preparation is a ceremonial one. The Tepehuan apparently make no effort to ritually mark the completion of fields prior to seeding as have the Tarahumar in times past.

There seem to be no important differences between the Tepehuan and the Tarahumar regarding selection of seeds for planting (Table V).

Similarly, there are few basic differences between the two groups with respect to seeding techniques (Table VI), particularly in the practice of seeding maize and legumes in field plots. On the other hand, the Tepehuan tend to plant cucurbits in fields apart from corn, whereas the Tarahumar plant them amidst the corn. The Tepehuan and the Tarahumar also differ somewhat with respect to locales for growing *guajes*; the Tarahumar generally grow gourds in the corn fields, whereas the Tepehuan cultivate them not only in the fields but also in ant hills, trash heaps, and former corral sites. These differences do not seem important, and they indicate nothing in the way of possible influence between one group and the other. The major difference with respect to seeding practices is that the Tepehuan practice elaborate ceremonies to celebrate the seeding and completion of seeding and the Tarahumar do not. However, the Tarahumar do engage in ceremonies to "cure" the fields after the corn is several inches high, ceremonies to bring rain, and ceremonies to celebrate ripening of the corn and harvesting of the crops.[7] It may be that the Tarahumar once performed planting ceremonies which have become integrated with the elaborate fiestas described by Bennett and Zingg.[8] These fiestas involve what may be termed a ritual slaughter of animals that might be analogous to the ritual killing of a rat by some present-day Tepehuan at seeding time and to the ritual slaying of a child for the same reason not long ago. The traditions and historical records of both Tepehuan and Tarahumar include many references to the slaughter of human-kind for other than war purposes, and it is almost certain that such practices continued until very recent times. However, efforts of missionaries during the colonial period and pressure from mestizos and the government in more recent times virtually eliminated such killings. Lack of information about ritual infanticide and fratricide among the Tepehuan and the Tarahumar during the historical period precludes any statement of certainty about whether or not one group influenced the other regarding the slaughter of humans or animals in planting ceremonies. Even though the Tepehuan practice rather elaborate ceremonies to mark the end of seeding and the Tarahumar do not, the available evidence suggests that in seeding and planting practices neither group has exerted much influence on the other.

With respect to customs associated with the care and protection of growing crops (Table VII), nothing can be determined regarding the cultural effect of the Tepehuan and the Tarahumar upon one another. *Temporal* and irrigation agriculture are practiced by both groups, the former type being the most widespread. Just when irrigation of crops was initiated among these Indians is unknown, but it probably did not develop until after sixteenth-century missionaries arrived in the San Pablo Balleza country, the northern portion of the transitional area between the Tarahumar and the Tepehuan. The historical record indicates that Julio Pascual introduced irrigation techniques to the Tarahumar and the Tepehuan there in the mid-seventeenth century.[9] Based on this record, it would appear that irrigation methods spread from the San Pablo country to the rest of the Tepehuan and Tarahumar country. If irrigating techniques did spread from the east and if the practice of irrigation among the westerly Tepehuan and Tarahumar was not introduced from Sonora and Sinaloa on the west coast, then the diffusion of irrigation must have been prompted more by missionary activity than by Indian influence.

Whether the aboriginal Tepehuan and Tarahumar possessed crude wooden hoes is not known. However, there is some slight evidence of the use of a hoelike instrument among the Tarahumar in the eighteenth century; a "tip of a stick" called *maquiachi* was used to cut weeds growing in the corn fields.[10] On the basis of a comment made by Franciscan missionaries in the late eighteenth century, Beals suggested that the aboriginal Tepehuan used hoes or mattocks to till the soil.[11] However, as indicated elsewhere in this monograph (see Chapter 2, note 73), this reference seems more applicable to the Tarahumar than to the Tepehuan. Hence, nothing definite may be said concerning the diffusion of a hoelike implement from the Tepehuan to the Tarahumar, or vice versa, since the sole early reference to a Tepehuan term for the hoe is found in Rinaldini, another eighteenth-century reference.[12]

Practices common to both the Tepehuan and the Tarahumar are weeding done by men and women, the hilling of corn, construction of fences, use of scarecrows, construction of huts used by crop-watchers, use of poisons and traps, and certain ceremonies designed to promote precipitation or to provide protection against damage from lightning or hail. Weeding and hilling practices are of such antiquity that it is impossible to determine whether or not one group influenced the other. Construction of fences probably is, for the most part, a post-Columbian custom. There exists the possibility that brush fences might have been constructed in pre-Columbian times, particularly since there is an eighteenth-century reference to brush fences that were constructed about piles of corn being dried by the Tarahumar.[13] The construction of huts to be used by crop-watchers may be an ancient custom. However, there is nothing in the early historical literature to indicate the presence or absence of the trait among either the Tarahumar or the Tepehuan. Therefore, the question of whether or not either Indian group borrowed the custom, one from the other, is a moot one. The same statement is true for the utilization of ixtle fibers and dead birds as scarecrows and perhaps for some types of traps. The log and metal traps are, without doubt, recent innovations. That the Tepehuan deny any knowledge of the gopher trap which is so important among the Tarahumar is interesting in view of the damage done by gophers and moles to corn in the Tepehuan country. Both groups are much concerned with ceremonies intended to promote rainfall and to insure protection of crops from damage by hail or lightning; however, there are differences in the designs of these ceremonies. Whereas the Tarahumar carry out the ceremonies within the framework of public fiestas, the Tepehuan tend to perform them in private (except when there are public prayers held in the corn fields before a cross). Whereas the Tepehuan throw salt into the air to insure the protection of corn against damage by hail, the Tarahumar burn a plant (*Lepidium virginicum*) to achieve this end. Although the Tepehuan deny any knowledge of this plant, it grows in Chihuahua south of the Río Verde. Utilization of poisonous substances to destroy animals or birds in the corn fields may be of great antiquity among both groups; certainly, the custom seems to have long been practiced by the Tarahumar, who were said to poison crows with some substance in the eighteenth century.[14] Apparently, there is no early reference to a Tepehuan use of poison in a substance to be put out for predators, which may mean that the southern Chihuahua Tepehuan learned of the technique from their neighbors to the north. At present, the Tepehuan utilize two plants in the preparation of substances mixed with *nixtamal* and placed in the fields to kill rodents: a native(?) *yerba de la cucuracha* and the introduced *Ricinus communis*. There is no certainty as to which plant was utilized first in this fashion or whether the Tepehuan learned of the custom from the Tarahumar.

IV— FIELD PREPARATION

	Tepehuan	Tarahumar	Sources other than Pennington
Brush and brambles burned	x	Px;xxR	1777: Relación de Guaguachic
Trees girdled			
Stone axe	Px	Px	
Metal axe	x	x	
Trees left to rot for a season before being burned	x	x	
Axe handles manufactured from timber			
Ehretia elliptica		x	
Fraxinus papillosa		x	
F. velutina	x	x	
Quercus bolanyosensis	x		
Q. rugosa	x		
Stone terraces	x	x	
Crop rotation	x	PxxR	1777: Relación de Guaguachic
Digging stick used to work ground	x	Px;xxR,Z	1777: Relación de Guaguachic; Zingg (1940)
Plows manufactured from timber			
Pinus sp.	x	x	
Quercus albocincta		x	
Q. chihuahuensis	x	x	
Q. coccolobaefolia	x		
Q. incarnata		x	
Q. omissa		x	
Q. rugosa		x	
Q. viminea	x		

(cont'd)

FIELD PREPARATION (cont'd)

	Tepehuan	Tarahumar	Sources other than Pennington
Plow points			
Iron	x		
Fraxinus papillosa		x	
F. velutina		x	
Quercus incarnata		xxBZ	Bennett and Zingg (1935)
Q. oblongifolia		xxBZ	Bennett and Zingg (1935)
Plowing			
Men only		x	
Men and women	x		
Field plowed three times; the second and third plowings at right angles to the previous plowing	x		
Field plowed twice; the second plowing at right angles to the first		x	
Communal plowing		x	
Drag used for breaking clods	x	x	
Application of fertilizers			
Corn husks		x	
Ripe wheat stalks		x	
Bat guano	x	x	
Animal dung	x	x	
Ceremony at completion of field preparation			
Owner of field proceeds to house between dancing columns of neighbors		xxL	Lumholtz (1902)
Speech made by owner of field		xxL	Lumholtz (1902)
Tesgüino provided by owner of field		xxL	Lumholtz (1902)

V— SEED AVAILABILITY AND SELECTION

	Tepehuan	Tarahumar
Seed scarcity		
Corn	x	x
Beans	x	
Squash	x	
Wheat	x	x
Selection of seeds for planting		
Corn grains from tip of ear not used	x	x
Large grains of corn selected for seeding	x	x
Corn grains of mixed colors seeded together	x	
Corn grains of like colors seeded together	x	x
Seed corn selected at time of planting	x	
Cucurbit seeds separated into specific types prior to planting	x	
Legume seeds separated into specific types prior to planting	x	x

VI— SEED PLANTING

	Tepehuan	Tarahumar	Sources other than Pennington
Maize seeding			
Grains carried in basket	x	x	
Grains carried in cloth anchored at waist	x	x	
Grains carried in blanket		x	
Grains carried in leather bag		x	
One man as seeder	x	x	
Two men as seeders	x	x	
(cont'd)			

SEED PLANTING (cont'd)

	Tepehuan	Tarahumar	Sources other than Pennington
Maize seeding (cont'd)			
Men and women as seeders	x		
Men, women, and children as seeders	x		
Dibble used for punching holes in ground	Px	Px;xxR	1777: Relación de Guaguachic
Grains covered by foot movement	x	Px;xxR	1777: Relación de Guaguachic
Grains dropped in newly made furrow which is covered by plowman as he makes the adjacent furrow	x		
Legume seeding			
Beans carried in basket	x		
Beans carried in cloth anchored at waist	x		
One man as seeder	x		
Two men as seeders	x		
Two or more men as seeders	x		
Men and women as seeders	x		
Men, women, and children as seeders	x		
Dibble used for punching holes in ground	x	x	
Beans dropped in newly made furrow which is covered by plowman as he makes the adjacent furrow	x		
Seeded in field with corn	x	x	
Seeded in patch apart from corn	x	x	
Cucurbit seeding			
Seeded in field with corn		x	
Seeded in field apart from corn	x		
(cont'd)			

SEED PLANTING (cont'd)

	Tepehuan	Tarahumar	Sources other than Pennington
Guaje seeding			
Seeded in former corral site	x		
Seeded in trash heap	x		
Seeded in ant hill	x		
Seeded in field with corn	x	x	
Wheat seeding			
Grains carried in basket	x	x	
Grains carried in olla	x		
Grains carried in leather bag		x	
Grains carried in cloth bag	x		
Grains sowed in furrow that is covered by plowman as he makes the adjacent furrow		x	
Grains broadcast and covered by drag	x		
Drag drawn by oxen	x		
Drag drawn by men	x		
Planting ceremonies			
Cross placed upon hill near corn field on the day before planting	x		
Offerings placed before the cross	x		
Prayers said in field during planting	x		
Blood from rat sprinkled on corn grains	x		
Dead rat buried in center of corn field	x		
Small cross erected upon rat's grave	x		
Child's blood sprinkled on corn grains	x		
Child's body wrapped in maguey leaves and placed on side of field "upon which sun rises"	x		
Child's body roasted and eaten after planting	x		

(cont'd)

SEED PLANTING (cont'd)

	Tepehuan	Tarahumar	Sources other than Pennington
Ceremony at completion of planting			
Two men tied up, their arms in front	x		
Huacal filled with corn placed upon back of each man	x		
Cross from hill near corn field removed to center of planted field	x		
Noise-making (rattles, drum, violins, dynamite caps)	x		
Speeches by the two tied men	x		
Men untied and presented with olla of *tesgüino*	x		
Cross removed to habitation, placed upon an altar	x		
Dances	x		

VII— CARE AND PROTECTION OF GROWING CROPS

	Tepehuan	Tarahumar	Sources other than Pennington
Water requirements			
Temporal agriculture	x	x	
Irrigation agriculture	x	x	
Implements			
Wooden hoe	P?x;xxB	P?x;xxR	Beals (1932); 1777: Relación de Guazapares
Iron hoe	x	x	
Weeding			
Men	x	x	
Women	x	x	
Children	x		
(cont'd)			

CARE AND PROTECTION OF GROWING CROPS (cont'd)

	Tepehuan	Tarahumar	Sources other than Pennington
Hilling of corn	x	x	
Fences			
Rail	x	x	
Stone	x	x	
Brush	x	x	
Stakes planted close together, entwined with brush	x		
Scarecrows			
Saplings planted in field, hung with ixtle fiber	x		
Saplings planted in field, hung with white rags	x	x	
Leaves of Liliaceae spp. hung on fiber ropes supported by poles		x	
Dead birds hung on poles in field	x	x	
Poisons			
Seeds of *Ricinus communis crushed, added to nixtamal	x		
Poison prepared from yerba de la cucuracha added to nixtamal	x		
Commercial poison	x		
Unknown poison		P?xxR	1777: Relación de Guaguachic
Traps			
Figure-four release rock trap	x	x	
Figure-four release crate trap	x	x	
Gopher trap (buried in ground)		x	
Metal trap	x	x	
Log trap	x		
(cont'd)			

CARE AND PROTECTION OF GROWING CROPS (cont'd)

	Tepehuan	Tarahumar	Sources other than Pennington
Protection against hail			
Throwing salt into the air	x		
Lepidium virginicum burned in ceremony		x	
Protection against lightning (public fiesta)		xxBZ	Bennett and Zingg (1935)
Rain ceremonies			
Public fiesta		xxBZ	Bennett and Zingg (1935)
Ceremony held in private place in the forest	xxL		Lumholtz (1902)
Ceremony held in field before a cross	x		
"Curing" the fields after the crops are up		xxBZ	Bennett and Zingg (1935)
Protection of bean plants			
Stakes	x	x	
Women and children watch goats and chickens	x		
Rocks arranged about young bean plants	x		
Thatched hut built in field for corn-watchers		xL	Lumholtz (1902)
Shingled hut built in field for corn-watchers	x		

It is difficult to assess the importance of most of the differences between the Tepehuan and the Tarahumar with respect to harvesting and storage practices (Table VIII). However, two techniques are noteworthy: one, the use of a bone implement to remove ears of corn from the stalk, because it apparently has not diffused from the Tepehuan to the Tarahumar; the other, the use of round and square stone storage structures, because it apparently did diffuse, from the Tarahumar to the Tepehuan.

The Tarahumar apparently do not practice harvest ceremonies—at least there is no evidence of them. Bennett and Zingg noted no specific harvest ceremonies during their field work among the Tarahumar in the late 1920's; and the Tarahumar harvest ceremonies mentioned by Lumholtz seem to have been abandoned, as have some of the Tepehuan customs he noted.[15] Harvest ceremonies are certainly important among some of the present-day Tepehuan, but it appears that no elements of the rituals have been adopted by the Tarahumar.

One of the major differences between Tepehuan and Tarahumar modes of harvesting concerns the removal of ears of corn from the stalks. Whereas the Tarahumar remove the ears by hand, the Tepehuan pry them from the stalks with a bone implement anchored to the palm with thongs. It seems strange that the Tarahumar have not adopted this useful technique.

Another difference, but one that is probably not of importance, concerns the drying of corn. The Tepehuan normally dry it on the stalks or in piles on the ground near their habitations. The Tarahumar favor drying it on elevated wooden platforms or on a bed of shucks placed on a rock, upon which a small wooden corral is built to protect the corn from predators. The Tarahumar also dry beans on elevated platforms, whereas the Tepehuan tend to let them dry in fields. Both groups cut squash into strips and hang them for drying; the dried strips are rolled into balls and stored in a suitable place. Apparently, the Tarahumar make no effort to store whole squash as do the Tepehuan.

It is likely that two, and perhaps three, types of storage huts have diffused from the Tarahumar to at least some of the Tepehuan. The round and square stone storage structures found only among those Tepehuan who live on the south slopes of the great Río Verde Canyon are clearly related to similar structures found among the Tarahumar to the north.

There is apparently no evidence of use by the Tarahumar of the Tepehuan circular storage crib made of saplings and covered with a conical roof. And nothing can be stated with certainty about the appearance in western Chihuahua of log storage structures, whether separate from habitations, as is the custom among the Tarahumar, or as an integral part of habitations, as is generally the custom among the Tepehuan. Lumholtz was apparently the first traveler to comment on and describe in detail such structures, and he found them among both groups. Hence, nothing definite can be said about diffusion of the trait.

VIII— HARVESTING AND STORAGE OF FIELD CROPS

	Tepehuan	Tarahumar	Sources other than Pennington
Harvest ceremonies			
Offerings placed before crop	x		
Special harvest dance to celebrate a particularly good crop			
Man and woman chief participants	x		
Burden baskets filled with corn anchored to backs of man and woman whose arms are bound behind their backs	x		
Dances held in the field and near the house, with dancing about the bound couple	x		
Noise-making (rattles, violins, drums, dynamite caps)	x		
Tesgüino made from ears of corn from stalk that grew more than just a few ears	xxL	xxL	Lumholtz (1902)
Stalks of corn and squash plants strewn upon a dance patio; special dance held on the plant material	xxL	xxL	Lumholtz (1902)
Celebration held by owner of field that yielded particularly well			
Owner of field proceeds to house between dancing columns of neighbors		xxL	Lumholtz (1902)
Speech made by owner of field		xxL	Lumholtz (1902)
Tesgüino provided by owner of field		xxL	Lumholtz (1902)
Rat (see Table VI, page 251) exhumed from center of field	x		
Shaman spreads bones over the ground	x		
Fire built over the bones	x		
Ashes spread over the field	x		
Celebration held by owner of field			
Owner of field or his son tied on a horse	xxL		Lumholtz (1902)
Horse led to house where rider is greeted with rifle shot	xxL		Lumholtz (1902)
Tesgüino provided for company	xxL		Lumholtz (1902)
Noise-making (drum and violin)	xxL		Lumholtz (1902)
(cont'd)			

HARVESTING AND STORAGE OF FIELD CROPS (cont'd)

	Tepehuan	Tarahumar	Sources other than Pennington
Modes of harvesting			
Ears of corn pulled from stalk by hand		x	
Ears of corn pulled from stalk with bone instrument	x		
Wheat pulled up by roots and sheaved	x	x	
Beans pulled up by roots	x	x	
Preparations for storage			
Corn			
Dried on stalks in field	x		
Removed from field, dried on ground near habitation	x		
Dried on elevated wooden platform		x	
Dried on shucks inside small wooden corral built on a rock		x	
Dried on a boulder; the corn surrounded by tightly constructed brush fence		PxxR	1777: Relación de Guaguachic
Wheat			
Sheaves placed against sapling anchored on forked poles about 18" from ground for drying	x		
Sheaves dried on elevated wooden structure		x	
Threshed on elevated wooden structure	x		
Threshed on rock surface		x	
Threshed by being rolled back and forth by hand on blanket or hide		x	
Winnowed	x	x	
Beans			
Dried on elevated platform		x	
Dried in field	x		
Dried on boulder reached by ladder		xxBZ	Bennett and Zingg (1935)
Dried on rocky surface		x	
Threshed on elevated platform	x		
(cont'd)			

HARVESTING AND STORAGE OF FIELD CROPS (cont'd)

	Tepehuan	Tarahumar	Sources other than Pennington
Preparations for storage (cont'd)			
Squash			
Cut into strips, hung to dry, then rolled into balls	x	x	
Whole squash stored for several months in storehouse	x		
Storage huts			
Log storage crib separate from house	x	x	
Log storage crib in house	x		
Round stone structure	x	Px;xxZ	Zingg (1940)
Square stone structure	x	x	
Combination stone and log structure	x	x	
Plank storage hut		x	
Storage crib built on face of cliff		x	
Storage crib built in cave		Px;xxZ	Zingg (1940)
Subterranean granary		PxxZ	Zingg (1940)
Circular crib made of saplings, covered with funnel-shaped frame heaped with brush	x		
Seed storage			
In shucks suspended from ceiling	x		
In covered ollas	x		
In *guajes* closed by corncob stoppers	x		
In bits of cloth suspended from ceiling	x		
In baskets	x	x	
In leather bags		x	

Some Tarahumar make use of storage cribs built on the faces of cliffs, and analogues of these cribs exist, according to reports, in western Tepehuan canyons. However, the Tepehuan insist that these cribs were not built by themselves or their ancestors but were constructed by the Cocoyome who once lived in southern Chihuahua. The very antiquity of these cribs makes it impossible to suggest a diffusion of the trait from one group to another during the past several centuries.

The above data indicate that culture traits associated with agriculture, as such, among the Tepehuan and Tarahumar do not show much influence of either group upon the other.

HORTICULTURE

On the whole, there is little difference between the Tepehuan and Tarahumar emphasis on gardens. The principal garden products are tobacco, condiments, and greens (Table IX). Both groups cultivate certain introduced crops (sugar cane, sorghum, onions, mustard, cabbage, coriander, and watermelon) as well as representatives of the New World chiles, tobacco, and tomatoes. However, the apparent absence of the Old World vetchling (*Lathyrus vernus*), and the *chícharo* (*Pisum sativum*), chickpea (*Cicer arietinum*), and horsebean (*Vicia faba*) among the Tarahumar is difficult to understand in view of contacts between the two groups, particularly since the arrival of missionaries in Chihuahua. Absence of the New World peppergrass (*Lepidium virginicum*), the sunflower, and the introduced *Brassica juncea* among the Tepehuan is equally unexplainable. Both groups plow and weed garden plots, utilize seed beds for the initial growth of some garden plants, locate gardens in former corral sites, and irrigate. However, it is apparent that the Tepehuan take better care of their garden plots than do the Tarahumar. Fences of stones, brush, saplings, rails, shingles, and stalks of *ocotillo* are constructed by the Tepehuan. The Tarahumar, on the other hand, almost never fence garden plots; but when they do, rails are commonly used.

Introduced fruit trees (Table X) have generally found acceptance among both groups. Puzzling, however, is the absence among the Tepehuan of the native wild cherry (*Prunus capuli*), the two native plums (*Spondias mombín* and *S. purpurea*), and *Achras zapota*. And equally strange is the fact that the Tarahumar, who are expert at building huts and who are very concerned with food storage, do not construct log storage huts for apples.

IX— GARDEN CROPS

	Tepehuan	Tarahumar	Sources other than Pennington
Plants			
Gramineae			
Saccharum officinarum var.	x	x	
Sorghum vulgare varieties			
Chinese Amber	x		
Hegari	x		
Shallu	x		
Undetermined		x	
Liliaceae			
Allium Ampeloprasum	x		
A. Cepa	x	xxP	Plancarte (1954)
A. sativum		xxP	Plancarte (1954)
Amaranthaceae			
Amaranthus blitoides		P?xxR	1777: Relación de Guaguachic
A. Palmeri		P?xxR	1777: Relación de Guaguachic
A. retroflexus		P?xxR	1777: Relación de Guaguachic
Cruciferae			
Brassica campestris	x	x	
B. juncea		x	
B. oleracea	x	x	
Lepidium virginicum		x	
Leguminosae			
Cicer arietinum	x		
Lathyrus vernus	x		
Pisum sativum	x		
Vicia faba	x		
(cont'd)			

GARDEN CROPS (cont'd)

	Tepehuan	Tarahumar	Sources other than Pennington
Plants (cont'd)			
Cactaceae			
Opuntia sp.	x		
O. sp.	x		
Umbelliferae			
*Coriandrum sativum	x	x	
Solanaceae			
Capsicum annuum	x	x	
Lycopersicon esculentum	x	x	
Nicotiana tabacum	x	x	
Solanum tuberosum	x		
Cucurbitaceae			
*Citrullus vulgaris	x	x	
Compositae			
Helianthus annuus		x	
*Lactuca sativa	x		
Techniques			
Gardens fenced			
Stones	x		
Brush	x		
Saplings	x		
Rails	x	x	
Long shingles	x		
Stalks of *ocotillo*	x		
Irrigated gardens	x	x	
(cont'd)			

GARDEN CROPS (cont'd)

	Tepehuan	Tarahumar	Sources other than Pennington
Techniques (cont'd)			
Nonirrigated gardens	x	x	
Seed beds			
Shallow basket		x	
In ground	x	x	
Gardens located in former corrals	x	x	
Plowing	x	x	
Weeding	x	x	

X— FRUIT TREES AND STORAGE

	Tepehuan	Tarahumar	Sources other than Pennington
Trees			
Moraceae			
*Ficus carica	x	x	
Morus microphylla		x	
Lauraceae			
Persea americana	x	x	
Rosaceae			
*Cydonia oblonga	x	x	
*Malus baccata	x	x	
(cont'd)			

FRUIT TREES AND STORAGE (cont'd)

	Tepehuan	Tarahumar	Sources other than Pennington
Rosaceae (cont'd)			
M. sylvestris	x	x	
Prunus americana	x	x	
P. armeniaca		x	
P. capuli		x	
P. Persica	x	x	
P. Sargentii		x	
Pyrus communis	x	x	
Leguminosae			
Tamarindus indica		xxP	Plancarte (1954)
Rutaceae			
Citrus aurantifolia var.		x	
C. aurantium var.	x	x	
C. decumana var.	x		
C. limonium var.	x	x	
Punicaceae			
Punica granatum	x	x	
Anacardiaceae			
Mangifera indica		xxP	Plancarte (1954)
Spondias mombín		x	
S. purpurea		x	
Sapotaceae			
Achras zapota		x	
(cont'd)			

FRUIT TREES AND STORAGE (cont'd)

	Tepehuan	Tarahumar	Sources other than Pennington
Preservation Techniques			
Apricots dried for storage		x	
Apples dried for storage	x		
Apples stored in corn crib		x	
Apples stored in specially constructed log crib	x		
Peaches dried for storage		x	

The above data hardly indicate much influence of either the Tepehuan or the Tarahumar upon one another. There is a possibility that most of the fruit trees common today among the Tepehuan reached extreme-southern Chihuahua by way of the Tarahumar; this explanation would be consistent with statements by the Tepehuan, who insist that fruit trees were not common at the beginning of the twentieth century, and with historical evidence of a long use by the Tarahumar of fruit trees introduced by Jesuit missionaries. However, a better explanation of the spread of fruit trees throughout Tepehuan country during the past six decades relates to the increase in and the influence of the mestizo population south of the Río Verde.

FOOD PREPARATION AND BEVERAGES

There is little in the preparation of food from field and garden products (Table XI) to indicate an influence of either the Tepehuan or the Tarahumar upon one another. Corn dishes prepared by both groups are more or less the same. *Yoríki* and *pozole*, which are but variants of atole dishes, are not prepared by the Tarahumar. The Tepehuan emphasis on wheat foods undoubtedly reflects more attention to the cultivation of wheat than is common among the Tarahumar. The crude stone oven used by the Tepehuan is analogous to well-made stone ovens used by the mestizos who live south of the Río Verde. Most of the important squash dishes are prepared in identical fashions by the Tepehuan and the Tarahumar. However, some dishes are made by one but not the other. There is no evidence that the Tepehuan fry a cake of toasted squash seeds on the comal, nor do they boil green squash until it thickens, then cool and slice it for frying. Also, the Tepehuan apparently do not use dried squash in preparing a liquid in which meat or potatoes are cooked. The Tarahumar apparently do not boil or fry squash flowers as do the Tepehuan. The Tepehuan emphasize the cultivation of beans more than the Tarahumar do; yet, the Tepehuan seem not as interested as the Tarahumar in a variety of bean dishes. The Tepehuan rarely fry beans and only infrequently stuff large tortillas with them.

Regarding techniques in the preparation of foodstuffs from field and garden products, there is only one major difference between the Tepehuan and the Tarahumar: the pouch-shaped olla used by virtually all the Tarahumar for parching corn is apparently not used by the Tepehuan, who prefer an ordinary olla or a comal for this purpose. It is clear that the Tarahumar are more interested in utilizing plants as a source of substances that give variety to the common foods than the Tepehuan. This is strange in view of the fact that the environments north and south of the Río Verde are not really very different with respect to plant life.

The available evidence pertaining to beverages prepared by the Tepehuan and the Tarahumar (Table XII) indicates that both groups give much attention to the preparation of fermented drinks. However, the Tepehuan do not utilize as many or the variety of plants as sources of basic ingredients and catalysts as the Tarahumar. And there are certain differences in the techniques involved in preparing the all-important *tesgüino*. If indeed the Tarahumar have exerted much cultural influence on the Tepehuan, it is then difficult to explain the relatively few plants used by the Tepehuan in preparing this fermented beverage and the rather simple processes they follow in brewing it. Certainly, within the Tepehuan environment there is no lack of the same species of plants that provide ingredients for Tarahumar *tesgüino*. There is nothing in the historical record to suggest that, with respect to *tesgüino* brewing methods, the Tarahumar influenced the Tepehuan or vice versa. A pre-Columbian tradition of fermented beverages among the Tepehuan and the Tarahumar cannot be documented, but the use of these beverages dates back to at least the seventeenth century. The Tepehuan and Tarahumar who lived at San Pablo (modern-day Balleza, Chihuahua) prepared fermented drinks from maize and maguey (the hearts or crowns?).[16]

XI– FOODS PREPARED FROM FIELD AND GARDEN PRODUCTS

	Tepehuan	Tarahumar	Sources other than Pennington
Foods			
Corn foods			
Pinole	x	x	
Esquiate	x	x	
Atole	x	x	
Yoríki	x		
Pozole	x		
Tortillas	x	x	
Tamales	x	x	
Esquite	x	x	
Boiled fresh corn	x	x	
Roasted fresh corn	x	x	
Wheat foods			
Pinole	x	x	
Esquiate	x		
Tortillas	x		
Tamales	x		
Wheat "bread" baked in crude oven	x		
Wheat "bread" baked on comal		x	
Squash foods			
Boiled dried strips	x	x	
Boiled green squash	x	x	
Boiled green squash until thick, then cooled and sliced, fried on comal		x	
Boiled ripe squash	x	x	
Roasted ripe squash	x	x	
Toasted seeds	x	x	
(cont'd)			

FOODS PREPARED FROM FIELD AND GARDEN PRODUCTS (cont'd)

	Tepehuan	Tarahumar	Sources other than Pennington
Squash foods (cont'd)			
Toasted seeds prepared as a cake and fried on comal		xxBZ	Bennett and Zingg (1935)
Dried squash boiled to prepare liquid in which meat or potatoes are cooked		x	
Flowers boiled or fried	x		
Bean and pea dishes			
Dried beans soaked	x?		
Boiled beans	x	x	
Toasted dried beans ground, mixed with water		x	
Boiled beans fried on comal	x	x	
Boiled beans stuffed into thick tortilla	x	x	
Green beans snapped and boiled	x	x	
Green beans baked in ashes	x		
Boiled peas	x		
Miscellaneous dishes			
Boiled cabbage	x		
Boiled potatoes	x	x	
Baked potatoes	x	x	
Techniques			
Dried corn removed from ears by rubbing cobs together	x	x	
Green corn removed from cob with knife	x	x	
Shucks removed from green corn before roasting	x	x	

(cont'd)

FOODS PREPARED FROM FIELD AND GARDEN PRODUCTS (cont'd)

	Tepehuan	Tarahumar	Sources other than Pennington
Techniques (cont'd)			
Corn grains parched in olla containing sand	x	x	
Pouch-shaped olla used		x	
Lime prepared from oak ashes	x	x	
Lime prepared from limestone rock	x	x	
Rind of squash used as "spoon"	x	x	
Corn parched on comal	x		
Plants and Trees That Supply Additive Substances For Prepared Foods			
Equisetaceae			
Equisetum laevigatum (leaves)		x	
Gramineae			
Sorghum vulgare varieties (seeds)	x		
Zea mays (crushed plumes of young stalks)	x		
Liliaceae			
Nothoscordum bivalve (roots, leaves)	x		
Yucca decipiens (flower stems)	x		
Yucca sp. (seeds?)		xxAC	Ascher and Clune (1960)
Amaryllidaceae			
Agave spp. (roots)	x		
Salicaceae			
Salix Bonplandiana (catkins)		x	
S. Gooddingii (catkins)		x	
S. lasiolepis (catkins)		x	
(cont'd)			

FOODS PREPARED FROM FIELD AND GARDEN PRODUCTS (cont'd)

	Tepehuan	Tarahumar	Sources other than Pennington
Additive Substances (cont'd)			
Fagaceae			
Quercus arizonica (acorns)	x		
Ulmaceae			
Celtis monoica (flowers)		x	
Ulmus LeSueurii (fruits)		x	
U. mexicana (fruits)		x	
Moraceae			
Ficus Goldmannii (fruits)		x	
F. padifolia (fruits)		x	
F. radulina (fruits)		x	
Polygonaceae			
Eriogonum atrorubens (roots)		x	
Chenopodiaceae			
Chenopodium album (leaves)		x	
C. ambrosioides var. (leaves)	x		
C. Fremontii (leaves)	x		
Amaranthaceae			
Amaranthus Palmeri (seeds)		x	
A. retroflexus (seeds)		x	
Iresine cassiniaeformis (flowers, seeds)		x	
Nyctaginaceae			
Mirabilis Jalapa (leaves)		x	
(cont'd)			

FOODS PREPARED FROM FIELD AND GARDEN PRODUCTS (cont'd)

	Tepehuan	Tarahumar	Sources other than Pennington
Additive Substances (cont'd)			
Lauraceae			
Persea Liebmanni (crushed seeds)	x		
Leguminosae			
Acacia cymbispina (seeds)		x	
Cicer arietinum (fruits)	x		
Cologania humifusa (leaves)		x	
Crotalaria incana (leaves)	x		
C. ovalis (leaves)		x	
Lupinus Havardii (flowers)	x		
Pithecellobium dulce (arils)		x	
Phaseolus Metcalfei (seeds)		x	
Prosopis juliflora (pods)		x	
Willardia mexicana (dried gum)		xxBZ	Bennett and Zingg (1935)
Cruciferae			
Brassica campestris (leaves)	x		
B. Kaber (leaves)	x		
Lepidium virginicum (leaves)		x	
Raphanus Raphanistrum (leaves)	x		
Rosaceae			
Prunus brachybotrya (seeds)		x	
P. capuli (leaves)		x	
Oxalidaceae			
Oxalis albicans (leaves)	x		
Euphorbiaceae			
Acalypha phleoides (leaves)		x	
(cont'd)			

FOODS PREPARED FROM FIELD AND GARDEN PRODUCTS (cont'd)

	Tepehuan	Tarahumar	Sources other than Pennington
Additive Substances (cont'd)			
Malvaceae			
Gossypium mexicanum (pods)		xxBZ	Bennett and Zingg (1935)
Bombacaceae			
Ceiba acuminata (pods and seeds)		x	
Onagraceae			
Oenothera grandis (leaves)	x		
O. laciniata (leaves)		x	
O. rosea (leaves)	x		
O. triloba (leaves)	x	x	
Cactaceae			
Lemaireocereus Thurberi (fruits)		x	
Pachycereus pecten-aboriginum (fruits)		x	
Opuntia spp. (leaves)	x		
Umbelliferae			
*Coriandrum sativum (leaves)	x		
Tauschia nudicaulis (leaves)	x		
Pyrolaceae			
Chimaphila umbellata (leaves)	x		
Ericaceae			
Arbutus arizonica (flowers)		x	
A. glandulosa (flowers)		x	
A. xalapensis (flowers)		x	
Arctostaphylos pungens (seeds)		x	
(cont'd)			

FOODS PREPARED FROM FIELD AND GARDEN PRODUCTS (cont'd)

	Tepehuan	Tarahumar	Sources other than Pennington
Additive Substances (cont'd)			
Oleaceae			
Fraxinus papillosa (leaves)		x	
F. velutina (leaves)		x	
Hydrophyllaceae			
Phacelia teucriifolia (leaves)	x		
Verbenaceae			
Lippia Berlandieri (leaves)	x	x	
L. Palmeri (leaves)	x		
Labiatae			
Mentha canadensis (leaves)	x		
Solanaceae			
Capsicum annuum (fruits)	x	x	
C. baccatum (fruits)	x	x	
Acanthaceae			
Jacobinia candicans (flowers)		x	
Plantaginaceae			
Plantago argyrea (leaves)		x	
P. galeottiana (leaves)		x	
P. major (leaves)		x	
Compositae			
Cirsium mexicanum (leaves)	x		
Helianthus annuus (leaves)		x	
Sonchus oleraceus (leaves)	x	x	
S. asper (leaves)		x	

XII– BEVERAGES

	Tepehuan	Tarahumar	Sources other than Pennington
Basic Ingredients			
Gramineae			
Saccharum officinarum var.			
Fresh stalks	x		
Sprouts	x		
Sorghum vulgare varieties			
Fresh stalks	x		
Sprouts	x		
Triticum aestivum var.			
Sprouts	x		
Zea mays			
Fresh stalks	Px	Px	
Sprouts	Px	Px	
Liliaceae			
Dasylirion durangense (hearts)		Px	
D. Wheeleri (hearts)	Px		
Amaryllidaceae			
Agave bovicornuta (hearts)		Px	
A. lecheguilla (hearts)		Px	
A. Patonii (hearts)		Px	
A. Schottii (hearts)		Px	
A. sp. (hearts)	Px		
A. sp. (hearts)	Px		
A. sp. (hearts)	Px		
A. sp. (hearts)	Px		
Lauraceae			
Persea Liebmanni (seeds)	x		
(cont'd)			

BEVERAGES (cont'd)

	Tepehuan	Tarahumar	Sources other than Pennington
Basic Ingredients(cont'd)			
Platanaceae			
Platanus Wrightii (bark)	x		
Rosaceae			
Malus baccata (fruits)		x	
M. sylvestris (fruits)		x	
Prunus Persica (fruits)	x		
Leguminosae			
Prosopis juliflora (fruits)		x	
Cactaceae			
Ariocarpus fissuratus (juice)		x	
Cephalocereus leucocephalus (fruits)		x	
Ferocactus sp. (fruits)		x	
Lemaireocereus Thurberi (fruits)		x	
Lophophora Williamsii (juice)		x	
Pachycereus pecten-aboriginum (fruits)		x	
Ericaceae			
Arbutus arizonica (fruits)		x	
A. glandulosa (fruits)		x	
A. xalapensis (fruits)		x	
Labiatae			
Salvia tiliaefolia (seeds)		x	
Rubiaceae			
Randia laevigata (fruits)	x		
(cont'd)			

BEVERAGES (cont'd)

	Tepehuan	Tarahumar	Sources other than Pennington
Catalysts			
Selaginellaceae			
Selaginella cuspidata (entire plant)		xxBZ	Bennett and Zingg (1935)
Gramineae			
Bromus arizonicus (stems)	x	x	
B. molliformis (stems)	x		
B. sp. (stems)	x		
Cyperaceae			
Fimbristylis sp. (entire plant)		xxBZ	Bennett and Zingg (1935)
Fagaceae			
Quercus crassifolia (bark)	x		
Leguminosae			
Phaseolus Metcalfei (roots)		x	
Plumbago scandens (roots)		x	
Pyrolaceae			
Chimaphila dasystemma (leaves)		x	
C. maculata (leaves)	x		
C. umbellata (leaves)	x		
Solanaceae			
Datura meteloides (leaves)		x	
Rubiaceae			
Coutarea pterosperma (bark)		x	
Randia echinocarpa (bark)	x	x	
R. laevigata (bark)	x	x	
R. Watsoni (bark)		x	
(cont'd)			

BEVERAGES (cont'd)

	Tepehuan	Tarahumar	Sources other than Pennington
Catalysts (cont'd)			
Compositae			
Hieracium Fendleri (roots)		x	
Stevia serrata (leaves)		x	
Usneaceae			
Usnea subfusca (entire plant)		x	
U. variolosa (entire plant)		x	
Unidentified species	x		
Techniques			
Seed beds			
Pine needle	x	x	
Basket	x	x	
In ground	x	x	
Within habitations	x	x	
Outside habitations	x	x	
Dried corn used for preparing tesgüino	x		
Sprouts crushed on metate	x	x	
Stalks crushed in hollowed-out log	x	x	
Stalks crushed in rock depression	x	x	
Stalks crushed with oak mallet		x	
Stalks crushed with wooden club	x		
Blanket used to soak up juice from hollowed-out log or rock depression		x	
(cont'd)			

BEVERAGES (cont'd)

	Tepehuan	Tarahumar	Sources other than Pennington
Techniques (cont'd)			
Guaje used for removal of juice from hollowed-out log or rock depression	x	x	
Pounded stalks placed on lattice anchored above container; water poured over stalks		x	
Squeezing net used to extract juice from crushed stalks		x	
Juice from crushed stalks poured through basket	x		
Catalysts added as sprouts are crushed on metate	x	x	
Catalysts added to boiling mixture	x	x	
Mixture removed from olla several times during boiling process and strained through basket	x	x	
Fresh batches of tesgüino added to fermenting tesgüino		x	
Tesgüino fermented in hollowed-out pumpkin		PxxS	Circa 1767: Steffel (1809)
Jars of tesgüino buried in pit in habitation		PxxA	1744: Abeé
Flowers of Bouvardia ternifolia decorate olla in which tesgüino is fermenting	x		

HUNTING AND TRAPPING

Basically, there are few important differences between the Tepehuan and the Tarahumar regarding weapons and techniques that pertain to hunting and trapping (Table XIII), and some of the differences may be a reflection of insufficient field data. However, the Tarahumar apparently do not manufacture the medium-sized bows that measure approximately thirty inches long, and they apparently do not wrap their bows with skin or green bark as the Tepehuan do. The Tepehuan do not utilize white pigment for decorating bows and arrows, and they claim never to have done so. The differences in types of woods utilized in the manufacture of bows and arrows seem to be related to personal preferences and to the distribution and availability of suitable woods. Foreshafted arrows are much less common among the Tepehuan than among the Tarahumar, and the Tarahumar apparently make greater use of arrowheads than do the Tepehuan. Both old and young Tepehuan are familiar with the techniques of arrow-poisoning practiced by the Tarahumar, but they claim the Tepehuan never followed this custom. Hunting and trapping techniques employed by both groups are very similar.

It seems clear that the basic elements of hunting and trapping customs followed by contemporary Tepehuan and Tarahumar are so ancient that it is impossible to speculate on which group influenced the other with respect to these traits.

XIII— HUNTING AND TRAPPING

	Tepehuan	Tarahumar	Sources other than Pennington
Weapons			
Rifles (rare)	x	x	
Bows			
Large bow (about 48" long)	Px	Px	
Medium bow (about 30" long)	x		
Diminutive bow (about 17" long)	x	x	
Woods used in bow			
Caesalpinia platyloba		x	
(cont'd)			

HUNTING AND TRAPPING (cont'd)

	Tepehuan	Tarahumar	Sources other than Pennington
Woods used in bow (cont'd)			
Fraxinus papillosa		x	
F. velutina		x	
Guazuma ulmifolia	x		
Haematoxylon brasiletto	x	x	
Morus microphylla	x	x	
Populus angustifolia		x	
Tecoma stans	x	x	
Ulmus divaricata		x	
Other woods	x	x	
Bows wrapped			
With skin	x		
With green bark	x		
Tips of bow notched	x	x	
Bows painted			
With red pigment	x	x	
With white pigment		x	
Paint tubes for pigments		Px;xxZ	Zingg (1940)
Bow strings			
Sinew from back of deer	x	x	
Vegetal fiber (ixtle)	x	x	
Rawhide	x		
Hair from cow's tail	x		
Modes of holding bow for shooting arrow			
Horizontally	x	x	
Vertically	x	x	
(cont'd)			

HUNTING AND TRAPPING (cont'd)

	Tepehuan	Tarahumar	Sources other than Pennington
Weapons (cont'd)			
Arrows without heads or foreshafts			
Woods used			
Cercocarpus montanus		x	
Fraxinus velutina	x	x	
Garrya laurifolia	x		
Lonicera pilosa		x	
Mahonia fascicularis	x		
Rhamnus sp.		x	
Tecoma stans		x	
Other woods	x		
Reeds used			
Arundo donax		x	
Phragmites communis	x	x	
Other reeds	x	x	
Feathered			
Two halved feathers	x	x	
Three halved feathers	x	x	
Featherless	x	x	
Tipped with corncob		x	
Blunt-tipped	x	x	
Painted			
With red pigment	x	x	
With white pigment		x	
Arrows with heads but no foreshafts			
Woods used			
Ceanothus azureus	x		
Cercocarpus montanus		x	
Fraxinus velutina	x		
Garrya laurifolia	x		
Lonicera pilosa		x	
Mahonia fascicularis	x		
Rhamnus sp.		x	
Tecoma stans		x	
Other woods	x	x	
(cont'd)			

HUNTING AND TRAPPING (cont'd)

	Tepehuan	Tarahumar	Sources other than Pennington
Arrows (heads, no foreshafts) (cont'd)			
Feathered			
Two halved feathers	x	x	
Three halved feathers	x	x	
Painted			
With red pigment	x	x	
With white pigment		x	
Foreshafted arrows			
Woods used			
Berberis Fremontii	x		
Cercocarpus montanus		x	
Garrya laurifolia	x		
G. ovata	x		
Ipomoea arborescens	x		
Lonicera pilosa		x	
Rhamnus sp.		x	
Other woods	x	Px;xxB	Brooks et al. (1962)
Reeds used			
Arundo donax		x	
Phragmites communis	x	x	
Other reeds	x	x	
Feathered			
Two halved feathers	x	x	
Three halved feathers	x	x	
Painted			
With red pigment	x	x	
With white pigment		x	
Arrow-straighteners			
Stone	x	PxxZ	Zingg (1940)
Wood		x	
Piece of pottery	x		
(cont'd)			

HUNTING AND TRAPPING (cont'd)

	Tepehuan	Tarahumar	Sources other than Pennington
Weapons (cont'd)			
Arrowheads			
Flint	x	x	
Obsidian	Px;xxB	Px;xxS	Brooks et al. (1962); Circa 1767: Steffel (1809)
Wood			
Berberis Fremontii	x		
Garrya laurifolia	x		
G. ovata	x	x	
Ipomoea arborescens	x		
Other woods	x	x	
Hafting			
Gut	x		
Sinew from back of deer	x	x	
Vegetal fiber (ixtle)	x	x	
Arrow poisons			
Vegetal matter		x	
Animal matter		x	
Wooden clubs	x	x	
Stone axes or clubs	x	x	
Lances	Px;xxB	Px;xxP	Brooks et al. (1962); 1645: Pérez de Ribas (1944)
Slings			
Pouch and string of vegetal fiber	x	x	
Pouch and string of rawhide	x	x	
Quivers	x	Px;xxS	Circa 1767: Steffel (1809)
(cont'd)			

HUNTING AND TRAPPING (cont'd)

	Tepehuan	Tarahumar	Sources other than Pennington
Weapons (cont'd)			
Wrist guards			
Bone		PxxR	1777: Relación de Guaguachic
Rawhide	x	x	
Techniques			
Dancing before hunting expedition	x		
Offerings made to "master" of hunt before hunting	x		
Dogs			
Individual hunting	x	x	
Communal hunting	x	x	
Fire drives		x	
Drives			
Deer into converging stake fences	x		
Deer over cliff	x	x	
Peccaries over cliff	x		
Running down game			
Deer	x	x	
Rabbits	x	x	
Turkeys	x	x	
Fawn-calls in rutting season	x		
Deer masks as decoy	x		
Individuals stationed on deer trails	x	x	
Individuals stationed near water holes	x		
(cont'd)			

HUNTING AND TRAPPING (cont'd)

	Tepehuan	Tarahumar	Sources other than Pennington
Techniques (cont'd)			
Pitfalls			
Coyotes	x		
Wolves	x		
Stakes in ground so that deer will be impaled			
Placed on trail	x	x	
Placed beyond fence jumped by animals	x	x	
Placed near entrance of corral	x		
Snares			
Birds		x	
Deer	x	x	
Gophers and moles		x	
Deadfalls (figure-four release)			
Stone	x	x	
Inverted fruit crate	x		
Inverted *cajete*	x		
Steel traps	x	x	
Conical brush traps			
Sprung by turkey	x	x	
Sprung by hunter		x	
Turkey clubbed to death in trap	x		
Log traps		x	
Sticks or arrows used to extract animals from burrows	x	x	
"Smothering" animals in nest with smoke	x	x	
Commercial poison	x	x	

The animals sought by the Tepehuan and the Tarahumar (Table XIV), whether as a source of food or skins or because the animals are predators, are virtually the same kinds except for the mule deer and opossum of Tarahumar country. The Tepehuan claim to know of these creatures but insist that they do not appear in extreme-southern Chihuahua. Absence of the mule deer may be related to the fact that mestizos with guns have tried to eliminate the deer as a predator within the past several decades. The Tepehuan statement that the opossum does not appear south of the Río Verde in Chihuahua is corroborated by the mestizos.[17] Of some interest is that although the Tepehuan appear to be as interested as the Tarahumar in medicinal preparations, they apparently make no use of animal fat—from wild or domestic animals—in preparing poultices, a very common practice among the Tarahumar. Whatever the origin of this practice among the Tarahumar, the custom apparently has not spread south of the Río Verde, at least not among the Tepehuan.

Almost all birds common to the high country of western Chihuahua and to the canyons that break away to the west are hunted by the Tepehuan and the Tarahumar for various reasons: the desire for food, the demand for feathers that are used in some fashion, the use of the creatures for medicinal purposes, or because the birds damage crops and are predators (Table XV). The most striking difference regarding attitudes towards birds is the superstitious beliefs held by the Tepehuan about certain birds. For example, there seems to be no evidence that the Tarahumar refrain from eating certain birds because of a fear that sons will not be born or that male children will die.

The above data suggest that, as is the case with weapons and techniques associated with hunting and trapping, there is no evidence that either the Tepehuan or the Tarahumar have much influenced one another as far as utilization of wild animals and birds is concerned. The same interpretation seems to be true for fishing activities (Table XVI), which, for the most part, are characterized by customs that appear to be rather ancient (probably dating back to pre-Columbian times) and so old that it is impossible to determine which group first practiced these customs. Differences in fishing activities appear to be of only minor importance. The Tepehuan display a certain interest in fishing and in fish as food, but they do not, as a whole, emphasize this food source as much as the Tarahumar do. In part, this may be because streams of the Tepehuan country, particularly those of the uplands, are not well stocked with fish. The Tepehuan favor hook-and-line fishing, whereas the Tarahumar do not. However, the Tarahumar must have once used the hook-and-line method since a cactus-spine fishhook has been recovered from an archeological site that is clearly within the Tarahumar country.[18] The funnel-shaped trap made of reeds is common among the Tarahumar, but it is apparently neither fashioned nor used in Tepehuan country. The Tepehuan display no interest in making seines,

XIV— ANIMALS HUNTED

	Tepehuan			Tarahumar			
	Food	Predator	Skin	Food	Predator	Skin	Medicine
Cottontails	x	x		x		x	
Hares				x		x	
Squirrels	x	x		x	x		
Armadillos	x						
Moles	x	x			x		
Gophers					x		
Rodents (small, field)	x	x		x	x		
Skunks	x	x		x			x
Bobcats		x					
Pumas		x	x		x		
Jaguarundis	x	x					
Jaguars			x		x	x	
Ocelots	x	x	x				
Otters	x		x	x		x	x
Ring-tailed cats		x	x				x
Raccoons	x	x	x				x
Coatis	x	x					x
Badgers				x	x		x
Opossums							x
Gray foxes		x	x		x	x	
Coyotes		x	x			x	x
Wolves		x		x	x		
Peccaries	x	x		x	x		
Bears	x	x	x		x	x	x
Mule deer				x		x	
White-tailed deer	x	x	x	x		x	

from either vegetable fibers or blankets, as the Tarahumar do. The Tarahumar reed-tipped spear used in taking fish is unknown among the Tepehuan, and they do not utilize the throwing stick that Lumholtz recorded as a weapon used by the Tarahumar to spear fish.[19]

Tepehuan techniques for stupefying fish differ but little from those practiced by the Tarahumar, and in some instances, the Tepehuan use the same species of plants. It is certain that there is a greater variety and number of plants used as piscicidal agents among the Tarahumar. However, this may be explained in that the Tarahumar habitat apparently supports a greater variety of plants than the Tepehuan habitat.

XV— FOWLING

	Tepehuan					Tarahumar				Sources other than Pennington
	Food	Predator	Medicine	Feathers	Superstitions	Food	Predator	Medicine	Feathers	
Turkeys	x					x				
Chachalacas	x					x				
Pheasants (several varieties)	x					x				
Horned guans								xxR		1777: Relación de Nabogame
Kingfishers	x									
Cranes						x				
Ducks						x				
Whimbrels	x									
Herons	x									
Crows	x	x				xxT	x			Thord-Gray (1955)
Hawks Red-tailed	x	x								
Sparrow	x	x								
(cont'd)										

FOWLING (cont'd)

	Tepehuan					Tarahumar				Sources other than Pennington
	Food	Predator	Medicine	Feathers	Superstitions	Food	Predator	Medicine	Feathers	
Hawks (cont'd)										
Pipíkoli	x	x								
Gavilán de la tierra		x		x						
Hawk variety						x				
Owls										
Tecolote	x				x					
Lechuza	x				x					
Pica metate		x								
Buho	x	x								
Owl varieties (several)						x?				
Woodpeckers										
Acorn	x									
Spotted-chested	x									
Red-breasted, yellow-bellied	x									
Ivory-billed			x						x	
Hairy woodpecker					x					
Woodpecker variety					x					
Woodpecker variety					x					
Meadowlarks	x									
Blackbirds						xxL				Lumholtz (1902)
Pigeons						x				
Doves										
Paloma torcáz	x									
Paloma del monte	x									
Quail varieties (several)	x					x				
Upland plovers	x									
Golondrinas			x			x				
Hummingbirds	x					x				
(cont'd)										

FOWLING (cont'd)

	Tepehuan					Tarahumar				Sources other than Pennington
	Food	Predator	Medicine	Feathers	Superstitions	Food	Predator	Medicine	Feathers	
Magpies						x				
Macaws									x	
Eagles		x					x			
Sopilotes		x					x			
Blue Jays					x					
Saltaparedes					x					
Miscellaneous birds										
Water bird with very long tail					x					
Meadow bird with red, black, and white feathers					x					
Water bird with very large bill					x					

XVI– FISHING

	Tepehuan	Tarahumar	Sources other than Pennington
Hook-and-line			
Metal hook	x		
Bone hook	x		
Cactus-spine hook	x	PxxC	Clune (1960)
Ixtle-fiber line	x		
(cont'd)			

FISHING (cont'd)

	Tepehuan	Tarahumar	Sources other than Pennington
Hook-and-line (cont'd)			
Yucca-fiber leader		PxxC	Clune (1960)
Leaves and fruits of *Datura meteloides* crushed and rubbed on lower portion of ixtle-fiber leader	x		
Throwing sticks		xxL	Lumholtz (1902)
Diminutive bows and arrows	x	x	
Reeds tipped with cactus thorns or wire		x	
Dynamite caps	x	x	
Fish trapped behind crude earth and stone dam	x	x	
Funnel-shaped traps of vegetal materials			
*Arundo donax		x	
Phragmites communis		x	
Converging stone walls closed by weirs of vegetal materials			
*Arundo donax		x	
Phragmites communis		x	
Ptelea aquilina		xxL	Lumholtz (1902)
Salix Gooddingii	x		
jarilla del río	x		
Seines			
Vegetal fiber		x	
Blanket		xxL	Lumholtz (1902)
Offerings made to "master" of fish	xxL	xxL	Lumholtz (1902)
(cont'd)			

FISHING (cont'd)

	Tepehuan	Tarahumar	Sources other than Pennington
Fish stupefaction			
Within stone corral	x	x	
Behind stone or earthen dam	x	x	
Plant material crushed, placed in basket, sloshed in stream	x	x	
Crushed plant material thrown into stream behind dam	x	x	
Plants used			
Liliaceae			
Yucca decipiens		x	
Amaryllidaceae			
Agave bovicornuta		x	
A. lecheguilla		x	
A. Schottii		x	
A. sp.	x		
A. sp.	x		
A. sp.	x		
Iridaceae			
Sisyrinchium arizonicum		x	
Juglandaceae			
Carya illinoensis		x	
Juglans major	x	x	
Polygonaceae			
Polygonum pensylvanicum		x	
P. punctatum		x	
Papaveraceae			
Argemone ochroleuca subsp. *ochroleuca*	x		
Rosaceae			
Licania retifolia	x		
Prunus capuli	x	x	
*P. Persica		x	
P. serotina	x		
P. virens	x		
Leguminosae			
Brongniartia sp.	x		
Lupinus sp.	x		
Mimosa dysocarpa		x	
(cont'd)			

FISHING (cont'd)

	Tepehuan	Tarahumar	Sources other than Pennington
Leguminosae (cont'd)			
Phaseolus salicifolius (?)	x		
Tephrosia leiocarpa		x	
T. nicaraguensis		xxBZ	Bennett and Zingg (1935)
T. Thurberi	x		
Rutaceae			
Casimiroa edulis		xxBZ	Bennett and Zingg (1935)
C. sapota		xxBZ	Bennett and Zingg (1935)
Euphorbiaceae			
Hura crepitans	x		
Sapium biloculare		x	
Sebastiana Pringlei		x	
Umbelliferae			
Conium maculatum		x	
Ligusticum Porteri		x	
Polemoniaceae			
Ipomopsis Thurberi (?)		x	
Gilia Macombii		xxG	Gajdusek (1954)
Compositae			
Baccharis glutinosa		x	
Cacalia decomposita		xxBZ	Bennett and Zingg (1935)
Dyssodia anomala		x	
Senecio Hartwegii		x	
Stevia salicifolia		x	
Viguiera decurrens		x	
Zexmenia podocephala	x	x	
Unidentified specimens			
anači		x	
yerba del piojo de los puercos	x		
yerba del pescado	x		
yerba loca	x		

COLLECTED FOODS

There are only minor dissimilarities in the list of plant species sought for their fruits and nuts by the Tepehuan and the Tarahumar (Table XVII). Some of the differences are no doubt reflections of taste and environment, but others are difficult to explain. Moreover, the differences mentioned herein may result only from insufficient field data. The Tepehuan are familiar with the juniper, which is so common in Tarahumar country; but they insist that juniper berries, which can be found in Tepehuan country south of the Río Verde, are not eaten—at least not by the Indians. Both groups toast and eat most acorns from the many species of oaks in western and southern Chihuahua without any further preparation. However, the Tepehuan do cook, rinse, and crush *Quercus arizonica* acorns as an added ingredient in meal used to make tortillas. Somewhat puzzling is the inattention of the Tepehuan to hackberry fruits; the trees are very common south of the Río Verde except in high and flattish uplands that are usually pine dominated. The great fig trees that are so numerous in western canyons of the Tarahumar country, such as *Ficus petiolaris, F. cotinifolia, F. padifolia*, and *F. radulina*, also grow in profusion along the Río Verde tributary canyons at lower elevations and in western Tepehuan canyons, but the Tepehuan claim that their fruits are not eaten. This disregard of a food source is inexplicable, but no more so than *Persea Liebmanni* fruits being eaten apparently only by the Tepehuan and *Rivina humilis* fruits being consumed only by the Tarahumar. Particularly difficult to understand is the Tepehuan statement that fruits of the *guamúchil* (*Pithecellobium dulce*), which appears south of the Río Verde, are not eaten; the flavorsome fruit of this tree is much esteemed by the Tarahumar.

Available data indicate that the Tarahumar make far more use of wild plants and trees as a source of leaves eaten as *quelites* than do the Tepehuan (Table XVIII); this disparity may indicate either the more varied habitat north of the Río Verde or simply a difference in taste and custom. Rather striking is that the Tepehuan apparently do not utilize the leaves of some very common trees in their habitat, such as various *Quercus* species and two widely distributed species of the Salicaceae family, *Salix lasiolepis* and *S. Bonplandiana*. Because the Tepehuan frequently experience hunger due to a scarcity of food supply, it seems strange that they have not learned from the Tarahumar about these additional sources of *quelites*.

The above data suggest that there is little with respect to collected fruits, nuts, and *quelites* to indicate Tepehuan or Tarahumar influence upon one another. This statement is also true regarding toasted seeds in the Indian diet (Table XIX). According to available data, not one out of the nine varieties of seeds collected by the Tarahumar is sought by the Tepehuan.

XVII— FRUITS AND NUTS COLLECTED

	Tepehuan	Tarahumar	Sources other than Pennington
Pinaceae			
Pinus ayacahuite	x	x	
P. cembroides		x	
P. Engelmanni	x		
P. leiophylla	x		
P. reflexa		x	
Cupressaceae			
Juniperus pachyphloea		x	
Liliaceae			
Yucca decipiens	x		
Juglandaceae			
Carya illinoensis		x	
Juglans major	x	x	
Fagaceae			
Quercus albocincta	x	x	
Q. arizonica	x		
Q. chihuahuensis	x		
Q. crassifolia	x		
Q. durifolia		x	
Q. Emoryi		x	
Q. Endlichiana	x		
Q. hypoleucoides	x	x	
Q. omissa	x	x	
Q. rugosa	x		
Q. Watsoni		x	
Q. sp.	x		
(cont'd)			

FRUITS AND NUTS COLLECTED (cont'd)

	Tepehuan	Tarahumar	Sources other than Pennington
Ulmaceae			
Celtis iguanaeus		x	
C. monoica		x	
C. reticulata		x	
Ulmus divaricata		x	
U. LeSueurii		x	
U. mexicana		x	
Moraceae			
Ficus cotinifolia		x	
F. Goldmannii		x	
F. padifolia		x	
F. petiolaris		x	
F. radulina		x	
Morus microphylla	x	x	
Loranthaceae			
Phoradendron Engelmanni		x	
P. scaberrimum	x		
P. sp.	x		
Struthanthus diversifolius	x		
Lauraceae			
Persea Liebmanni	x		
Phytolaccaceae			
Rivina humilis		x	
Rosaceae			
Crataegus sp. af. *mexicana*	x		
(cont'd)			

FRUITS AND NUTS COLLECTED (cont'd)

	Tepehuan	Tarahumar	Sources other than Pennington
Rosaceae (cont'd)			
Fragaria mexicana		x	
F. vesca	x		
Licania retifolia	x		
Potentilla Thurberi		x	
Prunus brachybotrya		xxBZ	Bennett and Zingg (1935)
P. capuli	x	x	
P. serotina	x		
P. virens	x		
Rubus idaeus var. *strigosus*		x	
R. sp	x		
R. sp.	x		
Leguminosae			
Pithecellobium dulce		x	
Rutaceae			
Casimiroa edulis		xxBZ	Bennett and Zingg (1935)
C. sapota		xxBZ	Bennett and Zingg (1935)
Citrus medica		xxBZ	Bennett and Zingg (1935)
Malpighiaceae			
Thryallis glauca		x	
Rhamnaceae			
Karwinskia Humboldtiana	x	x	
Rhamnus serrata (?)	x		
Zizyphus acuminata		x	
(cont'd)			

FRUITS AND NUTS COLLECTED (cont'd)

	Tepehuan	Tarahumar	Sources other than Pennington
Vitaceae			
Vitis arizonica	x	x	
V. bourgaeana	x		
V. rupestris	x		
Sterculiaceae			
Guazuma ulmifolia		x	
Cactaceae			
Cephalocereus leucocephalus		x	
Echinocereus dasyacanthus		x	
E. sp. af. Reichenbachii (?)	x		
E. sp. af. triglochidiatus (?)	x		
Ferocactus sp.		x	
F. sp.		x	
Lemaireocereus Thurberi		x	
Opuntia sp.		x	
O. sp.		x	
O. sp.		x	
O. sp.		x	
O. sp.		x	
O. sp.	x		
O. sp.	x		
Pachycereus pecten-aboriginum	x	x	
Myrtaceae			
Eugenia capuli		xxBZ	Bennett and Zingg (1935)
Psidium guajava	x	xxBZ	Bennett and Zingg (1935)
(cont'd)			

FRUITS AND NUTS COLLECTED (cont'd)

	Tepehuan	Tarahumar	Sources other than Pennington
Ericaceae			
Arbutus arizonica	x	x	
A. glandulosa	x	x	
A. xalapensis	x	x	
Arctostaphylos pungens	x	x	
Gaultheria glaucifolia		xxBZ	Bennett and Zingg (1935)
G. sp.	x	x	
Vaccinium confertum	x		
Sapotaceae			
Achras zapota	x	x	
A. sp.		x	
Asclepiadaceae			
Asclepias sordida	x		
A. strictiflora	x		
Convolvulaceae			
Ipomoea arborescens		xxBZ	Bennett and Zingg (1935)
Verbenaceae			
Lantana involucrata		xxBZ	Bennett and Zingg (1935)
Vitex mollis		x	
Solanaceae			
Chamaesaracha sp.	x		
Physalis sordida		x	
P. sp. af. *sordida*		x	
P. viscosa	x		
P. sp.		x	
P. sp.	x		
(cont'd)			

FRUITS AND NUTS COLLECTED (cont'd)

	Tepehuan	Tarahumar	Sources other than Pennington
Solanaceae (cont'd)			
Saracha jaltomata	x	x	
Solanum gracile	x		
*S. nigrum	x		
S. podiflorum	x		
Bignoniaceae			
Crescentia alata		xxBZ	Bennett and Zingg (1935)
Rubiaceae			
Randia echinocarpa	x	x	
R. laevigata	x	x	
R. Watsoni	x		
Rubus trivialis	x		
Caprifoliaceae			
Lonicera involucrata	x		
L. pilosa	x		
Unidentified specimens			
tuna colorada	x		
nakíši	x		
kasti návoi	x		
chapote	x		

XVIII— QUELITES COLLECTED

	Tepehuan	Tarahumar	Sources other than Pennington
Fagaceae			
Quercus durifolia		x	
Q. epileuca		x	
Q. hypoleucoides		x	
Salicaceae			
Salix Bonplandiana		x	
S. lasiolepis		x	
Ulmaceae			
Celtis monoica		x	
Moraceae			
Morus microphylla	x	x	
Polygonaceae			
Eriogonum sp.	x		
Rumex altissimus	x		
R. crispus	x		
*R. pulcher	x		
Urticaceae			
Urtica gracilis		x	
Chenopodiaceae			
Chenopodium album	x	x	
C. ambrosioides		x	
C. ambrosioides var.	x		
C. Berlandieri var. sinuatum (?)	x		
C. incanum (?)	x		
(cont'd)			

QUELITES COLLECTED (cont'd)

	Tepehuan	Tarahumar	Sources other than Pennington
Amaranthaceae			
Amaranthus blitoides		x	
A. hybridus		x	
A. leucocarpus	x		
A. Palmeri (?)	x		
A. Powellii	x		
A. retroflexus		x	
Phytolaccaceae			
Phytolacca icosandra	x		
Portulacaceae			
*Portulaca oleracea	x	x	
Cruciferae			
*Brassica campestris	x	x	
*B. juncea		x	
Descurainia pinnata	x	x	
Lepidium virginicum		x	
*Nasturtium officinale	x		
Roripa mexicana		x	
R. islandica	x		
Geraniaceae			
*Erodium cicutarium		x	
Oxalidaceae			
Oxalis albicans	x		
O. decaphylla		x	
O. divergens		x	
O. stricta	x		
(cont'd)			

QUELITES COLLECTED (cont'd)

	Tepehuan	Tarahumar	Sources other than Pennington
Euphorbiaceae			
Tragia nepetaefolia		x	
Violaceae			
Viola umbracticola		x	
Begoniaceae			
Begonia gracilis		x	
Onagraceae			
Oenothera laciniata		x	
O. rosea	x		
O. triloba		x	
Umbelliferae			
Arracacia edulis		x	
*Coriandrum sativum	x		
Eryngium Carlinae		x	
Osmorhiza radicans	x		
Tauschia nudicaulis	x		
Oleaceae			
Fraxinus papillosa		x	
F. velutina	x	x	
Asclepiadaceae			
Asclepias brachystephana		x	
A. glaucescens		x	
A. sp.		x	
Matelea sp.		x	
Convolvulaceae			
Ipomoea purpurea		xxBZ	Bennett and Zingg (1935)
(cont'd)			

QUELITES COLLECTED (cont'd)

	Tepehuan	Tarahumar	Sources other than Pennington
Hydrophyllaceae			
Phacelia congesta (?)	x		
P. teucriifolia	x		
Verbenaceae			
Lippia Berlandieri		x	
L. Palmeri		x	
L. sp.		xxBZ	Bennett and Zingg (1935)
Labiatae			
Mentha canadensis		x	
M. sp.		x	
Solanaceae			
*Solanum nigrum		xxBZ	Bennett and Zingg (1935)
Scrophulariaceae			
Mimulus guttatus	x	x	
Martyniaceae			
Martynia fragans		x	
Plantaginaceae			
Plantago argyrea		x	
P. galeottiana		x	
P. hirtella		x	
*P. major		x	
P. sp.	x		
Compositae			
Bidens Bigelovii		x	
Cirsium mexicanum	x		
(cont'd)			

QUELITES COLLECTED (cont'd)

	Tepehuan	Tarahumar	Sources other than Pennington
Compositae (cont'd)			
Cosmos Pringlei		x	
Eclipta alba		x	
Hieracium Fendleri		x	
*Sonchus asper		x	
*S. oleraceus	x		
Viguiera helianthoides		x	
Unidentified specimens			
kuči	x		
okata ívagi	x		
chichiquelite		x	
begonia		x	
ipasote		x	
orégano serrano		x	
sepé		x	
čoríkari		x	
borobé		x	
kujúbari		x	
nawábori		x	
wipáka		x	
bajisočuri		x	

XIX— SEEDS COLLECTED FOR TOASTING

	Tepehuan	Tarahumar	Sources other than Pennington
Equisetaceae			
Equisetum laevigatum		x	
Liliaceae			
Yucca sp. (?)		PxxAC	Ascher and Clune (1960)
Leguminosae			
Acacia cymbispina		x	
Caesalpinia pulcherrima		x	
Calliandra humilis var. *reticulata*		x	
Crotalaria incana	x		
Phaseolus Metcalfei		x	
Bombacaceae			
Ceiba acuminata		x	
Sterculiaceae			
Guazuma ulmifolia		x	
Martyniaceae			
Martynia fragans		x	
Compositae			
Helianthus annuus		x	

There is generally little difference in emphasis between the Tepehuan and the Tarahumar with respect to roots collected as food (Table XX). The important contrast pertains to techniques utilized in baking the hearts or crowns of certain Liliaceae and Amaryllidaceae species. Earth ovens are utilized by both groups, but only the Tarahumar favor baking the roots in an open oven. The Tepehuan insist that they have never used an open oven. Why this practical technique has not spread from the Tarahumar to the Tepehuan is not known.

XX— ROOTS COLLECTED

	Tepehuan	Tarahumar
Roots		
Palmae		
Sabal uresana		x
Liliaceae		
Dasylirion durangense		x
D. Wheeleri	x	x
Yucca decipiens	x	
Amaryllidaceae		
Agave bovicornuta		x
A. chihuahuana		x
A. Hartmani		x
A. Patonii		x
A. Schottii		x
A. sp.	x	
A. sp.	x	
A. sp.	x	
A. sp.	x	
Bravoa sp.	x	
Polygonaceae		
Eriogonum atrorubens		x
Oxalidaceae		
Oxalis decaphylla		x
Bombacaceae		
Ceiba acuminata	x	x
Umbelliferae		
Prionosciadium serratum		x
(cont'd		

ROOTS COLLECTED (cont'd)

	Tepehuan	Tarahumar
Convolvulaceae		
Exogonium bracteatum	x	x
Solanaceae		
Solanum cardiophyllum	x	
S. sp.	x	
S. sp.	x	
Valerianaceae		
Valeriana sp.	x	
Unidentified specimens		
contra yerba	x	
camote		x
camotito		x
burrero		x
calcomete		x
aríkari		x
Preparation		
Roots roasted on bed of embers		x
Open ovens		
Lined with stones		x
Fire built on stones		x
Layer of grass or pine needles placed on stones		x
Roots placed in oven, covered with hot stones		x
Earth ovens		
Lined with stones	x	x
(cont'd)		

ROOTS COLLECTED (cont'd)

	Tepehuan	Tarahumar
Earth ovens (cont'd)		
Fire built on stones	x	x
Lined with grass		x
Lined with pine needles		x
Lined with *Agave* sp. leaves		x
Lined with Liliaceae sp. leaves		x
Lined with Cactaceae sp. stalks		x
Roots placed in oven, covered with pine needles or grass		x
Roots placed in oven, covered with *Arbutus* sp. limbs	x	
Earth piled on covered roots	x	x
Fire built on mound of earth	x	x
Baked roots of Liliaceae spp. and Agave spp. eaten immediately after baking	x	x
Baked roots of Liliaceae spp. and Agave spp. cooled, sliced, and stored	x	x
Baked roots of Liliaceae spp. and Agave spp. pounded on metate until digestible matter separates from fibrous matter	x	x
Digestible matter eaten immediately	x	x
Digestible matter formed into cakes and stored	x	x
Stored digestible matter boiled as food	x	x

The available evidence suggests that the Tepehuan are somewhat more selective than the Tarahumar regarding most miscellaneous sources of food (Table XXI). Not one Tepehuan would admit ever to have eaten a fly, locust, grasshopper, corn worm, tadpole, toad, or lizard—all of which are certainly not ignored as food by the Tarahumar. However, this repugnant attitude of the Tepehuan toward such foodstuffs does not extend to snakes or newly hatched birds—a vague distinction suggesting that, once, the Tepehuan would eat almost anything, the same as the Tarahumar do today. The Tarahumar gather "wild honey" from the hives of escaped bees found in caves or trees. These escaped bees are probably the *Apis mellifera* recorded among the Tepehuan in 1960 as an *abeja silvestre* or a *mosco de enjambre chiquito*. However, it is strange that the Tarahumar apparently do not eat the waxy substance that is found in the underground nest of the bumble bee (*Bombus formosus*). They utilize this substance only as incense. It is equally strange that the Tepehuan do not pit-bake the young leaves of certain agaves, a common practice among the Tarahumar.

The total evidence concerning collected foods utilized by the Tepehuan and the Tarahumar indicates that neither group has really influenced the other, at least within recent times; the cultural pattern regarding collected foods must have been established many centuries ago.

XXI— MISCELLANEOUS FOODS COLLECTED

	Tepehuan	Tarahumar
Sweets		
Honey		
Mosco de enjambre	x	
Mosco de enjambre chiquito (*Apis mellifera*)	x	
Dávurai	x	
Bumble bees (*Bombus formosus*)	x	
Wasps (*Polybia diguetana*)	x	
Hive sought in caves or trees	x	x
(cont'd)		

MISCELLANEOUS FOODS COLLECTED (cont'd)

	Tepehuan	Tarahumar
Honey (cont'd)		
Hive sought underground	x	
Hive removed from place of origin to tree near habitation	x	
From flowers		
Eriogonum atrorubens		x
Macromeria Thurberi		x
Insects		
Flies		x
Locusts		x
Grasshoppers		x
Corn worms		x
Grubs found on trees		
Arbutus arizonica	x	x
A. glandulosa	x	x
A. xalapensis	x	
Reptiles		
Snakes	x	x
Lizards		x
Tadpoles		x
Toads		x
Plant Substances		
Fungi	x	x
(cont'd)		

MISCELLANEOUS FOODS COLLECTED (cont'd)

	Tepehuan	Tarahumar
Plant Substances (cont'd)		
Stalks		
Agave Patonii		x
A. Schottii		x
A. sp.	x	
A. sp.	x	
A. sp.	x	
A. sp.	x	
Dasylirion durangense		x
D. Wheeleri		x
Yucca decipiens	x	
Leaves		
Agave chihuahuana		x
A. Hartmani		x
A. lecheguilla		x
A. Patonii		x
A. Schottii		x
Echinocereus sp. var. *triglochidiatus* (?)	x	
Ferocactus sp.	x	
Root as chewing gum		
Euphorbia sp.		x

ANIMAL HUSBANDRY

Both the Tepehuan and the Tarahumar utilize domestic animals and poultry in virtually the same fashion (Table XXII), and since it is known that cattle have been common in the Chihuahua uplands since the 1600's,[20,21] nothing can be said with certainty concerning the influence of one group upon the other.

XXII— ANIMAL HUSBANDRY

	Tepehuan	Tarahumar
Animals		
Cattle		
Oxen	x	x
Cows	x	x
Square corral	x	x
Octagonal corral	x	x
Ears slit to indicate ownership	x	x
Sheep and goats		
Sheep	x	x
Goats	x	x
Maintained in cave at night	x	x
Maintained in covered log corral at night	x	x
Herded by women and children		x
Herded by men, youths, and dogs	x	
Horses		
Pack animal	x	x
Riding animal	x	x
Burros		
Pack animal	x	x
Riding animal	x	x
Mules	x	x
Pigs		
Permitted to roam at will except during crop season	x	x
Penned during crop season	x	x
Penned for fattening	x	
Ears slit to indicate ownership	x	
(cont'd)		

ANIMAL HUSBANDRY (cont'd)

	Tepehuan	Tarahumar
Animals (cont'd)		
Dogs		
Pet	x	x
Watchdog	x	x
Herding animal	x	
Castrated	x	
Given name	x	
Cats	x	x
Poultry		
Maintained in elevated coops at night	x	x
Nests built (occasionally)	x	
Domestic Animals as Food		
Cattle		
Oxen sacrificed, then eaten	x	x
Cows sacrificed, then eaten	x	x
Portions of cattle considered food		
Blood	x	x
Heart	x	x
Lungs	x	x
Intestines	x	x
Brains	x	x
Milk	x	x
Liver		x
Stomach		x
Testicles		x
Meat roasted	x	x
Meat stewed	x	x
(cont'd)		

ANIMAL HUSBANDRY (cont'd)

	Tepehuan	Tarahumar
Domestic Animals as Food (cont'd)		
Sheep and goats		
Sheep sacrificed, then eaten	x	x
Goats sacrificed, then eaten	x	x
Portions of sheep and goats considered food		
Lungs	x	
Kidneys	x	
Heart	x	x
Intestines	x	x
Testicles	x	x
Brains		x
Blood	x	x
Meat roasted	x	x
Meat stewed	x	x
Pigs		
Portions of pigs considered food		
Blood	x	x
Chicharrones	x	x
Intestines	x	x
Kidneys	x	
Lungs	x	
Heart		x
Liver		x
Stomach		x
Hoofs		x
Lard rendered	x	
Horse meat eaten		x
Mule meat eaten		x
Dogs eaten		x
Condiments added to dishes made from blood		
*Allium Ampeloprasum	x	
*A. Cepa	x	
(cont'd)		

ANIMAL HUSBANDRY (cont'd)

	Tepehuan	Tarahumar
Condiments added (cont'd)		
Capsicum annuum	x	x
C. baccatum	x	x
Coriandrum sativum	x	
Lippia Berlandieri	x	x
Mentha canadensis		x
Salvia sp.	x	
Cheese		
From goat's milk	x	x
From cow's milk	x	x
Curdling agents		
Portion of cow's stomach	x	x
Portion of goat's stomach	x	x
Portion of deer's stomach	x	x
Begonia gracilis leaves		x
Oxalis albicans leaves		x
O. decaphylla leaves		x
Solanum diversifolium leaves		x
Yucca decipiens leaves		x
"Honey" ants		x

MUSICAL INSTRUMENTS AND BATONS OF THE GOVERNORS

Both the Tepehuan and the Tarahumar utilize flutes, rasping sticks, musical bows, drums, violins, and rattles as musical or noise-making instruments (Table XXIII). However, too little is known about the antiquity and use of these items in western Chihuahua to make a definite statement about their diffusion from one group to the other. The only indication of precedence between the two groups is that precise references to most of these instruments are somewhat earlier for the Tarahumar than for the Tepehuan.

Lumholtz wrote about the use of flutes and rasping sticks by the Tarahumar in the late 1890's and noted that they possessed both instruments when the Spaniards arrived in northwestern Mexico.[22] Mason referred to a flute among the Tepehuan in the early 1950's,[23] and Tepehuan of the 1960's claimed that the flute and rasping stick were much used at the beginning of the twentieth century; since that time, use of both instruments has declined. There is apparently nothing in the archeological record of western Chihuahua to indicate great antiquity for either the flute or the rasping stick. Contrary to the notion of a pre-Columbian or an early post-Columbian use of the flute by Tarahumar is that Steffel's eighteenth-century Tarahumar dictionary includes no comment on the flute, whereas other musical instruments are mentioned in detail.[24] On the other hand, Rinaldini's eighteenth-century Tepehuan dictionary does give a specific Indian name for the *flauta*: *cucuitajare*,[25] which is clearly related to the term used today, *kukuitusajaroi*. This evidence might be interpreted as meaning that the Tepehuan used a reed flute earlier than the Tarahumar and that the trait spread to them from the Tepehuan. This interpretation is probably incorrect because, during historical times, it has been the western Tarahumar—the canyon Indians for the most part—who have made the most use of reed flutes, and these people were probably not known to Steffel, who spent most of his missionary life in eastern Tarahumar country, particularly at San Francisco de Borja.[26] Therefore, about all that can be stated is that the flute probably was used by the Tepehuan and the Tarahumar in post-Contact times. The evidence is too inconclusive to comment on the possible diffusion of the flute from one group to another. And, certainly, nothing can be said with exactitude about the rasping stick.

Archeological evidence does suggest an antiquity for a crude musical bow among the Tarahumar. Bennett and Zingg found such evidence in what were, without doubt, rather early post-Columbian sites.[27,28] There is apparently no further comment on anything that approximates a musical bow used by the Tepehuan until the 1960's; one end of an ordinary bow is held in the mouth, and the tightened bow string is plucked with an arrow. The absence of an historical comment on musical bows among the Tepehuan may mean that the present technique was borrowed from the Tarahumar.

Evidence for the antiquity of the drum among the Tepehuan and the Tarahumar is inconclusive. When Bennett and Zingg were among the Tarahumar in the 1920's, two types of drums were known.[29] One type was what may be termed a crude snare drum; it was manufactured from a circle of easily bent wood to which drumheads of buckskin were attached. The other type existed only in memory and was made by hollowing out a portion of a tree trunk and enclosing both ends with buckskin. Contrary to the notion of a great antiquity for the drum among the Tarahumar is that Steffel does not even mention a

Trommel in his very complete Tarahumar dictionary written circa 1767 and published in 1809. Furthermore, the fact that the word *tambor* does not appear in Rinaldini's eighteenth-century Tepehuan dictionary suggests that the drum is recent among the Tepehuan. Apparently, the first specific reference to Tepehuan drums is that made by Lumholtz in the 1890's.[30] However, if the drum was not an aboriginal item among the Tarahumar and the Tepehuan and if it spread among the two groups after the arrival of the Spaniards, then the drum is still probably older than is generally believed. If Spaniards were the impetus for adoption of the drum, as they surely were in the case of the violin, then both instruments were probably disseminated among the Tepehuan and the Tarahumar at about the same time when, after 1600, Spanish missionaries (and soldiers?) entered what is today southern Chihuahua. Jesuits established missions at San Miguel de Las Bocas in 1630 and at San Gerónimo de Huejotitlán and San Pablo Balleza in 1639, locales at which the Tepehuan and the Tarahumar lived and freely mingled.[31,32]

That rattles have been manufactured by the Tarahumar for several centuries is certain in view of Ratkay's seventeenth-century references to hollow gourd rattles[33] and the finding of gourd rattles in early post-Conquest archeological sites excavated by Bennett and Zingg.[34] The record for the Tepehuan is not clear since the only historical reference to a rattle is that made by Rinaldini in the eighteenth century.[35] The above data suggest that perhaps the gourd rattle spread from the Tarahumar to the Tepehuan. Contrary to this notion, however, is the lack of evidence that the Tepehuan have ever made use of pebble-filled wooden, leather pouch, or cocoon rattles. All of these types are preferred noise-makers among the Tarahumar. The Tepehuan seem to be as fond of rattles as the Tarahumar; but, if the gourd rattle did spread from the Tarahumar to the Tepehuan, then why did not the other types diffuse as well?

Both the Tepehuan and the Tarahumar acknowledge and respect the badges of authority carried by *gobernadores* on official duty. However, little is known about the antiquity of this trait among the Tepehuan. There is archeological evidence of an immediate post-Contact use of such sticks by the Tarahumar;[36] the archeological material resembles the modern-day badges of authority. Steffel referred to canes carried by Tarahumar *gobernadores* in the eighteenth century.[37] The lack of historical comments concerning batons of authority among the Tepehuan might be interpreted as meaning that the custom diffused from the Tarahumar southward to the Tepehuan. Such an assumption would be hazardous since almost nothing is known about badges of authority as a tradition in the greater Southwest.[38]

XXIII— MUSICAL INSTRUMENTS

	Tepehuan	Tarahumar
Flutes		
Fashioned from *Arundo donax*	x	x
Convex mouthpiece	x	x
One to four stops	x	x
Rasping sticks		
Notched stick from *Haematoxylon brasiletto*	x	
Unnotched stick from *H. brasiletto* used as rasp on notched stick	x	
Notched stick of easily worked wood		x
Gourd resonator		x
Olla used as resonator		x
Musical bows		
One end of ordinary bow held in mouth, bow string struck lightly with an arrow	x	
Length of cane (*Arundo donax*) pegged at ends, sheep or goat gut anchored to pegs; cane held in mouth, twanged in manner of a jew's-harp		x
Drums		
Hollow-log drum with skin heads	x	x
Drum from circular band of easily worked wood, covered with skin		x
Hole in side of drum	x	x
Drum decorated with ochre	x	x
Violins		
Woods used in bows and violins *Arctostaphylos pungens*	x	x
Fraxinus papillosa		x
(cont'd)		

MUSICAL INSTRUMENTS (cont'd)

	Tepehuan	Tarahumar
Woods used in bows and violins (cont'd)		
F. velutina	x	x
Garrya laurifolia	x	
G. ovata	x	
Ipomoea arborescens	x	
Pinus chihuahuana	x	x
P. Lumholtzii		x
P. reflexa	x	x
Salix Bonplandiana		x
S. Gooddingii		x
Sassafridium macrophyllum		x
Thevetia sp.	x	
Violin tinted with dye prepared from *Alnus oblongifolia* wood	x	
Bow strings		
Gut	x	x
Horsehair	x	x
Violin strings		
Gut	x	x
Horsehair	x	x
Wire	x	x
Rattles		
Prepared from *Cucurbita foetidissima* fruits	x	x
Prepared from leaf-shaped pieces of *Fraxinus papillosa* and *F. velutina* glued together with mixture from roots of *Cooperia Drummondi*		x
Gourd rattle filled with pebbles	x	x
Wooden rattle filled with pebbles		x
Pouch rattle (leather) filled with pebbles		x
Cocoon rattle filled with tiny pebbles		x
Bones strung on a cord		x
Deer hoofs strung on a cord		x

GAMES

Games (Table XXIV) of dexterity, chance, and throwing or shooting skills are played by the Tepehuan and the Tarahumar. The pre-eminent game is the kickball race, which involves two teams of runners who kick two balls around a designated course. As played today, the game is virtually the same among the Tepehuan and the Tarahumar. There are apparently no important differences regarding numbers of people who may participate, activities of team captains, wearing of distinctive decoration by each team, woods used for the balls, marking of balls so that neither team will be confused, dimensions of the racecourse, restrictions during races, and betting. There are some differences in that the Tepehuan lack rattling belts, ceremonies held prior to races, food restrictions prior to a race (except that of *tesgüino*), foods eaten to impart vigor, and certain stimulants that are taken during the Tarahumar race. These traits probably were once common to the Tepehuan but were abandoned because these Indians have been more subjected to mestizo pressures than have the Tarahumar. It is not likely that kickball was played by the aboriginal Tepehuan and Tarahumar since the first mention of the game is found in the eighteenth-century accounts of Rinaldini[39] (Tepehuan) and Steffel[40] (Tarahumar).

Additional evidence for a post-Columbian development of kickball among the Tarahumar is provided by the fact that the game is not mentioned in the rather complete account of Tarahumar culture that appears in Ratkay's 1683 account of the Tarahumar missions and in Neumann's *Historia Sediton- ium . . .* written circa 1725 and his letters written between 1681 and 1689. Instead, emphasis was placed on a rubber-ball game which Ratkay describes in detail.[41] Steffel also described the rubber-ball game in the eighteenth century.[42] Therefore, we may be certain that the game persisted among the Tarahumar until at least the eighteenth century, after which time it must have been abandoned—for what reason has not been determined. However, the well-known attempts of the missionaries to eradicate gambling games may have been at least partially responsible for the abandonment. The record of this game among the Tepehuan is not clear. Rinaldini referred to a rubber-ball game that was called *ulé* or *uláma* by the eighteenth-century Tepehuan;[43] this name was also used to designate the game as played among the Tarahumar according to Ratkay[44] and Steffel.[45] Rinaldini's reference to the game among the Tepehuan of Chihuahua should be accurate; he spent most of his missionary life among the Tepehuan at Nabogame, remaining there for more than twenty years.[46]

The above data indicate that the aboriginal Tepehuan and Tarahumar probably played the rubber-ball game (*ulé* or *uláma*) and probably did not play kickball. The rubber-ball game was abandoned for some reason and was replaced by the kickball race, which must have diffused into western Chihuahua from the west or the north, from people who did play kickball in aboriginal times.[47] In any case, there is no definite information about whether the Tepehuan or the Tarahumar influenced each other with respect to either the kickball or the rubber-ball game.

There is no evidence that present-day Tepehuan women play a game in which a wooden ball is tossed forward with a forked stick; this game is played by Tarahumar women. However, Tepehuan women do participate in a hoop race that is much like the one run by Tarahumar women. The Tepehuan women also participate in a stick race in which two sticks anchored together by thongs are tossed forward; the stick race is also played by Tarahumar women. Historical data are too incomplete to allow a statement of certainty about whether or not either group influenced the other with respect to these games. Apparently, the only historical references to the hoop race run by Tarahumar women are those found in nineteenth-century comments by Lumholtz[48] and Watson.[49]

The rough *tákuari* of the Tepehuan is played today in about the same fashion as is the *tácuri* (*palillo*) of the Tarahumar. For the Tarahumar, the earliest historical reference to the game is apparently that of Lumholtz, who noted that only women played and that the game involved two women who strove to reach one goal.[50] For the Tepehuan, there is the eighteenth-century reference by Rinaldini to terms that are clearly akin to the present Tepehuan and Tarahumar words for the game. Rinaldini's terms include *toccare, toccalianta, toccarudañi, tocca'daraga,* and *toccarudaragaquer.*[51] The early reference to this game among the Tepehuan and the similarity between present-day Tepehuan and Tarahumar names for the game suggest that perhaps the game did spread from the Tepehuan to the Tarahumar.

Cuatro or *quoits,* a game that involves the tossing of disks into holes, is played by both groups. The earliest historical reference to this game is apparently that of Lumholtz, who noted that late nineteenth-century Tarahumar placed many bets on the sport.[52] There is a current tradition among the Tepehuan that the game was derived from the Cocoyome, those legendary people who presumably once lived in western Chihuahua. Evidence for the influence of either group upon the other with respect to this game is inconclusive. Such is also the case for the knuckle-bone game that is played by the Tepehuan and the Tarahumar. Apparently, the sole historical reference to this game is that of Lumholtz.[53]

By far the most important game of chance played by the Tepehuan and the Tarahumar is *quince* or *patole,* and there are relatively few differences between how the game is played by each group. Detailed references to the game are lacking in the historical literature; the only ones are somewhat obscure references to a *patole* played by the Tarahumar in Steffel's time (eighteenth century) and Rinaldini's reference to a specific name for the game and the place where it was played by the eighteenth-century Tepehuan. The *patole* noted by Steffel was played only by women, and the sticks used were knocked from a hat rather than bounced or tipped from a rock in the middle of the playing court.[54] Rinaldini's reference must be considered as evidence that eighteenth-century Tepehuan south of the Río Verde played the game. The current Tepehuan name for the game, *suligari*, is certainly related to Rinaldini's term, *suligarague* (*juego de los patoles*), and to his term for the place where the game was played, *suligaragaquer* (*lugares adonde juegan al patole*).[55] All of these terms, eighteenth-century and present-day, are related to those used by Nabogame Tepehuan for the game when Lumholtz visited Chihuahua in the 1890's. At that time, the game was called *intuvigai zuli gairagai*, which meant "game straight throwing."[56]

Two factors make impossible a definite statement about whether or not the Tepehuan or the Tarahumar influenced one another with respect to *patole*: the paucity of historical references to the game for both groups and the record of its wide distribution in the greater American Southwest during post-Columbian times.[57]

Despite the lack of historical references to an arrow or archery game among the Tarahumar, it undoubtedly is as old among these Indians as it is among the Tepehuan. Rinaldini referred to an arrow game (*juego de las flechas*) as *vupi* or *vuparaga*,[58] terms that are clearly related to *vupadami*, the present name for the game. Apparently, Lumholtz was the first observer to note an arrow game among the Tarahumar.[59] In any case, not enough is known about the history of this game among the Chihuahua folk to warrant a positive statement concerning the influence of Tepehuan or Tarahumar upon each other.

XXIV– GAMES

	Tepehuan	Tarahumar	Sources other than Pennington
Games of Dexterity			
Kickball races			
Participants			
Males only	x	x	
Players from same locale	x	x	
Players from different locales	x	x	
(cont'd)			

GAMES (cont'd)

	Tepehuan	Tarahumar	Sources other than Pennington
Kickball races (cont'd)			
Teams			
3 to 10 men per team		x	
3 to 20 men per team	x		
Captain of team	x	x	
Assistant who searches for lost ball	x		
Distinctive decorations worn by team members			
Headband of red cloth		xxL	Lumholtz (1902)
Headband of white cloth		xxL	Lumholtz (1902)
White face paint	x	x	
Legs painted with white stripes	x	x	
Feathers worn		xxL	Lumholtz (1902)
Rattling belts			
Sections of reed (*Arundo donax*) filled with pebbles, affixed to leather belt		x	
Deer hoofs affixed to leather belt		x	
Team members spend night before important race in a particular place	x	x	
Balls			
Woods used			
Alnus Pringlei		x	
Arbutus arizonica	x		
A. glandulosa		x	
A. xalapensis	x		
Ficus petiolaris	x		
Guazuma ulmifolia	x	x	
Persea americana	x		
Populus tremuloides		x	
Quercus arizonica		x	
Thevetia sp.	x		
Wimmeria sp.	x		
Balls marked in distinctive fashion			
Red ochre	x	x	
White pigment	x	x	
Green pigment from vegetal compound			
Juglans major leaves	x		
Opuntia sp. leaves	x		
Persea americana leaves	x		
(cont'd)			

GAMES (cont'd)

	Tepehuan	Tarahumar	Sources other than Pennington
Balls (cont'd)			
Fruits of *Cucurbita foetidissima* used by children as kickballs		x	
Sticks used to pry balls from crevices in rocks or when wedged in exposed roots		x	
Balls removed from crevices in rocks or from exposed roots by hand	x	x	
Spectators assist in locating balls		x	
Racecourses			
Long course	x	x	
Short course	x	x	
Circuit	x	x	
Straight	x		
Level terrain	x		
Rough terrain	x	x	
Marked by stones		x	
Marked by notched trees		x	
Marked by men standing at turning points	x	x	
Course laid out at elevations below promontories where spectators view race		x	
Judges posted along course to prevent cheating	x	x	
Preparations for race			
Ceremonies			
Shaman presides		x	
Runners stand before a cross		x	
Offerings placed on blanket near cross		x	
Incense burned		x	
Songs sung about the gray fox		xxL	Lumholtz (1902)
Food restrictions			
Fatty foods forbidden		x	
Eggs forbidden		x	
Potatoes forbidden		x	
Food consumed by runners prepared by relatives		x	
Tesgüino forbidden for 24-hour period prior to race	x		
(cont'd)			

GAMES (cont'd)

	Tepehuan	Tarahumar	Sources other than Pennington
Food restrictions (cont'd)			
Tesgüino forbidden for several days before race		xxL	Lumholtz (1902)
Foods eaten to impart vigor			
Rabbits		x	
Deer		x	
Turkeys		x	
Chaparral cocks		x	
Continence for 24-hour period prior to race	x		
Runners questioned relative to sexual relations		xxL	Lumholtz (1902)
Restrictions during race			
If runner rests he must make up circuits or lengths		x	
Game forfeited if runner kicks ball of opposing team	x		
Ball cannot be touched with hand except for removal from cracks, roots, or brush	x	x	
Stimulants			
Ariocarpus fissuratus chewed		x	
Epithelantha micromeris fruits chewed		x	
Lophophora Williamsii chewed		x	
L. Williamsii used in wash applied to legs of runners	x		
Esquiate given to runners	x		
Pinole given to runners	x	x	
Tesgüino given to runners	x		
Atole given to runners		x	
Wash from *Carex* sp. applied to legs of runners	x		
Thorny branches of *Acacia pennatula* used to switch legs of runners	x		
Legs rubbed with chewed roots of ball cactus		x	
Ball cactus root carried by runners		x	
Legs rubbed with compound of plant substance mixed with suet		xxBZ	Bennett and Zingg (1935)

(cont'd)

GAMES (cont'd)

	Tepehuan	Tarahumar	Sources other than Pennington
Stimulants (cont'd)			
Legs bathed with wash from *Juniperus pachyphloea* leaves		x	
Cheating			
Runners kick ball of opposing team		x	
Runners trip one another		x	
Calliandra humilis var. *reticulata* chewed; breath blown into faces of opposing team members		x	
Other herbs used in similar fashion	x		
Drinks from certain herbs to counteract effect of *Calliandra humilis* var. *reticulata*		x	
Betting			
Land	x	x	
Cattle	x	x	
Sheep and goats	x	x	
Other personal property	x	x	
Custodian of bets		x	
Bets piled in particular place before start of race	x		
Stones piled up to indicate number of circuits run		x	
Scratches made in earth to indicate number of circuits run		x	
Ulé	PxxRi	PxxRa,S	1743: Rinaldini (1743); 1683: Ratkay; Circa 1767: Steffel (1809)
Women's ball games		x	
Wooden balls		x	
Balls tossed forward with forked sticks		x	
Balls tossed forward with carved wooden forks with long handles		x	
(cont'd)			

GAMES (cont'd)

	Tepehuan	Tarahumar	Sources other than Pennington
Games of Dexterity (cont'd)			
Women's hoop races			
2 players	x	x	
2 teams, each with 2 or more players		x	
Hoops from branches			
Arbutus arizonica	x		
A. xalapensis	x		
Caesalpinia platyloba		x	
Ficus petiolaris	x		
Holodiscus dumosus		x	
Morus microphylla	x	x	
Pinus leiophylla	x		
Salix Gooddingii	x		
Hoops from other materials			
Grapevines		x	
Plaited *Dasylirion simplex* leaves	x		
Plaited *D. Wheeleri* leaves	x		
Plaited *D.* or *Yucca* sp. leaves		x	
Plaited *Nolina durangensis* leaves	x		
Plaited *N. matapensis* leaves	x		
Plaited *Yucca decipiens* leaves	x		
Stems of *Fouquieria fasciculata* (?)	x		
Hoops decorated with colored rags for identification		x	
Hoops wrapped with rags	x		
Hoops wrapped with ixtle fiber	x		
Throwing sticks from *Populus tremuloides*		x	
Straight throwing sticks	x	x	
Racecourses			
Straight	x	x	
Circuit	x	x	
Betting	x	x	

(cont'd)

GAMES (cont'd)

	Tepehuan	Tarahumar	Sources other than Pennington
Games of Dexterity (cont'd)			
Women's stick games			
2 sticks tied together with leather thong or fiber cord	x	x	
Racecourses			
Straight	x	x	
Circuit	x	x	
Team members			
5 to 10		x	
Dependent on size and importance of gathering	x		
Betting	x	x	
Tákuari or palillo			
Participants			
Women only		xxL	Lumholtz (1902)
Men only		x	
Men and women	x		
Teams			
2 players		xxL	Lumholtz (1902)
2 teams, each with 6 to 10 players	x	x	
Courts			
Laid out on level field	x	x	
Laid out on rough terrain		x	
Definite markers at ends of field if 2 goals	x	x	
Definite markers at goal end of field if 1 goal		x	
Balls			
Wood	x	x	
Buried in center of playing field before start of game; dug from ground by opposing captains at start of game		x	
Tossed in air at start of game	x		
Spoon-shaped end of wooden club used to toss ball	x	x	
(cont'd)			

GAMES (cont'd)

	Tepehuan	Tarahumar	Sources other than Pennington
Games of Dexterity (cont'd)			
Cuatro			
2 players	x		
2 teams, each with 2 to 3 members		x	
2 holes about 25 feet apart	x		
2 holes about 30 to 40 feet apart		x	
Stick thrust into ground behind each hole		x	
2 stone disks, each marked in some fashion, assigned to each player	x	x	
2 pottery disks, each marked in some fashion, assigned to each player		x	
Scoring points awarded according to proximity of disks to holes	x	x	
Disk in hole counts 4 points	x	x	
1 disk near hole counts 1 point	x		
2 disks near hole counts 2 points	x		
1 disk covering another disk in hole counts 0 points		x	
2 disks upon disk in hole counts 4 points	x		
Player with 2 disks nearer hole than opponent's disks doubles score		x	
Game of 12 points	x		
Game of between 10 and 14 points		x	
Betting		x	
Games of Chance			
Knuckle-bone games			
Knuckle bone of deer	x	x	
Bone tossed in air, points awarded according to position of astragal on ground			
1 side up counts 0 points	x		
Another side up counts ½ point	x		
(cont'd)			

GAMES (cont'd)

	Tepehuan	Tarahumar	Sources other than Pennington
Points awarded (cont'd)			
Another side up counts 1 point	x		
Another side up counts 2 points	x		
Astragal on end counts 12 points	x		
Astragal on end counts 10 points	x		
Front of astragal up counts 5 points		x	
Back of astragal up counts 4 points		x	
Bottom of astragal up counts 2 points		x	
Top of astragal up counts 0 points		x	
Game of 12 points	x	xxL	Lumholtz (1902)
Game of 20 to 40 points		x	
Count of points kept by placing grains of corn within ring scratched in earth		xxL	Lumholtz (1902)
Quince or patole			
Men and women play	x	x	
Square court with 2 tails at opposite corners	x		
Rectangular court with 2 tails at opposite corners		x	
Total of 46 holes	x	x	
1 pawn to each player	x		
2 pawns to each player		x	
4 canes to determine points	x	x	
Slit cane segments	x		
Round cane segments	x		
4 wooden sticks to determine points		x	
Geometric designs to designate canes or sticks as *Quince*, *Catorce*, *Cuatro*, and *Seis*	x	x	
Canes tinted with black or red paint	x		
Canes held vertically in fist, struck against stone at side of court	x		
(cont'd)			

GAMES (cont'd)

	Tepehuan	Tarahumar	Sources other than Pennington
Quince or patole (cont'd)			
Sticks bounced or tipped from stone in center of court		x	
Values of counts			
All sticks or canes up counts 5 points	x	xxBZ	Bennett and Zingg (1935)
All sticks or canes down counts 10 points	x	xxBZ	Bennett and Zingg (1935)
2 sticks or canes up, 2 down counts 2 points	x	xxBZ	Bennett and Zingg (1935)
3 sticks or canes up, 1 down counts 3 points	x	xxBZ	Bennett and Zingg (1935)
Seis up, 3 down counts 6 points	x	xxBZ	Bennett and Zingg (1935)
Cuatro up, 3 down counts 4 points	x	xxBZ	Bennett and Zingg (1935)
Catorce up, 3 down counts 14 points	x	xxBZ	Bennett and Zingg (1935)
Quince up, 3 down counts 15 points	x	xxBZ	Bennett and Zingg (1935)
Restrictions			
If player's pawn comes to rest in opponent's hole then opponent must return to starting point	x	x	
Player may use only 2 or 3 points between certain spaces	x		
In final stretch of game only certain counts, as 1, 2, or 3, may be used to move pawn		x	
If 14 points made at certain positions, pawn may move only 1 hole	x		
If count of 1 or 14 made when player's remaining pawn is in last hole of tail, pawn is removed to starting point		x	
Catorce may be valued at 1 or 14, according to wish of player	x	xxBZ	Bennett and Zingg (1935)
(cont'd)			

GAMES (cont'd)

	Tepehuan	Tarahumar	Sources other than Pennington

Restrictions (cont'd)
  Players move about court in
    opposite directions
	x	xxBZ	Bennett and Zingg (1935)

Throwing or Shooting Games			
Archery			

Arrows aimed at target-arrow shot
  into ground about 50 yards
  from starting point
		xxL	Lumholtz (1902)

Arrows shot at line marked in ground some distance from participants	x	x	
Arrows shot at hat placed on ground some distance from participants	x		
Betting	x		
Sticks			
Male and female participants		x	
Sticks thrown toward goal stick cast by lead player		x	
Points awarded according to proximity of thrown stick to goal stick		x	
Game of 10 points		x	

MEDICINAL PLANTS

The Tepehuan and their near-neighbors, the Tarahumar, make much use of their natural environment as a source of plants utilized for medicinal purposes, and they apparently have done so for a very long time. The first specific references to utilization of medicinal plants among the Tarahumar are found in the eighteenth-century (1777) *Relaciones* written at Tónachic, Nabogame, Guazapares, Batopilillas, and Cusihuiriachic. No one can say whether or not such utilization represents aboriginal customs or missionary influence. The *Relación de Nabogame* refers to specific medicinal plants at Nabogame; hence, they must have been used by the Tepehuan who were living, along with some Tarahumar, at the Nabogame mission located south of the Río Verde.

It is interesting that in spite of the fact that the Tepehuan and the Tarahumar live in rather similar environments (in uplands and in canyons), the same plants utilized by both groups for medicinal purposes are few in number (Table XXV). The duplicates are, in almost all instances, the most widely distributed of the medicinal plants in western and southern Chihuahua. Particularly noteworthy are *Equisetum laevigatum*, *Pinus ayacahuite*, *Populus tremuloides*, *Chenopodium ambrosioides*, *Prunus capuli*, *Erythrina flabelliformis*, *Lysiloma Watsoni*, *Ricinus communis* (an introduced plant), *Karwinskia Humboldtiana*, *Arctostaphylos pungens*, *Mentha canadensis*, *Solanum nigrum*, and *Coutarea pterosperma*. In view of the very obvious and keen interest in medicinal plants on the part of both the Tepehuan and the Tarahumar, it seems strange that there is not more overlap in their use of this plant resource—even when allowance is made for the fact that the specimen collections may not be entirely representative of the actual situation regarding medicinal plant utilization.

XXV— MEDICINAL PLANTS

	Tepehuan	Tarahumar	Sources other than Pennington
Polypodiaceae			
Asplenium monanthes	x		
Cheilanthes Kaulfussii		x	
C. tomentosa		x	
Dryopteris normalis		x	
D. pilosa	x		
Notholaena candida		xxBZ	Bennett and Zingg (1935)
Pteridium aquilinum var. *pubescens*	x		
Woodsia mexicana		x	
Equisetaceae			
Equisetum laevigatum	x	x	
Pinaceae			
Cupressus arizonica		x	
Pinus arizonica	x		
(cont'd)			

MEDICINAL PLANTS (cont'd)

	Tepehuan	Tarahumar	Sources other than Pennington
Pinaceae (cont'd)			
P. ayacahuite	x	x	
P. Engelmanni	x		
P. Lumholtzii		x	
P. leiophylla	x		
P. reflexa		x	
Cupressaceae			
Juniperus pachyphloea		x	
J. sp.	x		
Gramineae			
Eleusine indica	x		
Mühlenbergia dumosa	x		
M. Porteri		x	
Phragmites communis		x	
Cyperaceae			
Fimbristylis sp.		xxBZ	Bennett and Zingg (1935)
Commelinaceae			
Commelina erecta	x		
Tradescantia sp.	x		
Liliaceae			
Dasylirion Wheeleri		x	
Hypoxis hirsuta	x		
Amaryllidaceae			
Agave bovicornuta	x	x	
Amaryllis sp.	x		
(cont'd)			

MEDICINAL PLANTS (cont'd)

	Tepehuan	Tarahumar	Sources other than Pennington
Orchidaceae			
Malaxis sp.	x		
Salicaceae			
Populus tremuloides	x	x	
Piperaceae			
Piper sp.		xxBZ	Bennett and Zingg (1935)
Fagaceae			
Quercus arizonica		x	
Q. chihuahuensis		x	
Q. crassifolia	x		
Q. Endlichiana	x		
Q. viminea	x		
Moraceae			
Ficus petiolaris		x	
Loranthaceae			
Struthanthus diversifolius	x		
Tillandsia Benthamiania		xxBZ	Bennett and Zingg (1935)
T. Karwinskyana		xxBZ	Bennett and Zingg (1935)
T. sp.		xxBZ	Bennett and Zingg (1935)
Aristolochiaceae			
Aristolochia brevipes		xxBZ	Bennett and Zingg (1935)
Polygonaceae			
Eriogonum atrorubens		x	
E. undulatum		x	
(cont'd)			

MEDICINAL PLANTS (cont'd)

	Tepehuan	Tarahumar	Sources other than Pennington
Chenopodiaceae			
Chenopodium ambrosioides	x	x	
Amaranthaceae			
Alternanthera repens	x	x	
Nyctaginaceae			
Boerhaavia mirabilis	x		
Pisonia capitata		xxBZ	Bennett and Zingg (1935)
Caryophyllaceae			
Silene sp.	x		
Stellaria sp.	x		
Ranunculaceae			
Ranunculus Forreri	x		
R. sp.	x		
Thalictrum Fendleri	x	x	
T. sp.		x	
Magnoliaceae			
Magnolia Schiedeana	x		
Lauraceae			
Litsea glaucescens		x	
Persea americana	x		
Papaveraceae			
Argemone ochroleuca subsp. ochroleuca	x		
Bocconia arborea	x		
*Papaver Rhoeas	x		
(cont'd)			

MEDICINAL PLANTS (cont'd)

	Tepehuan	Tarahumar	Sources other than Pennington
Cruciferae			
Brassica campestris	x		
Lepidium virginicum	x		
Nasturtium officinale	x		
Crassulaceae			
Echeveria simulans	x		
Saxifragaceae			
Ribes neglectum		x	
Platanaceae			
Platanus glabrata		xxBZ	Bennett and Zingg (1935)
P. Wrightii		x	
Krameriaceae			
Krameria sp.		xxBZ	Bennett and Zingg (1935)
Hydrangeaceae			
Hydrangea Oerstedii	x		
H. sp.	x		
Rosaceae			
Cercocarpus montanus		x	
Potentilla Thurberi	x		
P. sp. af. exsul	x		
P. sp.	x		
Prunus capuli	x	x	
Purshia tridentata		x	
Leguminosae			
Acacia cochliacantha	x		
(cont'd)			

MEDICINAL PLANTS (cont'd)

	Tepehuan	Tarahumar	Sources other than Pennington
Leguminosae (cont'd)			
A. cymbispina		x	
A. Farnesiana		x	
A. pennatula	x		
Brongniartia sp.	x		
Caesalpinia mexicana		xxBZ	Bennett and Zingg (1935)
C. pulcherrima		x	
Calliandra eriophylla		x	
C. humilis var. reticulata		x	
Cassia leptadenia	x		
Cologania angustifolia	x		
Dalea polygonoides		x	
D. sp.	x		
Erythrina flabelliformis	x	x	
Eysenhardtia polystachya		x	
Haematoxylon brasiletto		x	
*Lathyrus vernus	x		
Lupinus Havardii	x		
Lysiloma Watsoni	x	x	
*Melilotus indica	x	x	
Phaseolus Metcalfei		x	
Psoralea pentaphylla	x		
P. sp.	x		
Rhynchosia pyramidalis	x	x	
Senecio sp.	x		
Tephrosia leiocarpa		x	
T. nicaraguensis	x		
(cont'd)			

MEDICINAL PLANTS (cont'd)

	Tepehuan	Tarahumar	Sources other than Pennington
Leguminosae (cont'd)			
T. Thurberi	x		
Willardia mexicana		x	
Zornia diphylla	x	x	
Geraniaceae			
*Erodium cicutarium		x	
Oxalidaceae			
Oxalis albicans	x		
O. Dillenii	x		
O. sordida	x		
O. sp.	x		
Rutaceae			
Ruta chalapensis		x	
Ptelea trifoliata		x	
Burseraceae			
Bursera grandifolia		x	
Polygalaceae			
Monnina sp.	x		
Polygala sp.	x		
Euphorbiaceae			
Hura crepitans	x		
Euphorbia heterophylla		xxBZ	Bennett and Zingg (1935)
E. maculata	x		
E. trichocardia	x		
E. sp.		x	
(cont'd)			

MEDICINAL PLANTS (cont'd)

	Tepehuan	Tarahumar	Sources other than Pennington
Euphorbiaceae (cont'd)			
Croton niveus		x	
Jatropha cordata		x	
J. curcas		x	
Poinsettia radicans	x		
*Ricinus communis	x	x	
Sapium biloculare		x	
Sebastiana Pringlei		x	
Tragia nepetaefolia	x		
T. ramosa		x	
Anacardiaceae			
Elaphrium grandifolium		xxBZ	Bennett and Zingg (1935)
Sapindaceae			
Cardiospermum halicacabum		x	
Serjania mexicana		x	
Rhamnaceae			
Karwinskia Humboldtiana		x	
Vitaceae			
Vitis arizonica	x		
V. rupestris	x		
Cissus sp.		xxBZ	Bennett and Zingg (1935)
Malvaceae			
Malva parviflora		x	
*M. rotundifolia	x		
Malvaviscus arboreus	x		
Sida cordifolia	x		
(cont'd)			

MEDICINAL PLANTS (cont'd)

	Tepehuan	Tarahumar	Sources other than Pennington
Sterculiaceae			
Guazuma ulmifolia	x		
Waltheria americana (?)	x		
Fouquieraceae			
Fouquieria fasciculata (?)	x		
Cistaceae			
Helianthemum glomeratum	x		
Onagraceae			
Epilobium glandulosum	x		
Oenothera rosea	x		
Turneraceae			
Turnera ulmifolia	x		
Cactaceae			
Ariocarpus fissuratus		x	
Lophophora Williamsii		x	
Umbelliferae			
Conium sp.	x		
Eryngium Carlinae		x	
E. Hemsleyanum	x		
E. humile	x		
E. sp.	x		
E. sp. af. *heterophyllum*		x	
E. yuccaefolium	x		
Ligusticum Porteri		x	
Pyrolaceae			
Chimaphila maculata	x		
(cont'd)			

MEDICINAL PLANTS (cont'd)

	Tepehuan	Tarahumar	Sources other than Pennington
Ericaceae			
Arctostaphylos pungens	x	x	
Primulaceae			
*Anagallis arvensis	x		
Plumbaginaceae			
Plumbago scandens		x	
Loganiaceae			
Buddleia cordata		x	
B. sessiliflora	x		
B. sp.		xxBZ	Bennett and Zingg (1935)
B. tomentella	x		
Mascagnia macroptera		x	
Thryallis glauca		x	
Apocynaceae			
Macrosiphonia sp.	x		
Plumeria acutifolia		xxBZ	Bennett and Zingg (1935)
Stemmadenia Palmeri	x	x	
Asclepiadaceae			
Asclepias atropurpurea	x		
A. hypoleuca	x		
A. Linaria	x		
A. sp. af. *quinquedentata*	x		
A. sp.		xxBZ	Bennett and Zingg (1935)
Matelea sp.		x	
(cont'd)			

MEDICINAL PLANTS (cont'd)

	Tepehuan	Tarahumar	Sources other than Pennington
Convolvulaceae			
Dichondra argentea		xxBZ	Bennett and Zingg (1935)
D. repens		x	
Polemoniaceae			
Leptodactylon sp.	x		
Loeselia sp.	x		
Boraginaceae			
Lithospermum incisum	x		
Verbenaceae			
Lantana involucrata		xxBZ	Bennett and Zingg (1935)
Verbena carolina		x	
V. ciliata	x		
V. elegans	x		
V. elegans var. asperata	x		
V. sp.	x		
V. Wrightii		xxBZ	Bennett and Zingg (1935)
Labiatae			
Agastache pallida		xxBZ	Bennett and Zingg (1935)
Hedeoma dentata		x	
Hyptis albida		x	
H. Emoryi		xxBZ	Bennett and Zingg (1935)
Mentha canadensis	x	x	
M. rotundifolia	x		
M. sp.		x	
*Prunella vulgaris	x		
Salvia azurea	x		
(cont'd)			

MEDICINAL PLANTS (cont'd)

	Tepehuan	Tarahumar	Sources other than Pennington
Solanaceae			
Datura meteloides		x	
D. stramonium	x		
Nicotiana glauca		x	
Solanum diversifolium		x	
S. madrense	x		
*S. nigrum	x	x	
S. podiflorum	x		
S. rostratum		x	
S. verbascifolium		x	
S. sp.	x		
Scrophulariaceae			
Castilleja indivisa	x		
C. sp.	x		
Mimulus guttatus	x		
Pentstemon barbatus	x		
Bignoniaceae			
Crescentia alata		xxBZ	Bennett and Zingg (1935)
Tabebuia Palmeri		x	
Tecoma stans		x	
Acanthaceae			
Elytraria imbricata		x	
Plantaginaceae			
*Plantago major		x	
P. sp.	x		
P. sp.	x		
(cont'd)			

MEDICINAL PLANTS (cont'd)

	Tepehuan	Tarahumar	Sources other than Pennington
Rubiaceae			
Bouvardia glaberrima		x	
Coutarea pterosperma	x	x	
C. latiflora		x	
Galium aparine	x		
G. sp.	x		
G. triflorum	x		
Hedyotis sp.	x		
Caprifoliaceae			
Sambucus caerulea	x		
S. canadensis	x		
Lobeliaceae			
Lobelia laxiflora	x		
Compositae			
Artemisia dracunculoides	x		
A. ludoviciana var. *mexicana*	x	x	
A. mexicana	x		
Aster intricatus	x		
Astranthium mexicanum	x		
Baccharis glutinosa		x	
Berlandiera lyrata var. *macrophylla*		x	
B. sp.	x		
Bidens ferulaefolia (?)	x		
Brickellia laciniata	x		
Cacalia decomposita		x	
Cirsium mexicanum	x		
Chromolepis heterophylla	x		
Cosmos Pringlei		x	

(cont'd)

MEDICINAL PLANTS (cont'd)

	Tepehuan	Tarahumar	Sources other than Pennington
Compositae (cont'd)			
Erigeron sp.	x		
Eupatorium sp.		xxBZ	Bennett and Zingg (1935)
Franseria acanthicarpa	x		
F. sp.	x		
Galinsoga ciliata	x		
Gnaphalium Macounii	x		
G. sp.	x		
G. sp.		xxBZ	Bennett and Zingg (1935)
G. Wrightii	x		
Hieracium sp.		xxBZ	Bennett and Zingg (1935)
Pectis stenophylla		x	
Pinaropappus roseus	x		
Ratibida mexicana		x	
Senecio Hartwegii		x	
S. sp. af. *actinella*	x		
Stevia salicifolia		x	
S. serrata		x	
S. stenophylla	x		
Tagetes jaliscana	x		
T. lucida		x	
Tithonia fruticosa		x	
Trixis sp. af. *radialis*	x		
Viguiera decurrens		x	
Zexmenia podocephala	x	x	
Usneaceae			
Parmelia caperata		x	
P. reticulata	x		

SKINS

Skins from deer, cows, oxen, and goats are processed by the Tepehuan and the Tarahumar for use in manufacturing sandals, ropes, quirts, quivers, tumplines, nets for carrying baskets, sleeping and sitting mats, saddle pads and blankets, aprons used by arrieros, small and large bags, slings, and wrist guards (Table XXVI). The antiquity for most of these articles among the Tepehuan and the Tarahumar cannot be determined; there are only a few historical references in the literature that might pertain to leather goods. If sandals, quivers, small or large bags, slings, and wrist guards were used by aboriginal Tepehuan and Tarahumar, then the articles must have been manufactured primarily from deer skin that was processed in some fashion.

In a seventeenth-century account of the Tepehuan, there is an indirect reference to a quiver: Pérez de Ribas described bows and arrows at length and commented on how the Indians rarely went about without these weapons.[60]

XXVI– UTILIZATION OF SKINS

	Tepehuan	Tarahumar	Sources other than Pennington
Articles manufactured from skins			
Sandals	x	x	
Ropes	x	x	
Quirts	x	x	
Quivers	x	Px;xxS	Circa 1767: Steffel (1809)
Tumplines	x	x	
Nets for carrying baskets	x	x	
Sleeping and sitting mats	x	x	
Saddle pads and blankets	x	x	
Aprons used by arrieros	x		
Small bags	x	x	
Slings	x	x	
Wrist guards	x	x	
(cont'd)			

UTILIZATION OF SKINS (cont'd)

	Tepehuan	Tarahumar	Sources other than Pennington
Preparation of skins			
Tanning agents (bark)			
Acacia pennatula	x		
Lysiloma Watsoni		x	
Pithecellobium dulce		x	
Quercus albocincta	x	x	
Q. candicans	x		
Q. crassifolia	x		
Q. durifolia	x	x	
Q. Emoryi		x	
Q. Endlichiana	x		
Q. fulva		x	
Q. omissa	x		
Wimmeria sp. (?)	x		
Skin soaked in stream until hair removed		xxS	Schwatka (1893)
Skin stretched over beam and scraped with sharpened stone		xxS	Schwatka (1893)
Skin staked on ground, dried for several days	x	x	
Skin scraped with sharp knife or stone	x	x	
Skin soaked in hollowed-out log or rock container filled with lime solution	x	x	
Skin wrung out, placed in hollowed-out log	x		
Skin wrung out, placed in hollowed-out rock	x		
Bark placed in container with skin, covered with water	x	x	
Skin soaked with tanning agent about two weeks	x	x	
Skin removed from water, wrung out by hand	x		
Skin removed from water, beaten with stick to expel moisture		x	
Brains rubbed on skin	x	x	
(cont'd)			

UTILIZATION OF SKINS (cont'd)

	Tepehuan	Tarahumar	Sources other than Pennington
Preparation of skins (cont'd)			
Brains and salt rubbed on skin		x	
Intestines rubbed on skin	x		
Squash seeds and salt rubbed on skin		x	
Remaining hair scraped from skin with sharp knife or stone	x		
Skin rolled up, worked back and forth on smooth surface	x		
Skin spread on smooth surface, rolled with log	x	x	
Skin worked by hand to soften		x	
Implements used in manufacturing leather goods			
Wooden awl	x		
Wooden needle	x		
Bone needle		x	
Bone awl		Px;xxZ	Zingg (1940)

Presumably, the arrows were carried in a quiver. Reference to another leather article appears in the eighteenth-century Tepehuan dictionary written by Rinaldini, who gives the Indian term for a sling: *bagguivinajare*.[61] Evidence for the antiquity of leather goods among the Tarahumar is hardly more substantial in spite of the fact that the oldest archeological sites investigated by Bennett and Zingg yielded bone awls not unlike those used today in working with processed skins.[62] Exactly what these awls were used for cannot be determined, but they might have been used in the manufacture of some form of buckskin clothing and skin bags, which are mentioned in eighteenth-century accounts of the Tarahumar.[63,64,65] Or, they might have been used in manufacturing prototypes of the hide sandals mentioned by Steffel in the eighteenth century[66] or perhaps those of the quivers which were carried by eighteenth-century Tarahumar.[67,68] It seems likely that the wide use of leather by the Tepehuan and the Tarahumar in the manufacture of sandals, ropes, quirts, tumplines, nets for carrying baskets, saddle pads and blankets, aprons, and perhaps even sleeping and

sitting mats developed only after the introduction of cattle and more sophisticated techniques for processing skins.

The above data pertaining to skin utilization among the Tepehuan and the
Tarahumar suggest nothing of importance with respect to influence of either
group upon the other.

FIBERS

The Tepehuan and the Tarahumar utilize vegetable and animal fibers
(Table XXVII) in the manufacture of baskets, sleeping and sitting mats, hats,
thatch, sandals, and cordage to be used in nets for canteens and carrying baskets and for rope and headbands. Formerly, the Indians utilized vegetable fibers in the manufacture of clothing.

Contemporary, historical, and archeological evidences suggest that the
use of plant fibers has long constituted a basic cultural element among the
Tepehuan and the Tarahumar. Leaves from the two most important sources of
fibers for basket-making in highland Chihuahua, species of *Dasylirion* and *Nolina*, are processed in virtually the same fashion by the Tepehuan and the Tarahumar. Round and square, double- and single-twilled baskets are made by both
groups. Twilled basketry is certainly aboriginal among the Tarahumar,[69] who
also made mud and grass baskets in pre-Columbian times. Pre-Columbian Tarahumar sites have yielded coiled basketry with bark as a sewing element,[70] and a
pre-Columbian Tepehuan site has yielded basketry covered with pitch.[71] This
same site has also yielded plaited basketry. Funnel-shaped carrying devices are
currently manufactured by the Tepehuan and the Tarahumar with few differences in the techniques used. Nothing is known of the antiquity of these carrying baskets except that they date back to at least the late nineteenth century.[72]
There is no doubt but that both groups made sleeping or sitting mats from fibers in aboriginal times; remains of such mats have been found in Chihuahua[73,74,75] and in northern Durango[76] pre-Columbian sites. Today the Tepehuan and the Tarahumar wear single- and double-twilled hats, but there are no
data to indicate how long such hats have been worn or by what mode the hats
were introduced into western Chihuahua. Only the Tarahumar utilize thatch,
and this custom is apparently restricted to Indians of the western canyons.
Both groups occasionally manufacture crude sandals from *Yucca decipiens*
leaves. The trait seems to be relatively ancient among the Tarahumar since
immediate post-Columbian sites have yielded specimens of a primitive sandal
made of yucca fiber.[77] Whether or not the aboriginal Tarahumar and Tepehuan
wore footgear of any type is uncertain. There is apparently no specific reference to footgear among the Tepehuan until the middle of the eighteenth cen-

tury, and this reference is obscure, giving only the Indian term for *abarca de madera*.[78] Fonte,[79] the first missionary who reached the Tarahumar, did not mention footgear, and Neumann commented in 1682 that men and women went barefooted for the most part.[80] The antiquity of fiber cordage among the Tepehuan and the Tarahumar is without question. Remains of ixtle (pita from *Agave* species), fibers from *Apocynum* species, fronds of a *Washingtonia* species, and fibers from a *Yucca* species have been found in what are presumed to be pre-Columbian and early post-Contact Tarahumar sites.[81,82,83] Remains of ixtle, bear grass, *Gossypium*, and *Yucca* fibers have been found in the northern Durango Río Zape site.[84]

There are relatively few differences in processing techniques followed by the Tepehuan and the Tarahumar in preparing raw materials for the manufacture of cordage. Both groups use the introduced *tarabilla* for making cordage and rope, and this instrument must have reached both of them at about the same time when the Spaniards came in numbers to Chihuahua in the first half of the seventeenth century.

The above data pertaining to fibers suggest that their utilization is an ancient custom among the Tepehuan and the Tarahumar. Therefore, nothing can be said with exactitude about whether or not one of the two groups influenced the other with respect to cordage.

XXVII– UTILIZATION OF FIBERS

	Tepehuan	Tarahumar	Sources other than Pennington
Baskets			
Fibers used for twilled basket			
Dasylirion durangense		x	
D. simplex	x	x	
D. Wheeleri	x	x	
Nolina matapensis	x	x	
N. durangensis	x	x	
Sabal uresana		x	
Yucca decipiens	x	x	
Round double-twilled basket	x	x	
Square double-twilled basket	x	x	
Round single-twilled basket	x	x	
(cont'd)			

UTILIZATION OF FIBERS (cont'd)

	Tepehuan	Tarahumar	Sources other than Pennington
Baskets (cont'd)			
Square single-twilled basket	x	x	
Cover for twilled basket	x	Px;xxBZ	Bennett and Zingg (1935)
Mud and grass basket		PxxZ	Zingg (1940)
Coiled basket with bark sewing element		PxxZ	Zingg (1940)
Coiled basket covered with pitch	PxxB		Brooks et al. (1962)
Plaited basketry	PxxB		Brooks et al. (1962)
Conical carrying basket			
Oak frame	x	x	
Net of hide strips	x	x	
Net of *Salix Gooddingii* branches	x		
Net of *Fouquieria fasciculata* (?) branches	x		
Net of ixtle fibers	x		
Round carrying basket			
Oak frame	x		
Net of hide strips	x		
Net of *Fouquieria fasciculata* (?) branches	x		
Net of ixtle fibers	x		
Sleeping and sitting mats			
Fibers used			
Agave sp.		PxxZ	Zingg (1940)
*Arundo donax	x	x;xxAC,C	Ascher and Clune (1960); Clune (1960)
Dasylirion durangense		x	
D. simplex		x	
D. Wheeleri	x	x	
Nolina durangensis		x	
N. sp.		PxxZ	Zingg (1940)
Sabal uresana		x	
Washingtonia sp.(?)		PxxAC,C	Ascher and Clune (1960); Clune (1960)
(cont'd)			

UTILIZATION OF FIBERS (cont'd)

	Tepehuan	Tarahumar	Sources other than Pennington
Fibers used (cont'd)			
Yucca decipiens		x	
Y. sp.		PxxZ	Zingg (1940)
Unknown species	PxxB	PxxR	Brooks et al. (1962); 1778: Relación de Santa Eulalia
Hats			
Fibers used			
Dasylirion simplex	x		
D. Wheeleri		x	
Nolina durangensis		x	
N. matapensis	x	x	
Sabal uresana		x	
Types of hats			
Single-twilled	x	x	
Double-twilled	x	x	
Thatch			
Fibers used			
*Arundo donax		x	
Dasylirion durangense		x	
D. simplex		x	
D. Wheeleri		x	
Nolina durangensis		x	
N. matapensis		x	
Phragmites communis		x	
Sabal uresana		x	
Yucca decipiens		x	
Sandals			
Fibers used			
Yucca decipiens	x	x	
Y. sp.		PxxZ	Zingg (1940)
Cordage			
Sources of fibers			
Plants and trees			
Agave lecheguilla (ixtle)		x	
A. Patonii (ixtle)		x	
(cont'd)			

UTILIZATION OF FIBERS (cont'd)

	Tepehuan	Tarahumar	Sources other than Pennington
Plants and trees (cont'd)			
A. Schottii (ixtle)		x	
A. sp. (ixtle)	PxxB	PxxZ	Brooks et al. (1962); Zingg (1940)
A. sp. (ixtle)	x		
A. sp. (ixtle)	x		
A. sp. (ixtle)	x		
Apocynum sp. (fibers)		PxxO	O'Neale (1948)
Bear grass (leaves)	PxxB		Brooks et al. (1962)
Ceiba acuminata (?) (fibers)		PxxR	1777: Relación de Batopilillas
Cornus stolonifera (branches)		x	
Gossypium sp. (fibers)	PxxB		Brooks et al. (1962)
Guazuma ulmifolia (bark)		x	
Washingtonia sp. (fronds)		PxxC	Clune (1960)
Yucca decipiens (leaves)	x		
Y. sp. (leaves)	PxxB	PxxZ	Brooks et al. (1962); Zingg (1940)
Animal fibers			
Goat hair	x	x	
Hair from horse's tail	x	x	
Hair from cow's tail	x	x	
Articles made from cordage			
Ropes	x	x	
Nets for canteens	x	x	
Nets for carrying baskets	x		
Heavy cordage			
Goat hair	x	x	
Hair from cow's tail	x	x	
Hair from horse's tail	x	x	
Cornus stolonifera branches		x	
Processing of plant fibers			
Fibers removed from green leaves	x	x	
Fibers removed from dried leaves		x	
Dried leaves beaten with mallet or stone to loosen fibers		x	
(cont'd)			

UTILIZATION OF FIBERS (cont'd)

	Tepehuan	Tarahumar	Sources other than Pennington
Processing of plant fibers (cont'd)			
Green leaves boiled or baked to loosen fibers		x	
Leaves anchored to post or sapling, scraped with sharp stone or knife	x		
Green leaves sun-dried, pulp knocked from leaves with mallet		x	
Fibers washed and dried	x	x	
Fibers rolled on thigh for thin cordage	x	x	
Tarabilla used for ixtle cordage	x		
Processing of animal fibers (hair)			
Tarabilla used for cordage	x	xxBZ	Bennett and Zingg (1935)

CLOTHING AND PERSONAL ADORNMENT

Clothing (Table XXVIII) worn by the Tepehuan resembles that of the mestizos more than does the typical clothing of the Tarahumar. However, some articles of clothing worn today by the Tarahumar and the Tepehuan are, without doubt, analogues of articles worn by both groups in pre-Columbian and post-Contact times. Even so, there is insufficient historical and archeological evidence to indicate whether or not either group influenced the other with respect to wearing apparel.

Conservative adult Tarahumar and Tepehuan males wear either a cotton-cloth or woolen sash as a belt. The cotton-cloth belt is simply a rag wrapped around the waist and knotted at the side or in the front, whereas the woolen sash is woven from native wool on the horizontal loom that is typical of upland Chihuahua. Nothing definite is known concerning the antiquity of these belts or sashes. However, the woolen sashes certainly date back to the nineteenth century since they are pictured in Lumholtz.[85]

There is some slight archeological evidence that aboriginal Tarahumar wore headbands made from pita fiber or from palm fronds of a *Washingtonia* species.[86,87,88] Furthermore, it seems likely that the aboriginal Tarahumar also made headbands by plaiting the leaves of *Yucca, Nolina,* and *Sabal uresana* species just as is done today. Aboriginal Tarahumar may have worn mesh hairnets; a fine specimen that resembles the hairnets common to the American Southwest was found in a pre-Columbian Tarahumar site by Bennett and Zingg.[89]

Loincloths made from skins and pita fiber were worn by the Tarahumar in the very early colonial period[90,91] and no doubt were also worn in pre-Columbian times. Pre-Contact Tarahumar must have worn a kind of poncho prepared from ixtle fiber; a seventeenth-century account by Neumann refers to a garment that was put on over the head and worn over the shoulders.[92] The assumption that aboriginal Tarahumar wore pita garments is substantiated by finds of poncho-like apparel made of pita in ancient Basketmaker sites.[93] It seems certain that the small "poncho" worn today by Tarahumar males represents a modern adaptation of the ancient and larger garment.

The above data suggest, at least for the Tarahumar males, that their headbands, loincloths, and poncho-like garments date back to pre-Columbian times. For the Tepehuan, the record is not quite as clear. However, in spite of a lack of specific references to their articles of clothing, the pre-Columbian Tepehuan probably wore the same type of clothing as the Tarahumar. The Tepehuan were producing cotton at the time of contact as is evident from a reference to *vestidos de algodón* in an account of 1596.[94] There is also the very explicit comment by Pérez de Ribas that the early seventeenth-century Tepehuan grew cotton and secured pita from plants growing in nearby uplands; the fibers were woven into *faldellines* and mantas.[95] Additional evidence of the fibers used by pre-Columbian Tepehuan is found in material recovered from the Río Zape site. Agave and yucca leaf fragments are common in the older levels, but cotton string appears only in the late pre-Columbian strata.[96]

Tarahumar and Tepehuan women frequently wear a cotton-cloth or woolen sash and a cotton-cloth or fiber headband as well. Tepehuan women are distinct from Tarahumar women in that the former frequently wear bandanas about their heads. This style of head covering apparently never appears among Tarahumar women except for those who live on close terms with the mestizos or those who live in or near Jesuit missions. There is a further distinction between Tepehuan and Tarahumar women in that the Tepehuan generally wear shorter skirts than the Tarahumar. Also, the Tepehuan woman often wears a one-piece cotton dress, a style which has not been documented among the Tarahumar. Blanket skirts of wool were worn by Tarahumar women in the late nineteenth century according to Lumholtz.[97] Without doubt, these skirts were analogous to the very narrow blanket skirts worn by Tarahumar women at Cerocahui in the eighteenth century.[98] And probably, the eighteenth-century woolen skirts were analogous to the pita-fiber aprons found in the Basketmaker sites by Bennett and Zingg.[99] The above reference to Tepehuan *faldellines* (aprons or skirts) and mantas, made by Pérez de Ribas in the eighteenth century, does seem to suggest that aboriginal Tepehuan women wore certain kinds of garments. Against this assumption, however, is his subsequent comment that priests made efforts to obtain apparel for nude Indians in northern Durango.[100] These Indians might have been upland Indians living to the west and northwest of Durango City in areas that can hardly grow cotton. South of the Río Verde in Chihuahua, cotton can be cultivated only in the very warm, western canyons.

There can be no doubt about the antiquity of the loom among the Tepehuan and the Tarahumar. Pita-fiber blankets have been found in the oldest of Tarahumar sites, labeled as Basketmaker sites by Bennett and Zingg,[101] which certainly date back to pre-Columbian times. A fired clay whorl has been recovered from one of these sites, and a post-Contact site has yielded a wooden spindle not unlike those used today by the Tarahumar.[102] For the Tepehuan, the record is less clear. There is an indirect reference to a loom in that seventeenth-century statement by Pérez de Ribas about the *faldellines* and mantas worn by Tepehuan women,[103] and there were certain wooden objects removed from the Río Zape site in northern Durango that resemble shuttles and battens used in weaving.[104] Whether pre-Columbian Tepehuan and Tarahumar used a vertical or a horizontal loom cannot be stated with certainty; it was probably a horizontal loom in view of the fact that present-day Tepehuan and Tarahumar utilize that type.

The antiquity for use of native plants in the preparation of dyestuffs (Table XXVIII) is not determined. However, the Tarahumar certainly practice this trait today more than the Tepehuan. There is some evidence that pre-Columbian Tarahumar used dyestuffs. The Chihuahua textiles studied by O'Neale[105] and Kasha[106] are believed to be pre-Columbian; the textiles reveal evidences of an orange and a greenish-black dyestuff.

Commercial soap is not readily available to either the Tepehuan or the Tarahumar. Therefore, both groups utilize plant substances as detergents (Table XXVIII). Nothing can be stated with certainty about the antiquity of this trait in the uplands of Chihuahua or about whether the trait spread from one of the Indian groups to the other. With respect to making soap, a major distinction between the Tepehuan and the Tarahumar exists: some of the Tepehuan make soap from melted fat, whereas the Tarahumar do not. The rendering of fat by the Tepehuan definitely represents a custom borrowed from the mestizos.

Feathers have long been used for personal adornment by the Tepehuan and the Tarahumar as is evidenced by comments made by Pérez de Ribas in the seventeenth century.[107] Without doubt, the trait was an aboriginal one.

The Tepehuan and the Tarahumar utilize pine-cone combs and have done so for centuries. Rinaldini gives the eighteenth-century Tepehuan term for this comb,[108] and Palmer found nineteenth-century Tarahumar using such a device.[109] Both groups utilize dried immature fruits of *Pachycereus pecten-aboriginum* in dressing their hair. This practice may represent an ancient custom since the nineteenth-century Tarahumar collected these cacti fruits for use as hairbrushes.[110]

Tattooing was once common among the Tarahumar,[111,112] but there is no evidence that the Tepehuan have ever practiced this custom. Present-day Tepehuan and Tarahumar use various seeds and tiny marine shells for making necklaces. The antiquity of necklaces among both groups is demonstrated by pre-Columbian archeological evidence.[113,114] However, it seems strange that the Tepehuan apparently never make use of the handsome seeds of Job's Tears (*Coix Lacryma-Jobi*) as beads; this plant is one of the important cultivated plants among the Tarahumar.

Basically, there is almost nothing in the archival or historical record to indicate significant influence of the Tepehuan or Tarahumar upon one another with respect to clothing and personal adornment.

XXVIII– CLOTHING AND PERSONAL ADORNMENT

	Tepehuan	Tarahumar	Sources other than Pennington
Clothing worn by men and youths			
Belts			
Cotton cloth	x	x	
Woolen sash	x	x	
Leather (commercial belt)	x	x	
Headbands			
Woolen circlet		x;xxR	1683: Ratkay
Ixtle fiber	x	Px;xxZ	Zingg (1940)
Palm fronds (*Washingtonia* sp.)		PxxC,AC	Clune (1960); Ascher and Clune (1960)
Plaited leaves of *Yucca* spp.		x	
Plaited leaves of *Nolina* spp.		x	
Plaited leaves of *Sabal uresana*		x	
Hairnets			
Mesh net of fiber cordage		PxxZ	Zingg (1940)
(cont'd)			

CLOTHING AND PERSONAL ADORNMENT (cont'd)

	Tepehuan	Tarahumar	Sources other than Pennington
Clothing worn (cont'd)			
Loincloths			
Cotton cloth	Px;xxP,C	x	1645: Pérez de Ribas (1944); 1596: Carta Anua
Animal skin		PxxN	1682: Neumann
Fiber cordage		PxxN	1682: Neumann
Blanket		xxR	1777: Relación de Guaguachic
Shirts			
Cotton (commercial shirt)	x	x	
Cotton (made by women)	x	x	
Underwear			
Cotton drawers (made by women)	x		
Trousers			
Cotton (commercial trousers)	x	x	
Cotton (made by women)	x		
Blanket		xxR	1777: Relación de Guaguachic
Buckskin		PxxR	1777: Relación de Guaguachic
Blankets			
Woolen blanket wrapped about body	x	x	
Pita-fiber blanket		PxxZ	Zingg (1940)
Unknown material	PxxB		Brooks et al. (1962)
Poncho-like garment (ixtle?)		PxxN	1682: Neumann
Hats			
Commercial	x		
Twilled (made by women)	x	x	
Kerchief worn about neck			
Cotton cloth (white)	x	x	
Bandana	x		
Sandals			
Fiber	x	PxxZ	Zingg (1940)
Animal skin	x	x	
Rubber tire	x	x	
Leather thongs	x	x	
Fiber thongs	x	x	
(cont'd)			

CLOTHING AND PERSONAL ADORNMENT (cont'd)

	Tepehuan	Tarahumar	Sources other than Pennington
Clothing worn by women and girls			
Belts			
Cotton cloth	x	x	
Woolen sash	x	x	
Headbands			
Cotton cloth	x	x	
Bandana	x		
Fiber	x	Px;xxZ	Zingg (1940)
Skirts			
Long cotton skirt (commercial fabric)		x	
Short cotton skirt (commercial fabric)	x		
Blanket skirt (woolen)	x	xxL	Lumholtz (1902)
Pita-fiber skirt or apron	PxxP	PxxZ	1645: Pérez de Ribas (1944); Zingg (1940)
Cotton skirt or apron	PxxP		1645: Pérez de Ribas (1944)
Poncho-like cotton garment	x		
One-piece cotton dress	x		
Weaving			
Source of wool			
Sheep	x	x	
Goats	x	x	
Whorls			
Wooden	x	Px;xxZ	Zingg (1940)
Clay		PxxZ	Zingg (1940)
Horizontal loom	x	x	
Dyestuffs from vegetal sources			
Acacia Farnesiana		x	
Alnus acuminata		x	
*Erodium cicutarium		x	
Erythrina flabelliformis		x	
Haematoxylon brasiletto		x	
Haplopappus australis		xxBZ	Bennett and Zingg (1935)
(cont'd)			

CLOTHING AND PERSONAL ADORNMENT (cont'd)

	Tepehuan	Tarahumar	Sources other than Pennington
Dyestuffs (cont'd)			
Indigofera suffruticosa		x	
Iostephane heterophylla		x	
Mahonia sp.	x		
Manihot sp.		x	
Pithecellobium dulce		x	
Sideranthus australis		xxBZ	Bennett and Zingg (1935)
Usnea subfusca		x	
U. variolosa		x	
Unidentified specimens			
sepé		x	
siyóname		x	
acetilla	x		
Detergents			
Plant substances			
Agave bovicornuta	x		
A. lecheguilla		x	
A. Patonii		x	
A. Schottii		x	
A. sp.	x		
Cucurbita foetidissima		x	
Dyssodia anomala		x	
Fouquieria fasciculata		xxBZ	Bennett and Zingg (1935)
Phytolacca icosandra	x		
P. americana	x		
Pinus Engelmanni	x		
*Ricinus communis	x		
Sicyos parviflorus		x	
Yucca decipiens	x	x	
Special detergents for washing hair			
Abutilon trisulcatum		xxBZ	Bennett and Zingg (1935)
Agave sp.	x		
Senecio sp.	x		
Sida rhombifolia		xxBZ	Bennett and Zingg (1935)
Yucca sp.	x		
(cont'd)			

CLOTHING AND PERSONAL ADORNMENT (cont'd)

	Tepehuan	Tarahumar	Sources other than Pennington
Detergents (cont'd)			
Soap from rendered fat	x		
Hair styles			
Page-boy bob			
Men	x	x	
Women	x	x	
Hair worn long (men)	x	Px;xxR	1683: Ratkay
Braided hair (men and women)		PxxR	1777: Relación de Guaguachic
Braided hair (women)	x		
Combs and brushes			
Pine-cone comb	Px;xxR	x	1743: Rinaldini (1743)
Cactus-fruit brush	x	x	
Feathers worn	Px;xxP	Px;xxP	1645: Pérez de Ribas (1944)
Tattooing		PxxR	1683: Ratkay
Necklaces			
Arbutus arizonica seeds		x	
A. glandulosa seeds		x	
*Coix Lacryma-Jobi seeds		x	
Erythrina flabelliformis seeds	x	x	
Beads fashioned from *Ptelea trifoliata* wood		x	
Crosses fashioned from *P. trifoliata* wood		x	
Marine mollusks	Px;xxB	Px;xxZ	Brooks et al. (1962); Zingg (1940)
Olivella beads	PxxB		Brooks et al. (1962)

HOUSEHOLD ARTICLES

Essential household articles (Table XXIX), such as gourd containers, pottery, and metates, are apparently so ancient in both Tepehuan and Tarahumar culture that it is impossible to determine whether or not one group influenced the other with respect to these items. Certainly, the available evidence does not suggest much influence of either group upon the other as far as the past few centuries are concerned. A relative antiquity for the gourd container among the Tarahumar is evidenced by remains of such articles in a pre-Columbian site studied by Bennett and Zingg;[115] antiquity for the *guaje* among the Tepehuan is indicated by fragments of *Lagenaria siceraria* recovered from the Río Zape site in Durango.[116] The ancient Tarahumar manufactured bowls, dippers, and storage containers from gourds and, presumably, so did the Tepehuan. Present-day Tepehuan and Tarahumar manufacture carrying nets for canteens from pita fiber, but there is nothing in the archeological record to indicate the antiquity of this particular trait. Apparently, neither group decorates gourd utensils today; however, the Tarahumar did so formerly.[117] The Tarahumar prepare glue for mending *guaje* containers from substances obtained from either *Nolina matapensis*, *N. durangensis*, *Cooperia Drummondi*, or *Phaseolus Metcalfei*. Of these plants, only *Nolina matapensis* is utilized for a similar purpose by the Tepehuan, which is puzzling because all four species appear in Chihuahua south of the Río Verde. The Tepehuan claim not to know *Nolina durangensis*, *Cooperia Drummondi*, or *Phaseolus Metcalfei* as sources for adhesive preparations. This circumstance certainly does not suggest a Tarahumar influence upon the Tepehuan. Also, there is no evidence of the Tepehuan influencing the Tarahumar in the use of the bottle gourd. Apparently, nowhere north of the Río Verde do the six distinct varieties of *Lagenaria siceraria* cultivated by the Tepehuan appear.

There is no conclusive evidence that pre-Columbian Tepehuan and Tarahumar utilized pottery extensively; however, both groups did make pottery as is evidenced by materials recovered from the Waterfall Cave site in Chihuahua[118] and in the Río Zape site of northern Durango.[119] There are relatively few differences between the present techniques of the Tepehuan and the Tarahumar for manufacturing the crude pottery that serves the Chihuahua Indian folk. The one significant difference—and it may reflect a mestizo influence south of the Río Verde—is that the Tepehuan make pottery in a greater variety of shapes than the Tarahumar.

The antiquity of the metate and its associated upper grinding stone among the Tepehuan and the Tarahumar is indicated by materials recovered from the Río Zape[120] and Waterfall Cave[121] sites. Abrading stones and a crude stone knife have been recovered from pre-Columbian Tarahumar sites,[122] but no such articles have been found in pre-Columbian Tepehuan material. However, the Río Zape site has yielded choppers and hammerstones,[123] evidence enough that the aboriginal Tepehuan worked in stone. These ancient Tepehuan may also have made stone idols. Unquestionably, the multiplicity of references to these items being found north of Durango City in the early colonial period allows this speculation.

It is relatively certain that the ancient Tarahumar used wood for manufacturing household articles since they did work with wood in fashioning such items as supports for their habitations. A site designated by Bennett and Zingg as being Basketmaker in point of time has yielded a wooden stool-like artifact[124] that resembles sleeping boards currently manufactured by the Tarahumar. Also, the ancient Tarahumar probably fashioned headrests much as the Chihuahua Tarahumar and Tepehuan do today. The stone axes, which are still found here and there in western Chihuahua, would have served as well in the manufacture of headrests and sleeping boards as they no doubt did in the preparation of house supports. Although there is no direct evidence that ancient Tepehuan manufactured either headrests or sleeping boards, it is reasonable to assume that they did.

It seems unlikely that either ancient group carved wooden spoons or bowls; no suitable tool for such a craft has been recorded. However, nothing is known for certain regarding the antiquity of wooden spoons and bowls among the Indians of Chihuahua. The first mention of wooden spoons is apparently that of Lumholtz, who wrote that those used by the Tepehuan were brought in by Aztec and Otomi traders from southern Mexico.[125] If Lumholtz' observation was in fact correct, then it is possible that neither the Tepehuan nor the Tarahumar made wooden spoons until the beginning of the twentieth century.

XXIX– HOUSEHOLD ARTICLES

	Tepehuan	Tarahumar	Sources other than Pennington

Gourd utensils
 	
 Fruits used
   Crescentia alata
   Lagenaria siceraria
 	
 (cont'd)
	
	 Px;xxB
		
		 PxxZ
		 Px;xxZ
			
			 Zingg (1940)
			 Brooks et al. (1962);
			 Zingg (1940)

HOUSEHOLD ARTICLES (cont'd)

	Tepehuan	Tarahumar	Sources other than Pennington
Gourd utensils (cont'd)			
Articles made			
Bowls	x	Px;xxZ	Zingg (1940)
Canteens	x	x	
Dippers	x	Px;xxZ	Zingg (1940)
Storage containers	x	Px;xxZ	Zingg (1940)
Corncob stoppers	x	x	
Stoppers from other materials		PxxZ	Zingg (1940)
Carrying nets for canteens	x	x	
Decorated		PxxZ	Zingg (1940)
Utensils mended			
Glue from portions of vegetal material			
Cooperia Drummondi		x	
Nolina durangensis		x	
N. matapensis	x	x	
Phaseolus Metcalfei		x	
Ixtle fiber		Px;xxZ	Zingg (1940)
Ceramics	Px;xxB	Px;xxAC	Brooks et al. (1962); Ascher and Clune (1960)
Bowls	x	x	
Comals	x	x	
Dye pots		x	
Griddles	x	x	
Incense jugs	x	x	
Ollas			
Made by women	x	x	
Made by men	x	x	
Large olla with constricted center	x		
Tempering agents			
Crushed sherds	x	x	
Sand	x	x	
(cont'd)			

HOUSEHOLD ARTICLES (cont'd)

	Tepehuan	Tarahumar	Sources other than Pennington
Ollas (cont'd)			
Handles			
Regular handle	x	x	
Projection	x		
Dried in sun	x	x	
Dried in shade	x		
Firing materials			
Manure	x	x	
Oak	x	x	
Pine		x	
Smoothing agents			
Stone	x	PxxR	1777: Relación de Guaguachic
Broken bit of pottery	x		
Erythrina flabelliformis bean	x		
Small gourd		x	
Beading on rim	x		
Decorated with pigments			
Red	PxxB	Px;xxAC	Brooks et al. (1962); Ascher and Clune (1960)
Black		Px;xxAC	Ascher and Clune (1960)
Green		PxxR	1777: Relación de Cusihuiriachic
Mended with glue prepared from *Nolina matapensis*	x		
Stone artifacts			
Metates	Px;xxB	Px;xxAC	Brooks et al. (1962); Ascher and Clune (1960)
Wooden stand used for metate	x		
Grinding stones			
Manufactured		x	
Obtained from stream bed	x		
Square	x	x	
Round	x	x	
Stone knives	x	Px;xxZ	Zingg (1940)
(cont'd)			

HOUSEHOLD ARTICLES (cont'd)

	Tepehuan	Tarahumar	Sources other than Pennington
Stone artifacts (cont'd)			
Pestles		x	
Abrading stones		Px;xxZ	Zingg (1940)
Choppers	PxxB		Brooks et al. (1962)
Hammerstones	PxxB		Brooks et al. (1962)
Stone axes	x	x	
Stone idols	P?xxP		1645: Pérez de Ribas (1944)
Wooden artifacts			
Bowls			
Woods used			
Arbutus arizonica	x	x	
A. glandulosa	x	x	
A. xalapensis	x		
Guazuma ulmifolia		x	
Ficus petiolaris		x	
F. radulina		x	
Platanus Wrightii		x	
Populus angustifolia		x	
P. tremuloides		x	
Salix sp.	x		
Spoons			
Woods used			
Arbutus arizonica	x	x	
A. glandulosa	x	x	
A. xalapensis	x		
Ficus petiolaris		x	
F. radulina		x	
Guazuma ulmifolia		x	
Platanus Wrightii		x	
Populus angustifolia		x	
P. tremuloides		x	
Thevetia sp.	x		
(cont'd)			

HOUSEHOLD ARTICLES (cont'd)

	Tepehuan	Tarahumar	Sources other than Pennington
Wooden artifacts (cont'd)			
Troughs			
Woods used			
Pinus sp.	x	x	
Populus angustifolia		x	
P. tremuloides		x	
Stools	x		
Headrests	x	Px;xxBZ	Bennett and Zingg (1935)
Sleeping boards		x	
Fire drills		Px;xxBZ	Bennett and Zingg (1935)
Benches	x		
Crude wooden chairs with leather-strip seats	x		
Brooms			
Stems of *Mühlenbergia Emersleyi*	x	x	

HABITATIONS

Present-day Tepehuan and Tarahumar make much use of pine timber in the building of log structures which have locked corners. However, characteristics of the wooden structures (Table XXX) made by each group differ to such an extent that any notion of either group influencing the other in building techniques is negated. Whereas the Tarahumar invariably construct a one-room log dwelling, the Tepehuan commonly construct a two- or three-room dwelling. The Tarahumar never construct the high gabled roof so typical of Tepehuan log dwellings. Nor do the Tarahumar utilize shingles, which are nearly always used on roofs for Tepehuan habitations. The Tarahumar prefer *canoas* as a roofing element. They almost never have storage rooms within their dwellings, whereas most Tepehuan multiroom structures do. The antiquity of log structures is not determined, but they date back to at least the late nineteenth century, at which time Lumholtz described and photographed such habitations.[126] In any case, there is little in the record or the present landscape to warrant a positive statement about the influence of either Tepehuan or Tarahumar upon the other.

The use of timber for constructing habitations is very old among the Tarahumar and the Tepehuan as is evidenced in Zingg's account of pre-Columbian Tarahumar sites[127] and in the account of seventeenth-century Tepehuan by Pérez de Ribas.[128] Such timber undoubtedly was processed with stone axes.

Antiquity for the use of caves (abundant in western Chihuahua and in northern and northwestern Durango) as dwelling sites by the Tarahumar and the Tepehuan is without question. The evidence is in archeological and historical data.[129,130,131,132] We know that the ancient Tarahumar constructed multiroomed structures in caves, and it is likely that the ancient Tepehuan living south of the Río Verde did likewise. In the western canyons now inhabited by the Tepehuan, there are many caves containing the ruins of multiroomed structures. However, we cannot be certain that these ancient cave sites were ever occupied by the Tepehuan. They might have been occupied by the Tubar and the Zoe, who are known historically to have been in the vicinity of southwestern Chihuahua. Additional evidence, albeit tenuous, that the Tepehuan once lived in caves is obtained from stories told by present-day Tepehuan of multiroomed structures in large caves that are located in the rough country southeast of Guadalupe y Calvo.

The antiquity of stone and mud (mortar?) structures among the Tepehuan and the Tarahumar is certain. Pérez de Ribas referred to dwellings of stone and mud (*piedra y barro*) built by northern Durango Tepehuan,[133] and Zingg has described stone habitations with plastered adobe mud floors built in caves once occupied by the Tarahumar.[134]

There is evidence of a relatively great antiquity for the utilization of brush huts by both Tepehuan and Tarahumar. This statement is based on the assumption that the house types described by early missionaries were part of an ancient tradition. There must have been little difference between the crude *jacalillos* or *chozas* constructed by the seventeenth-century Tepehuan of northern Durango[135] and the straw and branch huts mentioned by seventeenth-century missionaries who lived among the Tarahumar.[136,137]

The above data, pertaining to the important house types—past and present—common to the Tepehuan and to the Tarahumar, suggest that, in very ancient times, both groups utilized brush and branches, stone and mud (mortar?), and saplings in the construction of habitations. Both groups occupied caves. These customs are so ancient that it is impossible to determine whether or not one group influenced the other. The use of logs in construction of dwellings and storage cribs must have developed among the Tepehuan and the Tarahumar within the past century, but nothing can be said with certainty about which group first built such structures. Irrespective of this particular point, the two groups differ considerably with respect to types of log structures built.

XXX— HABITATIONS

	Tepehuan	Tarahumar	Sources other than Pennington
Log structures			
1-room structure with slightly slanting roof of *canoas* or smoothed logs	x	x	
1-room structure with steeply slanted roof of *canoas* or smoothed logs	x	x	
1-room structure with shingle roof	x		
1-room structure with "porch"	x	x	
1-room structure with low gable roof of *canoas* or smoothed logs	x		
1-room structure with low gable roof of shingles	x		
1-room structure with high gable roof centered over structure, projected beyond dwelling to form "porch"	x		
Multiroom structure with high gable roof centered over structure, projected beyond dwelling to form "porch"	x		
Shingle structures			
1-room shingle-sided structure with gabled shingled roof	x		
Multiroom shingle-sided structure with gabled shingled roof	x		
Small shingle-sided structure as dwelling for people protecting crops from predators	x		
Stone and mud structures	PxxP	PxxZ	1645: Pérez de Ribas (1944); Zingg (1940)
Stone and adobe structures	x		
Stone and wood structures			
Rectangular stone and wood structure with walls of stones wedged between evenly spaced upright posts anchored in ground, with roof of *canoas* or smoothed logs		x	
(cont'd)			

HABITATIONS (cont'd)

	Tepehuan	Tarahumar	Sources other than Pennington
Stone and wood structures (cont'd)			
Rectangular stone structure with roof of *canoas* or smoothed logs	x	x	
Small gable-on-the-ground structure with end walls of stone, with side walls of logs or *canoas* resting against a ridgepole		x	
Cave dwellings			
Open cave dwelling	PxxB,R	Px;xxZ	Brooks et al. (1962); 1605: Relación de Martín Peláez; Zingg (1940)
Cave dwelling with opening partially walled up with stones		Px;xxZ	Zingg (1940)
Round stone dwelling in cave		PxxZ	Zingg (1940)
Square stone dwelling in cave		PxxZ	Zingg (1940)
2-story stone dwelling in cave		PxxZ	Zingg (1940)
Miscellaneous structures and materials			
Rush hut (conical?)	PxxP	PxxN	1645: Pérez de Ribas (1944); 1681: Neumann
Branches used for hut (conical?)	PxxP	PxxN,R	1645: Pérez de Ribas (1944); 1681: Neumann; 1683: Ratkay
Wood and saplings	PxxP		1645: Pérez de Ribas (1944)
Thatch	PxxP	x	1645: Pérez de Ribas (1944)
Side walls constructed of *Fouquieria fasciculata* (?) branches	x		
Apertures			
Windows			
Stone house		x	
Log house		x	
(cont'd)			

HABITATIONS (cont'd)

	Tepehuan	Tarahumar	Sources other than Pennington
Apertures (cont'd)			
Doors			
Stone house	x	x	
Log house	x	x	
Shingle house	x		
Roofs			
Slanted roof of *canoas*	x	x	
Gabled roof of *canoas*	x		
Combination of *canoas* and earth	x	x	
Shingle roof affixed with pine nails	x		
Shingle roof held down with stones	x		
Thatch roof		x	
Cooking platforms	x		
Habitation abandoned on death of occupant	P?xxP	PxxN	1645: Pérez de Ribas (1944); 1681: Neumann
Wooden cross anchored to house roof	x		
Incense bowl placed before wooden cross on rooftop	x		
Fire maintained continuously within habitation	Px;xxP	x	1645: Pérez de Ribas (1944)

CONCLUSIONS

Approximately 8,000 Tepehuan and about 50,000 Tarahumar[138] live to-day in western Chihuahua amidst approximately 100,000 mestizos.[139] Within the two *municipios* (Guadalupe y Calvo and Morelos) that contain the most Tepehuan, the ratio of mestizo to Indian is probably about four to one. Within those *municipios* that contain significant numbers of Tarahumar, the ratio of mestizo to Indian is less than one to one, with more Indians in each *municipio* than mestizos. But in both instances, among the Tepehuan and among the Tara-humar, the mestizo element is the dominant one regarding economic matters and political control.

Dominance of mestizo folk in population south of the Río Verde (in Tepehuan country) and in political control on both sides of the Río Verde is a situation that no doubt has developed within the past century. Probably, the next century will be marked by an ever-increasing dominance by mestizos not only with respect to population but also with respect to economic matters, particularly in the field of lumbering activities. Increasing dominance in the number of mestizos coupled with increasing activity on the part of the national government in an effort to bring Indian peoples into the mainstream of Mexi-can cultural and economic development may promote even further merging of Indians and mestizos. And this fusion could alter a situation that has obtained in the Mexican northwest since the sixteenth century.

The available evidence suggests that, since the Conquest, the Tepehuan and the Tarahumar have maintained their integrity with respect to language and culture while, at the same time, making full use of significant European introductions such as plows, axes, stock, certain plant life, and clothing styles. And while the two groups have maintained an Indian integrity despite several centuries of contacts with outsiders, they have also maintained tribal identities despite their living side by side. The data offered herein concerning Tepehuan and Tarahumar material culture do not suggest a significant influence of either group upon the other within historic times or even in the late pre-Columbian period. The basic cultural elements of these two conservative groups are, with-out doubt, so much a part of ancient tradition that any firm lines of influence—now or in the past—between the Tepehuan and the Tarahumar are not discernible.

CHAPTER 10 NOTES

1— Riley and Winters (1963), 177-78.

2— Most of the data concerning the Tepehuan and the Tarahumar found in Tables III through XXX are based on my field work among the Chihuahua Tepehuan in 1960 and 1965 and among the Tarahumar in 1955. Other data are taken from archival materials and published sources. In general, where my field data parallel the findings of other investigators, no specific references are indicated in the Tables. However, where an "xx" is followed by a letter, as "xxB," the datum is taken from the source indicated by author or manuscript and date of publication. Complete references are given in the Bibliography. A pre-Columbian trait is indicated by a "P" preceding the "x" or "xx." Existence of a pre-Columbian trait is based on archeological evidence or on a reasonable interpretation of very early historical documents. Introduced plants are asterisked.

3— Anderson and Cutler [1955; 1960].

4— Cutler [1966].

5— Lumholtz (1902), I, 429.

6— Bennett and Zingg [(1935), 174] refer to a use of *Gossypium mexicanum* pods in the preparation of a corn dish. However, nothing is said about whether this cotton plant was cultivated or wild. *Gossypium mexicanum* is known to appear in the wild state [Standley (1920-1926), 785]. There is no evidence of cotton materials in pre-Columbian Tarahumar archeological sites [Bennett and Zingg (1935), 174].

7— Bennett and Zingg (1935), 29-30.

8— Ibid., 269-90.

9— 1651: Pascual. "Noticias de las misiones sacadas . . . ," in *Doc.* (1857), 4th series, III, 179-209.

10— 1777: Relación de Guazapares.

11— Beals (1932), 163.

12— 1743: Rinaldini (1743), 3, 13.

13— 1777: Relación de Guaguachic.

14— Ibid.

15— Lumholtz (1902), I, 214-15, 431.

16— 1662: Figueroa. "Puntos de Anua . . . ," in *Doc.* (1857), 4th series, III, 219. See Pennington [(1963)b, 153] for a comment on the antiquity of maize *tesgüino* among the Tarahumar.

17— That the opossum does not appear south of the Río Verde seems incredible. The creature is certainly common north of the river.

18— Clune (1960), 274.

19— Lumholtz (1902), I, 400.

20— 1682: Letter of Joseph Neumann, February 20.

21— 1683: Letter of Juan Bautista Ancieta, March 20.

22— Lumholtz (1902), I, 264.

23— Mason (1952), 45.

24— Circa 1767: Steffel (1809).

25— 1743: Rinaldini (1743), 62.

26— Burrus (1963), 102.

27— Bennett and Zingg (1935), 68-69.

28— Zingg (1940), 63-64.

29— Bennett and Zingg (1935), 67.

30— Lumholtz (1902), I, 431.

31— 1662: Carta Anua.

32— Decorme (1941), II, 260.

33— 1683: Ratkay. An account of the Tarahumar missions. . . .

34— Zingg (1940), 63.

35— 1743: Rinaldini (1743), 130.

36— Zingg (1940), 62-63.

37— Circa 1767: Steffel (1809), 312.

38— For example, we really do not know if the trait is aboriginal. We do know that Spanish soldiers and missionaries presented badges of authority to Indian leaders in the American Southwest. Kino presented canes of office to Cocomaricopa along the Río Gila in the late seventeenth century [1746: Sedelmayr. "Relación, 1746," in *Jacobo Sedelmayr, Missionary, Frontiersman, Explorer* . . . (1955), 19, 29, 45]. Manje records distribution of canes as badges of office between 1694 and 1701 [1693-1721: Manje (1954), 10, 12, 31, 40, 42, 120, 214]. Then, there is that vexing matter of the derivation of the place-name Cusihuiriachic (an important Tarahumar center of the seventeenth and eighteenth centuries). The name stems from a combination of *kuši* (*palo* or *poste*, stick), *wirí* (*está erguido*, standing), and a euphonic *a* and *či* (*de lugar*, place of); it means *el palo parado*, or "place of the standing stick." I once wrote [Pennington (1963)b, 161] that the name might have been given to the place because the Spaniards presented a badge of authority to an important Indian there. I now wonder whether this observation really has merit. The sticks carried by the pre-Columbian (and immediate post-Columbian?) traders who roamed between central Mexico and the far north, particularly Casas Grandes, might be involved in the place-name of Cusihuiriachic. It lies on the eastern margin of the high sierras of western Chihuahua and would have been a fine stopping point for traders moving north or south who wished to avoid the desert country to the east. That Cusihuiriachic was a trading place is suggested by a comment found in an eighteenth-century account (1777: Relación de Cusihuiriachic) indicating that a great variety of pottery was available at the site, something that apparently never was common at other Tarahumar centers.

39— 1743: Rinaldini (1743), 11, 33, 77.

40— Circa 1767: Steffel (1809), 342-43.

41— 1683: Ratkay. An account of the Tarahumar missions. . . .

42— Circa 1767: Steffel (1809), 343.

43— 1743: Rinaldini (1743), 67-77.

44— 1683: Ratkay. An account of the Tarahumar missions. . . .

45— Circa 1767: Steffel (1809), 343.

46— Decorme (1941), II, 234, note 19.

47— See Culin [(1907), 665-95] for a discussion of the kickball race among Indians of the American Southwest and the Mexican northwest coast (Sonora and Sinaloa).

48— Lumholtz (1902), I, 294.

49— Watson (1886), 425.

50— Lumholtz (1902), I, 278.

51— 1743: Rinaldini (1743), 76-77.

52— Lumholtz (1902), I, 277.

53— Ibid., 278.

54— Circa 1767: Steffel (1809), 342-43.

55— 1743: Rinaldini (1743), 77.

56— Reported in Culin [(1907), 154].

57— Ibid., 146-152.

58— 1743: Rinaldini (1743), 76.

59— Lumholtz (1902), I, 276-77.

60— 1645: Pérez de Ribas (1944), III, 143.

61— 1743: Rinaldini (1743), 91.

62— Zingg (1940), 16.

63— 1777: Relación de Tutuaca.

64— 1777: Relación de Guaguachic.

65— 1777: Relación de Cusihuiriachic.

66— Circa 1767: Steffel (1809), 341.

67— Ibid., 304.

68— 1777: Relación de Cusihuiriachic.

69— Zingg (1940), 15-16, 25-26, 37.

70— Ibid., 15-16.

71— Brooks et al. (1962), 358.

72— Lumholtz (1902), I, 424.

73— Zingg (1940), 28-31.

74— Ascher and Clune (1960), 272.

75— Clune (1960), 274.

76— Brooks et al. (1962), 358.

77— Zingg (1940), 51.

78— 1743: Rinaldini (1743), 1.

79— 1645: Pérez de Ribas (1944), III, 159-60.

80— 1682: Letter of Joseph Neumann, February 20.

81— Zingg (1940), 8-9, 20, 24.

82— O'Neale (1948), 106.

83— Clune (1960), 274-77.

84— Brooks et al. (1962), 358-61.

85— Lumholtz (1902), I, 205, 219.

86— Zingg (1940), 96.

87— Clune (1960), 274.

88— Ascher and Clune (1960), 272.

89— Zingg (1940), 32.

90— 1682: Letter of Joseph Neumann, February 20.

91— 1777: Relación de Guaguachic.

92— 1682: Letter of Joseph Neumann, February 20.

93— Zingg (1940), 24.

94— 1596: Carta Anua.

95— 1645: Pérez de Ribas (1944), III, 137.

96— Brooks et al. (1962), 357-59.

97— Lumholtz (1902), I, 150.

98— 1777: Relación de Cerocahui.

99— Zingg (1940), 20.

100— 1645: Pérez de Ribas (1944), III, 137, 237.

101— Zingg (1940), 8-9, 37.

102— Ibid., 56.

103— 1645: Pérez de Ribas (1944), III, 137.

104— Brooks et al. (1962), 358.

105— O'Neale (1948).

106— Kasha (1948).

107— 1645: Pérez de Ribas (1944), III, 153, 155, 160, 190.

108— 1743: Rinaldini (1743), 106.

109— Watson (1886), 429-30.

110— Ibid.

111— 1683: Ratkay. An account of the Tarahumar missions. . . .

112— Circa 1767: Steffel (1809), 330-31.

113— Brooks et al. (1962), 358.

114— Zingg (1940), 51-52.

115— Ibid., 38.

116— Brooks et al. (1962), 367.

117— Zingg (1940), 38.

118— Ascher and Clune (1960), 271.

119— Brooks et al. (1962), 359.

120— Ibid., 359.

121— Ascher and Clune (1960), 272.

122— Zingg (1940), 31, 62.

123— Brooks et al. (1962), 359.

124— Zingg (1940), 35.

125— Lumholtz (1902), I, 430.

126— Ibid., 158, 424-25.

127— Zingg (1940), 46-48.

128— 1645: Pérez de Ribas (1944), III, 137, 204.

129— Zingg (1940), 46-48.

130— Brooks et al. (1962).

131— 1605: Relación de Martín Peláez.

132— 1645: Pérez de Ribas (1944), III, 159.

133— Ibid., 137.

134— Zingg (1940), 46-48.

135— 1645: Pérez de Ribas (1944), III, 227.

136— 1681: Letter of Joseph Neumann, January 15.

137— 1683: Ratkay. An account of the Tarahumar missions. . . .

138— For a comment on the Tarahumar population since the Spaniards arrived in Chihuahua, see Pennington [(1963)b, 23-24].

139— It is, of course, impossible to really determine how many mestizos there are in that portion of Chihuahua occupied by considerable numbers of Tepehuan and Tarahumar. However, some notion of the approximate mestizo population may be obtained from census data for 1960 by noting the number of only Spanish-speaking people within certain *municipios* [Mexico. . . . *VIII Censo General de Población, 1960.* . . . *Estado de Chihuahua* (1963), 610-12]. Within those *municipios* which certainly contain significant numbers of Tepehuan and Tarahumar, there were about 100,000 people (mestizos?) who spoke no *lengua indígena*.

BIBLIOGRAPHY

This bibliography is divided into two parts: General References and Primary Sources. Note references with author followed by publication date can be found in the General Reference section; references with a date followed by a colon can be found in the Primary Sources section which is arranged chronologically under Civil and Military Records, Franciscan Records, and Jesuit Records.

GENERAL REFERENCES

ALMADA, FRANCISCO R.
  1945 — *Geografía del Estado de Chihuahua.* Chihuahua.

ANDERSON, EDGAR, and
HUGH CUTLER
  1955 — Letter to Campbell W. Pennington, November 10, 1955.
  1960 — Letter to Campbell W. Pennington, August 9, 1960.

ASCHER, ROBERT, and
FRANCIS J. CLUNE, JR.
  1960 — "Waterfall Cave, Southern Chihuahua, Mexico," *American Antiquity*, XXVI, No. 2, pp.270-74.

BAILEY, LIBERTY H., and
ETHEL Z. BAILEY (compilers)
  1941 — *Hortus Second, A Concise Dictionary of Gardening, General Horticulture and Cultivated Plants in North America.* New edition, rev. and reset, April, 1941. New York: Macmillan Co.

BANCROFT, HUBERT H.
  1884-1889 — *History of the North Mexican States.* 2 vols. ("The Works of Hubert Howe Bancroft," Vols. XV-XVI.) San Francisco: A. L. Bancroft & Co.

BARLOW, ROBERT H., and
GEORGE T. SMISOR (eds.)
  1943 — *Nombre de Dios, Durango; Two Documents in Náhuatl Concerning Its Foundation.* Sacramento: House of Tlaloc.

BASAURI, CARLOS
  1929 — *Monografía de los Tarahumares.* México: Talleres Gráficos de la Nación.
  1940 — *La Población Indígena de México, Etnografía.* 3 vols. México: Secretaría de Educación Pública.

BASCOM, BURTON W., JR.
  1965 — "Proto-Tepiman (Tepehuán-Piman)." Unpublished Ph.D. dissertation, University of Washington.

BEALS, RALPH L.
  1932 — *The Comparative Ethnology of Northern Mexico Before 1750.* ("Ibero-Americana," No. 2.) Berkeley: University of California Press.

BEAN, TARLETON H.
  1898 — "Notes on Mexican Fishes Obtained by Dr. Carl Lumholtz," *Bulletin of the American Museum of Natural History*, X, pp.165-68.

BENNETT, WENDELL C., and
ROBERT M. ZINGG

1935— *The Tarahumara, An Indian Tribe of Northern Mexico.* Chicago: University of Chicago Press.

BLAKE, EMMET R.

1953— *Birds of Mexico: A Guide for Field Identification.* Chicago: University of Chicago.

BRAMBILA, DAVID

1953— *Gramática Rarámuri.* México: Editorial Buena Prensa.

BRAND, DONALD D.

1936— *Notes to Accompany a Vegetation Map of Northwest Mexico.* ("University of New Mexico Bulletin, Biological Series," Vol. IV, No. 4.) Albuquerque: University of New Mexico Press.

1939— "Notes on the Geography and Archaeology of Zape, Durango," in *So Live the Works of Men: Seventieth Anniversary Volume Honoring Edgar Lee Hewett,* Donald D. Brand and Fred E. Harvey (eds.), pp. 75-105. Albuquerque: Printed by the University of New Mexico Press.

BROOKS, RICHARD H., et al.

1962— "Plant Material from a Cave on the Río Zape, Durango, Mexico," *American Antiquity,* XXVII, No. 3, pp. 356-69.

BRUMAN, HENRY J.

1940— "Aboriginal Drink Areas in New Spain." Unpublished Ph.D. dissertation, University of California, Berkeley.

BURRUS, ERNEST J. (ed.)

1963— *Misiones Norteñas Mexicanas de la Compañía de Jesús, 1751-1757.* ("Biblioteca Histórica Mexicana de Obras Inéditas," Nu. 25.) México: Antigua Librería Robredo de José Porrúa e Hijos, Sucs.

CARDOSO, JOAQUIN

1948— *¡Sangre en los Tepehuanes . . . !* México: Editorial Buena Prensa.

CARTER, GEORGE F., and
EDGAR ANDERSON

1945— "A Preliminary Survey of Maize in the Southwestern United States," *Annals of the Missouri Botanical Garden,* XXXII, No. 3, pp. 297-323.

CERDA SILVA, ROBERT DE LA

1943— "Los Tepehuanes," *Rivista Mexicana de Sociología,* V, Nu. 4, pp. 541-67.

CLAUS, EDWARD P.

1956— *Gathercoal and Wirth Pharmacognosy.* 3rd ed. rev. Philadelphia: Lea & Febiger.

CLUNE, DORRIS

1960— "Textiles and Matting from Waterfall Cave, Chihuahua," *American Antiquity,* XXVI, No. 2, pp. 274-77.

CULIN, STEWART

1907— *Games of the North American Indians.* ("Twenty-fourth Annual Report of the Bureau of American Ethnology, 1902-1903.") Washington, D.C.: Government Printing Office.

CUTLER, HUGH

1960a— "Cultivated Plant Remains from Waterfall Cave, Chihuahua," *American Antiquity,* XXVI, No. 2, pp. 277-79.

1960b— Letter to Campbell W. Pennington, August 1, 1960.

1966— Letter to Campbell W. Pennington, March 7, 1966.

DARLINGTON, CYRIL D., and
E. K. JANAKI AMMAL

1945— *Chromosome Atlas of Cultivated Plants.* London: G. Allen & Unwin, Inc.

DECORME, GERARD

1941– *La Obra de Los Jesuítas Mexicanos Durante la Epoca Colonial, 1572-1767.* 2 vols. México: Antigua Librería Robredo de J. Porrúa e Hijos.

DUNNE, PETER MASTEN

1944– *Pioneer Jesuits in Northern Mexico.* Berkeley: University of California Press.

1948– *Early Jesuit Missions in Tarahumara.* Berkeley: University of California Press.

GAJDUSEK, D. CARLETON

1954– "Tarahumar Indian Piscicide: *Gilia macombii* Torrey," *Science,* CXX, No. 3115, p. 436.

GAMIZ, EVERARDO

1948– *Monografía de la Nación Tepehuana que Habita en la Región Sur del Estado de Durango.* México: Ediciones Gámiz.

GENTRY, HOWARD S.

1942– *Rio Mayo Plants, A Study of the Flora and Vegetation of the Valley of the Rio Mayo, Sonora.* ("Carnegie Institution of Washington Publications," No. 527.) Washington, D.C.

1963– *The Warihio Indians of Sonora-Chihuahua.* ("Anthropological Papers," No. 65; "Bureau of American Ethnology Bulletins," No. 186, pp. 69-144.) Washington, D.C.: Government Printing Office.

GRAY, ASA

1950– *Manual of Botany.* Largely rewritten and expanded by Merritt L. Fernald and others. 8th (centennial) ed. New York: American Book Co.

HEWETT, EDGAR LEE

1936– *Ancient Life in Mexico and Central America.* New York: Bobbs-Merrill Co.

HOVEY, EDMUND O.

1907– "A Geological Reconnaissance in the Western Sierra Madre of the State of Chihuahua, Mexico," *Bulletin of the American Museum of Natural History,* XXIII, pp. 401-42.

KAPLAN, LAWRENCE

1961– Letter to Campbell W. Pennington, March 15, 1961.

KASHA, MICHAEL

1948– "Chemical Notes on the Coloring Matter of Chihuahua Textiles in Pre-Columbian Mexico," appendix in *Textiles of Pre-Columbian Chihuahua,* Lila M. O'Neale, pp. 151-57. ("Contributions to American Anthropology and History," Vol. IX, No. 45; "Carnegie Institution of Washington Publications," No. 574, pp. 95-161.) Washington, D.C.

KELLEY, J. CHARLES

1956– "Settlement Patterns in North-Central Mexico," in *Prehistoric Settlement Patterns in the New World,* Gordon R. Willey (ed.), pp. 128-39. ("Viking Fund Publications in Anthropology," No. 23.) New York: Wenner-Gren Foundation for Anthropological Research.

KING, R. E.

1939– "Geological Reconnaissance in Northern Sierra Madre Occidental of Mexico," *Bulletin of the Geological Society of America,* L, No. 11, pp. 1625-1722.

LEOPOLD, ALDO S.

1959– *Wildlife of Mexico, The Game Birds and Animals.* Berkeley: University of California Press.

LUMHOLTZ, CARL S.

1894– "The Tarahumaris," 3 parts, *Scribner's Magazine,* XVI, Nos. 1, 3, 4, pp. 31-48, 296-311, 438-56.

1902– *Unknown Mexico.* 2 vols. New York: C. Scribner's Sons.

MacNEISH, RICHARD S.

1964– "The Origins of New World Civilization," *Scientific American*, CCXI, No. 5, pp. 29-37.

MASON, J. ALDEN

1917 – "Tepecano, A Piman Language of Western Mexico," *Annals of the New York Academy of Sciences*, XXV, pp. 309-416.

1948 – "The Tepehuán and Other Aborigines of the Mexican Sierra Madre Occidental," *América Indígena*, VIII, Nu. 4, pp. 289-300.

1952 – "Notes and Observations on the Tepehuán," *América Indígena*, XII, Nu. 1, pp. 33-53.

MASON, J. ALDEN, and DAVID M. BRUGGE

1958 – "Notes on the Lower Pima," in *Miscellanea Paul Rivet, Octogenario Dictata*, Vol. 1, pp. 277-97. México: Universidad Nacional Autónoma de México.

MECHAM, JOHN L.

1927 – *Francisco de Ibarra and Nueva Vizcaya*. Durham: Duke University Press.

MENDIZABEL, MIGUEL OTHON DE

1946-1947 – *Obras Completas*. 6 vols. México.

MEXICO. DIRECCION GENERAL DE ESTADISTICA.

1952 – *VII Censo General de Población, 1950, 6 de Junio de 1960. Estado de Chihuahua*. México.

1963 – *VIII Censo General de Población, 1960, 8 de Junio de 1960. Estado de Chihuahua; Estado de Durango; Estado de Jalisco; Estado de Nayarit*. México.

MUENSCHER, WALTER C.

1947 – *Poisonous Plants of the United States*. New York: Macmillan Co.

O'NEALE, LILA M.

1948 – *Textiles of Pre-Columbian Chihuahua*. ("Contributions to American Anthropology and History," Vol. IX, No. 45; "Carnegie Institution of Washington Publications," No. 574, pp. 95-161.) Washington, D.C.

PAMMEL, LOUIS H.

1911 – *A Manual of Poisonous Plants*. Cedar Rapids, Iowa: Torch Press.

PENNINGTON, CAMPBELL W.

1963a – "Medicinal Plants Utilized by the Tepehuán of Southern Chihuahua," *América Indígena*, XXIII, Nu. 1, pp. 31-47.

1963b – *The Tarahumar of Mexico, Their Environment and Material Culture*. Salt Lake City: University of Utah Press.

PERDUE, ROBERT E., JR.

1958 – "Arundo donax – Source of Musical Reeds and Industrial Cellulose," *Economic Botany*, XII, No. 4, pp. 368-404.

PIMENTEL, FRANCISCO

1874-1875 – *Cuadro Descriptivo y Comparativo de las Lenguas Indígenas de México*. 3 vols. 2d. ed. México: Tip. de I. Epstein.

PLANCARTE, FRANCISCO M.

1954 – *El Problema Indígena Tarahumara*. ("Memorias del Instituto Nacional Indigenista," Vol. V.) México.

QUINBY, J. ROY

1960 – Letter to Campbell W. Pennington, August 23, 1960.

RILEY, CARROLL L., and JOHN HOBGOOD

1959 – "A Recent Nativistic Movement Among the Southern Tepehuán Indians," *Southwestern Journal of Anthropology*, XV, No. 4, pp. 355-60.

RILEY, CARROLL L., and HOWARD D. WINTERS

1963 – "The Prehistoric Tepehuán of Northern Mexico," *Southwestern Journal of Anthropology*, XIX, No. 2, pp. 177-85.

ROUAIX, PASTOR

1946 – *Diccionario Geográfico, Histórico y Biográfico del Estado de Durango*. ("Instituto Panamericano de Geografía e Historia, Publicaciones," Nu. 80.) México.

SANTOSCOY, ALBERTO

1899 – *Nayarit; Colección de Documentos Inéditos, Históricos y Etnográficos, Acerca de la Sierra de Ese Nombre*. Guadalajara.

SAUER, CARL

1934 – *The Distribution of Aboriginal Tribes and Languages in Northwestern Mexico*. ("Ibero-Americana," No. 5.) Berkeley: University of California Press.

SCHWATKA, FREDERICK

1893 – *In the Land of Cave and Cliff Dwellers*. New York: Cassell Publishing Co.

SEINE, T. O.

1960 – Letter to Campbell W. Pennington, August 27, 1960.

STANDLEY, PAUL

1920-1926 – *Trees and Shrubs of Mexico*. 5 parts. ("United States National Museum, Contributions from the United States National Herbarium," Vol. XXIII.) Washington, D.C.: Government Printing Office.

THOMAS, CYRUS, and
JOHN R. SWANTON

1911 – *Indian Languages of Mexico and Central America*. ("Bureau of American Ethnology Bulletins," No. 44.) Washington, D.C.: Government Printing Office.

THORD-GRAY, I.

1955 – *Tarahumara-English, English-Tarahumara Dictionary and an Introduction to the Tarahumara Grammar*. Coral Gables, Florida: University of Miami Press.

VINALL, H. N., J. C. STEPHENS, and
J. H. MARTIN

1936 – *Identification, History, and Distribution of Common Sorghum Varieties*. ("United States Department of Agriculture Technical Bulletins," No. 506.) Washington, D.C.: Government Printing Office.

WALL, MONROE E., et al.

1957 – "Steroidal Sapogenins, XLIII; Survey of Plants for Steroidal Sapogenins and Other Constituents," *Journal of the American Pharmaceutical Association*, scientific edition, XLVI, No. 11, pp. 653-84.

1959 – "Steroidal Sapogenins, LV; Survey of Plants for Steroidal Sapogenins and Other Constituents," *Journal of the American Pharmaceutical Association*, scientific edition, XLVIII, No. 12, pp. 695-722.

WATSON, SERENO

1886 – "List of Plants Collected by Dr. Edward Palmer in Southwestern Chihuahua, Mexico in 1885," *Proceedings of the American Academy of Arts and Sciences*, XXI, pp. 414-55.

WEED, WALTER H.

1902 – "Notes on Certain Mines in the States of Chihuahua, Sinaloa and Sonora, Mexico," *Transactions of the American Institution of Mining and Engineers*, XXXII, pp. 396-443.

WELLHAUSEN, EDWIN J., et al.

1952 – *Races of Maize in Mexico, Their Origin, Characteristics and Distribution*. Cambridge: Bussey Institution of Harvard University.

WEST, ROBERT C.

1949 – *The Mining Community in Northern New Spain: The Parral Mining District*. ("Ibero-Americana," No. 30.) Berkeley: University of California Press.

WHITAKER, THOMAS W.

1960 – Letter to Campbell W. Pennington, August 2, 1960.

WILLIS, JOHN C.

   1931– *A Dictionary of the Flowering Plants and Ferns.* 6th ed., rev. Cambridge, England: The University Press.

ZINGG, ROBERT M.

   1940– *Report on Archaeology of Southern Chihuahua.* ("Contributions of the University of Denver," No. 3; "Center of Latin American Studies Publications," No. 1.) Denver.

PRIMARY SOURCES

There are primary source materials pertaining to the Tepehuan scattered among civil, military, and ecclesiastical records of northern New Spain. However, only the most important materials have been published. I have used originals or copies of records which are available in the Bancroft Library (University of California at Berkeley), in the Stevens Collection (University of Texas, Latin American Collection), in the Parral Archive, Hidalgo del Parral, Chihuahua, and in the national archives in Mexico City. In addition, I have used photocopies (made from microfilms of the original documents) of certain seventeenth- and eighteenth-century documents which concern northwestern Mexico; these photocopies are in the Department of Geography, University of California at Berkeley.

Primary source material which has been published is identified according to publisher, author or translator. Abbreviations used in indicating the location of unpublished and published material are given below.

B.C.– Bolton Collection. Transcripts in Bancroft Library, University of California, Berkeley.

Col. – Pacheco, Joaquín F., and Francisco de Cárdenas (eds.). *Colección de Documentos Inéditos, Relativos al Descubrimiento, Conquista y Organización de las Antiguas Posesiones Españolas de América y Oceanía, Sacados de los Archivos del Reino, y Muy Especialmente del de Indias.* 42 vols. Madrid, 1864-1884.

Doc. – Documentos Para la Historia de Méjico. 21 vols. in 4 series. Méjico: Impr. de J. R. Navarro, 1853-1857.

Hackett– Hackett, Charles W. (ed.). *Historical Documents Relating to New Mexico, Nueva Vizcaya and Approaches Thereto, to 1773*, collected by Adolph F. A. Bandelier and Fanny R. Bandelier. Spanish texts and English translations, edited . . . by Charles W. Hackett. ("Carnegie Institution of Washington Publications," No. 330, Vol. II.) Washington, D.C., 1926.

MS. – Parral Archive. Hidalgo del Parral, Chihuahua.

P.C.– Pastells Collection (microfilm). St. Louis University, Pious XII Library, St. Louis, Missouri.

Photo. – Photocopy in Department of Geography, University of California, Berkeley.

Santoscoy– Santoscoy, Alberto. *Nayarit; Colección de Documentos Inéditos, Historicos y Etnográficos, Acerca de la Sierra de Ese Nombre.* Guadalajara, 1899.

CIVIL AND MILITARY RECORDS

1554– "Relación de los descubrimientos conquistas y poblaciones hechas por el Gobernador Francisco de Ybarra en las provincias de Copala, Nueva Vizcaya y Chiametla," in *Col.*, XIV (1870), 463-84.

1562– "Información acerca de la rebelión de los Indios Zacatecas y Guachichiles a pedimento de Pedro Ahumada Samano, 1562," in *Colección de Documentos Inéditos Para la Historia de Ibero-América*, Santiago Montoto de Sedas (ed.), pp. 237-358. ("Colección de Documentos Inéditos Para la Historia de Hispano-América," Vol. I.) Madrid: Editorial Ibero-Africano-Americana, 1927.

1562– "Relación de Pedro de Ahumada," in *Nombre de Dios, Durango; Two Documents in Náhuatl Concerning Its Foundation*, Robert H. Barlow and George T.

Smisor (eds.), pp. 53-63. Sacramento: House of Tlaloc, 1943.

1563 — "Memorial de los Indios de Nombre de Dios, Durango, acerca de sus servicios al Rey, circa 1563," in *Nombre de Dios, Durango; Two Documents in Náhuatl Concerning Its Foundation*, Robert H. Barlow and George T. Smisor (eds.), pp. 3-45. Sacramento: House of Tlaloc, 1943.

1575 — "Relación hecha por Joan de Miranda, Clerigo, al Doctor Orozco, Presidente de la Audiencia de Guadalajara: sobre la tierra y población que hay desde las minas de San Martín a las de Santa Bárbara, que este último entonces estaba poblada," in *Col.*, XVI (1871), 563-70.

1584 — Obregón, Baltasar de. *Obregón's History of 16th Century Explorations in Western America, Entitled Chronicle, Commentary, or Relation of the Ancient and Modern Discoveries in New Spain and New Mexico, Mexico, 1584.* Translated, edited and annotated by George P. Hammond and Agapito Rey. Los Angeles: Wetzel Publishing Co., Inc., 1928.

1604 — Memorial de Francisco de Hordiñola, Governador de la Nueva Vizcaya al Excelentísimo Marqués de Montesclaros, Virrey de la Nueva España que mande su excelencia proveer las cossas necessarias y aqui conthenidas para el bien y augmento de estas provincias y conversión los naturales y de la población. Photo.

1605 — Carta de la Audiencia de Guadalajara a su Magestad sobre el fruto alcanzado por los religiosos de San Francisco en la conversión de los naturales Guainamotas y de los de San Agustin—en los naturales de San Pedro de Analco, y sobre la inconveniencia de quitar dicha Audiencia, 28 Abril 1605. P.C.

1606 — Real cedula á la Audiencia de la Nueva Galicia para que aliente la entrada y conversión de los Indios Guainamotas, Coras y de San Pedro de Analco, 1606 Marzo 27. P.C.

1616-1618 — "Relación breve y succinta de los sucesos que ha tenido la guerra de los Tepehuanes de la governación de la Nueva Vizcaya desde 15 de Noviembre de 1616 hasta 16 de Mayo de 1618," in Hackett (1926), II,100-13.

1617 — "Relación de la guerra de los Tepeguanes este mes de Diciembre de 1617," *Ramo de Historia*, CCCXI. México: Archivo General de la Nación.

1617 — "Servicios hechos a su Magestad por el Cappitán Don Hierónimo Valasquez Davila," in Hackett (1926), II, 94-97.

1618 — "Carta del Alonso del Valle, 1618," in *Doc.* (1857), 4th series, II, 90-129.

1620-1622 — "Papeles del Almirante Matheo de Vesga, 1620-1622," in Hackett (1926), II,119-36.

1625 — "Razón y minuta de los Yndios que se administran en las Provincias de la Nueba Vizcaia por los vicarios veneficiados y rrelixiosos de San Francisco y Compañía de Jesús que hoy estan bautizados," in Hackett (1926), II, 152-59.

1669 — Registro de un sitio que llaman Valsequillo en terrenos de Huejotitlán. MS.

1678 — "El lizenciado Don Lope de Sierra Ossorio oidor de la Real Audiencia de México, Gobernador y Capitán General que fué del Reino de la Nueva Vizcaia, informa a vuestra Magestad el estado de las cossas de aquel reino, 1678," in Hackett (1926), II, 210-17.

Circa 1683 — "Extracto de papel que formo el Señor Don Lope de Sierra sobre las cossas tocantes al reyno de la Nueba Vizcaya," in Hackett (1926), II, 218-27.

1685 — Autos de la fundación de un pueblo en las Bocas Viejas por los indios Tarahumaras y Tepehuanes. MS.

1693-1721 — Manje, Juan Mateo. *Unknown Arizona and Sonora, 1693-1721*; from the Francisco Fernández del Castillo version of *Luz de Tierra Incógnita*. An English translation of Part 2 by Harry J.

Karns and associates. Tucson: Arizona Silhouettes, 1954.

1715— Actas de la visita que en los pueblos de la nación Tepehuana practicó su Capitán General Don Francisco Javier Díaz por orden del Gobernador Don Manuel San Juan de Santa Cruz. MS.

FRANCISCAN RECORDS

Circa 1587— "Relación de las cosas que sucedieron al Padre Fray Alonso Ponce en las Provincias de la Nueva España," Miguel Salva and the Marqués de la Fuensante del Valle (eds.), in *Colección de Documentos Inéditos Para la Historia de España* (112 vols., Madrid: Impr. de la Viuda de Calero, 1842-1895), LVIII, 1-559.

1604— Barrio, Francisco del. Relación de las cosas sucedidas en las serranias de Choras y Tepehuanes e de las custumbres y ritos de estas naciones y de la dispusición y sitios de sus tierras. Photo.

Circa 1650— "Información rendide por el P. Antonio Arias y Saavedra, acerca del estado de la Sierra del Nayarit en el siglo XVII," in Santoscoy (1899), 7-35.

Circa 1650— Tello, Antonio. *Libro Segundo de la Crónica Miscelanea*. Guadalajara: Impr. de la Republica Literaria, de C. L. de Guevara y Ca., 1891.

1737— Arlegui, José de. *Crónica de la Provincia de N.S.P.S. Francisco de Zacatecas*. México: Reimpresa por Cumplido, 1851.

1769— "Visita de la Misión de San Juan Peyotlán por D. José Antonio Bugarín, 1769," in Santoscoy (1899), 35-56.

1777— Relación de Batopilillas. Photo.

1777— Relación de Cerocahui. Photo.

1777— Relación de Cusihuiriachic. Photo.

1777— Relación de Guaguachic. Photo.

1777— Relación de Guazapares. Photo.

1777— Relación de Indé. Photo.

1777— Relación de Nabogame. Photo.

1777— Relación de San Miguel de las Bocas. Photo.

1777— Relación de Tónachic. Photo.

1777— Relación de Tutuaca. Photo.

1777-1825— Patentes y comunicaciones que se refieren a la Tarahumara, 1777-1825. Copy in the Convento de Guadalupe, Guadalupe, Zacatecas.

1778— Descripción Topográfica de las misiones de propaganda fide de Nuestra Señora de Guadalupe de Zacatecas la Sierra Madre. [I have used a copy found in the Convento de Guadalupe, Guadalupe, Zacatecas; this version differs somewhat from that published in *Doc.* (1857), 4th series, IV, 92-131.]

1778— Relación de Santa Eulalia de Chihuahua. Photo.

1784— "Expediente de real orden sobre el estado de las misiones californias," in *Crónicas y Relaciones del Occidente de México*, Fernando Ocaranza (2 vols., México: Antigua Librería Robredo, de J. Porrúa e Hijos, 1937-1939), II, 329-56.

1788— Alcocer, José Antonio. *Bosquejo de la Historia del Colegio de Nuestra Señora de Guadalupe y Sus Misiones, Año de 1788*, Rafael Cervantes (ed.). México: Editorial Porrúa, 1958.

JESUIT RECORDS

1595— Carta Anua. B.C.

1596— Carta Anua. B.C.

1597— Carta Anua. B.C.

1598— Carta Anua. B.C.

1602— Carta Anua. B.C.

1602— Mota y Escobar, Alonso de la. *Descripción Geográfica de los Reinos de Nueva Galicia, Nueva Vizcaya y Nuevo León*. 2d. ed. México: P. Robredo, 1940.

1604— Carta Anua. B.C.

1605— Relación de Martín Peláez. Photo.

1611— Dabertzhofer, Chrysostomo. *Drey Neue Relationes.* Augsburg, 1611. (I have used the English translation found in the Bolton Collection, Bancroft Library, University of California, Berkeley.)

1645— Pérez de Ribas, Andrés. *Historia de los Triunfos de Nuestra Santa Fe Entre Gentes las Más Bárbaras y Fieras del Nuevo Orbe.* 3 vols. México: Editorial Layac, 1944.

1651— Pascual, Julio. "Noticias de las misiones sacadas de la Anua 1651," in *Doc.* (1857), 4th series, III, 179-209.

1662— Carta Anua. B.C.

1662— Figueroa, Gerónimo de. "Puntos de Anua de estos diez años que he asistido en este partido de San Pablo," in *Doc.* (1857), 4th series, III, 217-21.

1678— Relación de las Misiones que la Compañía tiene en el Reyno y Provincias de la Nueva Vizcaya en la Nueva España, echa el año de 1678 con ocasión de la Visita General dellas que por orden del Padre Provincial Tomás Altamirano hizo el Padre Visitador Juan Hortíz Zapata de la misma Compañía. B.C.

1681— Letter of Joseph Neumann, January 15. B.C.

1682— Letter of Joseph Neumann, February 20. B.C.

1683— Letter of Juan Bautista Ancieta, March 20. B.C.

1683— Ratkay, Juan María. An account of the Tarahumar missions and a description of the tribe of the Tarahumaras and of their country. B.C.

1686— Letter of Joseph Neumann, July 29. B.C.

1690— Letter of Joseph Neumann, February 4. B.C.

1690— Padrón de las personas de confesión que tiene este partido de San Gerónimo Guexotitlán, año de 1690. B.C.

1693— Letter of Joseph Neumann, September 16. B.C.

1695— Letter of Joseph Neumann, July 6. B.C.

1698— Letter of Joseph Neumann, April 23. B.C.

1725— "Carta del Padre San Juan de Guendulain al Provincial Gaspar Roder," in *Doc.* (1857), 4th series, IV, 22-33.

Circa 1725— Neumann, Joseph. Historia Seditonum quas adversus Societatis Jesu missionarios eorumque auxiliatores noverunt nationes indicae ac potissimum Tarahumara in America Septentionali regnoque Novae Cantabriae, jam toto ad fiden catholicam propemodum redacto. Prefacio 15 Abril 1724. Translated into English by Marion Reynolds. B.C.

1743— Rinaldini, Benito. *Arte de la Lengua Tepeguana.* México, 1743.

1744— Abeé, Juan Isidro Feinz de. An account of the founding of Cárichic. B.C.

1746— Sedelmayr, Jacobo. "Relación, 1746," in *Jacobo Sedelmayr, Missionary, Frontiersman, Explorer in Arizona and Sonora,* pp. 15-53. Four original manuscript narratives, 1744-1751, translated and annotated by Peter Masten Dunne. Tucson: Arizona Pioneers Historical Society, 1955.

Circa 1750— Relación de la fundación y aumento y estado presente de estas dos misiones Nabogame y Baborigame (Benito Rinaldini). Stevens Collection, No. 1771, University of Texas Latin American Collection, Austin, Texas.

1763— Noticia de la Visita General de P. Ignacio Lizasoain Visitador General de las Misiones de esta Provincia de Nueva España, que comenzio dia quatro de Abril de 1761 años y se concluyo a fines de Henero en 1763 con algunas notas y addiciones q. pueden servir para el conocimiento de estas Missiones, y Provincias de ellas. Stevens Collection, No. 47, University of Texas Latin American Collection, Austin, Texas.

1765— Tamarón y Romeral, Pedro. *Demostración del Vastísimo Obispado de la Nueva Vizcaya—1765; Durango, Sinaloa, Arizona, Nuevo México, Chihuahua y Porciones de Texas, Coahuila y Zacatecas*, Vito Alessio Robles (ed.). ("Biblioteca Histórica Mexicana de Obras Inéditos," Nu. 7.) México: Antigua Librería Robredo, de J. Porrúa e Hijos, 1937.

Circa 1767— Steffel, Matthäus. "Tarahumarisches Wörterbuch nebst Einigen Nachrichten von den Sitten und Gebräuchen der Tarahumaren, in Neu-Biscaya, in der Audiencia Guadalaxara im Vice-Königreiche Alt-Mexico oder Neu Spanien," in *Nachrichten von Verschiedenen Ländern des Spanischen Amerika*, Christoph G. von Murr (ed.), Part I, No. 11, pp. 293-374. Halle, 1809.

1780— Alegre, Francisco Javier. *Historia de la Provincia de la Compañia de Jesús de Nueva España*. 4 vols. Nueva ed. por Ernst J. Burrus y Felix Zubillaga. ("Bibliotheca Instituti Historici S.J.," Vol. 9, No. 13.) Roma: Institutum Historicum, 1956-1960.

INDEX

Campbell W. Pennington is Professor of Geography at Southern Illinois University, Carbondale, Illinois. His degrees include the B.A. and M.A. in History and Sociology from the University of Texas and the Ph.D. in Geography from the University of California at Berkeley.